THE
RING OF WORDS

PHILIP LIESON MILLER is former Chief of the Music Division of the New York Public Library, Senior Record Critic of *American Record Guide*, and a regular contributor to *High Fidelity, The Saturday Review, The Musical Quarterly, Notes,* and *The Library Journal* (of which he is the regular record critic). He is the author of the volume on vocal music of *The Guide to Long Playing Records*. Born and raised in Woodland, New York, he acquired an early interest in recorded songs, and later studied voice at the Platt School of Music and piano and theory at the Neighborhood Music School in New York. After winning a Juilliard Scholarship in voice, he studied at the Institute of Musical Art and began working in the Music Division of the New York Public Library. Mr. Miller also has been a President of the Music Library Association.

THE
RING OF WORDS
AN ANTHOLOGY OF SONG TEXTS

THE ORIGINAL TEXTS
SELECTED AND TRANSLATED
WITH AN INTRODUCTION BY
PHILIP L. MILLER

The Norton Library
W · W · NORTON & COMPANY · INC ·
NEW YORK

To the Memory of Povla Frijsh

The Ring of Words was originally published in 1963

FIRST PUBLISHED IN THE NORTON LIBRARY 1973
BY ARRANGEMENT WITH DOUBLEDAY & COMPANY, INC.

The texts of *Beau soir* and *Romance* by Paul Bourget are reprinted by permission of Librairie Alphonse Lemerre, Paris; the text of *Poème d'un jour* by Charles-Jean Grandmougin is reprinted by permission of Librairie Fischbacher, Paris; the text of *Au cimitière* by Jean Richepin is reprinted by permission of the Société des Gens de Lettres de France; the texts of *L'alba separa dalla luce l'ombra* by Gabriele D'Annunzio and *Nebbie* and *Notte* by Ada Negri are reprinted by permission of Arnoldo Mondadori Editore, Milan; the texts of *Befreit* and *Wiegenlied* by Richard Dehmel are reprinted by permission of Frau Vera Tügel-Dehmel, Blankense; the texts of *Haugtussa* by Arne Garborg, *Mot kveld* by Andreas Grimelund Jynge, and *Der skreg en fugl Mens jeg venter* and *Og jeg vil ha mig en hjertenskjaer* by Vilhelm Andreas Wexels Krag are reprinted by permission of H. Aschehoug & Co., Oslo; the text of *I Würzburg ringe de Klokker til Fest* is reprinted by permission of E. Spang-Hanssen, Charlottenlund; the text of *Med en primula veris* by John Olaf Paulsen is reprinted by permission of B. Dybwad Brochmann, Bergen; the texts of *Amor y odio, Callejero, La maja dolorosa, El majo discreto, El majo olvidado, El majo timido* and *El mirar de la maja* by Fernando Periquet y Zuaznabar are reprinted by permission of the Sociedad General de Autores de España; the texts of the 7 *Canciones Populares Espanolas* of Manuel de Falla are reprinted by permission of Editions Max Eschig, Paris.

Library of Congress Cataloging in Publication Data

Miller, Philip Lieson, 1906–   comp. and tr.
   The ring of words.

   (The Norton library)
   German, French, Italian, Spanish, Russian, Norwegian, and Swedish, with English translations.
   Reprint of the 1966 ed.
   1. Songs—Texts. I. Title.
[ML54.6.M5R5   1973]   781.9'6   72-10270
ISBN 0-393-00677-8

PRINTED IN THE UNITED STATES OF AMERICA

1 2 3 4 5 6 7 8 9 0

Bright is the ring of words
    When the right man rings them,
Fair the fall of songs
    When the singer sings them.
Still they are carolled and said —
    On wings they are carried —
After the singer is dead
    And the maker buried.

ROBERT LOUIS STEVENSON

SPOOF

CONTENTS

FRENCH

Contents

THE ART SONG

INTRODUCTION

"Song. In relation to the study of music, a song may be defined as a short metrical composition, whose meaning is conveyed by the combined force of words and melody. The song, therefore, belongs equally to poetry and music." So begins the famous article by Mrs. Edmund Wodehouse in the earlier editions of *Grove's Dictionary of Music and Musicians*. Yet of the few attempts that have been made to write the history of the song, not one has approached the subject as a combined art, with poetry as the inspiration of music. To be sure, if one studies the literature and the music of the middle ages one comes on the same names, for then poetry and music were conceived as one —indeed, not only did the poet set his own verses to music, but he sang them himself, perhaps to his own accompaniment on a stringed instrument. Then as each of these arts unfolded it became a considerable thing in itself: the art of the poet, of the composer and of the musical performer, each grew to ever greater complexity and to ever greater subtlety.

Yet the two creative arts did not drift completely apart, since for centuries music remained predominantly vocal. In the madrigal literature of the Renaissance we find, over and over, the names of such famous poets as Petrarch and Dante. The care with which their texts were set, the descriptive detail that colors the vocal lines, is well known to anyone who has enjoyed singing madrigals. But as these part-songs were written primarily for the pleasure of the singers (there were in those days no audiences as we have them today) the modern listener may miss many of the details. In writing for the church, composers drew on the timeless texts of the liturgy and the Bible. The very familiarity of these texts, and the impersonality of the Latin language, tempted them to indulge in more and more elaborate counterpoint. Spurious though it may be, the story of the composition of Palestrina's *Missa Papae Marcelli* in a conscious effort to prove how distinctly words could be set in polyphonic music, is not without significance. To hurry on through the years, the birth of Italian monody, and of opera itself, were attempts to bring together, on equal terms, the sister arts of poetry and music.

In this discussion of the art song we will limit ourselves to music for one voice and piano, occasionally with the addition of an obbligato instrument. In setting such limits, of course, we rule out the whole magnificent literature of the lute song, and early German lieder by such masters as Albert, Erlebach, Telemann, even Johann Sebastian Bach (with such a gem as *Bist du bei mir* composed for voice and figured bass). Classic Italian arias, well known in the various anthologies, and cantatas by French and Italian masters, must also be denied a place.

The nineteenth-century German lied was the result of a fusion of three elements. If it had its primary source in one genius, the man must certainly have been the poet Goethe, for while he is called the greatest of the German Classicists, he stands at the head of the Romantic movement. Goethe is to German literature what Shakespeare is to English; except for Heine he has inspired more songs than any other poet. Other Romanticists, such as Eichendorff, Rückert, Mörike and Heyse, were responsible for an unprecedented outpouring of lyrical verse, and by a happy coincidence the right composers were ready to take advantage of this. The third factor was a new instrument called the pianoforte. Cristofori had invented the piano in Florence some time around 1709, and though as early as 1726 J. S. Bach had been shown, but not convinced by, a piano made in Germany by Silbermann, it remained for the composers of the later eighteenth century to explore the possibilities of the new instrument. Mozart, Haydn, and Carl Philipp Emanuel Bach were enthusiastic pioneers, and, as we know, Beethoven charted his explorations in an unparalleled series of sonatas. In the best songs of Mozart and Haydn we find the piano on equal terms with the voice; many of Schubert's descriptive and coloristic effects are in his piano parts. Schumann, going further, was often accused in his own time of writing piano pieces with vocal parts added.

In a sense, the development of the French mélodie received its impetus from the German lied. The songs and piano pieces of Schubert and Schumann had taken immediate hold on the French imagination, and their influence was promptly felt. France, too, was enjoying a sunburst of lyrical poetry. Victor Hugo, Théophile Gautier, Charles Baudelaire and Paul Verlaine furnished the inspiration for much fine music, from Berlioz and

Gounod to Duparc, Fauré and Debussy. Across the channel, England was slower in making its contribution. Under the not always beneficial influence of Mendelssohn, the Victorians delighted in a salon-type ballad, sometimes set with fair success to the poetry of Tennyson and Kingsley, until Stanford and Parry started the trend back to older and often greater poets, such as Blake, Herrick, Lovelace, and of course Shakespeare. With the coming of Vaughan Williams and Holst, English music borrowed a new depth from its own folk song. Stevenson and Housman became favorite poets. American composers in the first quarter of the present century progressed from Longfellow through Kipling and Whitman to the more contemporary Sara Teasdale, Tagore, Masefield, and "Fiona MacLeod." Scandinavian songs, especially those of Grieg, were unfortunately long known abroad in German and English translations that did scant justice to the poetry of Ibsen, Krag, Vinje, and Hans Christian Andersen. And Russian settings of Pushkin, Lermontov and others suffered under a similar handicap outside their own country. It may be significant that few Italian and Spanish poets of the nineteenth and twentieth centuries are well known internationally, for neither have the song repertories of these countries established themselves as have the German and the French.

But there are two schools of thought as to the importance of poetry in song. To some authorities, who remind us that poetry contains its own music, any attempt to combine the two arts is pure lily-gilding. For instance, Jacques Barzun, lecturing on *Words and Music* at The Library of Congress in 1951, put it this way: "Music's same power to present the sensations missing from the verbal signs of an experience explains why as a general rule the text of the best songs and operas is inferior in its kind to the musical setting. A great poem is complete in itself and needs no additions from another art. Great music is complete in itself, and only a disagreeable overlap of intentions can result from its being harnessed to great literature. Fortunately, many musicians have shown a certain indifference to poetic expression and thus have expended their powers on verse that was literal and required to be made into art. We then enjoy both the independent beauty of the music and the pleasure of its adaptation to a rudimentary conception in words."

And introducing a symposium on *Sound and Poetry* (Columbia University Press, 1957) Northrup Frye writes: "When we listen to a reading of Dylan Thomas, say the reading of Pea-

cock's *Song of Dinas Vawr*, which is in the Harvard Collection,
we are struck by the slowness of the reading. The words have
it all their own way here: they organize the rhythm, and are
not subordinated to a continuous stress beat. Next we are struck
by the importance of the features which are traditional in
poetry but have little place in music as such. One is an approxi-
mately regular pattern of pitch accent, which has been replaced
by stress accent in music. The other is an emphasis on the vary-
ing sonority of vowels, which in Classical poetry would take the
regular form of a quantitative meter. The equivalent in English
might better be described as quality, the sense that some kind
of irregular patterning of vowel-sounds is present.

"These elements of pitch, accent and quality of assonance are
a part of chanting, and singing and chanting are, in modern
times, radically different methods of associating melos and
lexis. When a poem is set to music and sung, its rhythm is taken
over by music. When it is chanted, all musical elements are
subordinated to the words. We notice that poets who, like Yeats,
want their poems chanted are precisely those who are most
suspicious of musical settings."

No one, certainly, would hold that it is enough to set a "great"
text to music. If this were so, then Dudley Buck's *To be, or not
to be* would not have been forgotten even in its own generation.
On the other hand, fond as one may become of Schumann's
Frauenliebe und Leben cycle, one admires it less than *Dichterliebe*, not simply because the music of the one is superior to
that of the other—beyond question Heine was a finer poet than
Chamisso. Nowadays one does not take *Frauenliebe* too seri-
ously because of the text—*Così non fan tutte*. Yet it seems fair
enough to concede that poetry of great philosophical depth, of
involved symbolism or intellectual significance, is not too likely
to translate successfully into song, for song is essentially a
lyrical art form. Even so, to take a single example from Goethe
the philosopher, Schubert's *Prometheus* is a fine song, and surely
Wolf's is a great one.

Goethe is often cited as an example of the great poet—the
great *musical* poet—with no ear for music. We are told that his
favorite composers were his friends Reichardt and Zelter, who
pleased him by writing music so modest that it would not inter-
fere with his verse, though we also know that he admired
Mozart. The sad story of the Schubert songs has perhaps been
too often told. In 1816 Josef von Spaun and several others of
Schubert's most faithful friends undertook to send a sheaf of

the Goethe settings to the poet. In the course of time the manuscript was returned without comment. In justice it should be remembered that Goethe was now sixty-seven, and that a group of friends around him watched very carefully over the things he got to see. Furthermore, as Maurice J. E. Brown puts it in his biography of Schubert, Spaun's letter was "so obsequious in tone that only a man whose head had been turned by praise would fail to be nauseated by it." It is then by no means certain that Goethe ever saw the songs. So much for his lack of appreciation.

Another popular Schubert bromide is that he could set a menu card to music. To bear this out the critic will point to numerous less than first-rate verses to be found among Schubert's 603 songs. But consider that this total number includes also fifty-nine Goethe poems, some set several times; six by Heine, whom Schubert discovered only in his last year; thirteen by Klopstock, a very great man in his day; thirty-one by Schiller; five by Rückert; and so on. And which are Schubert's masterpieces? *Erlkönig, Gretchen am Spinnrade, An Schwager Kronos, Heidenröslein,* the two *Wandrers Nachtlieder, Ganymed, Der Musensohn, Rastlose Liebe?*—these are a few by Goethe. *Der Doppelgänger, Am Meer, Der Atlas?*—these are by Heine. *Gruppe aus dem Tartarus?*—certainly the finest of all Schiller settings. *Dem Unendlichen?*—by Klopstock. Nor should we dismiss too casually such a poet as Wilhelm Müller— of the *Schöne Müllerin* and *Winterreise* cycles—quaint, old-fashioned and sentimental though he may be, his poems had a strong influence on Heine, and there is life in them even today. If the greatest and most perfect of Schubert's lieder are inspired by genuine poetry, it is equally true that his most conspicuous failures fall into the "menu" class.

Though Schubert remains the warmest and most lovable of the lieder composers, Hugo Wolf is now generally acknowledged the master of masters. Here is a musician whose literary taste is above reproach, one who became so absorbed in the poetry that caught his imagination that he would concentrate on one poet at a time until he had exhausted such material as he could respond to. His reading of his favorite poets—Mörike, Goethe, Eichendorff, Heyse and Geibel of the Spanish and Italian *Liederbücher*—was said to be positively demonic; when the creative urge was on him he worked at white heat. Composing at such speed he himself could hardly have been conscious of all the details that would someday be studied in his music. Only recently have the songs of Wolf begun to be generally known, for with a few exceptions they were too difficult for the once flourishing amateur singer and pianist, nor have many of them been considered "grateful" enough for the recital singer. It remained for the phonograph record to build an audience for Wolf, and it has provided the ideal way for the mere listener to enjoy and study him. One hears less and less the old charge that his music lacks melody—a stock answer to the exaggerated claims of his admirers that his vocal line always follows exactly the shape, meaning and inflection of the poem. The mastery and significance of his piano parts (here, especially, though to a large extent in all the lieder repertoire, the word "accompaniment" is inappropriate) and the way in which they set the stage, color, underline, or even argue with the voice—these things are no longer questioned. Of course it is possible to point out flaws even in Wolf's setting of words: what is important is that in his songs text and music remain inseparable in the memory to an extent unequaled by those of any other composer.

If Wolf, then, represents the literary approach to song writing, there are other lieder composers of real stature whose approach is fundamentally musical. One thinks especially of Beethoven and Brahms. Beethoven's songs have suffered neglect and a degree of condescension, partly because they are dwarfed by his achievements in other fields. Yet his little cycle *An die ferne Geliebte* has made its way into the affections of lieder enthusiasts, and his *Kennst du das Land* is one of the best. But in setting Goethe's *Wonne der Wehmut* he could write a lovely slow movement, perfectly appropriate to a violin and piano sonata. Robert Franz was more successful in making us feel the words of this poem. *Adelaide*, more properly a cantata than a song, is oversized for Matthisson's text; Schubert's little known setting is simpler and warmer. But if Beethoven here repeats words and phrases endlessly in the interests of musical form, he carries these excesses to absurd lengths in a little conceit called *Der Kuss*. The song is charming enough—a pastorale in which the lover threatens to kiss his Chloe. She tells him if he kisses her she will scream. He does and she does—but a long while after. This is the kind of humor that hardly bears repeating, but Beethoven labors the point in order to balance his composition. *Der Kuss* may be good music, and it is an attractive piece, but it is music rather than song.

Brahms has come in for a good deal of abuse, and has been set up as the anti-christ, largely because of Wolf's dislike for him. This hatred goes back to an early interview Wolf had with Brahms (whom he had up to that time admired) in which the older man advised the younger to do some studying. Had Brahms acknowledged the youthful genius in his headstrong caller all might have been different. But it is true that the two masters approached the song from opposite poles. The most self-critical of musicians, Brahms carefully selected his texts, but was more concerned with a poem as a whole than with the individual words and lines that composed it. It is not true that he was insensitive to poetic details, but he saw them as they fitted into the musical whole. Perhaps the most famous of his sins is the break in the opening line of *Wie bist du, meine König* (he himself may thus be to blame for the frequency with which this song is listed on programs as *Wie bist du, meine König?*); the singer who would do justice to the lied is required somehow to bridge the rest to the second phrase, a thing which can be done, as such artists as Elisabeth Schumann and Heinrich Schlusnus used to demonstrate. Again in the equally well-known *Minnelied*—beginning *Holder klingt der Vogelsang* —Brahms has set the line so that *klingt* becomes the important word, which is, of course, ridiculous. But his reason for doing so appears later in the song. He must have conceived the melody in the first place for the third stanza—*Traute, minnigliche Frau* —for here it fits perfectly. Be all this as it may, the climax on the repeated words *Mög' in Wonne blühen* would ensure the success of this musically rich lied.

The perfect song, by the standards of Wolf, is one in which the text is so well set that the hearer, assuming that he understands the language, grasps the meaning at once, without the necessity of repeating the poet's words. A folk song stands the test of time because words and music are so wedded that one remembers them together, even though the form is strophic, and there may be endless stanzas of text sung to the repeated melody. The song achieves a kind of perfection while passing from mouth to mouth, perhaps with slight changes each time it is sung, until it fairly sings itself. This is the ideal toward which every composer should strive, no matter how broad or how musically involved his conception may be. As we have seen, not even Wolf has a perfect score in this.

By these standards, then, the quality of the song is closely related to the quality of the poetry. No one better understood the art of setting words to music than Sir Arthur Sullivan. When he worked with Gilbert the results were delightful; but there was a very serious side to Sullivan. Deeply moved by a poem of the then eminent Adelaide Procter (he happened to read it while watching at the bedside of his dying brother) Sullivan composed a song which nearly a century later is by no means forgotten. If we accept the idea behind it, *The Lost Chord* is something of a masterpiece, for the melody fits the words like a glove, and the organlike background is a perfect stage setting.

Whatever the quality in a poem that makes it right for musical setting, a composer's success may be measured in terms of inevitability—the conviction that the poem was destined for just this music, and that the music could have been written only for the poem. Yet it is not difficult to point to numerous instances where two or more composers have achieved this sense in widely differing settings of the same poem. Loewe, looking over Schubert's *Erlkönig*, is said to have exclaimed: "Man kann es auch anders machen" (One can do this another way) and to have proceeded to prove his point. The result was good enough to convince many judges—Richard Wagner among them—that Loewe had written the greater song. As a song—the faithful setting of words—we can certainly make a strong case for Loewe's achievement, for he maintains Goethe's meter (as Schubert did not) and achieves an eerie effect in the voice of the Erlking unlike anything else in music. And though the hoofbeats of his horse (prophetic, it has been noted, of the *Walküre*) have not the maddening drive of Schubert's, they set the stage admirably. The real test is that, though as a piece of music the Schubert song is notably superior, we can easily forget it when we hear the Loewe.

Heine's *Lorelei* is familiar in the strophic setting of Silcher, so simple and folk-like that for many of us it has long since become the type of German folk song. Even the fact that the words of the second stanza fit the tune rather awkwardly bothers no one: it is hard to think of the poem without this melody. For atmosphere there is nothing more than the peaceful flow of the tune, perhaps suggestive of the Rhine. Compare this with the Liszt setting, in the form of a *scena dramatica*, opening with a recitative and proceeding to a sensuous cantabile depicting the siren herself, then after a dramatic shipwreck and a return to the recitative, the ominously melodious close. Consider the numerous (and admirable) settings of Verlaine's *Clair de lune*—Fauré's in the form of a minuet, evoking at once the pale semireality of a Watteau canvas; Debussy's more voluptuous yet more subdued, with the voice rising at the end like the very fountain the words describe; the remarkable song of Joseph Szulc, in which the fountain plays in stately languor throughout.

Loewe was right: there are many ways of setting a poem to music.

I have avoided referring to my subject as the "Romantic song," though the temptation to do so has been strong. For surely the great flowering of the lied and of the mélodie, even the modern English song, though it blossomed later, belong to the Romantic period of the nineteenth century. Now as we look backward upon that period, gratefully conserving the good things it has left us, we may wonder what the future of the lied may be. Today many composers are seeking new directions, often so conscientiously that little of their most careful work survives its world premiere. The voice is required to do things for which the only excuse is that they have not been done before, things far beyond the limits of what we call singing. Schoenberg's *Sprechstimme*, a compromise between singing and pitchless speech, seems to have been succeeded by wide and unvainly intervals supported by unlikely progressions. When such music is set to poetry one hardly hears the words, much less follows their sense. Stravinsky, acknowledged the most eminent composer of our day, sets English texts as he formerly (and more justifiably) set Latin, with regard for neither line nor accent. All this presupposes more and more highly developed professionalism on the part of our performers, and inevitably the end of the amateur singer who did so much in other days to make at least a limited repertory familiar.

And what of contemporary poets? Are they providing usable texts for songs? Are their techniques sufficiently in harmony with those of our composers to make a new union possible? To attempt an answer would be dangerous. It is interesting that a poet of Auden's stature should have taken to writing opera librettos; the fact that Benjamin Britten has found congenial texts in some of Auden's poems may not be unrelated. And, tragically, Dylan Thomas, whose poems are so rich in verbal music, was planning at the time of his death to provide a libretto for Stravinsky. So long as some quality of lyricism remains in poetry, the possibility of musical setting is not at an end. And the number of younger composers who today are interesting themselves in the song is an encouraging sign.

Povla Frijsh, one of the great interpreters, has told us that whenever she decided to add a song to her repertoire she began by memorizing the words. She never allowed her pupils to begin to sing before they had done likewise. In this way she shed light upon the composer's work. The present collection has been planned with this in mind. Wherever possible the texts are given as they appear in the collected works of the poets, or in anthologies; changes made by the chief composers are noted as they occur. Each poem is the occasion for a song, sometimes many songs. Some are first-rate poetry, others are minor but nonetheless genuine, a few merely curios. It is hoped that the reader, aside from using the anthology as a help to his concert going and record listening, may find pleasure in savoring the original texts as poetry. This is the way to the heart of the songs

The poems included in this book have been selected on the basis of the more or less standard song repertoire, not necessarily according to my own preference. Every connoisseur will miss some of his favorites and no doubt question the inclusion of others for which he cares less. For this I can only offer my sincere apologies and note the exigencies of space. In making the English translations it has been my aim to keep as close to the original poems as possible, but at the same time to stay within the boundaries of readable English. Generally the English versions are given line by line, and as often as feasible the word order has been retained, so that the meaning of the original words may be made reasonably clear. Occasionally it has seemed permissible to read between the lines—some of the German poetry is notably obscure—and where compound verbs are split between two or three lines a compromise has been necessary. In such cases, and in others where strict literalness results in a sort of pidgin English, I have preferred to keep my translation readable. There are variants of several of the poems which can be found in the Appendix. The Scandinavian poems have been translated for me by Miss Aasta Wendelbo, the Russian by Mrs. Alexandria Vodarsky-Shiraeff, and the Spanish by Miss Henrietta Yurchenco. Herbert Weinstock, my very understanding editor, and my wife have done more than I can say to make the book possible. And I owe a special word of gratitude to Mrs. Wallace Ferguson, Professor Frederick Stewart, Dr. Edward Kravitt, Mr. Fred Kleeberg, Mr. Gunter Kossodo, Mrs. Maria Claudia Grant, Professor Harry Zohn, Professor Otto Albrecht, Mr. Fujio Ishii, Dr. Emanuel Winternitz, and the late Dr. Curt Sachs, for suggestions, encouragement, and corrections.

GERMAN SONGS

ALLMERS, HERMANN
1821–1902

Ich ruhe still im hohen grünen Gras
Und sende lange meinen Blick nach oben,
Von Grillen rings umschwirrt ohn' Unterlass,
Von Himmelsbläue wundersam umwoben.

Und schöne weisse Wolken ziehn dahin
Durchs tiefe Blau, wie schöne stille Träume;—
Mir ist, als ob ich längst gestorben bin
Und ziehe selig mit durch ew'ge Räume.

JOHANNES BRAHMS, Op. 86, no. 2. The first words of the second stanza—*Und schöne weisse*—have been changed to *Die schönen weissen*. . . .

It is amusing to recall that this infinitely peaceful setting, so full of the atmosphere of the country on a summer day, did not please the poet, who found it pretentious and artificial. Admitting its fine musical craftsmanship, he missed in it the mood and the feelings he

BIERBAUM, OTTO JULIUS
1865–1910

FREUNDLICHE VISION

Nicht im Schlafe hab ich das geträumt,
Hell am Tage sah ichs schön vor mir:
Eine Wiese voller Margeritten;
Tief ein weisses Haus in grünen Büschen;
Götterbilder leuchten aus dem Laube.
Und ich geh mit Einer, die mich lieb hat,
Ruhigen Gemütes in die Kühle
Dieses weissen Hauses, in den Frieden,
Der voll Schönheit wartet, dass wir kommen.

RICHARD STRAUSS, Op. 48, no. 1.

German writer interested in legendary lore. His poems are notable chiefly for his love of nature.

ALONE IN THE FIELDS

I lie still in the tall green grass
and gaze a long time upward—
crickets chirping around me ceaselessly,
heaven's blue miraculously woven about me.

And beautiful white clouds drift yonder
through the deep blue, like lovely silent dreams.
It seems to me as though I have long been dead,
and am drifting blissfully with them through the eternal spaces.

---

had tried to express in his simple poem. His preference was for an amateurish and now forgotten setting by Gerhard Focken.

An interesting experiment is a more modern setting by the American Charles Ives, who is careful to point out, in his collection of 114 songs, that in making new music for texts that have previously inspired masterpieces, he is simply trying his hand and not offering competition.

Studied philosophy, law, and Chinese, and for a time worked as a journalist. Applied the technique of modern impressionism to older forms and subjects. Belonged to the Naturalistic school of German literature.

PLEASANT REVERIE

Not in sleep did I dream this;
in broad daylight I saw it beautiful before me:
a meadow full of daisies,
a white house deep in the green bushes;
sculptured gods shine through the foliage.
And I walk with one who loves me,
my soul content in the cool
of this white house, where peace,
full of beauty, awaits our coming.

TRAUM DURCH DIE DÄMMERUNG

Weite Wiesen im Dämmergrau;
Die Sonne verglomm, die Sterne ziehn;
Nun geh ich zu der schönsten Frau,
Weit über Wiesen im Dämmergrau,
Tief in den Busch von Jasmin.

Durch Dämmergrau in der Liebe Land;
Ich gehe nicht schnell, ich eile nicht;
Mich zieht ein weiches, samtenes Band
Durch Dämmergrau in der Liebe Land,
In ein blaues, mildes Licht.

RICHARD STRAUSS, Op. 29, no. 1. The third line of this setting reads *Nun geh ich hin zu der schönsten Frau*, and in the final repetition of the last line the order is changed to *In ein mildes, blaues Licht*.

BRUCHMANN, FRANZ, RITTER VON
1798–1867

AN DIE LEIER

Ich will von Atreus' Söhnen,
Von Kadmus will ich singen!
Doch meine Saiten tönen
Nur Liebe im Erklingen.

Ich tauschte um die Saiten,
Die Leier möcht' ich tauschen!
Alcidens Siegesschreiten
Sollt' ihrer Macht entrauschen!

Doch auch die Saiten tönen
Nur Liebe im Erklingen!
So lebt denn wohl, Heroen!
Denn meine Saiten tönen,
Statt Heldensang zu drohen,
Nur Liebe im Erklingen.

FRANZ PETER SCHUBERT, D. 737. At least one other setting exists, by P. Mirsch, Op. 1, no. 1. The poem is a translation from Anacreon.

DREAMING THROUGH THE TWILIGHT

Broad meadows in the twilight gray;
the sun has set, the stars appear;
now I go to the loveliest of women,
far over the meadows in the twilight gray,
deep into the jasmine bush.

Through the twilight gray to the land of love,
I do not go quickly, I do not hurry,
drawn by a fragile velvet ribbon,
through the twilight gray into the land of love,
into a blue, soft light.

Some critics consider the setting by Max Reger, Op. 35, no. 3,
superior to the famous Strauss song. Christian Sinding is among the
several others who have composed music for the poem.

One of Schubert's intimate friends, a student of law,
remembered now only for the songs Schubert made from
his poetry.

TO HIS LYRE

I will sing of the sons of Atreus,
of Cadmus will I sing!
But my strings sound
only strains of love.

I changed the strings about—
would I could change the lyre!—
On the triumphant strides of Alcides
it should spend its power.

But again my strings sound
only strains of love!
So farewell, heroes!
For my strings sound,
instead of threatening with heroic songs,
only strains of love.

CHAMISSO, ADALBERT VON
1781–1838

ROBERT SCHUMANN, Op. 42. Schumann's famous cycle includes eight of Chamisso's nine poems. The first seven of them, set by Carl Loewe, were published as his Op. 60. He also composed Nos. 8 and 9 in the same year (1836) but these were not published until many years later.

1

Seit ich ihn gesehen,
 Glaub ich blind zu sein;
Wo ich hin nur blicke,
 Seh' ich ihn allein;
Wie im wachen Traume
 Schwebt sein Bild mir vor,
Taucht aus tiefstem Dunkel
 Heller nur empor.

Sonst ist licht- und farblos
 Alles um mich her,
Nach der Schwester Spiele
 Nicht begehr' ich mehr,
Möchte lieber weinen
 Still im Kämmerlein;
Seit ich ihn gesehen,
 Glaub ich blind zu sein.

ROBERT SCHUMANN, Op. 42, no. 1.

2

Er, der Herrlichste von allen,
 Wie so milde, wie so gut!
Holde Lippen, klares Auge
 Heller Sinn und fester Mut.

So wie dort in blauer Tiefe,
 Hell und herrlich, jener Stern,
Also er an meinem Himmel,
 Hell und herrlich, hoch und fern.

Although born in France and acquiring German as a second tongue, Chamisso achieved great fame among the German Romantics. He served as botanist of the Romanzov expedition to Oceania and the Arctic. Founded, with Varnhagen von Ense, the *Berliner Musenalmanach* (1803), for which his earliest verses were written, and later the *Deutsche Musenalmanach* (1829), which introduced most of his later works. He was admired for his lyrical expression of the domestic emotions and for his powerful imagination.

WOMAN'S LOVE AND LIFE

Since I have seen him
I think myself blind;
wherever I look
I see him only.
As in a waking dream
his image hovers before me;
out of the deepest darkness
it rises ever more brightly.

There is no other light or color
in anything around me;
playing with my sisters
no longer delights me;
I would rather weep
quietly in my room.
Since I have seen him
I think myself blind.

He, the noblest of all—
how kind, how good!
Fine lips, clear eyes,
bright soul and strong spirit!

As yonder in the deep blue
that bright and glorious star,
so is he in my heaven,
bright and glorious, high and distant.

Wandle, wandle deine Bahnen;
  Nur betrachten deinen Schein,
Nur in Demut ihn betrachten,
  Selig nur und traurig sein!

Höre nicht mein stilles Beten,
  Deinem Glücke nur geweiht;
Darfst mich, niedre Magd, nicht kennen,
  Hoher Stern der Herrlichkeit!

Nur die Würdigste von allen
  Soll beglücken deine Wahl,
Und ich will die Hohe segnen,
  Segnen viele tausend Mal.

Will mich freuen dann und weinen,
  Selig, selig bin ich dann,
Sollte mir das Herz auch brechen,
  Brich, o Herz, was liegt daran!

ROBERT SCHUMANN, Op. 42, no. 2. In the last line of the second
stanza *hoch und fern* is changed to *hehr und fern*. In the second line
of the fifth stanza *Soll beglücken* becomes *Darf beglücken*. The repetition of the word *segnen* with which the last line of this stanza

3

Ich kann's nicht fassen, nicht glauben,
  Es hat ein Traum mich berückt;
Wie hätt' er doch unter allen
  Mich Arme erhöht und beglückt?

Mir war's—er habe gesprochen:
  Ich bin auf ewig dein—
Mir war's—ich träume noch immer,
  Es kann ja nimmer so sein.

O lass im Traum mich sterben
  Gewiegt an seiner Brust,
Den seligsten Tod mich schlürfen
  In Tränen unendlicher Lust.

ROBERT SCHUMANN, Op. 42, no. 3. The third line of the final stanza

Go, go your way:
only let me contemplate your brilliance,
only in humility consider it,
only be blest and melancholy!

Do not listen to my quiet prayer,
dedicated only to your good fortune;
take no notice of me, the lowly maid,
o high and splendid star!

Only the worthiest of all
shall be favored by your choice;
and I will bless that exalted one,
bless her many thousand times.

I will rejoice, then, and weep,
for then I am happy—happy!
Even though my heart should break—
break, o heart, what can it matter?

begins is omitted. As so often in Schumann, the first stanza is
repeated at the end to complete the musical form, and the second
line, *Wie so milde, wie so gut*, is dwelt on once again to close the
song.

I cannot grasp or believe it;
I am beguiled by a dream.
How could he, from among them all,
have exalted and blessed so lowly a one as I?

It seemed to me—he spoke:
"I am yours forever"—
it seemed to me—I am still dreaming,
it cannot ever be so.

O let me perish in my dream,
lulled upon his breast!
Let me relish the most blessed death
in the endless happiness of tears.

reads: *Den seligen Tod mich schlürfen.* The first stanza is repeated
at the end with verbal and musical extensions.

4

Du Ring an meinem Finger,
  Mein goldenes Ringelein,
Ich drücke dich fromm an die Lippen,
  Dich fromm an das Herze mein.

Ich hatt' ihn ausgeträumet,
  Der Kindheit friedlichen Traum,
Ich fand allein mich verloren
  Im öden, unendlichen Raum.

Du Ring an meinem Finger,
  Da hast du mich erst belehrt,
Hast meinem Blick erschlossen
  Des Lebens unendlichen Wert.

Ich werd' ihm dienen, ihm leben,
  Ihm angehören ganz,
Hin selber mich geben und finden
  Verklärt mich in seinem Glanz.

Du Ring an meinem Finger,
  Mein goldenes Ringelein,
Ich drücke dich fromm an die Lippen,
  Dich fromm an das Herze mein.

ROBERT SCHUMANN, Op. 42, no. 4. There are a number of word-extensions to make the poem fit Schumann's melody: the last line of the first stanza becomes *Dich fromm an die Lippen, an das Herze mein*; the second line of the second stanza *Der Kindheit friedlichen schönen Traum*; the last line of the third stanza *Des Lebens unend-*

5

Helft mir, ihr Schwestern,
Freundlich mich schmücken,
Dient der Glücklichen heute mir.
Windet geschäftig
Mir um die Stirne
Noch der blühenden Myrte Zier.

O ring upon my finger,
my little golden ring,
I press you devoutly to my lips,
devoutly to my heart.

I had done with dreaming
the peaceful dream of childhood;
only to find myself lost
in endless desert space.

O ring upon my finger,
it was you who first taught me,
revealed to my sight
the infinite value of life.

I will serve him, live for him,
belong to him entirely,
give myself and find
myself transfigured in his light.

O ring upon my finger,
my little golden ring,
I press you devoutly to my lips,
devoutly to my heart.

---

lichen, tiefen Wert; in the last two lines of the fourth stanza *und finden Verklärt mich* is repeated; and again in the final line the composer makes it *Dich fromm an die Lippen, an das Herze mein*. There is one actual word change in the first line of the fourth stanza, which reads *Ich will ihm dienen. . . .*

Help me, sisters,
please, to adorn myself,
serve me, the happy one, today.
Busily wind
around my forehead
the blossoming myrtle wreath.

Als ich befriedigt,
Freudigen Herzens,
Dem Geliebten im Arme lag,
Immer noch rief er,
Sehnsucht im Herzen,
Ungeduldig den heut'gen Tag.

Helft mir, ihr Schwestern,
Helft mir verscheuchen
Eine törichte Bangigkeit;
Dass ich mit klarem
Aug' ihn empfange,
Ihn, die Quelle der Freudigkeit.

Bist, mein Geliebter,
Du mir erschienen,
Giebst du, Sonne, mir deinen Schein?
Lass mich in Andacht,
Lass mich in Demut
Mich verneigen dem Herren mein.

Streuet ihm, Schwestern,
Streuet ihm Blumen,
Bringt ihm knospende Rosen dar.
Aber euch, Schwestern,
Grüss' ich mit Wehmut,
Freudig scheidend aus eurer Schar.

ROBERT SCHUMANN, Op. 42, no. 5. In the second stanza the third
line reads *Sonst dem Geliebten im Arme lag.* In the final line of this
stanza *heut'gen* becomes *heutigen.* In the fourth stanza the order of
the third line is changed thus: *Giebst du mir, Sonne, deinen Schein.*

6

Süsser Freund, du blickest
Mich verwundert an,
Kannst es nicht begreifen,
Wie ich weinen kann;
Lass der feuchten Perlen
Ungewohnte Zier
Freudenhell erzittern
In den Wimpern mir.

As I lay peacefully,
happy in heart,
in my beloved's arms,
he was always crying out
with longing in his heart,
impatient for this day.

Help me, sisters,
help me to banish
a foolish anxiety,
so that I may with clear eye
receive him,
him, the source of happiness.

When you, my beloved,
appeared to me,
o sun, did you give me your light?
Let me in devotion,
let me in humility
bow before my lord.

Scatter flowers before him,
sisters,
bring him the budding roses.
But, sisters,
I greet you with sweet melancholy
as I happily take leave of your group.

The last two lines of this stanza are expanded thus: *Lass mich in Demut,/ Lass mich verneigen dem Herren mein.* In the third line of the final stanza *bringt* becomes *bringet*.

Dear friend, you look
at me in astonishment.
You don't understand
how I can weep!
Leave the moist pearls—
unwonted ornament—
to glisten, bright with happiness,
on my eyelashes.

Wie so bang mein Busen
  Wie so wonnevoll!
Wüsst' ich nur mit Worten,
  Wie ich's sagen soll;
Komm und birg dein Antlitz
  Hier an meiner Brust,
Will in's Ohr dir flüstern
  Alle meine Lust.

[Hab' ob manchen Zeichen
  Mutter schon gefragt,
Hat die gute Mutter
  Alles mir gesagt,
Hat mich unterwiesen
  Wie, nach allem Schein,
Bald für eine Wiege
  Muss gesorget sein.]

Weisst du nun die Tränen,
  Die ich weinen kann,
Sollst du nicht sie sehen,
  Du geliebter Mann;
Bleib' an meinem Herzen,
  Fühle dessen Schlag,
Dass ich fest und fester
  Nur dich drücken mag.

Hier an meinem Bette
  Hat die Wiege Raum,
Wo sie still verberge
  Meinen holden Traum;
Kommen wird der Morgen,
  Wo der Traum erwacht
Und daraus dein Bildnis
  Mir entgegen lacht.

ROBERT SCHUMANN, Op. 42, no. 6. The last two lines of the first
stanza read: *Freudig hell erzittern/In dem Auge mir.* The third

An meinem Herzen, an meiner Brust,
Du meine Wonne, du meine Lust!

How anxious I am,
how full of delight!
If only I had the words
to say it!
Come, and bury your face
here on my breast;
into your ear I will whisper
all my happiness.

[I have already asked mother
about the signs.
Good mother has
told me everything;
she has assured me
that, by all indications,
soon a cradle
will be needed.]

Now do you understand the tears
that I can weep?
Ought you not see them,
dearest man?
Rest upon my heart,
feel its beat,
and nearer and nearer
let me draw you.

Here by my bed
is place for the cradle
which shall quietly hide
my lovely dream.
The morning will come
when the dream awakens,
and from it your image
will smile at me.

---

stanza is omitted. After the fourth stanza the words *fest und fester*
are repeated, and after the final stanza *dein Bildnis*.

Upon my heart, upon my bosom,
Oh my joy, oh my rapture!

Das Glück ist die Liebe, die Lieb' ist das Glück,
Ich hab' es gesagt und nehm's nicht zurück.

Hab' überglücklich mich geschätzt,
Bin überglücklich aber jetzt.

Nur die da säugt, nur die da liebt
Das Kind, dem sie die Nahrung giebt,

Nur eine Mutter weiss allein,
Was lieben heisst und glücklich sein.

O wie bedaur' ich doch den Mann,
Der Mutterglück nicht fühlen kann!

Du schauest mich an und lächelst dazu,
Du lieber, lieber Engel du!

An meinem Herzen, an meiner Brust,
Du meine Wonne, du meine Lust!

ROBERT SCHUMANN, Op. 42, no. 7. The first words of the fourth
line are contracted to *Ich hab's gesagt*; in the fifth line *überglücklich*
is changed to *überschwenglich*; the order of the penultimate couplet

8

Nun hast du mir den ersten Schmerz getan,
    Der aber traf.
Du schläfst, du harter, unbarmherz'ger Mann,
    Den Todesschlaf.

Es blicket die Verlass'ne vor sich hin,
    Die Welt ist leer.
Geliebet hab' ich und gelebt, ich bin
    Nicht lebend mehr.

Ich zieh' mich in mein Inn'res still zurück,
    Der Schleier fällt,
Da hab' ich Dich und mein vergang'nes Glück,
    Du meine Welt!

ROBERT SCHUMANN, Op. 42, no. 8. In the third line of the final

Happiness is love, love is happiness,
I have said it before and I don't take it back.

I have thought myself over-happy,
but I am over-happy now.

Only she who gives suck, only she who loves
the child to whom she gives nourishment,

only a mother knows
what it is to love and to be fortunate.

O how I pity the man,
who cannot feel a mother's rapture.

You look at me and smile,
you dear, dear angel!

Upon my heart, upon my bosom,
oh my joy, oh my rapture!

---

is changed to *Du lieber, lieber Engel, du,/Du schauest mich an und lächelst dazu!*

Now you have hurt me for the first time—
really hurt me!
You sleep, hard pitiless man,
the sleep of death.

The forsaken one looks before her—
the world is empty.
I have loved and lived—I am
no longer alive.

I withdraw silently within myself.
The veil falls.
There I have *you* and my lost happiness,
O you, my world!

---

stanza *vergang'nes Glück* becomes *verlor'nes Glück.*

9

Traum der eig'nen Tage,
  Die nun ferne sind,
Tochter meiner Tochter,
  Du mein süsses Kind,
Nimm, bevor die Müde
  Deckt das Leichentuch,
Nimm in's frische Leben
  Meinen Segensspruch.

Siehst mich grau von Haaren,
  Abgezehrt und bleich,
Bin, wie du, gewesen
  Jung und wonnereich,
Liebte, wie du liebest,
  Ward, wie du, auch Braut,
Und auch du wirst altern,
  So wie ich ergraut.

Lass die Zeit im Fluge
  Wandeln fort und fort,
Nur beständig wahre
  Deines Busens Hort;
Hab' ich's einst gesprochen,
  Nehm ich's nicht zurück:
Glück ist nur die Liebe,
  Liebe nur das Glück.

Als ich, den ich liebte,
  In das Grab gelegt,
Hab' ich meine Liebe
  Treu in mir gehegt:
War mein Herz gebrochen,
  Blieb mir fest der Mut,
Und des Alters Asche
  Wahrt die heil'ge Glut.

Nimm, bevor die Müde
  Deckt das Leichentuch,
Nimm in's frische Leben
  Meinen Segensspruch:
Muss das Herz dir brechen,
  Bleibe fest dein Mut,
Sei der Schmerz der Liebe
  Dann dein höchstes Gut.

Dream of my own days
now long gone,
daughter of my daughter,
my sweet child,
take, before the weary one
is covered with the shroud,
take in your young life
my words of blessing.

Though you see me gray-haired,
wasted and faded,
I was once, like you,
young and charming.
I loved as you love,
like you, became a bride;
and you too will grow old
and gray as I.

Let time pass
on and on;
only steadfastly guard
the treasure in your breast.
I once said,
and I do not take it back:
happiness is only love,
love only happiness.

When I laid the one I loved
in his grave,
I cherished my love
faithfully within myself.
Though my heart was broken
my courage remained strong,
and the ashes of age
are kept aglow by the sacred fire.

Take, before the weary one
is covered with the shroud,
take in your young life
my words of blessing:
Though your heart must break,
keep your courage strong;
may the pain of love, then,
be your highest good.

This epilogue to Chamisso's cycle of poems was not set by Schumann.

DIE KARTENLEGERIN

Schlief die Mutter endlich ein
Über ihre Hauspostille?
Nadel, liege du nun stille:
Nähen, immer nähen,—nein!—
Legen will ich mir die Karten,
Ei, was hab' ich zu erwarten?
Ei, was wird das Ende sein?

Trüget mich die Ahnung nicht,
Zeigt sich Einer, den ich meine,—
Schön, da kommt er ja, der Eine,
Coeurbub kannte seine Pflicht.—
Eine reiche Witwe?—wehe!
Ja, er freit sie, ich vergehe!
O verruchter Bösewicht!

Herzeleid und viel Verdruss—
Eine Schul' und enge Mauern,
Carreaukönig, der bedauern,—
Und zuletzt mich trösten muss.—
Ein Geschenk auf art'ge Weise—
Er entführt mich—Eine Reise—
Geld und Lust im Überfluss!

Dieser Carreaukönig da
Muss ein Fürst sein oder König
Und es fehlt daran nur wenig,
Bin ich selber Fürstin ja.—
Hier ein Feind, der mir zu schaden
Sich bemüht bei seiner Gnaden,
Und ein Blonder steht mir nah.

Ein Geheimnis kommt zutag
Und ich flüchte noch bei Zeiten—
Fahret wohl, ihr Herrlichkeiten;
O das war ein harter Schlag!—
Hin ist einer, eine Menge
Bilden um mich ein Gedränge,
Dass ich kaum sie zählen mag.

THE FORTUNE-TELLER

Has mother finally gone to sleep
over her book of sermons?
Needle, lie still!
Sewing, eternal sewing—no!
I am going to lay out the cards—
well, what have I to look forward to?
well, what will the end be?

If my premonition isn't false,
The one I have in mind will appear.
Fine, there he comes, the one—
the Jack of Hearts knew his duty.
A rich widow?—Woe!
Yes, he woos her, I am undone!
O the infamous scoundrel!

Heartbreak and trouble!
A school and narrow walls—
the King of Diamonds, who pities me
and at last wants to comfort me.
A friendly gift—
he abducts me—a journey—
gold and pleasure in profusion!

This King of Diamonds
must be a prince or a king,
and there is only a little something lacking
for me to be a princess.
Here an enemy is trying to make trouble for me
with His Grace,
and there is a blond fellow standing by.

A secret come to light,
and I flee just in time.
Farewell, glories!
O that was a hard blow!
The one is gone, a crowd
gathers around me so thick
that I can hardly count them.

[Dieser hier im grauen Haar
  Ist ein Junker wohl vom Lande,
  Spröde halt' ich ihn am Bande
  Und ich führ' ihn zum Altar.—
  Nach Paris!—Ein lustig Leben!
  Brummt der Mann, so lach' ich eben,
  Bleibt doch alles, wie es war.—]

Kommt das grämliche Gesicht,
  Kommt die Alte da mit Keuchen,
  Lieb' und Lust mir zu verscheuchen,
  Eh' die Jugend mir gebricht?—
  Ach! die Mutter ist's, die aufwacht,
  Und den Mund zu schelten aufmacht,
  Nein, die Karten lügen nicht!

ROBERT SCHUMANN, Op. 31, no. 2. Chamisso's poem is a translation from the French of Béranger (see Appendix). There are many repeated lines in the Schumann setting, and the sixth stanza is omitted. In the first line of the fifth stanza *zutag* is changed to *zu*

DER SOLDAT

Es geht bei gedämpfter Trommel Klang;
Wie weit noch die Stätte! der Weg wie lang!
O wär' er zur Ruh und alles vorbei!
Ich glaub', es bricht mir das Herz entzwei.

Ich hab' in der Welt nur ihn geliebt,
Nur ihn, dem jetzt man den Tod doch giebt.
Bei klingendem Spiele wird paradiert,
Dazu bin auch ich kommandiert.

Nun schaut er auf zum letztenmal
In Gottes Sonne freudigen Strahl,
Nun binden sie ihm die Augen zu—
Dir schenke Gott die ewige Ruh!

Es haben die Neun wohl angelegt,
Acht Kugeln haben vorbeigefegt;
Sie zitterten alle vor Jammer und Schmerz—
Ich aber, ich traf ihn mitten ins Herz.

ROBERT SCHUMANN, Op. 40, no. 3. The poem is a translation from Hans Christian Andersen (see Appendix). Schumann makes two changes in the text: the first line of the last stanza reads *Es haben*

[This one here with the gray hair
is a country gentleman.
Primly I catch him
and lead him to the altar.
To Paris!—A merry life!
When the man grumbles, I laugh;
but everything remains as it was.]

Does the irritable face,
the old one with her coughing,
come to blight my love and pleasure
while I am still young?
Ah! it's mother waking up,
and she is opening her mouth to scold me—
No, the cards don't lie!

Tage, and in the last line the order is altered to *Dass ich sie kaum
zählen mag*. The first line of the final stanza is changed to *Kommt
das dumme Frau'ngesicht*.

THE SOLDIER

It is done to the sound of muffled drums;
how distant, still, the place! How long the way!
Oh if only he were at rest and all were over!
I believe it will break my heart in two.

In all the world I loved him only,
him only whom they now put to death.
With music and ceremony there will be a parade,
and I too am ordered to take part.

Now he looks up for the last time
in the joyous light of God's sun;
now they are blindfolding him—
God send you eternal rest!

The nine have taken good aim;
eight bullets have missed him.
They were all trembling with distress and pain—
but I, I shot straight to his heart.

---

dann Neun wohl angelegt; and in the final line *ins* becomes *in das*.
Another setting, by Friedrich Silcher, is in the style of a folk song.
Less well known is Edvard Grieg's song, set to the original Danish.

CLAUDIUS, MATTHIAS
1740–1815

DER TOD UND DAS MÄDCHEN

DAS MÄDCHEN

Vorüber, ach vorüber
Geh, wilder Knochenmann!
Ich bin noch jung! Geh, Lieber,
Und rühre mich nicht an!

DER TOD

Gib deine Hand, du schön und zart Gebild!
Bin Freund und komme nicht zu strafen.
Sei gutes Muts! Ich bin nicht wild!
Sollst sanft in meinen Armen schlafen!

FRANZ PETER SCHUBERT, D. 531.

COLLIN, MATTHÄUS VON
1779–1824

NACHTFEIER

Heil'ge Nacht, du sinkest nieder;
Nieder wallen auch die Träume,
Wie dein Licht durch diese Bäume,
Lieblich durch der Menschen Brust.

Die belauschen sie mit Lust;
Rufen, wenn der Tag erwacht:
Kehre wieder, heil'ge Nacht!
Holde Träume, kehret wieder!

FRANZ PETER SCHUBERT, D. 827. Schubert called his song *Nacht
und Träume* (*Night and dreams*). Lines 3 and 4 are changed to *Wie
dein Mondlicht durch die Räume,/Durch der menschen stille Brust*

A German poet who used the *nom de plume* of Asmus, from 1771 to 1775 he edited a newspaper called *Wandsbecker Bote*, in which he published many poems and essays. In his later days he became engrossed in religion.

DEATH AND THE MAIDEN

THE MAIDEN

Pass by, pass by,
go, horrible skeleton!
I am still young! Go, good man,
and do not touch me!

DEATH

Give me your hand, lovely and gentle creature!
I am your friend, and do not come to punish you.
Be of good cheer! I am not fierce!
You shall sleep softly in my arms!

Tutor to the Duke of Reichstadt, son of Napoleon I, and active in Austria as one of the early *Romantics*, Collin became editor of the *Jahrbücher der Literatur*. He was a friend of Schubert and a brother of Heinrich von Collin, author of *Coriolan*, for which Beethoven wrote his overture.

IN PRAISE OF NIGHT

Hallowed night, you are descending;
dreams, too, come drifting down—
like your light through these trees—
delightfully through the hearts of men.

They listen furtively with joy;
they call out when the day breaks:
Come back, hallowed night!
Gracious dreams, come back again!

Like your moonlight through space,/through the silent hearts of men).

CRAIGHER DE JACHELUTTA, JAKOB NIKOLAUS, REICHSFREIHERR VON

1797–1855

DIE JUNGE NONNE

Wie braust durch die Wipfel der heulende Sturm!
Es klirren die Balken, es zittert das Haus!
Es rollet der Donner, es leuchtet der Blitz,
Und finster die Nacht wie das Grab!

Immerhin, immerhin,
So tobt' es auch jüngst noch in mir!
Es brauste das Leben, wie jetzo der Sturm,
Es bebten die Glieder, wie jetzo das Haus,
Es flammte die Liebe, wie jetzo der Blitz,
Und finster die Brust wie das Grab!

Nun tobe, du wilder, gewalt'ger Sturm,
Im Herzen ist Friede, im Herzen ist Ruh,
Des Bräutigams harret die liebende Braut,
Gereinigt in prüfender Glut,
Der ewigen Liebe getraut.

Ich harre, mein Heiland, mit sehnendem Blick!
Komm, himmlischer Bräutigam, hole die Braut,
Erlöse die Seele von irdischer Haft!
Horch, friedlich ertönet das Glöcklein vom Turm!
Es lockt mir das süsse Getön
Allmächtig zu ewigen Höhn.
Alleluja!

FRANZ PETER SCHUBERT, D. 825. Schubert made his setting from a
manuscript copy of the poem which Craigher gave him when they
met in 1825. In 1828 the poet published it in his *Poetische Be-
trachtungen von Nicolaus*, making two minor changes: the second

An accountant who published many poems using the pseudonym Nicolaus, he became Belgian consul at Trieste and traveled in the East.

THE NOVICE

How the raging storm howls through the treetops!
The rafters rattle, the house trembles!
The thunder rolls, the lightning flashes,
and the night is gloomy as the grave!

Ever, ever so,
not long ago it raged within me!
Life blustered as now the storm;
my limbs shivered as now the house;
love flamed as now the lightning,
and my heart was gloomy as the grave!

Now rage, wild mighty storm:
in my heart there is peace, in my heart there is rest.
The loving bride awaits the bridegroom,
cleansed by the proving fire,
pledged to eternal love.

I wait, my Saviour, with longing eyes!
Come, Heavenly Bridegroom, come for the bride;
release the soul from earthly ties!
Hark! Peacefully the bell rings from the tower!
The sweet sound calls me
irresistibly to the eternal heights.
Alleluia!

---

line of the second stanza became *So tobt es noch jüngst auch in mir,* and in the fourth line of the final stanza he changed *vom Turm* to *am Turm.*

DAUMER, GEORG FRIEDRICH
1800–1875

BOTSCHAFT

Wehe, Lüftchen, lind und lieblich,
Um die Wange der Geliebten,
Spiele zart in ihrer Locke,
Eile nicht, hinweg zu fliehn!
Tut sie dann vielleicht die Frage,
Wie es um mich Armen stehe,
Sprich: "Unendlich war sein Wehe,
Höchst bedenklich seine Lage;
Aber jetzo kann er hoffen,
Wieder herrlich aufzuleben,
Denn du, Holde, denkst an ihn."

JOHANNES BRAHMS, Op. 47, no. 1.

NICHT MEHR ZU DIR ZU GEHEN

Nicht mehr zu dir zu gehen,
Beschloss ich und beschwor ich,
Und gehe jeden Abend,
Denn jede Kraft und jeden Halt verlor ich.

Ich möchte nicht mehr leben,
Möcht' augenblicks verderben,
Und möchte doch auch leben
Für dich, mit dir, und nimmer, nimmer sterben.

Ach rede, sprich ein Wort nur,
Ein einziges, ein klares;
Gieb Leben oder Tod mir,
Nur dein Gefühl enthülle mir, dein wahres!

JOHANNES BRAHMS, Op. 32, no. 2. In the second stanza Brahms
repeats the word *augenblicks*, and in the third the phrase *Nur dein
Gefühl.*

Known as a writer on religion, at first opposed to Christianity, Daumer became interested in Mohammedanism. He translated poems of Hafiz and other Oriental and Slavic writers. Later he became a Catholic.

THE MESSAGE

Drift, breezes, gently and lovingly
around the cheeks of the beloved;
play tenderly in her locks;
do not hasten to leave her.
Should she then perhaps ask the question
how I, poor man, fare,
say: "Endless was his suffering,
very grave was his condition;
but now he can hope
to come to glorious life again
because you, dear one, are thinking of him."

NEVER AGAIN TO GO TO YOU

Never again to go to you,
I resolved and I swore it;
and I go every evening,
for I have lost all power and all firmness.

I do not want to live any more,
I wish I could perish right now;
and yet I also want to live
for you, with you, and never, never die.

Ah speak, speak one word only,
a solitary, clear word;
give me life or death,
only let me know your feeling, your true feeling!

WIE BIST DU, MEINE KÖNIGIN

Wie bist du, meine Königin,
    Durch sanfte Güte wonnevoll!
Du lächle nur—Lenzdüfte weh'n
    Durch mein Gemüte wonnevoll.

Frisch aufgeblüter Rose Glanz
    Vergleich ich ihn dem deinigen?
Ach, über alles, was da blüht,
    Ist deine Blüte wonnevoll!

Durch tote Wüsten wandle hin,
    Und grüne Schatten breiten sich,
Ob fürchterliche Schwüle dort
    Ohn' Ende brüte, wonnevoll.

Lass mich vergeh'n in deinem Arm!
    Es ist in ihm ja selbst der Tod,
Ob auch die herbste Todesqual
    Die Brust durchwüte, wonnevoll.

JOHANNES BRAHMS, Op. 32, no. 9. At the end of each stanza the
word *wonnevoll* is repeated, this little refrain after the last stanza

WIR WANDELTEN

Wir wandelten, wir zwei zusammen;
Ich war so still und du so stille;
Ich gäbe viel, um zu erfahren,
Was du gedacht in jenem Fall.

Was ich gedacht—unausgesprochen
Verbleibe das! Nur Eines sag' ich:
So schön war Alles, was ich dachte,
So himmlisch-heiter war es all.

In meinem Haupte die Gedanken
Sie läuteten, wie goldne Glöckchen;
So wundersüss, so wunderlieblich
Ist in der Welt kein andrer Hall.

JOHANNES BRAHMS, Op. 96, no. 2.

HOW DELIGHTFUL, O MY QUEEN

How delightful you are, o my queen,
with your gentle graces!
You merely smile—fragrances of spring waft
through my soul delightfully.

The fresh lustre of the new-blown rose—
shall I compare it to yours?
Ah, above everything that blossoms
is your bloom delightful.

Through the barren desert I wander
and green shade spreads itself—
though horrible sultriness
endlessly broods there—delightfully.

Let me die in your arms!
In them indeed is death itself,
even though the bitterest pangs of death
rage through me, delightful.

becoming *Wonnevoll, wonne-wonnevoll*. In the first line of the second stanza Daumer's *Rose Glanz* becomes *Rosen Glanz*.

WE WALKED TOGETHER

We walked, we two together;
I was so silent and you were so silent.
I would give a good deal to know
what you were thinking then.

What I thought—unspoken
let it remain! Only one thing I say:
So beautiful was everything I thought,
so heavenly and serene was it all!

In my head the thoughts
rang like golden bells;
so marvelously sweet and lovely
is no other sound in the world.

DEHMEL, RICHARD

1863–1920

BEFREIT

Du wirst nicht weinen. Leise, leise
Wirst du lächeln; und wie zur Reise
Geb' ich dir Blick und Kuss zurück.
Unsre lieben vier Wände! Du hast sie bereitet,
Ich habe sie dir zur Welt geweitet—
O Glück!

Dann wirst du heiss meine Hände fassen
Und wirst mir deine Seele lassen,
Lässt unsern Kindern mich zurück.
Du schenkest mir dein ganzes Leben,
Ich will es ihnen wiedergeben—
O Glück!

Es wird sehr bald sein, wir wissen's beide.
Wir haben einander befreit vom Leide;
So geb' ich dich der Welt zurück.
Dann wirst du mir nur noch im Traum erscheinen
Und mich segnen und mit mir weinen—
O Glück!

RICHARD STRAUSS, Op. 39, no. 4. The third line in the last stanza

WIEGENLIED

Venus Mater:

Träume, träume, du mein süsses Leben,
von dem Himmel, der die Blumen bringt;
Blüten schimmern da, die beben
von dem Lied, das deine Mutter singt.

Träume, träume, Knospe meiner Sorgen,
von dem Tage, da die Blume spross;
von dem hellen Blütenmorgen,
da dein Seelchen sich der Welt erschloss.

A leader in German poetry in the period of transition from naturalism to neo-classicism, Dehmel produced work marked by descriptive and emotional power and intense feeling.

RELEASED

You will not cry. Gently, gently
you will smile, and as though going on a journey
I will return your glance and your kiss.
Our beloved four walls! You made them ready;
I have made of them a world for you—
O happiness!

Then you must warmly clasp my hands
and leave your soul with me,
as you leave me to our children.
You give me your whole life;
I shall give it back to them—
O happiness!

It will be very soon, we both know it.
We have set each other free from sorrow;
so I give you back to the world.
Then you will come to me again only in dreams,
and bless me and weep with me—
O happiness!

---

is altered to *So gab' ich dich der Welt zurück*, and the final *O Glück* is repeated.

CRADLE SONG

Dream, dream, my sweet life,
of heaven, which brings the flowers;
Blossoms glisten there; they quiver
to the song your mother sings.

Dream, dream, bud of my care,
of the day when the flower sprouted,
of the bright blossoming morning
when your little soul came into the world

Träume, träume, Blüte meiner Liebe,
von der stillen, von der heiligen Nacht,
da die Blume Seiner Liebe
diese Welt zum Himmel mir gemacht.

RICHARD STRAUSS, Op. 41, no. 1. The poem was also set by Hans

EICHENDORFF, JOSEPH, FREIHERR VON
1788–1857

LIEDERKREIS

ROBERT SCHUMANN, Op. 39. Schumann's cycle is made up of twelve
selected Eichendorff poems. Indeed, there is little connection between
them. But as a series of brief mood pictures they make a satisfying
group, and they are often sung together. They are therefore given
here in the order Schumann gave them.

I

IN DER FREMDE

Aus der Heimat hinter den Blitzen rot,
Da kommen die Wolken her,
Aber Vater und Mutter sind lange tot,
Es kennt mich dort keiner mehr.

Wie bald, wie bald kommt die stille Zeit,
Da ruhe ich auch, und über mir
Rauschet die schöne Waldeinsamkeit,
Und keiner mehr kennt mich auch hier.

2

ANDENKEN

Dein Bildnis wunderselig
Hab' ich im Herzensgrund,
Das sieht so frisch und fröhlich
Mich an zu jeder Stund'.

Dream, dream, bloom of my love,
of the silent holy night
when the flowering of his love
made this world a heaven for me.

Pfitzner, who gave it the title *Venus Mutter* (Op. 11, no. 4).

After studying law, Eichendorff spent some time in Paris and Vienna; in 1813 he joined Lützow's corps as a volunteer. One of the greatest of the later German Romanticists, he was especially successful in his shorter lyrics interpreting the moods and mysteries of nature.

SONG CYCLE

FAR FROM HOME

From my home beyond the lightning's flash,
the clouds drift over me.
But father and mother are long since dead,
and no one there remembers me any more.

How soon, how soon comes the quiet time
when I too shall rest; and over me
will rustle the lovely, lonely forest.
And no one will remember me any more even here.

ROBERT SCHUMANN, Op. 39, no. 1. The second stanza begins *Wie bald, ach wie bald*. The first word of the third line in this stanza is shortened to *rauscht*, and the last line becomes *Und keiner kennt mich mehr hier*. Among the several other composers who ventured to set this text was the young Johannes Brahms (Op. 3, no. 5), friend and protégé of Schumann. He seems to have taken his text from the already famous setting, for he makes exactly the same changes.

MEMORY

Your blessed image
I keep deep in my heart;
so gay and happy, it looks
at me all the time.

Mein Herz still in sich singet
Ein altes schönes Lied,
Das in die Luft sich schwinget
Und zu dir eilig zieht.

ROBERT SCHUMANN, Op. 39, no. 2. Schumann changes the title to
Intermezzo. There are some thirty-five settings listed in Challier's

3

WALDESGESPRÄCH

"Es ist schon spät, es wird schon kalt,
Was reitst du einsam durch den Wald?
Der Wald ist lang, du bist allein,
Du schöne Braut! Ich führ' dich heim!"

"Gross ist der Männer Trug und List,
Vor Schmerz mein Herz gebrochen ist,
Wohl irrt das Waldhorn her und hin,
O flieh! du weisst nicht, wer ich bin."

"So reich geschmückt ist Ross und Weib,
So wunderschön der junge Leib,
Jetzt kenn' ich dich—Gott steh' mir bei!
Du bist die Hexe Lorelei."—

"Du kennst mich wohl—von hohem Stein
Schaut still mein Schloss tief in den Rhein.
Es ist schon spät, es wird schon kalt,
Kommst nimmermehr aus diesem Wald!"

ROBERT SCHUMANN, Op. 39, no. 3. The first line reads *Es ist schon
spät, es ist schon kalt.* Among the fifteen or more other settings, that

4

DIE STILLE

Es weiss und rät es doch keiner,
Wie mir so wohl ist, so wohl!
Ach, wüsst' es nur einer, nur einer,
Kein Mensch es sonst wissen soll!

My heart sings softly to itself
an old, beautiful song
that soars into the air
and hastens to you.

Lieder-Katalog and its supplements.

DIALOGUE IN THE FOREST

"It is already late, it is growing cold;
why do you ride alone through the wood?
The forest is vast, you are alone;
beautiful bride! I will see you home!"

"Great are the deceit and the cunning of men;
my heart is wracked with pain;
the sound of the horn is all around us.
Begone! You do not know who I am."

"So richly adorned are both horse and lady,
so enchanting is your young body—
now I know you—God be with me!—
You are the sorceress Lorelei."

"You know me well—from a high cliff
my castle looks silently deep into the Rhine.
It is already late, it is growing cold.
Nevermore shall you leave this wood!"

---

of Adolf Jensen alone seems to be remembered.

THE SILENT GIRL

No one knows it or guesses it,
I am so happy, so happy!
I wish it were known to only one—only one—
no other mortal should know it!

So still ist's nicht draussen im Schnee,
So stumm und verschwiegen sind
Die Sterne nicht in der Höh',
Als meine Gedanken sind.

[Ich wünscht', es wäre schon Morgen,
Da fliegen zwei Lerchen auf,
Die überfliegen einander,
Mein Herze folgt ihrem Lauf.]

Ich wünscht', ich wäre ein Vöglein
Und zöge über das Meer,
Wohl über das Meer und weiter,
Bis dass ich im Himmel wär'!

ROBERT SCHUMANN, Op. 39, no. 4. The third stanza is omitted, and
the first is repeated in conclusion. The last word of the first stanza is
changed to *sollt'*.

5

MONDNACHT

Es war, als hätt der Himmel
Die Erde still geküsst,
Dass sie im Blütenschimmer
Von ihm nun träumen müsst.

Die Luft ging durch die Felder,
Die Ähren wogten sacht,
Es rauschten leis die Wälder,
So sternklar war die Nacht.

Und meine Seele spannte
Weit ihre Flügel aus,
Flog durch die stillen Lande,
Als flöge sie nach Haus.

ROBERT SCHUMANN, Op. 39, no. 5. Eichendorff's *nun träume*
müsst here becomes *nur träumen müsst*. There is an early setting of
the poem by Brahms, published without opus number many years
after its composition. It has two identical stanzas and a third in
contrast. Some words are repeated at the end of each stanza—*nu*
träumen müsst, So sternklar and *nach Haus, als flöge sie nach Haus*
In the third stanza *spannte weit* is also repeated. Like Schumann

It is not so quiet out in the snow,
not so reserved and silent
are the stars in the heavens,
as my thoughts.

[I wish it were already morning;
then two larks would fly up,
they would overtake each other—
my heart would follow them.]

I wish I were a bird
and could fly over the sea,
over the sea and farther
until I was in heaven!

Felix Mendelssohn-Bartholdy uses the first line for the title of his setting (Op. 99, no. 6), and he sets the entire poem, with many repetitions. Over thirty other settings have been published.

MOONLIT NIGHT

It seemed as though the heavens
had kissed the earth to silence,
so that, amid glistening flowers,
she must now dream heavenly dreams.

The breeze passed through the fields;
the corn stirred softly;
the forest rustled lightly,
so clear and starry was the night.

And my soul spread
wide its wings;
took flight through the silent land
as though it were flying home.

Brahms changes *nun* to *nur* in the last line of the first stanza, and in the third stanza, third line, *Lande* becomes *Räume*, thereby abolishing the poet's rhyme.

Of the more than forty other settings, mention may be made of those by Hummel (Op. 16, no. 4), Kalliwoda (Op. 7, no. 3), Lassen, Marschner (Op. 179, no. 2) and Emanuel Moór (Op. 43, no. 1).

6

SCHÖNE FREMDE

Es rauschen die Wipfel und schauern,
Als machten zu dieser Stund'
Um die halbversunkenen Mauern
Die alten Götter die Rund'.

Hier hinter den Myrtenbäumen
In heimlich dämmernder Pracht
Was sprichst du wirr wie in Träumen
Zu mir, phantastische Nacht?

Es funklen auf mich alle Sterne
Mit glühendem Liebesblick,
Es redet trunken die Ferne
Wie von künftigem, grossem Glück.—

7

AUF EINER BURG

Eingeschlafen auf der Lauer
Oben ist der alte Ritter;
Drüben gehen Regenschauer
Und der Wald rauscht durch das Gitter.

Eingewachsen Bart und Haare
Und versteinert Brust und Krause,
Sitzt er viele hundert Jahre
Oben in der stillen Klause.

Draussen ist es still und friedlich
Alle sind ins Tal gezogen,
Waldesvögel einsam singen
In den leeren Fensterbogen.

Eine Hochzeit fährt da unten
Auf dem Rhein im Sonnenscheine,
Musikanten spielen munter,
Und die schöne Braut die weinet.

BEWITCHING DISTANT LANDSCAPE

The treetops rustle and quiver
as though at this hour
about the ruined walls
the ancient gods were making their rounds.

Here beyond the myrtle trees
in the quiet shimmer of twilight,
what are you telling me, confused as in dreams,
fantastic night?

The stars all shine upon me
with the glow of love;
the far horizon speaks ecstatically
as if of great happiness to come.

ROBERT SCHUMANN, Op. 39, no. 6.

IN THE CASTLE

Asleep on guard
up there is the old knight;
showers pass over,
and the trees rustle through the grating.

Beard and hair grown long,
breast and collar petrified,
he sits for many hundred years
up there in his silent solitude.

Outside all is peaceful and quiet;
everyone has gone down into the valley.
Lonely forest birds sing
in the empty window arches.

A wedding procession moves below
along the Rhine in the sunshine.
The musicians are playing merrily,
and the beautiful bride is crying.

ROBERT SCHUMANN, Op. 39, no. 7.

8

ERINNERUNG

Ich hör' die Bächlein rauschen
Im Walde her und hin.
Im Walde, in dem Rauschen,
Ich weiss nicht, wo ich bin.

Die Nachtigallen schlagen
Hier in der Einsamkeit,
Als wollten sie was sagen
Von alter, schöner Zeit.

Die Mondesschimmer fliegen,
Als säh' ich unter mir
Das Schloss im Tale liegen,
Und ist doch so weit von hier!

Als müsste in den Garten,
Voll Rosen weiss und rot,
Mein' Liebste auf mich warten,
Und ist doch lange tot.

ROBERT SCHUMANN, Op. 39, no. 8. The composer's title is *In der Fremde* (*Away from Home*). The fourth line of the second stanza reads *Von der alten schönen Zeit*. In the final stanza, first line, *in den Garten* is changed to *in dem Garten*; in the third line *Mein' Liebste* becomes *Meine Liebste*. The final line appears as *Und ist doch so*

9

WEHMUT

Ich kann wohl manchmal singen,
Als ob ich fröhlich sei,
Doch heimlich Tränen dringen,
Da wird das Herz mir frei.

So lassen Nachtigallen,
Spielt draussen Frühlingsluft,
Der Sehnsucht Lied erschallen,
Aus ihres Käfigs Gruft.

REMEMBRANCE

I hear the brooks gushing
in the woods here and there;
in the rustling woods
I do not know where I am.

The nightingales sing
here in the loneliness,
as if they would speak to me
of the old and beautiful times.

In the flickering moonlight
I seem to see below me
the castle lying in the valley—
but it is far from here.

It seems that in the garden,
full of white and red roses,
my sweetheart must be waiting for me—
but she is long dead.

---

lange tot, but is twice repeated as Eichendorff had it—*Und ist doch lange tot*.

Other settings have been published by Robert Eitner (Op. 13, no. 1), Wilhelm Taubert (Op. 99, no. 2), Joseph Marx, Othmar Schoeck (Op. 17, no. 7), E. Jaques-Dalcroze (Op. 10, no. 3), Eric Meyer-Helmund, and more than a dozen others.

MELANCHOLY

I can sometimes sing
as though I were happy,
though secretly tears well up,
to relieve my heart.

Thus nightingales,
while the spring air plays outside,
sing their song of longing,
from the depths of their cage.

Da lauschen alle Herzen,
Und alles ist erfreut,
Doch keiner fühlt die Schmerzen,
Im Lied das tiefe Leid.

ROBERT SCHUMANN, Op. 39, no. 9. The second stanza begins *Es
en* and ends *Aus ihres Kerkers Gruft.*
Of nearly fifty other settings mention may be made of those by

10

ZWIELICHT

Dämmerung will die Flügel spreiten,
Schaurig rühren sich die Bäume,
Wolken ziehn wie schwere Träume—
Was will dieses Graun bedeuten?

Hast ein Reh du lieb vor andern,
Lass es nicht alleine grasen,
Jäger ziehn im Wald und blasen,
Stimmen hin und wieder wandern.

Hast du einen Freund hienieden,
Trau ihm nicht zu dieser Stunde,
Freundlich wohl mit Aug' und Munde,
Sinnt er Krieg im tück'schen Frieden.

Was heut müde gehet unter,
Hebt sich morgen neugeboren,
Manches bleibt in Nacht verloren—
Hüte dich, bleib wach und munter!

ROBERT SCHUMANN, Op. 39, no. 10. The first line of the final stanza

11

IM WALDE

Es zog eine Hochzeit den Berg entlang,
Ich hörte die Vögel schlagen,
Da blitzten viel Reiter, das Waldhorn klang,
Das war ein lustiges Jagen!

Every heart listens,
and everyone is made happy,
but no one feels the grief,
the deep sorrow in the song.

H. Esser (Op. 62, no. 3), A. M. Foerster (Op. 6, no. 2), G. Lange
(Op. 236), V. E. Nessler (Op. 21, no. 3), R. Radecke (Op. 23, no. 1),
A. von Fielitz (Op. 51, no. 1), and Charles C. Converse.

TWILIGHT

Twilight spreads its wings,
the trees stir eerily;
clouds drift like heavy dreams—
What does this shuddering mean?

If you have a favorite roe,
do not let him graze alone;
hunters are abroad in the woods, blowing their horns
and shouting back and forth.

If you have a friend on earth,
trust him not from this time forth!
Friendly in look and word,
he plans a quarrel in deceitful peace.

That which goes wearily down today
will arise tomorrow newborn.
Many are hopelessly lost in the night—
Be on guard—keep alert and vigilant!

---

reads: *Was heut' gehet müde unter*; in the third *bleibt* is changed to
geht, and in the fourth *bleib* becomes *sei*.

IN THE WOODS

A wedding procession moved along the mountain.
I heard the birds singing.
Many a horseman flashed, the hunting horn sounded—
that was a merry hunt!

Und eh' ich's gedacht, war alles verhallt,
Die Nacht bedecket die Runde,
Nur von den Bergen noch rauschet der Wald
Und mich schauert im Herzensgrunde.

ROBERT SCHUMANN, Op. 39, no. 11. In the final line *schauert*

12

FRÜHLINGSNACHT

Übern Garten durch die Lüfte
Hört ich Wandervögel ziehn,
Das bedeutet Frühlingsdüfte,
Unten fängts schon an zu blühn.

Jauchzen möcht ich, möchte weinen,
Ist mirs doch, als könnts nicht sein,
Alte Wunder wieder scheinen
Mit dem Mondesglanz herein.

Und der Mond, die Sterne sagen's,
Und in Träumen rauscht's der Hain,
Und die Nachtigallen schlagen's:
Sie ist deine, sie ist dein!

ROBERT SCHUMANN, Op. 39, no. 12. The first word in the song is
Über'm. In the second line of the third stanza *Träumen* is changed
to *Traume.*
In the setting of Adolf Jensen, as in that of Schumann, the first
word is *Über'm.* In the fourth line of the second stanza *Mondesglanz*

DER MUSIKANT

Wandern lieb' ich für mein Leben,
Lebe eben wie ich kann,
Wollt' ich mir auch Mühe geben,
Passt es mir doch gar nicht an.

Schöne alte Lieder weiss ich,
In der Kälte, ohne Schuh'
Draussen in die Saiten reiss' ich,
Weiss nicht, wo ich abends ruh'.

And before I realized it all sound had died away.
Night closed in.
Only the trees rustled on the mountain;
and I trembled deep in my heart.

---

becomes *schauert's*. The poem was also set by Nicolai Medtner (Op.
46, no. 4).

NIGHT IN SPRING

Over the garden, through the breezes,
I heard passage birds flying:
that presages fragrant spring.
Underfoot the flowers are already beginning to bloom.

I want to shout for joy! I want to weep!
I cannot believe what I feel;
old wonders appear again
in the light of the moon.

And the moon, the stars, are telling it,
and in my dreams the wood rustles it;
and the nightingales peal it forth:
She is yours! She is yours!

---

becomes *Mondenglanz*. As a coda, one line is repeated at the end—
Das bedeutet Frühlingsdüfte.
  The more than forty other composers include Curschmann (Op.
25, no. 1), Henselt (Op. 2, no. 3), Marschner (Op. 144, no. 1), and
Dessauer (Op. 53).

THE MUSICIAN

I love a wandering life;
I live any way I can.
I might worry about it,
but that sort of thing doesn't suit me.

I know beautiful old songs,
out in the cold, barefoot;
outdoors I pluck the strings,
but I don't know where I'll rest at night.

Manche Schöne macht wohl Augen,
Meinet, ich gefiel ihr sehr,
Wenn ich nur was wollte taugen,
So ein armer Lump nicht wär'.—

Mag dir Gott ein'n Mann bescheren,
Wohl mit Haus und Hof versehen!
Wenn wir zwei zusammen wären,
Möcht' mein Singen mir vergehn.

HUGO WOLF (Eichendorff Lieder 2).

VERSCHWIEGENE LIEBE

Über Wipfel und Saaten
In den Glanz hinein—
Wer mag sie erraten,
Wer holte sie ein?
Gedanken sich wiegen,
Die Nacht ist verschwiegen,
Gedanken sind frei.

Errät' es nur eine,
Wer an sie gedacht,
Beim Rauschen der Haine,
Wenn niemand mehr wacht,
Als die Wolken, die fliegen—
Mein Lieb ist verschwiegen
Und schön wie die Nacht.

HUGO WOLF (Eichendorff Lieder 3).

Many a beauty makes eyes at me,
as if to say I please her—
if only I amounted to something,
and weren't such a poor good-for-nothing.

May God send you a man
well provided with house and home!
If we two were to be together
I would forget how to sing.

SECRET LOVE

Over the treetops and the fields of grain,
in the moonlight—
who could guess them,
who hold them in check?
Thoughts are in motion,
the night is silent,
thoughts are unconfined.

May only one guess
who is thinking of her,
in the rustling of the grove
when no one else is awake.
As the clouds that soar,
my love is silent,
and lovely as the night.

GEIBEL, EMANUEL
1815–1884

DIE IHR SCHWEBET

Die ihr schwebet
Um diese Palmen
In Nacht und Wind,
Ihr heil'gen Engel,
Stillet die Wipfel!
Es schlummert mein Kind.

Ihr Palmen von Bethlehem
Im Windesbrausen,
Wie mögt ihr heute
So zornig sausen!
O rauscht nicht also!
Schweiget, neiget
Euch leis' und lind;
Stillet die Wipfel!
Es schlummert mein Kind.

Der Himmelsknabe
Duldet Beschwerde,
Ach, wie so müd' er ward
Vom Leid der Erde.
Ach nun im Schlaf ihm
Leise gesänftigt
Die Qual zerrinnt,
Stillet die Wipfel!
Es schlummert mein Kind.

Grimmige Kälte
Sauset hernieder,
Womit nur deck' ich
Des Kindleins Glieder!
O all ihr Engel,
Die ihr geflügelt
Wandelt im Wind,
Stillet die Wipfel!
Es schlummert mein Kind.

HUGO WOLF (*Spanisches Liederbuch*, no. 4). The text is a translation of Lope de Vega. Brahms also made a fine setting called
Geistliches Wiegenlied (Op. 97, no. 2), the second of his two songs

Son of a pastor in Lübeck and educated in theology, Geibel interested himself in classical and romance philosophy. He was one of a group of political poets who heralded the revolution of 1845, but he later hailed the establishment of the Empire in 1871. Notable for his lyrical poetry and his collaboration with Heyse in translating the poetry of the *Spanisches Liederbuch.*

YE HOVERING ANGELS

Ye who hover
about these palms
in the night and the wind,
ye holy angels,
quiet the treetops!
My child is asleep.

Ye palms of Bethlehem
in the blustering wind,
how can you today
howl so angrily?
O do not rustle so!
Be silent, bow down
softly and gently.
My child is asleep.
Quiet the treetops!

The Son of Heaven
must endure hardships;
Ah, how weary He is
from the sorrow of the world.
Ah, now in sleep
quietly comforted,
His torment disappears.
Quiet the treetops!
My child is asleep.

Bitter cold winds
rage on the earth;
how can I cover
my child's limbs!
O all ye angels
whose wings
bear you on the wind,
quiet the treetops!
My child is asleep.

for alto voice with viola and piano. The viola obbligato is based on the old German cradle hymn *Josef, lieber Josef mein.*

GELLERT, CHRISTIAN FÜRCHTEGOTT
1715–1769

DIE EHRE GOTTES AUS DER NATUR

Die Himmel rühmen des Ewigen Ehre;
    Ihr Schall pflanzt seinen Namen fort.
Ihn rühmt der Erdkreis, ihn preisen die Meere;
    Vernimm, o Mensch, ihr göttlich Wort.

Wer trägt der Himmel unzählbare Sterne?
    Wer führt die Sonn' aus ihrem Zelt?
Sie kommt und leuchtet und lacht uns von ferne
    Und läuft den Weg gleich als ein Held.

[Vernimm's und siehe die Wunder der Werke,
    Die die Natur dir ausgestellt!
Verkündigt Weisheit und Ordnung und Stärke
    Dir nicht den Herrn, den Herrn der Welt?

Kannst du der Wesen unzählbare Heere,
    Den kleinsten Staub fühllos beschaun?
Durch wen ist alles? O gib ihm die Ehre!
    "Mir," ruft der Herr, "sollst du vertraun.

Mein ist die Kraft, mein ist Himmel und Erde;
    An meinen Werken kennst du mich.
Ich bin's und werde sein, der ich sein werde,
    Dein Gott und Vater ewiglich.

Ich bin dein Schöpfer, bin Weisheit und Güte,
    Ein Gott der Ordnung und dein Heil;
Ich bin's! Mich liebe von ganzem Gemüte
    Und nimm an meiner Gnade teil!"]

LUDWIG VAN BEETHOVEN, Op. 48, no. 4. Beethoven set only the first two stanzas. Carl Philipp Emanuel Bach made a strophic setting to which any or all stanzas might be used.

Poet, theologian, and writer of fables. An exponent of rationalism and sentimentalism, Gellert is remembered chiefly for his *Fables and Aphorisms* and his *Spiritual Songs*.

NATURE'S PRAISE OF GOD

The heavens proclaim the glory of the Infinite;
their sound magnifies His name.
The earth praises Him, the sea extols Him:
heed, o man, their God-inspired word.

Who sustains the countless stars of heaven?
Who leads the sun out of its canopy?
It comes and lights us, laughing, from afar,
and goes its way like a hero.

[Consider and see the wonders of the works
which nature reveals to thee.
Do not wisdom and order and strength
make known to thee the Lord of the earth?

Canst thou contemplate the existence of countless
    multitudes,
or the smallest particle of dust, unmoved?
Who created it all? O give Him praise!
"In Me," cries the Lord, "shalt thou trust.

Mine is the strength, mine are heaven and earth;
by my works shalt thou know me.
I am and shall be that I shall be,
thy God and Father in eternity.

I am thy Creator, I am wisdom and goodness,
a God of Order, and thy Salvation.
I AM. Love me with thy whole soul,
and share in my grace."]

GILM ZU ROSENEGG, HERMANN VON
1812–1864

ALLERSEELEN

Stell auf den Tisch die duftenden Reseden,
Die letzten roten Astern trag herbei
Und lass uns wieder von der Liebe reden,
    Wie einst im Mai.

Gib mir die Hand, dass ich sie heimlich drücke,
Und wenn mans sieht, mir ist es einerlei:
Gib mir nur einen deiner süssen Blicke,
    Wie einst im Mai.

Es blüht und funkelt heut auf jedem Grabe,
Ein Tag im Jahr ist ja den Toten frei;
Komm an mein Herz, dass ich dich wieder habe,
    Wie einst im Mai.

RICHARD STRAUSS, Op. 10, no. 8. In this setting the last stanza begins *Es blüht und duftet heut*. In the somewhat less well-known, simpler setting by Eduard Lassen (Op. 85, no. 3), the second line of the final stanza reads *Ein Tag im Jahre ist den Toten frei*.

HABE DANK

Ja, du weisst es, teure Seele,
Dass ich fern von dir mich quäle;
Liebe macht die Herzen krank,
    Habe Dank.

Hielt ich nicht, der Freiheit Zecher,
Hoch den Amethystenbecher,
Und du segnetest den Trank,
    Habe Dank.

Und beschworst darin die Bösen,
Bis ich, was ich nie gewesen,
Heilig an das Herz dir sank,
    Habe Dank.

RICHARD STRAUSS, Op. 10, no. 1. Titled *Zueignung*. The first line of the second stanza is altered thus: *Einst hielt ich, der Freiheit*

Combined a fresh and genuine lyric talent with a fine sense
of form; known for his love and nature songs.

ALL SOULS' DAY

Place on the table the fragrant mignonettes,
bring in the last red asters,
and let us speak again of love,
as once in May.

Give me your hand, that I may secretly press it,
and if anyone sees, that matters not to me.
Give me only one of your sweet glances,
as once in May.

Every grave blooms and glows tonight:
one day in the year belongs to the dead.
Come to my heart, that I may hold you again,
as once in May.

Of more than thirty other composers the following may be mentioned: J. Pembauer (Op. 33, no. 2), L. Thuille (Op. 44, no. 4), A.
von Fielitz (Op. 29, no. 2), and Josef Stransky.

THANKS

Yes, you know it, dear soul,
that when I am away from you I am miserable;
love makes the heart sick.
Take my thanks.

Did not I, the tippler of liberty,
hold high the amethyst cup,
and you bless the draught?
Take my thanks.

And you exorcised the evils within it,
until I, blessed, as I had never been,
sank upon your heart.
Take my thanks.

Zecher. The third line of the last stanza reads: *Heilig, heilig ans
Herz dir sank.*

DIE NACHT

Aus dem Walde tritt die Nacht,
Aus den Bäumen schleicht sie leise,
Schaut sich um im weiten Kreise,
    Nun gib acht!

Alle Lichter dieser Welt,
Alle Blumen, alle Farben
Löscht sie aus und stiehlt die Garben
    Weg vom Feld.

Alles nimmt sie, was nur hold,
Nimmt das Silber weg des Stromes,
Nimmt vom Kupferdach des Domes
    Weg das Gold.

Ausgeplündert steht der Strauch;
Rücke näher, Seel an Seele,
O die Nacht, mir bangt, sie stehle
    Dich mir auch.

RICHARD STRAUSS, Op. 10, no. 3. In the third line *im* is changed to
in. In the third stanza, the rhyming words in lines two and three are

GOETHE, JOHANN WOLFGANG VON
1749–1832

AN SCHWAGER KRONOS

Spude dich, Kronos!
Fort den rasselnden Trott!
Bergab gleitet der Weg;
Ekles Schwindeln zögert
Mir vor die Stirne dein Zaudern.
Frisch, holpert es gleich,
Über Stock und Steine den Trott
Rasch ins Leben hinein!

THE NIGHT

Out of the forest steals the night,
out of the trees she slinks quietly,
looks round about—
now take care!

All the lights of this world,
all flowers, all colors
she extinguishes, and steals the sheaves
away from the fields.

She takes away all that is pleasing—
the silver from the river;
from the copper roof of the cathedral
she steals the gold.

The shrubbery is plundered—
come closer, soul to soul!
O the night, I fear, will steal
you too from me!

---

changed from *Stromes* and *Domes* to *Stroms* and *Doms*.

Generally acknowledged the greatest of German poets and
one of the towering intellects of all time. Goethe had a great
influence on the Romantic movement, studied painting and
science, and held several government positions. His writings
touch on all phases of literature, but he is perhaps most read
today as a poet combining dramatic power, philosophy,
and the purest lyricism. His influence on the German lied is
incalculable.

TO THE POSTILION CHRONOS

Hurry, Chronos!
Forth at a rattling trot!
The way leads downhill;
I am sick and giddy
from your delay.
Oh! Rough as it is,
jog at full speed,
swiftly into life.

Nun schon wieder
Den eratmenden Schritt
Mühsam Berg hinauf!
Auf denn, nicht träge denn,
Strebend und hoffend hinan!

Weit, hoch, herrlich der Blick
Rings ins Leben hinein,
Vom Gebirg zum Gebirg
Schwebet der ewige Geist,
Ewigen Lebens ahnevoll.

Seitwärts des Überdachs Schatten
Zieht dich an
Und ein Frischung verheissender Blick
Auf der Schwelle des Mädchens da.
Labe dich!—Mir auch, Mädchen,
Diesen schäumenden Trank,
Diesen frischen Gesundheitsblick!

Ab denn, rascher hinab!
Sieh, die Sonne sinkt!
Eh sie sinkt, eh mich Greisen
Ergreift im Moore Nebelduft,
Entzahnte Kiefer schnattern
Und das schlotternde Gebein:

Trunknen vom letzten Strahl
Reiss mich, ein Feuermeer
Mir im schäumenden Aug',
Mich geblendeten Taumelnden
In der Hölle nächtliches Tor!

Töne, Schwager, ins Horn,
Rassle den schallenden Trab,
Dass der Orkus vernehme: wir kommen,
Dass gleich an der Türe
Der Wirt uns freundlich empfange.

FRANZ PETER SCHUBERT, D. 369. The first two lines of the third
stanza are rearranged as follows: *Weit, hoch, herrlich rings den*

Now back again,
panting, stride
wearily up the mountain!
Up! Have done with sluggishness,
upward, striving and hoping!

Far, high, magnificent the view
of life around us;
from peak to peak
the eternal spirit soars,
presaging eternal life.

Along the way the shade of a shelter
draws you aside,
and a glimpse at a maiden's threshold
promises to revive you.
Refresh yourself!—For me also, maiden,
this foaming drink,
this bright healing glance!

On your way, then, faster downwards!
See, the sun is setting!
Before it sets, before I the old man
am seized by the mist in the moor,
before the chattering toothless jaws
and the shaky skeleton,

drunk with the last ray,
drag me, a sea of fire
in my watering eyes,
blinded and staggering,
to the dismal gate of hell!

Sound your horn, coachman!
Rattle at a resounding trot,
that Orcus may know we are coming!
That right at the door
the host may graciously greet us.

Blick ins Leben hinein.

ANAKREONS GRAB

Wo die Rose hier blüht, wo Reben um Lorbeer sich schlingen,
  Wo das Turtelchen lockt, wo sich das Grillchen ergötzt,
Welch ein Grab ist hier, das alle Götter mit Leben
  Schön bepflanzt und geziert? Es ist Anakreons Ruh.
Frühling, Sommer und Herbst genoss der glückliche Dichter;
  Vor dem Winter hat ihn endlich der Hügel geschützt.

HUGO WOLF (*Goethe Lieder*, no. 29). Also set by Alfred Valentin
Heuss.

ERLKÖNIG

Wer reitet so spät durch Nacht und Wind?
Es ist der Vater mit seinem Kind;
Er hat den Knaben wohl in dem Arm,
Er fasst ihn sicher, er hält ihn warm.

Mein Sohn, was birgst du so bang dein Gesicht?—
Siehst, Vater, du den Erlkönig nicht?
Den Erlenkönig mit Kron' und Schweif?—
  Mein Sohn, es ist ein Nebelstreif.—

"Du liebes Kind, komm, geh mit mir!
Gar schöne Spiele spiel' ich mit dir,
Manch bunte Blumen sind an dem Strand,
Meine Mutter hat manch gülden Gewand."

Mein Vater, mein Vater, und hörest du nicht,
Was Erlenkönig mir leise verspricht?—
Sei ruhig, bleibe ruhig, mein Kind:
In dürren Blättern säuselt der Wind.—

"Willst, feiner Knabe, du mit mir gehn?
Meine Töchter sollen dich warten schön;
Meine Töchter führen den nächtlichen Reihn
Und wiegen und tanzen und singen dich ein."

Mein Vater, mein Vater, und siehst du nicht dort
Erlkönigs Töchter am düstern Ort?—
Mein Sohn, mein Sohn, ich seh' es genau:
Es scheinen die alten Weiden so grau.—

ANACREON'S GRAVE

Here where the roses bloom, where vine and laurel
    intertwine,
where the turtle-dove coos, where the grasshopper
    rejoices,
what grave is this, that all the gods have beautifully
    planted
and decked with life? It is Anacreon's resting place.
Spring, summer, and autumn delighted the happy poet;
from the winter the mound at last has sheltered him.

THE ERLKING

Who rides so late through the night and the wind?
It is the father with his child;
he folds the boy close in his arms,
he clasps him securely, he holds him warmly.

"My son, why do you hide your face so anxiously?"
"Father, don't you see the Erlking?
The Erlking with his crown and his train?"
"My son, it is a streak of mist."

"Dear child, come, go with me!
I'll play the prettiest games with you.
Many colored flowers grow along the shore;
my mother has many golden garments."

"My father, my father, and don't you hear
the Erlking whispering promises to me?"
"Be quiet, stay quiet, my child;
the wind is rustling in the dead leaves."

"My handsome boy, will you come with me?
My daughters shall wait upon you;
my daughters lead off in the dance every night,
and cradle and dance and sing you to sleep."

"My father, my father, and don't you see there
the Erlking's daughters in the shadows?"
"My son, my son, I see it clearly;
the old willows look so gray."

"Ich liebe dich, mich reizt deine schöne Gestalt;
Und bist du nicht willig, so brauch' ich Gewalt."
Mein Vater, mein Vater, jetzt fasst er mich an!
Erlkönig hat mir ein Leids getan!—

Dem Vater grauset's, er reitet geschwind,
Er hält in Armen das ächzende Kind,
Erreicht den Hof mit Mühe und Not;
In seinen Armen das Kind war tot.

FRANZ SCHUBERT, D. 328. Goethe's poem was originally written a
part of a *Schauspiel* called *Die Fischerin*, and was set to rathe
simple music several times by the poet's contemporaries. There i
one slight textual change in the Schubert song: in the repetition o
the last line of stanza five *Und* becomes *Sie*.

Despite the celebrity and the undeniable greatness of Schubert'
song, there is considerable reason on the side of those critics—
Richard Wagner among them—who pronounce that of Carl Loewe
(Op. 1, no. 3) even greater. Less melodious than Schubert's, Loewe
is truer to the accentuation of the poem. Goethe, we remember, di
not approve of elaborate musical settings for his poems, preferrin
a strophic setting, such as that made for *Erlkönig* by Johann
Friedrich Reichardt. Reading the poem aloud, we cannot fail to be

GANYMED

Wie im Morgenglanze
Du rings mich anglühst,
Frühling, Geliebter!
Mit tausendfacher Liebeswonne
Sich an mein Herz drängt
Deiner ewigen Wärme
Heilig Gefühl,
Unendliche Schöne!

Dass ich dich fassen möcht'
In diesen Arm!

Ach, an deinem Busen
Lieg' ich, schmachte,
Und deine Blumen, dein Gras
Drängen sich an mein Herz.
Du kühlst den brennenden
Durst meines Busens,
Lieblicher Morgenwind,

"I love you, your beautiful figure delights me!
And if you are not willing, then I shall use force!"
"My father, my father, now he is taking hold of me!
The Erlking has hurt me!"

The father shudders, he rides swiftly on;
he holds in his arms the groaning child,
he reaches the courtyard weary and anxious:
in his arms the child was dead.

---

struck by the rhythm of the horse's hoof-beats in the poetic meter—
an effect ignored by Schubert, who provided this background in the
piano part. While following the structure of the poem, Loewe is
able at the same time to do considerable tone painting in the piano
part.

Challier's *Lieder-Katalog* lists some twenty-eight settings of this
poem. Perhaps the most curious and interesting of the lesser
Erlkönigs is that of Louis Spohr (Op. 154, Book II, no. 4), for bari-
tone, piano, and violin. The supernatural, it seems, is here the
province of the obbligato. The composer makes a number of changes
in the text. Also worthy of mention is the song pieced together by
Reinhold Becker out of sketches left by Beethoven, who had not
been satisfied with his setting.

GANYMEDE

In the splendor of the morning,
how you glow about me,
spring, beloved!
With love's thousandfold raptures
my heart is filled
by your eternal warmth's
hallowed emotion,
endless beauty!

O that I might hold you
in my arms!

Ah, on your bosom
I lie, languishing,
and your flowers, your grass,
press against my heart.
You cool the burning
thirst of my bosom,
lovely morning breeze.

Ruft drein die Nachtigall
Liebend nach mir aus dem Nebeltal.

Ich komm', ich komme!
Wohin? Ach, wohin?

Hinauf! Hinauf strebt's.
Es schweben die Wolken
Abwärts, die Wolken
Neigen sich der sehnenden Liebe.
Mir! Mir!
In eurem Schosse
Aufwärts!
Umfangend umfangen!
Aufwärts an deinen Busen,
All-liebender Vater!

HUGO WOLF (*Goethe Lieder*, no. 50). Both this great song and the Schubert setting (D. 544) deserve to be better known. There are a number of word changes in the Schubert. In the fifth line *Herz* is

---

GEHEIMES

Über meines Liebchens Äugeln
Stehn verwundert alle Leute;
Ich, der Wissende dagegen
Weiss recht gut, was das bedeute.

Denn es heisst: ich liebe diesen,
Und nicht etwa den und jenen.
Lasset nur, ihr lieben Leute,
Euer Wundern, euer Sehnen!

Ja, mit ungeheuren Mächten
Blicket sie wohl in die Runde;
Doch sie sucht nur zu verkünden
Ihm die nächste süsse Stunde.

FRANZ SCHUBERT, D. 719. The third line of the second stanza is

The nightingale calls
lovingly to me from the misty valley.

I come, I come!
Whither, ah whither?

Upward, upward I soar.
The clouds float
down, the clouds
bend down with yearning love
to me! To me!
Into their lap,
upwards!
Embraced, embracing!
Upwards to Thy bosom,
All-loving Father!

---

expanded to *Herze*; the twelfth line reads *Lieg' ich und schmachte*; the twenty-first becomes *Ach, wohin, wohin?*; the twenty-second, *Hinauf! strebt's hinauf.*

SECRET

My beloved's eyes
astonish everyone;
I, the authority on the subject,
know very well what this means.

For she is saying: I love this one,
and not at all that one or the other.
Leave off, good people,
your wondering and your desire.

Yes, with uncanny powers
she looks about her;
yet she only means to announce
to him the next sweet hour.

---

changed to *Lasset nur, ihr guten Leute.*

HARFENSPIELER-LIEDER

1

Wer sich der Einsamkeit ergibt,
Ach, der ist bald allein;
Ein jeder lebt, ein jeder liebt
Und lässt ihn seiner Pein.

Ja! lasst mich meiner Qual!
Und kann ich nur einmal
Recht einsam sein,
Dann bin ich nicht allein.

Es schleicht ein Liebender lauschend sacht
Ob seine Freundin allein?
So überschleicht bei Tag und Nacht
Mich Einsamen die Pein,

Mich Einsamen die Qual.
Ach, werd' ich erst einmal
Einsam im Grabe sein,
Da lässt sie mich allein!

HUGO WOLF (*Goethe Lieder*, no. 1). The first of the three "Songs of the Harper" from *Wilhelm Meister*. Of the various settings of these famous texts, those of Wolf are the most penetrating. Other

2

An die Türen will ich schleichen,
Still und sittsam will ich stehn;
Fromme Hand wird Nahrung reichen,
Und ich werde weiter gehn.
Jeder wird sich glücklich scheinen,
Wenn mein Bild vor ihm erscheint;
Eine Träne wird er weinen,
Und ich weiss nicht, was er weint.

HUGO WOLF (*Goethe Lieder*, no. 2). Also set by Reichardt, Schubert (*Gesänge des Harfners, III*, D. 479), Rubinstein (Op. 91,

SONGS OF THE HARP PLAYER

He who gives himself to solitude,
ah, he is soon alone;
others live, others love
and leave him to his torment.

Yes, leave me my affliction!
And if I can only once
be really lonely,
then I am not alone.

A lover steals softly and listens—
is his beloved alone?
So day and night
I the lonely one am stalked by pain,

I the lonely one am stalked by torment.
Ah, once I am
lonely in my grave,
they will leave me alone!

settings of no. 1 include those of Zelter (called simply *Harfenspieler*),
Schubert (*Gesänge des Harfners, I,* D. 478), Schumann (Op. 98a,
no. 6), and Rubinstein (Op. 91, no. 3).

I will steal to the doors;
quiet and humble will I stand;
an honest hand will offer me food,
and I will go my way.
Everyone will consider himself fortunate,
when my image appears to him;
one tear will he shed,
and I know not why he weeps.

no. 9), Medtner (*Aus Wilhelm Meister*) *An die Türen will ich
schleichen.* Op. 15, no. 2), and Musorgski, among others.

3

Wer nie sein Brot mit Tränen ass,
Wer nie die kummervollen Nächte
Auf seinem Bette weinend sass,
Der kennt euch nicht, ihr himmlischen Mächte.

Ihr führt ins Leben uns hinein,
Ihr lasst den Armen schuldig werden,
Dann überlasst ihr ihn der Pein;
Denn alle Schuld rächt sich auf Erden.

[Ihm färbt der Morgensonne Licht
Den reinen Horizont mit Flammen,
Und über seinem schuld'gen Haupte bricht
Das schöne Bild der ganzen Welt zusammen.]

HUGO WOLF (*Goethe Lieder*, no. 3). The third stanza as given here
is taken from a later part of the novel of *Wilhelm Meister*. Though
it fits well with the poem and has not infrequently been thus added,
it is not included in any of the musical settings actually examined.

HEIDENRÖSLEIN

Sah ein Knab' ein Röslein stehn,
Röslein auf der Heiden,
War so jung und morgenschön,
Lief er schnell, es nah zu sehn,
Sah's mit vielen Freuden.
Röslein, Röslein, Röslein rot,
Röslein auf der Heiden.

Knabe sprach: "Ich breche dich,
Röslein auf der Heiden!"
Röslein sprach: "Ich steche dich,
Dass du ewig denkst an mich,
Und ich will's nicht leiden."
Röslein, Röslein, Röslein rot,
Röslein auf der Heiden.

Und der wilde Knabe brach
's Röslein auf der Heiden;
Röslein wehrte sich und stach,
Half ihm doch kein Weh und Ach,

He who has never eaten his bread with tears,
who never sat through sorrowful nights
weeping on his bed,
he knows you not, ye heavenly powers!

You bring us into life;
you let the poor man go astray,
then leave him to his torture,
for every sin avenges itself upon this earth!

[For him the light of the morning sun colors
the clear horizon with flames;
then over his guilty head
the beautiful picture of the world collapses.]

The best of the other settings include Schubert (*Gesänge des Harfners, II*, D. 480), Schumann (*Wer nie sein Brot mit Tränen ass*, Op. 98a, no. 4), Reichardt, Zelter, Rubinstein (Op. 91, no. 2), Bungert (Op. 1, no. 1), Marschner (Op. 160, no. 4), and Nessler.

THE WILD ROSE

A lad saw a rosebud,
rosebud on the heath;
it was so young in its morning beauty
that he ran to look at it more closely;
he gazed at it with great pleasure.
Rosebud red,
rosebud on the heath.

The lad said: "I'll pick you,
rosebud on the heath!"
The rosebud said: "I'll prick you,
so that you will always think of me,
and I won't stand for it."
Rosebud red,
rosebud on the heath.

And the brutal lad picked
the rosebud on the heath;
the rosebud defended itself and pricked,
yet no grief and lamentation helped it:

Musst' es eben leiden.
Röslein, Röslein, Röslein rot,
Röslein auf der Heiden.

FRANZ SCHUBERT, D. 257. As familiar as the incomparable
Schubert song is the simple folk song setting by Heinrich Werner
(1827). The poem was of course included among the songs of
Reichardt, and Brahms gave it a simple strophic setting in his

LIEBHABER IN ALLEN GESTALTEN

Ich wollt', ich wär' ein Fisch,
So hurtig und frisch;
Und kämst du zu angeln,
Ich würde nicht mangeln.
Ich wollt', ich wär' ein Fisch,
So hurtig und frisch.

[Ich wollt', ich wär' ein Pferd,
Da wär' ich dir wert.
O, wär' ich ein Wagen,
Bequem dich zu tragen.
Ich wollt', ich wär' ein Pferd,
Da wär' ich dir wert.]

Ich wollt', ich wäre Gold,
Dir immer im Sold;
Und tätst du was kaufen,
Käm' ich wieder gelaufen.
Ich wollt', ich wäre Gold,
Dir immer im Sold.

[Ich wollt', ich wär' treu,
Mein Liebchen stets neu;
Ich wollt' mich verheissen,
Wollt' nimmer verreisen.
Ich wollt' ich wär' treu,
Mein Liebchen stets neu.

Ich wollt' ich wär' alt
Und runzlich und kalt;
Tätst du mir's versagen,
Da könnt' mich's nicht plagen.
Ich wollt' ich wär' alt
Und runzlich und kalt.

it simply had to suffer.
Rosebud red,
rosebud on the heath.

Volkskinderlieder (no. 6). Beethoven left a sketch, completed many years later by Henry Holden Huss. Other composers include Joseffy, Reissiger (Op. 79, no. 3), and Taubert (Op. 5, no. 2).

THE LOVER IN ALL SHAPES

I wish I were a fish,
so agile and lively;
if you were to come angling
I wouldn't fail you.
I wish I were a fish,
so agile and lively.

[I wish I were a horse,
that I might prove of worth to you.
Or were I a wagon
to carry you in comfort.
I wish I were a horse,
that I might prove of worth to you.]

I wish I were gold,
always at your service;
and if you wanted to buy something
I would come running back to you.
I wish I were gold,
always at your service.

[I wish I were faithful
to my sweetheart, ever new;
I would make a vow
never to leave you.
I wish I were faithful
to my sweetheart, ever new.

I wish I were old,
wrinkled and cold;
then if you were to refuse me
that wouldn't worry me.
I wish I were old,
wrinkled and cold.

Wär' ich Affe sogleich
Voll neckender Streich';
Hätt' was dich verdrossen,
So macht' ich dir Possen.
Wär' ich Affe sogleich
Voll neckender Streich'.

Wär' ich gut wie ein Schaf,
Wie der Löwe so brav;
Hätt' Augen wie's Lüchschen
Und Listen wie's Füchschen.
Wär' ich gut wie ein Schaf,
Wie der Löwe so brav.

Was alles ich wär',
Das gönnt' ich dir sehr;
Mit fürstlichen Gaben,
Du solltest mich haben.
Was alles ich wär',
Das gönnt' ich dir sehr.]

Doch bin ich, wie ich bin,
Und nimm mich nur hin!
Willst du bessre besitzen,
So lass dir sie schnitzen.
Ich bin nur, wie ich bin;
So nimm mich nur hin.

FRANZ PETER SCHUBERT, D. 558. The setting is strophic, but only
the first, third, and last stanzas are included in the music. The fourth

MEINE RUH IST HIN

Meine Ruh ist hin,
Mein Herz ist schwer;
Ich finde sie nimmer
Und nimmermehr.

Wo ich ihn nicht hab'
Ist mir das Grab,
Die ganze Welt
Ist mir vergällt.

Were I an ape forthwith,
full of teasing pranks!
If you were out of sorts,
I would play the clown.
Were I an ape forthwith,
full of teasing pranks!

Were I good as a sheep,
as stalwart as a lion;
had I eyes like a lynx
and cunning like a fox.
Were I good as a sheep
as stalwart as a lion.

Whatever I might be,
I would give myself to you freely;
with princely gifts
you should have me.
Whatever I might be,
I would give myself to you freely.]

But I am what I am,
so just take me!
If you want better lovers,
have them custom-carved for you.
I am only what I am,
so just take me.

---

line of the third stanza reads *Käm' ich gelaufen*, and the third line
of the final stanza is *Willst bessre besitzen.*

MY PEACE IS GONE

My peace is gone,
my heart is heavy;
I shall find it never,
never again.

Where I do not have him
it is like the grave to me,
the whole world
is bitter.

Mein armer Kopf
Ist mir verrückt,
Mein armer Sinn
Ist mir zerstückt.

Meine Ruh ist hin,
Mein Herz ist schwer;
Ich finde sie nimmer
Und nimmermehr.

Nach ihm nur schau' ich
Zum Fenster hinaus,
Nach ihm nur geh' ich
Aus dem Haus.

Sein hoher Gang,
Sein' edle Gestalt,
Seines Mundes Lächeln,
Seiner Augen Gewalt,

Und seiner Rede
Zauberfluss,
Sein Händedruck,
Und ach, sein Kuss!

Meine Ruh ist hin,
Mein Herz ist schwer;
Ich finde sie nimmer
Und nimmermehr.

Mein Busen drängt
Sich nach ihm hin;
Ach, dürft' ich fassen
Und halten ihn

Und küssen ihn,
So wie ich wollt',
An seinen Küssen
Vergehen sollt'!

FRANZ SCHUBERT, D. 118. This is the famous *Gretchen am Spinnrade*. Though no other setting is comparable, the composers include Loewe (Op. 9), Kreutzer, Spohr (Op. 25, no. 3), Zelter, Berlioz (Op. 24), Graben-Hoffmann (Op. 65), Curschmann (Op. 11,

My poor head
is deranged,
my poor mind
is distracted.

My peace is gone,
my heart is heavy;
I shall find it never,
never again.

Only for him
I look out of the window;
only for him I
leave the house.

His fine bearing,
his noble form,
the smile of his lips,
the power of his eyes,

and the magic flow
of his talk,
the clasp of his hands,
and ah, his kiss!

My peace is gone,
my heart is heavy;
I shall find it never,
never again.

My bosom yearns
for him,
ah, could I grasp him
and hold him

and kiss him
to my heart's content,
under his kisses
to swoon!

---

no. 5), Glinka, Macfarren (Op. 50), and Verdi (*Perduto ho la pace*).
Since the poem occurs in *Faust*, Gounod made a setting for his
opera, but this scene is usually omitted in performance.

MIGNON-LIEDER

I

Kennst du das Land, wo die Zitronen blühn,
Im dunkeln Laub die Gold-Orangen glühn,
Ein sanfter Wind vom blauen Himmel weht,
Die Myrte still und hoch der Lorbeer steht?
Kennst du es wohl?—Dahin! Dahin!
Möcht' ich mit dir, o mein Geliebter, ziehn.

Kennst du das Haus? Auf Säulen ruht sein Dach,
Es glänzt der Saal, es schimmert das Gemach,
Und Marmorbilder stehn und sehn mich an:
Was hat man dir, du armes Kind, getan?
Kennst du es wohl?—Dahin! Dahin
Möcht' ich mit dir, o mein Beschützer, ziehn.

Kennst du den Berg und seinen Wolkensteg?
Das Maultier sucht im Nebel seinen Weg;
In Höhlen wohnt der Drachen alte Brut;
Es stürzt der Fels und über ihn die Flut.
Kennst du ihn wohl?—Dahin! Dahin
Geht unser Weg! o Vater, lass uns ziehn!

HUGO WOLF (*Goethe Lieder*, no. 9). Though often criticized as over-elaborate, Wolf's is the greatest of the many settings of this great poem. Its closest rival is probably that of Schumann (Op. 98a, no. 1). Other settings include those of Schubert (D. 321), Beethoven (Op. 75, no. 1), Himmel, Liszt, Rubinstein (Op. 91, no. 4), Spohr

2

Heiss mich nicht reden, heiss mich schweigen,
Denn mein Geheimnis ist mir Pflicht;
Ich möchte dir mein ganzes Innre zeigen,
Allein das Schicksal will es nicht.

Zur rechten Zeit vertreibt der Sonne Lauf
Die finstre Nacht, und sie muss sich erhellen;
Der harte Fels schliesst seinen Busen auf,
Missgönnt der Erde nicht die tiefverborgnen Quellen.

SONGS OF MIGNON

Do you know the country where the lemon trees bloom
where among the dark leaves the golden oranges glow,
where a soft wind wafts from the blue heaven,
where the myrtle stands motionless and the laurel grows
   high?
Do you really know it?—There! There
I would go with you, my beloved.

Do you know the house? Its roof rests on columns;
the great hall shines, the rooms glitter,
and marble statues stand looking at me—
"What have they done to you, poor child?"
Do you really know it?—There! There
I would go with you, my protector.

Do you know the mountain and its cloud-veiled path?
The mule tries to find its way in the mist;
in the caves lives the ancient brood of dragons;
The cliff falls sheer and over it the torrent.
Do you really know it?—There! There
leads our way! O father, let us go!

(Op. 37, no. 1), Spontini, Tchaikovski (Op. 25, no. 3), Zelter,
Reichardt, Erich Wolff (Op. 15, no. 1), and Leopold Damrosch (Op.
17, no. 2). More familiar than any of these, but in a different
category, is the aria in Ambroise Thomas' opera *Mignon, Connais-
tu le pays?*

Do not ask me to speak, tell me to be silent,
for my secret is my duty;
I would reveal to you my inmost being,
but fate will not have it so.

At the appointed time the sun's course drives away
the gloomy night, and it cannot choose but brighten.
The hard rock opens its bosom;
It does not begrudge the earth its deep-hidden springs.

Ein jeder sucht im Arm des Freundes Ruh,
Dort kann die Brust in Klagen sich ergiessen;
Allein ein Schwur drückt mir die Lippen zu,
Und nur ein Gott vermag sie aufzuschliessen.

HUGO WOLF (*Goethe Lieder*, no. 5). Other composers include
Schubert (*Lied der Mignon, I,* D. 877), Schumann (Op. 98a, no. 5),

3

Nur wer die Sehnsucht kennt,
Weiss, was ich leide!
Allein und abgetrennt
Von aller Freude
Seh' ich ans Firmament
Nach jener Seite.
Ach! der mich liebt und kennt,
Ist in der Weite.
Es schwindelt mir, es brennt
Mein Eingeweide.
Nur wer die Sehnsucht kennt,
Weiss, was ich leide!

HUGO WOLF (*Goethe Lieder*, no. 6). The Wolf song is given preference here despite the great popularity of the smoother one by
Tchaikovski (Op. 6, no. 6; Russian translation by Meï. See Appendix.) Zelter made two settings of the text (called *Sehnsucht*), Schubert

4

So lasst mich scheinen, bis ich werde;
Zieht mir das weisse Kleid nicht aus!
Ich eile von der schönen Erde
Hinab in jenes feste Haus.

Dort ruh' ich eine kleine Stille,
Dann öffnet sich der frische Blick;
Ich lasse dann die reine Hülle,
Den Gürtel und den Kranz zurück.

Und jene himmlischen Gestalten,
Sie fragen nicht nach Mann und Weib,
Und keine Kleider, keine Falten
Umgeben den verklärten Leib.

Every man seeks rest in the arms of a friend,
for there he can pour out the troubles of his heart.
But a vow seals my lips,
and only a god can prevail upon me to open them.

Rubinstein (Op. 91, no. 10), Reichardt, and Zelter.

Only one who knows longing
can understand what I suffer!
alone and bereft
of all joy,
I look at the sky
yonder.
Ah, he who loves and understands me
is far away.
I faint. Fire burns
within me.
Only one who knows longing
can understand what I suffer!

---

three (D. 359, 877, 310), and Beethoven four. Others include
Schumann (Op. 98a, no. 3), Hiller (Op. 129, no. 3), Kreutzer (Op. 75),
Loewe (Op. 9), Proch (Op. 79, no. 2), Reichardt, Moór (Op. 13, no.
14), and Medtner (Meï translation, Op. 18, no. 4).

So let me seem, until I become so;
do not divest me of my white garment!
I am hastening from the beautiful earth
down to that impregnable house.

There I shall rest a little while in tranquillity,
then a fresh vision will open up;
I shall leave behind then the pure raiment,
the girdle and the wreath.

And those heavenly beings
do not concern themselves with man and woman,
and no garments, no robes,
cover the transfigured body.

Zwar lebt' ich ohne Sorg' und Mühe,
Doch fühlt' ich tiefen Schmerz genung.
Vor Kummer altert' ich zu frühe;
Macht mich auf ewig wieder jung!

HUGO WOLF (*Goethe Lieder*, no. 7). Schubert made three settings of this poem, the first entitled *Lied der Mignon, II* (D. 469), the second and third simply *Mignon* (D. 727 and 877). In some editions of all three settings the fourth line of the first stanza is changed to

DER MUSENSOHN

Durch Feld und Wald zu schweifen,
Mein Liedchen wegzupfeifen,
So geht's von Ort zu Ort!
Und nach dem Takte reget,
Und nach dem Mass beweget
Sich alles an mir fort.

Ich kann sie kaum erwarten,
Die erste Blum' im Garten,
Die erste Blüt' am Baum.
Sie grüssen meine Lieder,
Und kommt der Winter wieder,
Sing' ich noch jenen Traum.

Ich sing' ihn in der Weite,
Auf's Eises Läng' und Breite,
Da blüht der Winter schön!
Auch diese Blüte schwindet,
Und neue Freude findet
Sich auf bebauten Höhn.

Denn wie ich bei der Linde
Das junge Völkchen finde,
Sogleich erreg' ich sie.
Der stumpfe Bursche bläht sich,
Das steife Mädchen dreht sich
Nach meiner Melodie.

True, I have lived without trouble and toil,
yet I have felt deep pain enough.
Through sorrow I have aged too early—
O make me forever young again!

Hinab in jenes dunkle Haus. In the second setting, *fühlt'*, in the
second line of the final stanza, is changed to *fühl'*.

Other settings include those of Schumann (Op. 98a, no. 9),
Reichardt, and Rubinstein.

THE POET

To ramble through field and forest,
to pipe away my little song,
so it goes from place to place!
and to my beat
and to my measure
everything moves.

I can hardly wait
for the first flower in the garden,
the first bloom on the tree.
They greet my songs,
and when winter comes again
I am still singing of that dream.

I sing it far and wide
over the length and breadth of ice,
and winter blossoms beautifully!
These flowers also vanish,
and new happiness is found
in the upland farms.

For when under the linden
I find the young people,
at once I excite them.
The dull boy struts,
the stiff girl turns
to my melody.

Ihr gebt den Sohlen Flügel
Und treibt durch Tal und Hügel
Den Liebling weit von Haus.
Ihr lieben holden Musen,
Wann ruh' ich ihr am Busen
Auch endlich wieder aus?

FRANZ SCHUBERT, D. 764. The text was also set by Goethe's con-

PROMETHEUS

Bedecke deinen Himmel, Zeus,
Mit Wolkendunst
Und übe, dem Knaben gleich,
Der Disteln köpft,
An Eichen dich und Bergeshöhn!
Musst mir meine Erde
Doch lassen stehn
Und meine Hütte, die du nicht gebaut,
Und meinen Herd,
Um dessen Glut
Du mich beneidest.

Ich kenne nichts Ärmeres
Unter der Sonn', als euch, Götter!
Ihr nähret kümmerlich
Von Opfersteuern
Und Gebetshauch
Eure Majestät
Und darbtet, wären
Nicht Kinder und Bettler
Hoffnungsvolle Toren.

Da ich ein Kind war,
Nicht wusste, wo aus noch ein,
Kehrt' ich mein verirrtes Auge
Zur Sonne, als wenn drüber wär'
Ein Ohr, zu hören meine Klage,
Ein Herz, wie meins,
Sich des Bedrängten zu erbarmen.

You give wings to my feet
and drive over vale and hill
your loved one, far from home.
O dear, gentle muses,
when shall I rest again upon her bosom
at last?

---

temporaries Reichardt and Zelter.

PROMETHEUS

Cover your heavens, Zeus,
with misty clouds,
and play, like a boy
who pulls the heads off thistles,
with oaks and mountaintops!
But my earth
you must leave alone,
and my hut, which you did not build,
and my hearth,
whose fire
you envy.

I know nothing more wretched
under the sun, than you, gods!
You nourish miserably—
on required sacrifices
and the breath of prayer—
your majesty,
and you would starve, if
children and beggars
were not hopeful fools.

When I was a child,
and did not know out from in,
I would turn my wandering eyes
to the sun, as if above there were
an ear to hear my lament,
a heart, like mine,
to take pity on the distressed.

Wer half mir
Wider der Titanen Übermut?
Wer rettete vom Tode mich,
Von Sklaverei?
Hast du nicht alles selbst vollendet,
Heilig glühend Herz?
Und glühtest jung und gut,
Betrogen, Rettungsdank
Dem Schlafenden da droben?

Ich dich ehren? Wofür?
Hast du die Schmerzen gelindert
Je des Beladenen?
Hast du die Tränen gestillet
Je des Geängsteten?
Hat nicht mich zum Manne geschmiedet
Die Allmächtige Zeit
Und das ewige Schicksal,
Meine Herrn und deine?

Wähntest du etwa,
Ich sollte das Leben hassen,
In Wüsten fliehen,
Weil nicht alle
Blütenträume reiften?

Hier sitz' ich, forme Menschen
Nach meinem Bilde,
Ein Geschlecht, das mir gleich sei,
Zu leiden, zu weinen,
Zu geniessen und zu freuen sich
Und dein nicht zu achten,
Wie ich!

HUGO WOLF (*Goethe Lieder*, no. 49). This big work is more
properly a *scena dramatica* than a song; it was orchestrated by the
composer. Schubert's setting (D. 674) is an interesting attempt to
stretch the limits of the *lied* form. He makes a few changes: Stanza

RASTLOSE LIEBE

Dem Schnee, dem Regen,
Dem Wind entgegen,
Im Dampf der Klüfte,
Durch Nebeldüfte,
Immer zu! Immer zu!
Ohne Rast und Ruh!

Who helped me
against the arrogance of the Titans?
Who delivered me from death,
from slavery?
Have you not done it all yourself,
glowing, dedicated heart?
And with fine youthful ardor
were you not betrayed into thanks for your delivery
to the sleeping one above?

I honor you? What for?
Have you ever soothed the affliction
of the heavy-laden?
Have you ever stilled the tears
of the distressed?
Was I not forged into manhood
by omnipotent time
and eternal destiny,
my masters and yours?

Do you perhaps imagine
that I ought to hate life,
and fly into the desert
because not all
flowery dreams come true?

Here I sit, fashioning men
in my own image,
a species like myself
to suffer, to weep,
to enjoy and to rejoice,
and to ignore you,
even as I!

2, line 3, *Ihr nährt kümmerlich*; line 4, *Vom Opfersteuern*.
   The dramatic text was more simply set by J. F. Reichardt. A later
work is that of Julius Röntgen (Op. 99).

RESTLESS LOVE

Against the snow, the rain,
the wind,
in the mist of the ravines,
through the fragrant vapors,
ever on! Ever on!
Without rest or repose.

Lieber durch Leiden
Möcht' ich mich schlagen,
Als so viel Freuden
Des Lebens ertragen
Alle das Neigen
Von Herzen zu Herzen,
Ach, wie so eigen
Schaffet das Schmerzen!

Wie, soll ich fliehen?
Waldwärts ziehen?
Alles vergebens!
Krone des Lebens,
Glück ohne Ruh,
Liebe, bist du!

FRANZ SCHUBERT, D. 138. Stanza 2, line 2, reads *Wollt ich mich schlagen*; line 8, *Schaffet es Schmerzen*. Stanza 3, lines 1 and 2, *fliehen* and *ziehen* are contracted to *flieh'n* and *zieh'n*. In Robert Franz's song (Op. 33, no. 6), these same contractions are made, and the sixth line of the second stanza reads *Der Herzen zu Herzen.*

DAS VEILCHEN

Ein Veilchen auf der Wiese stand
Gebückt in sich und unbekannt;
Es war ein herzigs Veilchen
Da kam eine junge Schäferin
Mit leichtem Schritt und munterm Sinn
Daher, daher,
Die Wiese her und sang.

"Ach," denkt das Veilchen, "wär' ich nur
Die schönste Blume der Natur,
Ach, nur ein kleines Weilchen,
Bis mich das Liebchen abgepflückt
Und an dem Busen matt gedrückt!
Ach nur, ach nur
Ein Viertelstündchen lang!"

Rather would I struggle
through suffering
than to bear so much
of the world's joy.
All the inclining
of heart to heart,
ah, how in its own way
it causes pain!

What, shall I run away?
Flee to the woods?
All in vain!
Crown of life,
fortune without rest,
that is love!

Of forty or more other settings, the following may be mentioned: Himmel (Op. 21, no. 2), O. Jahn, Raff (Op. 98, no. 23), Reichardt, Reissiger (Op. 53, no. 1), Schumann (Op. 33b, no. 3), Taubert (Op. 9), Zelter, Backer-Grøndahl, and Othmar Schoeck (Op. 19a, no. 5).

THE VIOLET

A violet stood in the meadow,
modest and unknown;
it was a charming violet.
There came a young shepherdess,
light of foot and merry of heart,
this way, this way
along the meadow, and sang.

"Ah," thought the violet, "if I were only
the most beautiful flower in nature,
ah, only for a little while,
so that the sweet one might pick me
and press me till faint on her bosom!
Ah, only, only
for a quarter of an hour!"

Ach! aber ach! das Mädchen kam
Und nicht in acht das Veilchen nahm,
Ertrat das arme Veilchen.
Es sank und starb und freut' sich noch:
"Und sterb' ich denn, so sterb' ich doch
Durch sie, durch sie,
Zu ihren Füssen doch."

WOLFGANG AMADEUS MOZART, K. 476. Mozart's melody requires one slight change in the fourth line, where *eine* is shortened to *ein*. At the end the poem is extended with the words *Das arme Veilchen!*

WANDRERS NACHTLIED, I

Der du von dem Himmel bist,
Alles Leid und Schmerzen stillest,
Den, der doppelt elend ist,
Doppelt mit Erquickung füllest,
Ach, ich bin des Treibens müde!
Was soll all der Schmerz und Lust?
Süsser Friede,
Komm, ach komm in meine Brust!

FRANZ SCHUBERT, D. 224. In the second line *stillest* becomes *stillst*, and in the fourth *Erquickung* is changed to *Entzückung* and *füllest* is contracted to *füllst*.

Other composers include Hugo Wolf (*Lieder nach verschiedenen Dichtern*, no. 17), Franz Liszt, Joseph Marx (with slight verbal

WANDRERS NACHTLIED, II

Über allen Gipfeln
Ist Ruh,
In allen Wipfeln
Spürest du
Kaum einen Hauch;
Die Vöglein schweigen im Walde.
Warte nur, balde
Ruhest du auch.

FRANZ SCHUBERT, D. 768. Also set by Schumann (Op. 96, no. 1), Liszt, S. Herzog, Hiller (Op. 129, no. 11), Kuhlau, Nessler (Op. 34, no. 3), Panofka, F. Wüllner (Op. 5, no. 3), Zelter, Ansorge (Op. 19,

Ah, but ah! the maiden came
and did not notice the violet—
stepped on the poor violet.
It sank and died, and still rejoiced:
"Even though I die, yet I die
because of her, because of her,
right at her feet."

Es war ein herzigs Veilchen! Goethe's friend J. F. Reichardt also
made a setting, and there is a more modern one by Nicolai Medtner
(Op. 18, no. 5).

WANDERER'S NIGHT SONG

Thou that comest from heaven,
that dost quiet all sorrow and pain,
that dost the doubly wretched
doubly revive,
Ah, I am weary of striving!
Why all this pain and pleasure?
Sweet peace,
come, oh come to my breast!

---

changes), Reichardt (set for four voices), Götz (Op. 19, no. 6),
Medtner (Op. 15, no. 1), Raff, Pfitzner (Op. 40, no. 5), Mikuli (Op.
27, no. 4), Nessler (Op. 34, no. 2), Zelter, Rheinberger, C. Ansorge
(Op. 19, no. 2), and Mary Turner Salter.

WANDERER'S NIGHT SONG

Over all the mountain peaks
is peace,
in all the tree tops
you feel
hardly a breath;
the birds are silent in the forest.
Only wait, soon
you too shall rest.

---

no. 3), Medtner (Op. 6, no. 1), and Charles Ives (called *Ilmenau*),
along with more than sixty others.

WONNE DER WEHMUT

Trocknet nicht, trocknet nicht,
Tränen der ewigen Liebe!
Ach, nur dem halbgetrockneten Auge
Wie öde, wie tot die Welt ihm erscheint!
Trocknet nicht, trocknet nicht,
Tränen unglücklicher Liebe!

LUDWIG VAN BEETHOVEN, Op. 83, no. 1. Though Beethoven's song
is better known, Robert Franz's setting (Op. 33, no. 1) is one of his

GROTH, KLAUS
1819–1899

O WÜSST' ICH DOCH DEN WEG ZURÜCK

O wüsst' ich doch den Weg zurück,
Den lieben Weg zum Kinderland!
O warum sucht' ich nach dem Glück
Und liess der Mutter Hand?

O wie mich sehnet auszuruhn,
Von keinem Streben aufgeweckt,
Die müden Augen zuzutun,
Von Liebe sanft bedeckt!

Und nichts zu forschen, nichts zu spähn,
Und nur zu träumen leicht und lind,
Der Zeiten Wandel nicht zu sehn,
Zum zweiten Mal ein Kind!

O zeigt mir doch den Weg zurück,
Den lieben Weg zum Kinderland!
Vergebens such' ich nach dem Glück—
Ringsum ist öder Strand!

JOHANNES BRAHMS, Op. 63, no. 8. The second of three Klaus Groth

DELIGHT OF MELANCHOLY

Dry not, dry not,
tears of eternal love!
Ah, even to the half-dry eye
how barren, how dead the world appears!
Dry not, dry not!
Tears of unhappy love!

---

finest, and that of Schubert well worth a hearing. The Reichardt is
interesting as the work of the composer the poet preferred.

Poet honored in his day for popularizing the Low German
dialects. Was Professor of German Language and Literature at Kiel. He wrote in many German dialects, but his
work is notable chiefly for the effects he achieved in Low
German.

O THAT I KNEW THE WAY BACK

O that I knew the way back,
the charming way to the land of childhood!
O why did I seek after fortune
and let go of my mother's hand?

O how I long to go to sleep
undisturbed by any aspirations,
to close my tired eyes,
gently protected by love!

And to seek nothing, to notice nothing,
and only to dream, lightly and softly,
not to see the changing times,
once more to be a child!

O show me but the way back,
the charming way to the land of childhood!
In vain I seek after fortune—
around me is waste land.

---

songs to which Brahms gave the general title *Heimweh*.

WIE MELODIEN ZIEHT ES MIR

Wie Melodien zieht es
Mir leise durch den Sinn.
Wie Frühlingsblumen blüht es,
Und schwebt wie Duft dahin.

Doch kommt das Wort und fasst es
Und führt es vor das Aug',
Wie Nebelgrau erblasst es
Und schwindet wie ein Hauch.

Und dennoch ruht im Reime
Verborgen wohl ein Duft,
Den mild aus stillem Keime
Ein feuchtes Auge ruft.

JOHANNES BRAHMS, Op. 105, no. 1.

GRUPPE, OTTO FRIEDRICH
1806–1876

DAS MÄDCHEN SPRICHT

Schwalbe, sag' mir an,
ist's dein alter Mann,
mit dem du's Nest gebaut,
oder hast du jüngst
erst dich ihm vertraut?

Sag', was zwitschert ihr,
sag', was flüstert ihr
des Morgens so vertraut?
Gelt, du bist wohl auch
noch nicht lange Braut?

JOHANNES BRAHMS, Op. 107, no. 3.

LIKE MELODIES

Like melodies it runs
gently in my mind.
Like spring flowers it blooms
and drifts thither like fragrance.

Yet if a word comes and fixes it
and brings it before the eye,
like a gray mist it fades
and vanishes like a breath.

Nevertheless, there remains in the rhyme
a hidden fragrance,
which softly from the silent bud
can be brought forth by tears.

A student of natural science, philosophy, and the German
language, Gruppe was strongly influenced by Hegel, a fact
that had its effect upon his many-sided poetry.

THE MAIDEN SPEAKS

Swallow, tell me,
is it your last year's mate
with whom you have built your nest,
or have you recently
made your first vows to him?

Say, what are you twittering,
say, what are you whispering
so intimately this morning?
Surely, you too are
not yet long a bride?

HART, HEINRICH
1855-1906

WENN DU ES WÜSSTEST

Wenn du es wüsstest,
Was träumen heisst
Von brennenden Küssen,
Von Wandern und Ruhen
Mit der Geliebten,
Aug' in Auge
Und kosend und plaudernd,
Wenn du es wüsstest,
Du neigtest dein Herz.

Wenn du es wüsstest,
Was bangen heisst
In einsamen Nächten,
Umschauert vom Sturm,
Da niemand tröstet
Milden Mundes
Die kampfmüde Seele,
Wenn du es wüsstest,
Du kämst zu mir.

Wenn du es wüsstest,
Was leben heisst,
Umhaucht von der Gottheit
Weltschaffendem Atem,
Zu schweben empor,
Lichtgetragen,
Zu seligen Höhen—
Wenn du es wüsstest,
Du lebtest mit mir.

RICHARD STRAUSS, Op. 27, no. 2. Titled *Cäcilie*. In the last line of
the second stanza *kämst* is expanded to *kämest*. In the last stanza,

With his brother Julius was a leader in the German
Naturalist school. His ideal was a literature contemporary
in spirit and subject matter, one that should embrace understanding of modern science and avoid imitation of the
Romantics.

IF YOU BUT KNEW

If you but knew
what it is to dream
of burning kisses,
of roving and resting
with the one you love,
eye to eye,
and caressing and babbling;
if you but knew it,
you would incline your heart.

If you but knew
what it is to fret
in lonely nights,
while the rain is pouring,
and no one there to comfort
with soft words
your weary soul,
if you only knew it
you would come to me.

If you but knew
what it is to live
inspired by godhood's
world-creating breath,
to soar upward
borne on the light
to blessed heights—
if you but knew it,
you would live with me.

---

the third line before the end, *Höhen* is contracted to *Höh'n*.

HEINE, HEINRICH
1797–1856

DER ATLAS

Ich unglücksel'ger Atlas! eine Welt,
Die ganze Welt der Schmerzen, muss ich tragen,
Ich trage Unerträgliches, und brechen
Will mir das Herz im Leibe.

Du stolzes Herz! du hast es ja gewollt!
Du wolltest glücklich sein, unendlich glücklich,
Oder unendlich elend, stolzes Herz,
Und jetzo bist du elend.

FRANZ PETER SCHUBERT (*Schwanengesang*, D. 957, no. 8).

AUF FLÜGELN DES GESANGES

Auf Flügeln des Gesanges,
Herzliebchen, trag' ich dich fort,
Fort nach den Fluren des Ganges,
Dort weiss ich den schönsten Ort.

Dort liegt ein rotblühender Garten
Im stillen Mondenschein;
Die Lotosblumen erwarten
Ihr trautes Schwesterlein.

Die Veilchen kichern und kosen
Und schaun nach den Sternen empor;
Heimlich erzählen die Rosen
Sich duftende Märchen ins Ohr.

With Goethe, unquestionably the strongest poetic influence on the German lied. The pure lyricism of his poetry, usually combined with bitterness and a stinging wit, awakened a unique response in many composers, notably Schubert, Schumann, and Franz. After a short and disastrous career in business, he took to the law, being required at the time to embrace Christianity when so doing. This forsaking of his Jewish heritage is said to have affected his writings, and to have accounted for his political radicalism. His last years were spent in Paris, where he wrote in French as well as German.

ATLAS

I, wretched Atlas! A world,
the whole world of affliction, I must bear!
I endure the intolerable, though
the heart within my body break.

Arrogant heart! You have willed it so!
You wanted to be happy, endlessly happy,
or endlessly miserable, arrogant heart,
And now you are miserable.

ON WINGS OF SONG

On wings of song,
beloved, I carry you away,
away to the plains of the Ganges;
there I know the loveliest spot.

There lies a garden in full bloom
in the quiet moonlight;
the lotus flowers await
their dear sister.

The violets titter and flirt
and look up to the stars;
furtively the roses whisper
fragrant tales into each other's ears.

Es hüpfen herbei und lauschen
Die frommen, klugen Gazell'n;
Und in der Ferne rauschen
Des heiligen Stromes Well'n.

Dort wollen wir niedersinken
Unter dem Palmenbaum
Und Lieb' und Ruhe trinken
Und träumen seligen Traum.

FELIX MENDELSSOHN-BARTHOLDY, Op. 34, no. 2. The last line o
the fourth stanza reads *Des heil'gen Stromes Well'n*. In the third lin
of the final stanza later editions of the poem have *Liebe* for *Lieb*
Mendelssohn set the text as originally published.

AUS MEINEN GROSSEN SCHMERZEN

Aus meinen grossen Schmerzen
Mach' ich die kleinen Lieder;
Die heben ihr klingend Gefieder
Und flattern nach ihrem Herzen.

Sie fanden den Weg zur Trauten,
Doch kommen sie wieder und klagen,
Und klagen, und wollen nicht sagen,
Was sie im Herzen schauten.

ROBERT FRANZ, Op. 5, no. 1. Of twenty or more other settings

DICHTERLIEBE

ROBERT SCHUMANN, Op. 48. The poems which inspired this cycle
are all taken from Heine's *Lyrisches Intermezzo* (1822–1823), in
which are found the texts of most of the well-known Heine songs
Of the sixty-five poems in the set, Schumann chose sixteen, and

I

Im wunderschönen Monat Mai,
Als alle Knospen sprangen,
Da ist in meinem Herzen
Die Liebe aufgegangen.

And skipping by and listening
come the gentle, wise gazelles;
and in the distance ripple
the waves of the holy river.

There we will sink down
under the palmtree,
and drink of love and rest,
and dream blissful dreams.

The fame of Mendelssohn's melody has not kept others—over
twenty of them—from setting these words. The best-known names
are Taubert (Op. 12, no. 1), and Henry K. Hadley (Op. 14, no. 3).

OUT OF MY GREAT AFFLICTIONS

Out of my great afflictions
I make little songs;
they lift their sounding plumage
and fly to her heart.

They found their way to the beloved,
yet they come back and complain;
they complain and will not say
what they saw in her heart.

---

only an early one by Hugo Wolf calls for mention.

POET'S LOVE

---

though they do not tell a definite story, for the most part he has
kept them in Heine's order. Thus the first four poems of the
Lyrisches Intermezzo are the first four of *Dichterliebe*, and number
sixty-five in Heine is Schumann's number sixteen.

In the lovely month of May,
when all the buds were bursting,
then within my heart
love broke forth.

Im wunderschönen Monat Mai,
Als alle Vögel sangen,
Da hab' ich ihr gestanden
Mein Sehnen und Verlangen.

ROBERT SCHUMANN, Op. 48, no. 1. The first song in Schumann's cycle is by all odds the best known setting of a very much set poem. The Robert Franz song (Op. 25, no. 5) should not be overlooked. Of more than eighty others, perhaps the best-known composers are Kücken (Op. 17, no. 4), Nessler (Op. 21, no. 1), D. Popper (Op. 2,

2

Aus meinen Tränen spriessen
Viel blühende Blumen hervor,
Und meine Seufzer werden
Ein Nachtigallenchor.

Und wenn du mich lieb hast, Kindchen,
Schenk' ich dir die Blumen all,
Und vor deinem Fenster soll klingen
Das Lied der Nachtigall.

ROBERT SCHUMANN, Op. 48, no. 2. Of over thirty other composers, only the names of Frank Van der Stucken (Op. 4, no. 1) and

3

Die Rose, die Lilie, die Taube, die Sonne,
Die liebt' ich einst alle in Liebeswonne.
Ich lieb' sie nicht mehr, ich liebe alleine
Die Kleine, die Feine, die Reine, die Eine;
Sie selber, aller Liebe Bronne,
Ist Rose und Lilie und Taube und Sonne.

ROBERT SCHUMANN, Op. 48, no. 3. The fifth line reads: *Sie selber aller Liebe Wonne*. To complete his still very brief song, Schumann repeats a line and a half from the middle of the poem. The other

49092 *strophic*

In the lovely month of May,
when all the birds were singing,
then I confessed to her
my longing and desire.

---

no. 1), Ethelbert Nevin (Op. 2, no. 2), Henry K. Hadley (*'Twas in the glorious month of May*), John Ford Barbour (*'Twas in the lovely month of May*), James H. Rogers, W. G. Hammond, Ludwig Hartmann (Op. 13, no. 1), and Catharinus Elling (Op. 16, no. 2).

no prelude

From my tears spring up
many blooming flowers,
and my sighs become
a chorus of nightingales.

And if you love me, child,
I give you all the flowers,
and before your window shall sound
the song of the nightingale.

Alexander Borodin stand out.

The rose, the lily, the dove, the sun—
I once loved them all with ecstatic love.
I love them no more, I love only
the little one, the dainty one, the pure one, the One.
She alone, the well-spring of all love,
is rose and lily and dove and sun.

---

important setting is that of Robert Franz (Op. 34, no. 5), though Giacomo Meyerbeer is among the others who set the poem.

4

Wenn ich in deine Augen seh'
So schwindet all mein Leid und Weh;
Doch wenn ich küsse deinen Mund,
So werd' ich ganz und gar gesund.

Wenn ich mich lehn' an deine Brust,
Kommt's über mich wie Himmelslust;
Doch wenn du sprichst: Ich liebe dich!
So muss ich weinen bitterlich.

ROBERT SCHUMANN, Op. 48, no. 4. Robert Franz has also given us
a fine setting (Op. 44, no. 5), with the second line changed to *So
schwindet alles Leid und Weh!* The poem is found again among the
early songs of Hugo Wolf (1876) published posthumously. Here the
last line reads *Dann muss ich weinen bitterlich.*

5

Ich will meine Seele tauchen
In den Kelch der Lilie hinein;
Die Lilie soll klingend hauchen
Ein Lied von der Liebsten mein.

Das Lied soll schauern und beben
Wie der Kuss von ihrem Mund,
Den sie mir einst gegeben
In wunderbar süsser Stund'.

ROBERT SCHUMANN, Op. 48, no. 5. Again the name of Robert Franz
stands out among the other composers who have set this text (Op.
43, no. 4). Mention may also be made of O. Dresel (Op. 1, no. 1).

6

Im Rhein, im schönen Strome,
Da spiegelt sich in den Well'n
Mit seinem grossen Dome
Das grosse, heilige Köln.

Im Dom, da steht ein Bildnis
Auf goldenem Leder gemalt;
In meines Lebens Wildnis
Hat's freundlich hineingestrahlt.

When I look into your eyes
all my sorrow and pain disappear;
but when I kiss your mouth,
then I become wholly well.

When I lie upon your breast
a heavenly happiness comes over me;
but when you say: I love you!
then I must weep bitterly.

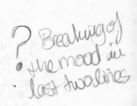

Of perhaps eighty other settings the following may be mentioned: Curschmann (Op. 16, no. 2), B. Tours (Op. 3, no. 1), A. Wilhelmj, L. Erlanger (Op. 21, no. 4), H. K. Hadley (Op. 14, no. 1), L. A. Coerne (Op. 57, no. 2), W. G. Hammond, and Ward Stephens.

I will dip my soul
into the chalice of the lily;
the lily shall breath
a song about my beloved.

The song shall quiver and palpitate
like the kiss of her mouth
that once she gave me
in a wonderfully sweet moment.

A. Fesca, A. Grünfeld (Op. 1, no. 1), D. Popper (Op. 2, no. 5), and Z. Fibich (Op. 3, no. 1).

The Rhine, the beautiful river,
reflects in its waves,
with its great cathedral,
the great holy city of Cologne.

In the cathedral there hangs a painting
painted on gilded leather;
in the confusion of my life
it has shone kindly down upon me.

Es schweben Blumen und Englein
Um unsre Liebe Frau;
Die Augen, die Lippen, die Wänglein,
Die gleichen der Liebsten genau.

ROBERT SCHUMANN, Op. 48, no. 6. Schumann follows Heine's
original version of the first line, *Im Rhein, im heiligen Strome*. The
third line of the final stanza is expanded thus: *Die Augen, die
Lippen, die Lippen, die Wänglein*. In another fine setting, Robert
Franz (Op. 18, no. 2) also follows the original first line. The second
line of the second stanza in his song is *Auf goldenem Grund*.

7

Ich grolle nicht, und wenn das Herz auch bricht,
Ewig verlornes Lieb! ich grolle nicht.
Wie du auch strahlst in Diamantenpracht,
Es fällt kein Strahl in deines Herzensnacht.

Das weiss ich längst. Ich sah dich ja im Traum,
Und sah die Nacht in deines Herzens Raum,
Und sah die Schlang', die dir am Herzen frisst,
Ich sah, mein Lieb, wie sehr du elend bist.

ROBERT SCHUMANN, Op. 48, no. 7. In the second stanza, the
rhyming words at the ends of the first and second lines are changed
to *Traume* and *Raume*. Because of the many word repetitions
Schumann's form is a very different thing from Heine's.

Charles Ives made a setting of this poem in 1899. Apparently using
Schumann rather than Heine for his source, he makes even more
repetitions and drifts even farther from the poet's form. In justice
perhaps his note to this song should be quoted: "The writer has

8

Und wüssten's die Blumen, die kleinen,
Wie tief verwundet mein Herz,
Sie würden mit mir weinen,
Zu heilen meinen Schmerz.

Und wüssten's die Nachtigallen,
Wie ich so traurig und krank,
Sie liessen fröhlich erschallen
Erquickenden Gesang.

Flowers and cherubs float
about Our dear Lady.
Her eyes, her lips, her cheeks
are exactly like those of my love.

---

gemalt. Franz Liszt (1856) favors the revised poem, but changes the last word of the second line to *Wellen*, and the fourth line to *Das grosse, das heilige Köln.*
Others include A. M. Foerster (Op. 6, no. 3), H. Proch (Op. 160, no. 1), and B. Shapleigh (Op. 32, no. 3).

I bear no grudge, even though my heart may break,
eternally lost love! I bear no grudge.
However you may shine in the splendor of your diamonds,
no ray of light falls in the darkness of your heart.

I have long known this. I saw you in a dream,
and saw the night within the void of your heart,
and saw the serpent that is eating your heart—
I saw, my love, how very miserable you are.

---

been severely criticized for attempting to put music to texts of songs, which are masterpieces of great composers. The song above and some of the others, were written primarily as studies. It should be unnecessary to say that they are not composed in the spirit of competition; neither Schumann, Brahms or Franz will be the one to suffer by comparison—another unnecessary statement. . . ."
At least ten other settings have been published.

And if the flowers knew, the little ones,
how deeply my heart is wounded,
they would weep with me
to heal my affliction.

And if the nightingales knew
how sad and sick I am,
they would cheerfully sound forth
their comforting song.

Und wüssten sie mein Wehe,
Die goldnen Sternelein,
Sie kämen aus ihrer Höhe,
Und sprächen Trost mir ein.

Die alle können's nicht wissen,
Nur Eine kennt meinen Schmerz:
Sie hat ja selbst zerrissen,
Zerrissen mir das Herz.

ROBERT SCHUMANN, Op. 48, no. 8. In the second line of the third
stanza *goldnen* becomes *goldenen*. The first line of the final stanza
begins *Sie alle.* . . .
Of nearly ninety other composers the following may be remem-

9

Das ist ein Flöten und Geigen,
Trompeten schmettern drein;
Da tanzt den Hochzeitreigen
Die Herzallerliebste mein.

Das ist ein Klingen und Dröhnen
Von Pauken und Schalmein;
Dazwischen schluchzen und stöhnen
Die guten Engelein.

ROBERT SCHUMANN, Op. 48, no. 9. The second line reads: *Trompeten schmettern darein*, and the third: *Da tanzt wohl den Hoch-*

10

Hör' ich das Liedchen klingen,
Das einst die Liebste sang,
So will mir die Brust zerspringen
Vor wildem Schmerzendrang.

Es treibt mich ein dunkles Sehnen
Hinauf zur Waldeshöh',
Dort löst sich auf in Tränen
Mein übergrosses Weh.

ROBERT SCHUMANN, Op. 48, no. 10. The fourth line of the first
stanza reads *Von wildem Schmerzendrang*. In the Franz song (Op. 5,
no. 11) the word becomes *Schmerzensdrang*. Edvard Grieg set a
Norwegian translation by Nordahl Rolfsen (Op. 39, no. 6). Others

And if my woes were known
to the golden stars,
they would come down from their heights
and speak consolation to me.

They cannot all understand it;
only one knows my suffering:
she herself, indeed, has broken,
broken my heart.

---

bered: A. Grünfeld (Op. 1, no. 4), F. Himmel (Op. 6, no. 3), M.
Moszkowski (Op. 13, no. 2), V. E. Nessler (Op. 43, no. 2), D. Popper
(Op. 2, no. 2), S. Thalberg, R. Hermann (Op. 1, no. 9), and A.
Reisenauer.

There is playing of flutes and fiddles,
trumpets blaring forth;
there in the wedding party,
my dearest love is dancing.

There is sounding and roaring
of drums and pipes;
and in the midst of it
the good angels sob and groan.

---

zeitreigen. The second line of the second stanza reads: *Ein Pauken
und ein Schalmei'n.* The last line is: *Die lieblichen Engelein.*

When I hear the song
that once my sweetheart sang,
my heart wants to burst
from the stress of savage pain.

An oppressive longing drives me
up to the wooded hilltop;
there I find release in tears
from my intolerable grief.

---

include Leopold Damrosch (Op. 10, no. 2), A. M. Foerster (Op. 6,
no. 4), A. Grünfeld (Op. 1, no. 2), G. Meyerbeer, B. Tours (Op. 3,
no. 5), A. Wilhelmj, B. O. Klein (Op. 59, no. 5), E. Lassen, and R.
Hermann (Op. 1, no. 4).

II

Ein Jüngling liebt ein Mädchen,
Die hat einen andern erwählt;
Der andre liebt eine andre
Und hat sich mit dieser vermählt.

Das Mädchen heiratet aus Ärger
Den ersten besten Mann,
Der ihr in den Weg gelaufen;
Der Jüngling ist übel dran.

Es ist eine alte Geschichte,
Doch bleibt sie immer neu;
Und wem sie just passieret,
Dem bricht das Herz entzwei.

ROBERT SCHUMANN, Op. 48, no. 11. In the original published version of the poem the last word of the first line was *Mägdlein*. In the first line of the second stanza Schumann has: *Das Mädchen nimmt*

I2

Am leuchtenden Sommermorgen
Geh' ich im Garten herum.
Es flüstern und sprechen die Blumen,
Ich aber, ich wandle stumm.

Es flüstern und sprechen die Blumen,
Und schaun mitleidig mich an:
Sei unserer Schwester nicht böse,
Du trauriger, blasser Mann.

ROBERT SCHUMANN, Op. 48, no. 12. In the fourth line of the first stanza Schumann follows Heine's original version: *Ich aber wandle stumm*. In the second stanza, third line, *unserer* is contracted to

13

Ich hab' im Traum geweinet,
Mir träumte, du lägest im Grab.
Ich wachte auf, und die Träne
Floss noch von der Wange herab.

A boy loves a girl
who has chosen another;
the other loves still another
and has married this one.

The girl weds out of spite
the first, most eligible man
who comes her way;
the boy is miserable over it.

It is an old story,
yet it remains ever new;
and whoever experiences it,
has his heart broken in two.

----

us Ärger. Other composers include E. Alnaes (Op. 6, no. 3), H.
Wuzél, and E. O. Nodnagel (Op. 36, no. 2).

In the bright summer morning
I walk about the garden.
The flowers are whispering and talking,
but I wander in silence.

The flowers are whispering and talking,
and they look pityingly at me:
"Don't be angry with our sister,
you doleful, pale man."

----

unsrer. Similarly Franz (Op. 11, no. 2) changes *schaun* to *schauen*
and *unserer* to *unsrer.* János Bókay and R. Hermann (Op. 1, no. 1)
are among more than twenty other composers.

I cried in my dream:
I dreamed that you lay in your grave.
I woke up, and the tears
were still streaming down my cheeks.

Ich hab' im Traum geweinet,
Mir träumt', du verliessest mich.
Ich wachte auf, und ich weinte
Noch lange bitterlich.

Ich hab' im Traum geweinet,
Mir träumte, du bliebest mir gut.
Ich wachte auf, und noch immer
Strömt meine Tränenflut.

ROBERT SCHUMANN, Op. 48, no. 13. Schumann follows Heine's
original in the second line of the third stanza: *Mir träumte, du
wärst mir noch gut.* Robert Franz (Op. 25, no. 3) does the same, and
in his song throughout the word *Traum* becomes *Traume.* The well-
known song by Georges Hué is set to the translation by Gérard de
Nerval (see Appendix).

14

Allnächtlich im Traume seh' ich dich,
Und sehe dich freundlich grüssen,
Und laut aufweinend stürz' ich mich
Zu deinen süssen Füssen.

Du siehst mich an wehmütiglich,
Und schüttelst das blonde Köpfchen;
Aus deinen Augen schleichen sich
Die Perlentränentröpfchen.

Du sagst mir heimlich ein leises Wort,
Und gibst mir den Strauss von Zypressen.
Ich wache auf, und der Strauss ist fort,
Und das Wort hab' ich vergessen.

ROBERT SCHUMANN, Op. 48, no. 14. In the first line of the second
stanza, for *siehst* read *siehest.* The last line of the song is contracted
thus: *Und's Wort hab' ich vergessen.*
In the Franz song (Op. 9, no. 4) the last stanza begins *Du sagest*

I cried in my dream:
I dreamed that you had forsaken me.
I woke up, and I cried
still long and bitterly.

I cried in my dream:
I dreamed that you still loved me.
I woke up, and still
the flood of my tears is streaming.

The following are selected from a list of more than one hundred names: J. Joachim, E. Lassen, C. Loewe (Op. 9), V. E. Nessler (Op. 43, no. 1), F. Ries (Op. 23, no. 1), S. Thalberg, J. Bókay, Alberto Jonas (Op. 17, no. 1), and Guy d'Hardelot (*Mes yeux pleuraient en rêve*).

Every night in my dreams I see you,
and see your friendly greeting;
and, loudly weeping, I throw myself
at your sweet feet.

You look at me sadly
and shake your little blond head;
from your eyes steal
teardrops like pearls.

You murmur intimately a quiet word to me,
and give me a spray of cypress.
I wake up and the spray is gone
and I have forgotten the word.

---

mir heimlich. Mendelssohn (Op. 86, no. 4) has in the second line *seh'* for *sehe*. The final line reads: *Und's Wort hab' ich vergessen*. There are settings by F. O. Dessoff, M. Lippold (Op. 33, no. 5), A. Buttykay (Op. 5, no. 1), S. Karg-Elert (Op. 53, no. 4), and others.

15

Aus alten Märchen winkt es
Hervor mit weisser Hand,
Da singt es und da klingt es
Von einem Zauberland,

Wo bunte Blumen blühen
Im goldnen Abendlicht,
Und lieblich duftend glühen
Mit bräutlichem Gesicht;—

Und grüne Bäume singen
Uralte Melodein,
Die Lüfte heimlich klingen,
Und Vögel schmettern drein;

Und Nebelbilder steigen
Wohl aus der Erd' hervor,
Und tanzen luft'gen Reigen
Im wunderlichen Chor;

Und blaue Funken brennen
An jedem Blatt und Reis,
Und rote Lichter rennen
im irren, wirren Kreis;

Und laute Quellen brechen
Aus wildem Marmorstein,
Und seltsam in den Bächen
Strahlt fort der Widerschein.

Ach, könnt' ich dorthin kommen,
Und dort mein Herz erfreun,
Und aller Qual entnommen,
Und frei und selig sein!

Ach! jenes Land der Wonne,
Das seh' ich oft im Traum;
Doch kommt die Morgensonne,
Zerfliesst's wie eitel Schaum.

ROBERT SCHUMANN, Op. 48, no. 15. Schumann set the poem as originally published; Heine made extensive alterations in later editions. In the later version the first line of the second stanza reads: *Wo grosse Blumen schmachten*, the third *Und zärtlich sich be-*

Out of the old fairy tales
a white hand beckons;
there are singing and sounding
from a magic country

where bright flowers bloom
in the golden evening light,
and in their lovely fragrance glow
like the visage of a bride;

and green trees sing
ancient melodies;
the breezes sound peacefully,
and the birds warble there;

and hazy images rise up
from the earth
and dance airy revels
in a mystical chorus;

and blue sparks burn
on every leaf and twig,
and red lights rush about
in confused, fantastic circles;

and noisy springs burst forth
out of rough marble,
and strangely in the streams
the reflection shines forth.

Ah, could I go there,
and there delight my heart,
removed from all torment,
and be free and blessed!

Ah, that land of rapture,
I often see it in dreams,
but when the morning sun rises
it vanishes like spraying foam.

---

trachten. The rest of the poem, shortened by two stanzas, can be
found in the Appendix. Other composers include M. Vogrich, T.
Luther-Schneider (Op. 3), F. Lev (Op. 53, no. 3), and L. Makray.

16

Die alten, bösen Lieder,
Die Träume schlimm und arg,
Die lasst uns jetzt begraben,
Holt einen grossen Sarg.

Hinein leg' ich gar manches,
Doch sag' ich noch nicht was;
Der Sarg muss sein noch grösser
Wie's Heidelberger Fass.

Und holt eine Totenbahre,
Von Brettern fest und dick;
Auch muss sie sein noch länger
Als wie zu Mainz die Brück'.

Und holt mir auch zwölf Riesen,
Die müssen noch stärker sein
Als wie der heil'ge Christoph
Im Dom zu Köln am Rhein.

Die sollen den Sarg forttragen
Und senken ins Meer hinab,
Denn solchem grossen Sarge
Gebührt ein grosses Grab.

Wisst ihr, warum der Sarg wohl
So gross und schwer mag sein?
Ich legt' auch meine Liebe
Und meinen Schmerz hinein.

ROBERT SCHUMANN, Op. 48, no. 16. The second line reads: *Die Träume bös' und arg*. The second line of the third stanza is: *Und Bretter fest und dick*. In the third line of the fourth stanza *der heil'ge*

DER DOPPELGÄNGER

Still ist die Nacht, es ruhen die Gassen,
In diesem Hause wohnte mein Schatz;
Sie hat schon längst die Stadt verlassen,
Doch steht noch das Haus auf demselben Platz.

The old evil songs,
the wicked, depraved dreams,
let us bury them now;
fetch a large coffin.

Therein I will put a great deal,
but I won't say yet of what;
the coffin must be even larger
than the Heidelberg Cask.

And fetch a bier
of strong thick boards;
they must also be even longer
than the bridge at Mainz.

And fetch me, too, twelve giants;
they must be even stronger
than Saint Christopher
in the cathedral at Cologne on the Rhine.

They shall bear the coffin out
and sink it into the sea,
for such a large coffin
deserves a large grave.

Do you know why the coffin
must be so large and heavy?
I have also laid my love
and my suffering in it.

Christoph becomes *der starke Christoph.* The third line of the last stanza reads : *Ich senkt' auch meine Liebe.*

MY DOUBLE

Still is the night, the streets are asleep.
In this house my love once lived.
She left the city long ago,
yet the house still stands on the same spot.

Da steht auch ein Mensch und starrt in die Höhe,
Und ringt die Hände vor Schmerzensgewalt;
Mir graust es, wenn ich sein Antlitz sehe—
Der Mond zeigt mir meine eigne Gestalt.

Du Doppelgänger! du bleicher Geselle!
Was äffst du nach mein Liebesleid,
Das mich gequält auf dieser Stelle
So manche Nacht in alter Zeit?

FRANZ PETER SCHUBERT (*Schwanengesang*, D. 957, no. 13).

DU BIST WIE EINE BLUME

Du bist wie eine Blume
So hold und schön und rein;
Ich schau' dich an, und Wehmut
Schleicht mir ins Herz hinein.

Mir ist, als ob ich die Hände
Aufs Haupt dir legen sollt',
Betend, dass Gott dich erhalte
So rein und schön und hold.

ROBERT SCHUMANN, Op. 25, no. 24. Published in more than two
hundred settings, this lyric is best known in the Schumann song,
though those of Rubinstein (Op. 32, no. 5) and Liszt are by no means
forgotten. In the last-named, the order of the third line of stanza
two is changed thus: *Betend, dass dich Gott erhalte.*

Slight verbal changes are common in the many other settings—
So rein, so schön, so hold, Und beten: das Gott . . ., dir legen soll,
etc. The better-known composers include A. Bungert (Op. 3, no. 2),
A. Goltermann (Op. 7, no. 5), M. Hauptmann (Op. 19, no. 2), G.
Henschel (Op. 37, no. 3), W. Kalliwoda (Op. 7, no. 1), W. Rust (Op.

DIE GRENADIERE

Nach Frankreich zogen zwei Grenadier',
Die waren in Russland gefangen;
Und als sie kamen ins deutsche Quartier,
Sie liessen die Köpfe hangen.

Da hörten sie beide die traurige Mär':
Dass Frankreich verloren gegangen,
Besiegt und zerschlagen das grosse Heer—
Und der Kaiser, der Kaiser gefangen.

Another man stands there looking up,
and rings his hands in agony.
I shudder to see his face—
the moonlight shows me my own figure.

O my double! Pale comrade!
Why do you ape my unhappy love
which tortured me upon this spot
so many nights in the olden time?

Other published settings include those of Molique (Op. 34) and Otterström.

YOU ARE LIKE A FLOWER

You are like a flower,
so sweet and fair and chaste;
I look upon you, and melancholy
creeps into my heart.

It seems to me as if I must
lay my hands upon your head,
praying that God will keep you
so chaste and fair and sweet.

14, no. 4), W. Taubert (Op. 186, no. 2), A. Thomas, F. Van der Stucken (Op. 1, no. 1), G. Sgambati, H. H. Huss, E. Tinel (Op. 38, no. 4), L. Halvorsen (Op. 2A, no. 1), F. W. Kücken, E. Nevin (Op. 2, no. 4) (*Oh fair, and sweet and holy*), J. Bókay, J. F. Barbour (*Thou'rt like a lovely flower*), C. W. Cadman (Op. 41, no. 1), O. Cantor (*Oh fair, oh sweet and holy*), G. W. Chadwick (Op. 11, no. 3), Clayton Johns, J. H. Rogers, W. G. Smith (*Thou'rt like unto a lovely flower*), Vernon Spencer, W. H. Thorley, and Graben-Hoffmann (Op. 74).

THE GRENADIERS

To France were returning two grenadiers
who had been captured in Russia;
and when they came to the German land
they hung their heads.

For there they heard the sad news
that France was lost,
the great army defeated and destroyed
and the Emperor a prisoner.

Da weinten zusammen die Grenadier'
Wohl ob der kläglichen Kunde.
Der eine sprach: "Wie weh wird mir,
Wie brennt meine alte Wunde!"

Der andre sprach: "Das Lied ist aus,
Auch ich möcht' mit dir sterben;
Doch hab' ich Weib und Kind zu Haus,
Die ohne mich verderben."

"Was schert mich Weib, was schert mich Kind,
Ich trage weit bessres Verlangen;
Lass sie betteln gehn, wenn sie hungrig sind—
Mein Kaiser, mein Kaiser gefangen!

Gewähr mir, Bruder, eine Bitt':
Wenn ich jetzt sterben werde,
So nimm meine Leiche nach Frankreich mit,
Begrab mich in Frankreichs Erde.

Das Ehrenkreuz am roten Band
Sollst du aufs Herz mir legen;
Die Flinte gib mir in die Hand,
Und gürt mir um den Degen.

So will ich liegen und horchen still,
Wie eine Schildwach', im Grabe,
Bis einst ich höre Kanonengebrüll
Und wiehernder Rosse Getrabe.

Dann reitet mein Kaiser wohl über mein Grab,
Viel Schwerter klirren und blitzen;
Dann steig' ich gewaffnet hervor aus dem Grab—
Den Kaiser, den Kaiser zu schützen!"

ROBERT SCHUMANN, Op. 49, no. 1. Titled *Die beiden Grenadiere*.
The third line of the second stanza reads *Besiegt und geschlagen das
tapfere Heer*. In the second line of the fifth stanza *bessres* is changed
to *besser*. Richard Wagner made a setting of Heine's own French

The grenadiers wept together
over the miserable tidings.
One spoke: "Woe is me!
How my old wound burns!"

The other said: "It is all over.
I too would like to die with you,
but I have a wife and child at home
who without me would perish."

"What do I care for wife and child?
I have more important concerns.
Let them go begging if they are hungry—
my Emperor is a prisoner!

"Brother, grant me one request,
if I must die now;
take my body to France with you,
bury me in French earth.

"My cross of honor, with the red ribbon,*
you must lay on my heart;
put my rifle in my hand,
and fasten my sword-belt around me.

"So will I lie still and listen,
like a sentry in the grave,
until I hear the noise of cannon
and the hoofs of whinnying horses.

"Then should my Emperor ride over my grave,
with many swords clanking and clashing;
then I shall arise, fully armed, from my grave,
to defend my Emperor!"

music Schumann uses for French National Anthem

* Instituted by Napoleon.

---

version of this poem (see Appendix), using, as Schumann did, the
strains of *La Marseillaise* at the climax of his song. A few other
settings have been published, including one by Reissiger.

DIE LORELEI

Ich weiss nicht, was soll es bedeuten,
Dass ich so traurig bin;
Ein Märchen aus alten Zeiten,
Das kommt mir nicht aus dem Sinn.

Die Luft ist kühl, und es dunkelt,
Und ruhig fliesst der Rhein;
Der Gipfel des Berges funkelt
Im Abendsonnenschein.

Die schönste Jungfrau sitzet
Dort oben wunderbar,
Ihr goldnes Geschmeide blitzet,
Sie kämmt ihr goldenes Haar.

Sie kämmt es mit goldenem Kamme
Und singt ein Lied dabei;
Das hat eine wundersame
Gewaltige Melodei.

Den Schiffer im kleinen Schiffe
Ergreift es mit wildem Weh;
Er schaut nicht die Felsenriffe,
Er schaut nur hinauf in die Höh'.

Ich glaube, die Wellen verschlingen
Am Ende Schiffer und Kahn;
Und das hat mit ihrem Singen
Die Lorelei getan.

FRANZ LISZT. There are two contractions: in line 1 *soll es* becomes *soll's*, and in the first line of the fourth stanza *goldenem* becomes *gold'nem*.

THE LORELEI

I do not know what it means
that I am so sad;
a tale of the olden times
will not go from my mind.

The air is cool and it is growing dark,
and the Rhine flows peacefully;
the peak of the mountain sparkles
in the evening sunlight.

The most beautiful girl is sitting
up over there;
her golden jewels shine,
she is combing her golden hair.

She is combing it with a golden comb
and also singing a song
that has a miraculously
powerful melody.

The boatman in his little boat
is seized with sore distress;
he does not look at the rocky reef,
he only looks upward.

I believe the waves
in the end devour the boatman and the boat;
and this with her singing
the Lorelei has done.

FRIEDRICH SILCHER. This setting is so simple and so familiar that
it is thought of as a folk song.

DIE LOTOSBLUME

Die Lotosblume ängstigt
Sich vor der Sonne Pracht,
Und mit gesenktem Haupte
Erwartet sie träumend die Nacht.

Der Mond, der ist ihr Buhle,
Er weckt sie mit seinem Licht,
Und ihm entschleiert sie freundlich
Ihr frommes Blumengesicht.

Sie blüht und glüht und leuchtet
Und starret stumm in die Höh';
Sie duftet und weinet und zittert
Vor Liebe und Liebesweh.

ROBERT SCHUMANN, Op. 25, no. 7. The first two lines of this setting
are a famous example of the triumph of music over poetry, or perhaps we should say of musicianship over music. Schumann has put a
half-measure rest between *ängstigt* and *sich*, thus requiring more
than ordinary sensitivity on the part of the singer to carry over the
sense. Nevertheless, the rest of the poem is set happily enough to
keep the song very much alive.

DAS MEER ERGLÄNZTE

Das Meer erglänzte weit hinaus
Im letzten Abendscheine;
Wir sassen am einsamen Fischerhaus,
Wir sassen stumm und alleine.

Der Nebel stieg, das Wasser schwoll,
Die Möwe flog hin und wieder;
Aus deinen Augen liebevoll
Fielen die Tränen nieder.

Ich sah sie fallen auf deine Hand
Und bin aufs Knie gesunken;
Ich hab' von deiner weissen Hand
Die Tränen fortgetrunken.

Seit jener Stund verzehrt sich mein Leib,
Die Seele stirbt vor Sehnen—
Mich hat das unglücksel'ge Weib
Vergiftet mit ihren Tränen.

FRANZ PETER SCHUBERT (*Schwanengesang*, D. 957, no. 12). Titled

THE LOTUS FLOWER

The lotus flower is fretful
before the glory of the sun,
and with her head hanging
waits, dreaming, for the night.

The moon, who is her lover,
wakes her with his light,
and for him she smilingly unveils
her innocent flower-face.

She blooms and glows and gleams,
and gazes silently upward;
she sends forth her fragrance, and weeps, and trembles,
with love and love's torment.

In the Robert Franz setting (Op. 25, no. 1), stanza 2, line 4, *frommes* is changed to *holdes*. A note under Charles Ives's song *The south wind* says: "Composed originally to *Die Lotosblume* but as the setting was unsatisfactory, the other words were written for it." Heine's text is printed in the music, very slightly modified. Numbered among the more than thirty other composers are R. Joseffy, W. Kienzl (Op. 8, no. 1), and C. Loewe (Op. 9).

THE BROAD SEA SPARKLED

The broad sea sparkled
in the last rays of the evening;
we were sitting by the deserted house of a fisherman;
we were sitting silent and alone.

The mist rose, the water swelled,
the gulls flew back and forth;
from your eyes, overflowing with love,
the tears fell.

I watched them fall upon your hand,
and I sank upon my knee;
from your white hand
I drank up the tears.

Since that hour my body wastes away,
my soul dies of longing—
the wretched woman
has poisoned me with her tears.

Am Meer. Among some eight other settings is one by Heinrich Proch (Op. 176).

DER TOD, DAS IST DIE KÜHLE NACHT

Der Tod, das ist die kühle Nacht,
Das Leben ist der schwüle Tag.
Es dunkelt schon, mich schläfert,
Der Tag hat mich müd' gemacht.

Über mein Bett erhebt sich ein Baum,
Drin singt die junge Nachtigall;
Sie singt von lauter Liebe,
Ich hör' es sogar im Traum.

JOHANNES BRAHMS, Op. 96, no. 1. Besides Brahms this text has been set by upwards of thirty composers, including A. Amadei (Op. 8, no. 3), A. Bungert (Op. 32, no. 6), N. Stcherbatcheff, Leo Blech,

HENCKELL, KARL

1864–1929

RUHE, MEINE SEELE

Nicht ein Lüftchen
Regt sich leise,
Sanft entschlummert
Ruht der Hain;
Durch der Blätter
Dunkle Hülle
Stiehlt sich lichter
Sonnenschein.
Ruhe, ruhe,
Meine Seele,
Deine Stürme
Gingen wild,
Hast getobt und
Hast gezittert,
Wie die Brandung,
Wenn sie schwillt!

DEATH IS THE COOL NIGHT

Death is the cool night,
life is the sultry day.
Already it is growing dark, I am sleepy;
the day has made me weary.

Over my bed there grows a tree;
in it the young nightingale sings;
she sings of nothing but love.
I hear it even in my dreams.

E. Meyer-Helmund (Op. 161), H. Drechsler (Op. 16, no. 2), E. Lassen, and Paul Ambrose (*A dream*, Op. 12, no. 3).

One of the group of *Jüngstdeutsche*, Henckell had a special interest in Socialism. His labor poems won him considerable reputation.

REST, MY SOUL

Not a breeze
is lightly stirring;
in soft sleep
the grove is at rest;
through the leaves'
dark cover
steal bright shafts of
sunshine.
Rest, rest,
my soul,
your storms
have raged wildly;
you have started up
and have trembled
like the seething
breakers!

Diese Zeiten
Sind gewaltig,
Bringen Herz und
Hirn in Not—
Ruhe, ruhe,
Meine Seele,
Und vergiss,
Was dich bedroht!

RICHARD STRAUSS, Op. 27, no. 1.

HEYSE, PAUL JOHANN LUDWIG
1830–1914

AM SONNTAG MORGEN

Am Sonntag Morgen, zierlich angetan,
Wohl weiss ich, wo du da bist hingegangen,
Und manche Leute waren, die dich sahn,
Und kamen dann zu mir, dich zu verklagen.
Als sie mir's sagten, hab' ich laut gelacht
Und in der Kammer dann geweint zu Nacht.
Als sie mir's sagten, fing ich an zu singen,
Um einsam dann die Hände wund zu ringen.

JOHANNES BRAHMS, Op. 49, no. 1. In the sixth line *zu Nacht* becomes *zur Nacht*. Hermann Götz (Op. 4, no. 5) and W. Riedel (Op.

AUCH KLEINE DINGE

Auch kleine Dinge können uns entzücken,
Auch kleine Dinge können teuer sein.
Bedenkt, wie gern wir uns mit Perlen schmücken.
Sie werden schwer bezahlt und sind nur klein.
Bedenkt, wie klein ist die Olivenfrucht,
Und wird um ihre Güte doch gesucht.
Denkt an die Rose nur, wie klein sie ist,
Und duftet doch so lieblich, wie ihr wisst.

HUGO WOLF (*Italienisches Liederbuch*, no. 1).

> These times
> are portentous,
> they try the heart
> and the brain to extremity—
> rest, rest,
> my soul,
> and forget
> the things that threaten you!

Celebrated for his *Novellen*, Heyse published much original and translated poetry. Son of a philologist, he was a specialist in the Romance languages and literature. To the student of song his greatest interest centers around his *Italienisches Liederbuch* and *Spanisches Liederbuch* (the latter written in collaboration with Emanuel Geibel), which contain his masterly translations. In his later years he became an outspoken opponent of the Naturalist and Impressionist schools of German literature. In 1910 he won the Nobel Prize for literature.

ON SUNDAY MORNING

On Sunday morning, dressed in your best,
I know very well where you went.
And many people there were who saw you
and then came to me to tell tales about you.
While they were telling me I laughed lustily;
but in my room I wept that night.
While they were telling me I began to sing,
only to wring my hands raw as soon as I was alone.

2, no. 1) have also set this poem.

EVEN LITTLE THINGS

Even little things can delight us;
even little things can be precious.
Think with what pleasure we bedeck ourselves with pearls;
they are very costly, yet very small.
Think how small is the olive,
and yet sought after for its excellence.
Only think of the rose, how small it is,
and yet so fragrant, as you know.

AUF DEM GRÜNEN BALKON

Auf dem grünen Balkon mein Mädchen
Schaut nach mir durchs Gitterlein.
Mit den Augen blinzelt sie freundlich,
Mit dem Finger sagt sie mir: Nein!

Glück, das nimmer ohne Wanken
Junger Liebe folgt hienieden,
Hat mir eine Lust beschieden,
Und auch da noch muss ich schwanken.
Schmeicheln hör' ich oder Zanken,
Komm' ich an ihr Fensterlädchen.
Immer nach dem Brauch der Mädchen.
Träuft ins Glück ein bisschen Pein:
Mit den Augen blinzelt sie freundlich,
Mit dem Finger sagt sie mir: Nein!

Wie sich nur in ihr vertragen
Ihre Kälte, meine Glut?
Weil in ihr mein Himmel ruht,
Seh' ich Trüb und Hell sich jagen.
In den Wind gehn meine Klagen,
Dass noch nie die süsse Kleine
Ihre Arme schlang um meine;
Doch sie hält mich hin so fein,—
Mit den Augen blinzelt sie freundlich,
Mit dem Finger sagt sie mir: Nein!

HUGO WOLF (*Spanisches Liederbuch*, Welt., no. 5).

BENEDEIT DIE SEL'GE MUTTER

Benedeit die sel'ge Mutter,
Die so lieblich dich geboren,
So an Schönheit auserkoren—
Meine Sehnsucht fliegt dir zu!
Du so lieblich von Gebärden,
Du die Holdeste der Erden,
Du mein Kleinod, meine Wonne,
Süsse, benedeit bist du!

ON THE LEAFY BALCONY

From her leafy balcony my sweetheart
looks at me through the lattice;
her eyes twinkle amiably;
with her finger she says: No!

Fortune, which never without swerving
follows young love here below,
has given me one happiness,
and yet even there I must hesitate.
I hear flattery or quarreling
whenever I come to her window.
It is always the way with girls
to mix a little pain with happiness.
Her eyes twinkle amiably;
with her finger she says: No!

How can she reconcile within herself
her coldness with my passion?
Since in her lies my heaven,
I see darkness stalking light;
my complaints go to the winds,
that never yet has the little sweetheart
entwined her arms with mine;
yet she keeps me at a distance so slyly—
her eyes twinkle amiably;
with her finger she says: No!

BLESSED BE THE HAPPY MOTHER

Blessed be the happy mother
of whom you were born so lovely,
of a beauty so elect
that I long for you!
You, so charming in bearing,
you, the most gracious on the earth,
you my jewel, my joy,
sweet one, blessed are you!

Wenn ich aus der Ferne schmachte
Und betrachte deine Schöne,
Siehe wie ich beb' und stöhne,
Dass ich kaum es bergen kann!
Und in meiner Brust gewaltsam
Fühl' ich Flammen sich empören,
Die den Frieden mir zerstören,
Ach, der Wahnsinn fasst mich an!

Hugo Wolf (*Italienisches Liederbuch*, no. 35).

DASS DOCH GEMALT ALL' DEINE REIZE WÄREN

Dass doch gemalt all' deine Reize wären,
Und dann der Heidenfürst das Bildnis fände.
Er würde dir ein gross Geschenk verehren,
Und legte seine Kron' in deine Hände.
Zum rechten Glauben müsste sich bekehren
Sein ganzes Reich bis an sein fernstes Ende.
Im ganzen Lande würd' es ausgeschrieben,
Christ soll' ein Jeder werden und dich lieben.
Ein jeder Heide flugs bekehrte sich
Und würd' ein guter Christ und liebte dich.

Hugo Wolf (*Italienisches Liederbuch*, no. 9). In the fifth line

GESEGNET SEI, DURCH DEN DIE WELT ENTSTUND

Gesegnet sei, durch den die Welt entstund;
Wie trefflich schuf er sie nach allen Seiten!
Er schuf das Meer mit endlos tiefem Grund,
Er schuf die Schiffe, die hinübergleiten,
Er schuf das Paradies mit ew'gem Licht,
Er schuf die Schönheit und dein Angesicht.

Hugo Wolf (*Italienisches Liederbuch*, no. 4).

When from afar I languish
and contemplate your beauty,
see how I tremble and sigh,
hardly able to conceal it!
And in my breast
I feel violent flames arising,
robbing me of my peace,
ah, madness seizes me!

WOULD THAT ALL YOUR CHARMS WERE PAINTED

Would that all your charms were painted,
and then that the heathen prince might find the portrait.
He would honor you with a great gift,
and lay his crown in your hands.
To the true faith must be converted
his whole kingdom to its remotest end.
Throughout the land it would be proclaimed:
Everyone must become a Christian and love you.
Each heathen straightway would be converted,
become a good Christian, and love you.

---

there is a contraction of the word *müsste* to *müsst'*.

BLESSED HE

Blessed He, by whom the world was created;
How excellently He made it in every way!
He created the bottomless sea;
He created the ships that glide over it;
He created Paradise with eternal light;
He created beauty and your face.

HERR, WAS TRÄGT DER BODEN HIER

Herr, was trägt der Boden hier,
Den du tränkst so bitterlich?
"Dornen, liebes Herz, für mich,
Und für dich der Blumen Zier."

Ach, wo solche Bäche rinnen,
Wird ein Garten da gedeihn?
"Ja, und wisse! Kränzelein,
Gar verschiedne, flicht man drinnen."

O mein Herr, zu wessen Zier
Windet man die Kränze? sprich!
"Die von Dornen sind für mich,
Die von Blumen reich' ich dir."

HUGO WOLF (*Spanisches Liederbuch, Geist.* no. 9). There is

IN DEM SCHATTEN MEINER LOCKEN

In dem Schatten meiner Locken
Schlief mir mein Geliebter ein.
Weck' ich ihn nun auf?—Ach nein!

Sorglich strählt' ich meine krausen
Locken täglich in der Frühe,
Doch umsonst ist meine Mühe,
Weil die Winde sie zersausen,
Lockenschatten, Windessausen
Schläferten den Liebsten ein.
Weck' ich ihn nun auf?—Ach nein!

Hören muss ich, wie ihn gräme,
Dass er schmachtet schon so lange,
Dass ihm Leben geb' und nehme
Diese meine braune Wange.
Und er nennt mich seine Schlange,
Und doch schlief er bei mir ein.
Weck' ich ihn nun auf?—Ach nein!

HUGO WOLF (*Spanisches Liederbuch*, Welt., no. 2). Wolf was
especially fond of this song, and he found a place for it in his opera
Der Corregidor. Brahms's setting (*Spanisches Lied*, Op. 6, no. 1),
using the same basic rhythmic pattern as Wolf, makes an interesting

LORD, WHAT WILL THE EARTH BRING FORTH

Lord, what will the earth bring forth,
that Thou waterest it so bitterly?
"Thorns, dear heart, for me,
and for you flowers to adorn yourself."

Ah, where such brooks flow,
will a garden flourish there?
"Yes, and be assured, wreaths
in great variety will be woven in it."

O my Lord, for whose adornment
will the wreaths be woven? Say!
"Those made of thorns are for me;
those of flowers I give to you."

---

another setting by G. Flügel (Op. 43, no. 7).

IN THE SHADOW OF MY CURLS

In the shadow of my curls
my lover lies asleep.
Shall I wake him? Ah, no!

Carefully I have combed my curly
locks every morning,
but my trouble is in vain,
because the winds dishevel them.
Shadow of curls, rush of wind,
put my lover to sleep.
Shall I wake him? Ah, no!

I must listen to his complaining
that he languished so long,
that his whole life depends
on these brown cheeks of mine.
And he calls me his serpent,
and yet he sleeps beside me.
Shall I wake him? Ah, no!

---

comparison. Here the third line of the third stanza reads *Dass ihm Leben gäb und nähme*. There are also settings by A. Jensen and M. Mayer (Op. 14, no. 2).

DER MOND HAT EINE SCHWERE KLAG' ERHOBEN

Der Mond hat eine schwere Klag' erhoben
Und vor dem Herrn die Sache kund gemacht:
Er wolle nicht mehr stehn am Himmel droben,
Du habest ihn um seinen Glanz gebracht.
Als er zuletzt das Sternenheer gezählt,
Da hab' es an der vollen Zahl gefehlt;
Zwei von den schönsten habest du entwendet:
Die beiden Augen dort, die mich verblendet.

HUGO WOLF (*Italienisches Liederbuch*, no. 7). Also set by A. Stöckel.

NUN WANDRE, MARIA
(Der heilige Joseph singt)

Nun wandre, Maria,
Nun wandre nur fort.
Schon krähen die Hähne,
Und nah ist der Ort.

Nun wandre, Geliebte,
Du Kleinod mein,
Und balde wir werden
In Bethlehem sein.
Dann ruhest du fein
Und schlummerst dort.
Schon krähen die Hähne
Und nah ist der Ort.

Wohl seh ich, Herrin,
Die Kraft dir schwinden;
Kann deine Schmerzen
Ach, kaum verwinden.
Getrost! Wohl finden
Wir Herberg dort.
Schon krähen die Hähne
Und nah ist der Ort.

THE MOON HAS COMPLAINED

The moon has lodged a grievous complaint
and brought the matter before the Lord:
he no longer wishes to remain up there in heaven,
since you have robbed him of some of his brightness.
When he last counted the host of stars
some of their full number were missing;
two of the most beautiful you have stolen:
those two eyes there, which dazzle me.

NOW COME ALONG MARY
(Saint Joseph sings)

Now come along, Mary,
keep on.
Already the cocks are crowing,
and we are nearly there.

Now come along, beloved,
my jewel,
and soon we shall be
in Bethlehem.
Then you shall have a good rest
and sleep there.
Already the cocks are crowing,
and we are nearly there.

I see very well, my Lady,
that your strength is failing,
I can hardly bear
your pain any longer.
Courage! Surely we shall find
shelter there.
Already the cocks are crowing,
and we are nearly there.

Wär erst bestanden
Dein Stündlein, Marie,
Die gute Botschaft
Gut lohnt' ich sie.
Das Eselein hie
Gäb' ich drum fort!
Schon krähen die Hähne,
Komm! Nah ist der Ort.

HUGO WOLF (*Spanisches Liederbuch, Geist.*, no. 3). Often called, after the "stage direction" that heads the poem, *Der heilige Joseph*

UND WILLST DU DEINEN LIEBSTEN STERBEN SEHEN

Und willst du deinen Liebsten sterben sehen,
So trage nicht dein Haar gelockt, du Holde.
Lass von den Schultern frei sie niederwehen;
Wie Fäden sehn sie aus von purem Golde.
Wie goldne Fäden, die der Wind bewegt—
    Schön sind die Haare, schön ist, die sie trägt!
Goldfäden, Seidenfäden ungezählt—
    Schön sind die Haare, schön ist, die sie strählt!

HUGO WOLF (*Italienisches Liederbuch*, no. 17).

WENN DU, MEIN LIEBSTER, STEIGST ZUM HIMMEL AUF

Wenn du, mein Liebster, steigst zum Himmel auf,
Trag' ich mein Herz dir in der Hand entgegen.
So liebevoll umarmst du mich darauf,
Dann woll'n wir uns dem Herrn zu Füssen legen.
Und sieht der Herrgott unsre Liebesschmerzen,
Macht er Ein Herz aus zwei verliebten Herzen,
Zu Einem Herzen fügt er zwei zusammen,
Im Paradies, umglänzt von Himmelsflammen.

HUGO WOLF (*Italienisches Liederbuch*, no. 36).

If only your time
were come, Mary,
the good news—
what would I give for it!
The donkey here,
I would part with him!
Already the cocks are crowing,
come! we are nearly there.

---

singt. There are also settings by M. Bruch (Op. 71), G. Flügel (Op. 43, no. 1), and A. Jensen (Op. 64, no. 1).

AND WOULD YOU SEE YOUR LOVER PERISH?

And would you see your lover perish?
Then do not wear your hair in curls, my dear.
Let it float freely down around your shoulders—
like threads of pure gold it seems.
Like golden threads caressed by the wind—
beautiful hair, beautiful she who wears it!
Golden threads, silken threads—numberless—
beautiful hair, beautiful she who combs it!

WHEN YOU, MY LOVE, ASCEND TO HEAVEN

When you, my love, ascend to heaven,
I shall carry my heart to you in my hand.
Lovingly you will thereupon embrace me,
then we shall lay ourselves at the feet of the Lord.
And when the Lord sees our love pangs,
He shall mold our two loving hearts into one.
Into one heart shall He fit our two together,
in Paradise, lighted by the fires of heaven.

HÖLTY, LUDWIG HEINRICH CHRISTOPH
1748–1776

AN DIE NACHTIGALL

Geuss nicht so laut der liebentflammten Lieder
  Tonreichen Schall
Vom Blütenast des Apfelbaums hernieder,
  O Nachtigall!
Du tönest mir mit deiner süssen Kehle
  Die Liebe wach;
Denn schon durchbebt die Tiefen meiner Seele
  Dein schmelzend Ach.

Dann flieht der Schlaf von Neuem dieses Lager,
  Ich starre dann,
Mit nassem Blick, und totenbleich und hager,
  Den Himmel an.
Fleuch, Nachtigall, in grüne Finsternisse,
  In's Haingesträuch,
Und spend' im Nest der treuen Gattin Küsse;
  Entfleuch, entfleuch!

JOHANNES BRAHMS, Op. 46, no. 4. The text was also set by

DIE MAINACHT

Wenn der silberne Mond durch die Gestreuche blickt
Und sein schlummerndes Licht über den Rasen geusst,
Und die Nachtigall flötet,
  Wandl' ich traurig von Busch zu Busch.

[Selig preis' ich dich dann, flötende Nachtigall,
Weil dein Weibchen mit dir wohnet in einem Nest,
Ihrem singenden Gatten
Tausend trauliche Küsse giebt.]

This gifted lyric poet was a founder and leader of the *Göttinger Dichterbund*. His poems show the influence of Uz, Klopstock, and the Volkslied, but are marked by a very personal strain of melancholy. They were not, however, published in the poet's lifetime, and were not always improved by the editing of Johann Heinrich Voss (1751–1826), who made extensive changes in them.

TO THE NIGHTINGALE

Do not pour so loudly your amorous songs'
rich strains
down from the blooming bough of the apple tree,
o nightingale!
With your sweet throat
you reawaken my love;
for already the depths of my soul are stirred
by your melting cry.

Then again I would lie sleepless,
staring up
with tear-filled eyes, and pale as death, and haggard,
to heaven above.
Flee, nightingale, into the green shadows,
into the grove,
and in your nest spend your kisses on your faithful wife.
Flee, ah flee!

Schubert (D. 196), J. F. Kittl (Op. 23, no. 2), and G. Trautmann (Op. 4, no. 1).

THE MAY NIGHT

When the silvery moon gleams through the copse,
and pours his slumbering light over the grass,
and the nightingale warbles,
I wander sadly from bush to bush.

[Then I count you blessed, o warbling nightingale,
for your wife shares your nest with you,
gives to her singing mate
a thousand tender kisses.]

Überhüllet von Laub, girret ein Taubenpaar
Sein Entzücken mir vor; aber ich wende mich,
   Suche dunklere Schatten,
   Und die einsame Träne rinnt.

Wann, o lächelndes Bild, welches wie Morgenrot
Durch die Seele mir strahlt, find' ich auf Erden dich?
   Und die einsame Träne
   Bebt mir heisser die Wang' herab!

JOHANNES BRAHMS, Op. 45, no. 2. The first word is changed from
Wenn to *Wann*. The last word in the second line is changed from
geusst to *streut* and the last word of the first line from *blickt* to
blinkt. The second stanza is omitted. In the Schubert setting

MINNELIED

Holder klingt der Vogelsang,
Wenn die Engelreine,
Die mein Jünglingsherz bezwang,
Wandelt durch die Haine.

Röter blühet Tal und Au,
Grüner wird der Rasen,
Wo die Finger meiner Frau
Maienblumen lasen.

Ohne sie ist alles tot,
Welk' sind Blüt' und Kräuter;
Und kein Frühlingsabendrot
Dünkt mich schön und heiter.

Traute, minnigliche Frau,
Wollest nimmer fliehen,
Dass mein Herz, gleich dieser Au,
Mög' in Wonne blühen!

(as edited by Johann Heinrich Voss, and published in 1804)

JOHANNES BRAHMS, Op. 71, no. 5. The poems of Hölty were published posthumously under the editorship of J. H. Voss, who did a
good deal of re-writing. *Minnelied* is an outstanding example of his
improvements (see Appendix). The various composers, of course,
set the Voss version. Brahms made no further changes, but in

Hidden by the foliage, a pair of doves
coos its delight near by; but I turn away,
seek deeper shadows,
and weep a lonely tear.

When, o smiling image, which like the light of morning
shines through my soul, shall I find you upon the earth?
And the lonely tear
trembles hotter down my cheek!

(D. 194), the same changes are made. Being strophic.in form, this
song includes all four stanzas. Of some half dozen others who set the
poem, Mendelssohn's sister, Fanny Hensel, may be mentioned.

LOVE SONG

More pleasing sounds the song of the birds
when the pure angel
who has conquered my heart
walks through the grove.

More brightly bloom valley and meadow,
greener grows the grass,
where my lady's fingers
gather May flowers.

Without her everything is dead,
faded are the blossoms and the plants;
and no spring twilight
seems to me beautiful and clear.

Dear, lovely lady,
do not ever leave me;
that my heart, like this meadow,
may bloom in rapture!

Mendelssohn (Op. 8, no. 1) we find the third line thus: *Die mein
junges Herz bezwang*; and the first line of the final stanza, *Traute,
heissgeliebte Frau*. In the second stanza Schubert (D. 429) has
*Grüner wird der Wasen,/Wo mir Blumen rot und blau, Ihre Hände
lasen*. Challier lists eight settings.

JACOBI, JOHANN GEORG
1740–1814

LITANEI

(auf das Fest aller Seelen)

Ruhn in Frieden alle Seelen,
Die vollbracht ein banges Quälen,
Die vollendet süssen Traum,
Lebenssatt, geboren kaum,
Aus der Welt hinüber schieden:
Alle Seelen ruhn in Frieden!

Die sich hier Gespielen suchten,
Öfter weinten, nimmer fluchten,
Wenn von ihrer treuen Hand
Keiner je den Druck verstand:
Alle, die von hinnen schieden,
Alle Seelen ruhn in Frieden!

Liebevoller Mädchen Seelen,
Deren Tränen nicht zu zählen,
Die ein falscher Freund verliess,
Und die blinde Welt verstiess:
Alle, die von hinnen schieden,
Alle Seelen ruhn in Frieden!

Und der Jüngling, dem, verborgen
Seine Braut am frühen Morgen,
Weil ihn Lieb' ins Grab gelegt,
Auf sein Grab die Kerze trägt:
Alle, die von hinnen schieden,
Alle Seelen ruhn in Frieden!

Alle Geister, die voll Klarheit,
Wurden Märtyrer der Wahrheit,
Kämpften für das Heiligtum,
Suchten nicht der Marter Ruhm:
Alle, die von hinnen schieden,
Alle Seelen ruhn in Frieden!

Editor successively of two periodicals, both named *Iris*, Jacobi published poems of Goethe, his brother F. H. Jacobi, Gleim, Klopstock, Herder, Jean Paul, Voss, and the brothers Stolberg. He himself contributed many admired sonnets and lyrics.

LITANY

(for All Souls Day)

Rest in peace, all souls:
who have done with anxious torment,
who have ended a sweet dream,
satiated with life, hardly born,
gone over from the world—
all souls rest in peace!

Those who sought for companions here,
who often wept, never cursed
if the grasp of their friendly hand
was never understood:
all who have departed,
all souls rest in peace!

The souls of lovely girls,
whose tears are not to be counted,
deserted by a false friend
and cast out by the blind world:
all who have departed,
all souls rest in peace!

And the youth, for whom secretly
in the early morning, his bride,
who once lovingly laid him in the grave,
takes a candle there:
all who have departed,
all souls rest in peace!

All those serene spirits
who became martyrs to the truth,
who fought for the right
without seeking the glory of martyrdom:
all who have departed,
all souls rest in peace!

Und die nie der Sonne lachten,
Unterm Mond auf Dornen wachten,
Gott, im reinen Himmels-Licht,
Einst zu sehn von Angesicht:
Alle, die von hinnen schieden,
Alle Seelen ruhn in Frieden!

Und die gern im Rosen-Garten
Bei dem Freuden-Becher harrten,
Aber dann, zur bösen Zeit,
Schmeckten seine Bitterkeit:
Alle, die von hinnen schieden,
Alle Seelen ruhn in Frieden!

Auch, die keinen Frieden kannten,
Aber Mut und Stärke sandten
Über leichenvolles Feld
In die halb entschlafne Welt:
Alle, die von hinnen schieden,
Alle Seelen ruhn in Frieden!

Ruhn in Frieden alle Seelen,
Die vollbracht ein banges Quälen,
Die vollendet süssen Traum,
Lebenssatt, geboren kaum,
Aus der Welt hinüber schieden:
Alle Seelen ruhn in Frieden!

FRANZ PETER SCHUBERT, D. 343. Though the poet's title has been restored by common usage, Schubert called his song *Am Tage Allerseelen*. The poet furnishes the following note: "On this feast Roman Catholics visit the graves of their loved ones, place lights upon them, and pray for the dead." As Schubert's setting is strophic, any

JEITTELES, ALOIS

1794–1858

AN DIE FERNE GELIEBTE

I

Auf dem Hügel sitz' ich, spähend
In das blaue Nebelland,
Nach den fernen Triften sehend,
Wo ich dich, Geliebte, fand.

And those upon whom the sun never smiled,
who under the moon lay sleepless upon thorns,
that in the clear light of heaven
they might one day see God face to face:
all who have departed,
all souls rest in peace!

And those who sought joy in the rose garden,
and in the cup of delight,
but then in evil days
tasted its bitterness:
all who have departed,
all souls rest in peace!

And those who knew no peace,
whom courage and strength sent
into the field of battle
in a darkening world:
all who have departed,
all souls rest in peace!

Rest in peace, all souls,
who have done with anxious torment,
who have ended a sweet dream,
satiated with life, hardly born,
gone over from the world—
all souls rest in peace!

---

of the stanzas might be used, and all are printed in the complete
edition of his works. Most familiar, however, and certainly the best,
are those published in the first (posthumous) edition. They are
stanzas 1, 3, 6.

A young physician whose poems were published in various
periodicals of his time. He became a hero in a cholera
epidemic in Brünn because he insisted on leaving his own
sickbed to care for those who needed his help.

TO THE DISTANT BELOVED

On the hill I sit, staring
into the blue, misty land,
looking for the distant pastures
where I found you, my beloved.

Weit bin ich von dir geschieden,
  trennend liegen Berg und Tal
Zwischen uns und unserm Frieden,
  Unserm Glück und uns'rer Qual.

Ach, den Blick kannst du nicht sehen,
  Der zu dir so glühend eilt,
Und die Seufzer, sie verwehen
  In dem Raume der uns teilt.

Will denn nichts mehr zu dir dringen,
  Nichts der Liebe Bote sein?
Singen will ich, Lieder singen,
  Die dir klagen meine Pein!

Denn vor Liedesklang entweichet
  Jeder Raum und jede Zeit,
Und ein liebend Herz erreichet,
  Was ein liebend Herz geweiht!

2

Wo die Berge so blau aus dem nebligen Grau
    schauen herein,
Wo die Sonne verglüht, wo die Wolke umzieht,
    möchte ich sein!
Dort im ruhigen Tal schweigen Schmerzen und Qual.
  Wo im Gestein
Still die Primel dort sinnt, weht so leise der Wind,
    möchte ich sein!
Hin zum sinnigen Wald drängt mich Liebesgewalt,
    innere Pein,
Ach, mich zög's nicht von hier, könnt'ich, Traute, bei dir
    ewiglich sein!

3

Leichte Segler in den Höhen,
  und du Bächlein klein und schmal,
könnt mein Liebchen ihr erspähen,
  grüsst sie mir viel tausendmal.

I am far away from you,
between us lie hill and valley,
between us and our peace,
our happiness and our torment.

Ah, you cannot see my eyes
searching so ardently for you,
and my sighs dispersed
in the space that separates us.

Will then nothing any longer reach you,
nothing be a messenger of love?
I will sing you songs
complaining of my agony!

For song effaces
all space and all time,
and a loving heart attains
that to which a loving heart consecrates itself.

p.151 repetition last stanza of last song = cyclic

Where the blue mountains
look down from the misty gray,
where the sun ceases to glow, where the cloud encircles,
there would I be!
There in the restful valley pain and affliction are still.
Wherever among the stones
silently the primrose meditates, wherever the winds stir so
    lightly,
there would I be!
To the dreaming forest love's power urges me on,
sickness of heart,
ah, I would not stir from here if, dear, I could
be forever with you!

Light clouds above,
and you, brooklet, small and narrow,
should my love espy you
greet her for me many thousand times.

Seht ihr Wolken sie dann gehen
sinnend in dem stillen Tal,
lasst mein Bild vor ihr entstehen
in dem luft'gen Himmelssaal.

Wird sie an den Büschen stehen,
die nun herbstlich falb und kahl,
klagt ihr, wie mir ist geschehen,
klagt ihr, Vöglein, meine Qual!

Stille Weste, bringt im Wehen
hin zu meiner Herzenswahl
meine Seufzer, die vergehen
wie der Sonne letzter Strahl.

Flüstr' ihr zu mein Liebesflehen,
lass sie, Bächlein klein und schmal,
treu in deinen Wogen sehen
meine Tränen ohne Zahl.

4

Diese Wolken in den Höhen,
Dieser Vöglein munt'rer Zug
Werden dich, o Huldin, sehen.
Nehmt mich mit im leichten Flug!

Diese Weste werden spielen
Scherzend dir um Wang' und Brust,
In den seid'nen Locken wühlen.
Teilt' ich mit euch diese Lust!

Hin zu dir von jenen Hügeln
Emsig dieses Bächlein eilt.
Wird ihr Bild sich in dir spiegeln,
Fliess zurück dann unverweilt!

5

Es kehret der Maien, es blühet die Au',
Die Lüfte, sie wehen so milde, so lau,
Geschwätzig die Bäche nun rinnen.
Die Schwalbe, die kehret zum wirtlichen Dach,
Sie baut sich so emsig ihr bräutlich Gemach,
Die Liebe soll wohnen da drinnen.

Ye clouds, if you see her walking
thoughtfully in the silent valley,
let my image arise before her
in the airy hall of heaven.

Should she stand by the bushes,
now withered and lifeless in the autumn,
lament to her of what has happened to me;
complain to her, little bird, of my torment!

Silent West Wind, as you drift
yonder to my heart's chosen one,
bear my sighs, which die
like the last rays of the sun.

Whisper to her my love's entreaty,
let her, brooklet small and narrow,
truly see in your rapids
my numberless tears.

These clouds above,
these birds in happy passage,
will see you, my goddess.
Take me with you in gentle flight!

This West Wind will drift
playfully about your cheek and bosom,
blow through your silken hair.
Oh that I could share this pleasure!

Away from that hill to you
eagerly this brooklet hurries.
If her image should be reflected in you,
flow back then without delay!

May comes again, the meadows are in bloom,
the breezes stir so gently, so warmly,
chattering, the brooks are now running.
The swallow returns to the hospitable roof,
she builds so eagerly her bridal chamber—
love must dwell in it.

Sie bringt sich geschäftig von Kreuz und von Quer,
Manch' weicheres Stück zu dem Brautbett hieher
Manch' wärmendes Stück für die Kleinen.
Nun wohnen die Gatten beisammen so treu,
Was Winter geschieden verband nun der Mai,
Was liebet, das weiss er zu einen.

Es kehret der Maien, es blühet die Au',
Die Lüfte, sie wehen so milde, so lau,
Nur ich kann nicht ziehen von hinnen.
Wenn Alles, was liebet, der Frühling vereint,
Nur unserer Liebe kein Frühling erscheint,
Und Tränen sind all ihr Gewinnen.

6

Nimm sie hin denn, diese Lieder,
Die ich dir, Geliebte, sang,
Singe sie dann Abends wieder
Zu der Laute süssem Klang!

Wenn das Dämm'rungsrot dann ziehet
Nach dem stillen blauen See,
Und sein letzter Strahl verglühet
Hinter jener Bergeshöh',

Und du singst, was ich gesungen,
Was mir aus der vollen Brust
Ohne Kunstgepräng' erklungen,
nur der Sehnsucht sich bewusst.

Dann vor diesen Liedern weichet,
Was geschieden uns so weit,
Und ein liebend Herz erreichet,
Was ein liebend Herz geweiht.

LUDWIG VAN BEETHOVEN, Op. 98.

She brings busily from all directions
many a soft piece here to the bridal bed,
many a piece to warm the little ones.
Now the couple live so faithfully together,
what winter has parted, May binds together;
whatever is in love, he can unite.

May comes again, the meadows are in bloom,
the breezes stir so gently, so warmly,
only I cannot go away from here.
Though all things in love are united by spring,
to our love alone no spring appears,
and tears are its only reward.

Take them, then, beloved, these songs
which I have sung to you.
Sing them again in the evening,
to the sweet sound of the lute!

When the red of twilight moves
toward the still blue lake,
and its last ray dies out
over yonder mountaintop,

and you sing what I have sung,
what from my full breast
has artlessly sounded,
conscious only of its longing,

then these songs will cause to yield
that which has kept us so far apart
and a loving heart attains
that to which a loving heart consecrates itself.

KELLER, GOTTFRIED
1819–1890

Du milchjunger Knabe,
Wie schaust du mich an?
Was haben deine Augen
Für eine Frage getan!

Alle Ratsherrn in der Stadt
Und alle Weisen der Welt
Bleiben stumm auf die Frage,
Die deine Augen gestellt!

Eine Meermuschel liegt
Auf dem Schrank meiner Bas':
Da halte dein Ohr d'ran,
Dann hörst du etwas!

DU MILCHJUNGER KNABE

Du milchjunger Knabe,
Wie siehst du mich an?
Was haben deine Augen
Für eine Frage getan!

Alle Ratsherrn der Stadt
Und alle Weisen der Welt
Bleiben stumm auf die Frage,
Die deine Augen gestellt!

Ein leeres Schneckhäusel,
Schau, liegt dort im Gras;
Da halte dein Ohr dran,
Drin brümmelt dir was!

JOHANNES BRAHMS, Op. 86, no. 1. Keller's original version of the poem was called *Therese,* whence Brahms's title. After this song had been published, Keller brought out a new edition of his works, making extensive alterations. It was the later (and by no means improved) version that Wolf set (*Lieder nach verschiedenen Dich-*

Most celebrated and influential of German-Swiss writers, author of many well-known short stories, and such novels as *Der grüne Heinrich*. His poems number some of the finest things in German lyric poetry.

THERESE

You infant!
Why do you look at me like that?
What kind of question
have your eyes been asking?

All the town councilors
and all the wise men in the world
remain silent at the question
put by your eyes!

A sea-shell lies
in my aunt's cupboard:
hold it up to your ear
and you'll hear something!

YOU INFANT!

You infant!
Why do you look at me like that?
What kind of question
have your eyes been asking?

All the town councilors
and all the wise men in the world
remain silent at the question
put by your eyes!

Look, an empty snail-shell
lies there in the grass.
Hold it up to your ear—
something in it will mutter to you!

---

tern, no. 9).

Other composers include Hans Pfitzner (Op. 33, no. 3), R. Fischhof, H. Sommer (Op. 16, no. 2), Christian Sinding, R. Schweizer (Op. 22, no. 1), and O. Vrieslander.

KERNER, JUSTINIUS ANDREAS CHRISTIAN
1786–1862

Wohlauf, noch getrunken
Den funkelnden Wein!
Ade nun, ihr Lieben!
Geschieden muss sein.
Ade nun, ihr Berge,
Du väterlich Haus!
Es treibt in die Ferne
Mich mächtig hinaus.

Die Sonne, sie bleibet
Am Himmel nicht stehn,
Es treibt sie durch Länder
Und Meere zu gehn.
Die Woge nicht haftet
Am einsamen Strand,
Die Stürme, sie brausen
Mit Macht durch das Land.

Mit eilenden Wolken
Der Vogel dort zieht
Und singt in der Ferne
Ein heimatlich Lied.
So treibt es den Burschen
Durch Wälder und Feld,
Zu gleichen der Mutter,
Der wandernden Welt.

Da grüssen ihn Vögel
Bekannt überm Meer,
Sie flogen von Fluren
Der Heimat hieher;
Da duften die Blumen
Vertraulich um ihn,
Sie trieben vom Lande
Die Lüfte dahin.

Poet and writer on medical subjects, Kerner, with Uhland and Schwab, produced the *Poetischer Almanach* for 1812 and *Deutscher Dichterwald* for 1813. His poetry especially appealed to Schumann.

WANDERLUST

Come, let us drain
the sparkling wine!
Farewell, companions,
now we must part!
Farewell to the mountains,
and to my father's house!
I feel an irresistible urge
to roam.

The sun does not stand
still in the heavens,
but feels the impulse
to wander over land and sea.
The wave is not fixed
to the lonely shore;
the storm blusters mightily
throughout the land.

With the hurrying clouds
up there the bird moves
and sings in the distance
a song of home.
So youth is impelled
through forest and field,
as is our mother,
the moving world.

There birds greet him
that he has known over seas,
They have flown here
from the meadows of home;
There the fragrance of the flowers
around him is familiar;
the breezes blow it
from his country.

Die Vögel, die kennen
Sein väterlich Haus.
Die Blumen einst pflanzt' er
Der Liebe zum Strauss,
Und Liebe, die folgt ihm,
Sie geht ihm zur Hand:
So wird ihm zur Heimat
Das ferneste Land.

ROBERT SCHUMANN, Op. 35, no. 3. Better known as *Wanderlied*.
The third line of the final stanza reads: *Die Blumen, die pflanzt' er*.

ZUR RUH', ZUR RUH'!

Zur Ruh', zur Ruh'
Ihr müden Glieder!
Schliesst fest euch zu,
Ihr Augenlider!
Ich bin allein,
Fort ist die Erde;
Nacht muss es sein,
Dass Licht mir werde.

O führt mich ganz,
Ihr innern Mächte,
Hin zu dem Glanz
Der tiefsten Nächte!
Fort aus dem Raum
Der Erdenschmerzen
Durch Nacht und Traum
Zum Mutterherzen!

HUGO WOLF (*Lieder nach verschiedenen Dichtern*, no. 18).

The birds know
his father's house;
the flowers he once planted
to make a posy for his love,
and the love that follows him
and is near at hand;
so the most distant land
becomes a home to him.

Challier lists four settings under *Wanderlied*.

TO REST!

To rest, to rest,
weary limbs!
Close tightly,
my eyelids!
I am alone,
gone is the earth;
night must it be
that light may come to me.

O lead me wholly,
ye inner powers,
on to the radiance
of the deepest nights!
Away from the bourne
of earthly pain,
through night and dreams
to the Mother-Heart!

KLOPSTOCK, FRIEDRICH GOTTLIEB

1724–1803

Wie erhebt sich das Herz, wenn es dich,
Unendlicher, denkt! wie sinkt es,
Wenns auf sich herunterschaut!
Elend schauts wehklagend dann, und Nacht und Tod!

Allein du rufst mich aus meiner Nacht, der in
    Elend, der im Tod hilft!
Dann denk ich es ganz, dass ewig mich schufst,
Herrlicher! den kein Preis, unten am Grab', oben am Thron,
Herr Herr Gott! den, dankend entflammt, kein Jubel genug
    besingt.

Weht, Bäume des Lebens, im Harfengetön!
Rausche mit ihnen ins Harfengetön, krystallner Strom!
Ihr lispelt, und rauscht, und, Harfen, ihr tönt
Nie es ganz! Gott ist es, den ihr preist!

Donnert, Welten, in feierlichem Gang, in der Posaunen Chor!
Du Orion, Wage, du auch!
Tönt all' ihr Sonnen auf der Strasse voll Glanz,
In der Posaunen Chor!

Ihr Welten, donnert
Und du, der Posaunen Chor, hallest
Nie es ganz, Gott; nie es ganz, Gott,
Gott, Gott ist es, den ihr preist!

FRANZ PETER SCHUBERT (D. 291). In the first line of the second
stanza, *Tod* is changed to *Tode*, and in the fourth line, one *Herr* is
dropped. The first line of the fourth stanza reads *Welten, donnert,*

Poet and dramatist, he was especially inspired by reading Milton in translation. He became the most revered and influential poet of his day, a fact acknowledged by such masters as Schiller and Goethe. It has been said that the revival of German literature began with Klopstock. Today he is remembered chiefly by his *Odes*; even in these shorter pieces his thoughts are grand, his style epic.

TO THE INFINITE

How my heart leaps when it thinks
on Thee, o Infinite One! How it sinks
when it looks down upon itself!
Mourning it sees, then, misery and night and death!

But Thou callest me out of my night, Thou who succorest
in misery and in death!
Then it comes over me that Thou createst me for eternity,
Noble One! for whom no praise, below in the grave,
above at the throne,
Lord, Lord God! glowing with thanks, no rejoicing
is sufficient.

Wave, trees of life, with the sound of the harp!
Roar with them in the sound of the harp, o crystal
streams!
No matter how it murmurs and throbs, harps, your sound
is never enough! God it is whom ye praise!

Thunder, worlds, in your solemn course; in the chorus
of trumpets,
thou, Orion, thou also, Libra!
Sound forth, all suns, in your shining row,
in the chorus of trumpets!

Ye worlds, thunder,
and you, chorus of trumpets, resound,
never enough, God, never enough, God,
God, God it is whom ye praise!

---

m *feierlichen Gang, | Welten donnert in der Posaunen Chor.* The econd line is omitted. The first two lines of the last stanza read hr *Welten, ihr donnert, | Du, der Posaunen Chor.*

KUGLER, FRANZ

1808–1858

STÄNDCHEN

Der Mond steht über dem Berge,
So recht für verliebte Leut';
Im Garten rieselt ein Brunnen,
Sonst Stille weit und breit.

Neben der Mauer im Schatten,
Da stehn der Studenten drei
Mit Flöt' und Geig' und Zither
Und singen und spielen dabei.

Die Klänge schleichen der Schönsten
Sacht in den Traum hinein,
Sie schaut den blonden Geliebten
Und lispelt: "Vergiss nicht mein!"

JOHANNES BRAHMS, Op. 106, no. 1. Also set by Franz Abt (Op.
105, no. 4).

LAPPE, KARL

1773–1843

IM ABENDROT

O wie schön ist deine Welt,
Vater, wenn sie golden strahlet,
Wenn dein Glanz hernieder fällt,
Und den Staub mit Schimmer malet;
Wenn das Rot, das in der Wolke blinkt,
In mein stilles Fenster sinkt.

Könnt' ich klagen, könnt' ich zagen,
Irre sein an Dir und mir?
Nein, ich will im Busen tragen,
Deinen Himmel schon allhier,
Und dies Herz, eh' es zusammenbricht,
Trinkt noch Glut und schlürft noch Licht.

FRANZ PETER SCHUBERT, D. 799.

Professor of art history and lecturer at the University of Berlin, Kugler wrote a famous history of art. Also published stories and poems.

SERENADE

The moon stands over the mountain,
just right for lovers;
a fountain plashes in the garden,
otherwise quiet, far and wide.

Alongside the wall in the shadows,
three students stand
with flute and fiddle and zither,
singing and playing.

The music steals to the fair one,
softly into her dream,
she sees her blond lover
and whispers, "Forget me not!"

Remembered now only for two Schubert songs—one of them certainly among the composer's loveliest—Lappe achieved some fame in his own day with his popular *Hütte und Pütte*.

IN THE EVENING GLOW

O how beautiful is Thy world,
Father, when it shines like gold;
when Thy radiance descends
and paints the dust with splendor;
when the red that gleams in the clouds
falls upon my silent window.

Could I complain, could I waver,
doubt Thee and myself?
No, I will carry in my breast
Thy heaven even here;
and this heart, ere it fails,
shall still drink in the warmth and relish the light.

LEMCKE, KARL VON

1831–1913

VERRAT

Ich stand in einer lauen Nacht
An einer grünen Linde,
Der Mond schien hell, der Wind ging sacht,
Der Giessbach floss geschwinde.

Die Linde stand vor Liebchens Haus,
Die Türe hört' ich knarren.
Mein Schatz liess sacht' ein Mannsbild 'raus:
"Lass morgen mich nicht harren;

Lass mich nicht harren, süsser Mann,
Wie hab' ich dich so gerne!
Ans Fenster klopfe leise an,
Mein Schatz ist in der Ferne!"

Lass ab vom Druck und Kuss, Feinslieb,
Du Schöner im Sammetkleide,
Nun spute dich, du feiner Dieb,
Ein Mann harrt auf der Heide.

Der Mond scheint hell, der Rasen grün
Ist gut zu unserm Begegnen,
Du trägst ein Schwert und nickst so kühn,
Dein' Liebschaft will ich segnen!—

Und als erschien der lichte Tag,
Was fand er auf der Heide!
Ein Toter in den Blumen lag
Zu einer Falschen Leide.

JOHANNES BRAHMS, Op. 105, no. 5. The poem is in the style of a
folk ballad, and Brahms heightens the effect by repeating certain

Lectured in aesthetics and the history of literature and art at Heidelberg, Munich, Amsterdam, and Stuttgart. Besides his poems, Lemcke published novels, using the pseudonym Carl Manno, and books on aesthetics and poetry.

TREACHERY

I stood one warm night
by a green linden tree;
the moon shone brightly, a light breeze stirred,
the mountain stream gushed swiftly.

The linden stood by my sweetheart's house;
I heard the door creak.
My sweetheart softly opened it for a man:
"Don't keep me waiting tomorrow!

"Don't keep me waiting, dearest,
oh, how I love you!
tap lightly at my window,
my lover is far away!"

Leave off your hugging and kissing, my dear,
and you, handsome one in the velvet suit,
now hurry, my fine thief,
a man is waiting on the heath.

The moon is bright, the greensward
is a good place for our meeting.
You carry a sword and you cut such a figure,
I want to give my blessing to your lovemaking!

And when the bright day dawned,
what did it disclose on the heath?
A dead man lay among the flowers,
to a false woman's distress.

---

end-words—*Geschwinde, ja Ferne, ja Leide,* etc.

LENAU, NIKOLAUS (NIKOLAUS FRANZ NIEMBSCH VON STREHLENAU)

1802–1850

Weil' auf mir, du dunkles Auge,
Übe deine ganze Macht,
Ernste, milde, träumerische,
Unergründlich süsse Nacht!

Nimm mit deinem Zauberdunkel
Diese Welt von hinnen mir,
Dass du über meinem Leben
Einsam schwebest für und für.

ROBERT FRANZ, Op. 9, no. 3. Some two hundred composers have
set this text, including Anton Rubinstein, Emil Sjögren (Op. 16
no. 2), Erik Meyer-Helmund (Op. 29, no. 3), Emanuel Moór (Op. 13

LILIENCRON, DETLEV VON

1844–1909

AUF DEM KIRCHHOF

Der Tag ging regenschwer und sturmbewegt,
Ich war an manch vergessenem Grab gewesen,
Verwittert Stein und Kreuz, die Kränze alt,
Die Namen überwachsen, kaum zu lesen.

At one time considered the greatest modern lyric poet of Austria, Lenau was a practicing physician. The elegiac mood predominant in his poetry reflects his agnosticism and his search for consolation in nature. Always restless, he even went to America in the hope of finding a better life, but returned to Germany disappointed. Lenau typifies the strain of pessimism in nineteenth-century poetry.

REQUEST

Rest on me, dark eyes,
bring your full power into play,
earnest, gentle, dreamy,
unfathomable sweet night!

Take with your magic darkness
this world away from me,
that over my life
you alone shall hover forever and forever.

---

no. 4), A. von Fielitz (Op. 11, no. 3), Felix Weingartner (Op. 16, no. 6), Leopold Damrosch (Op. 5, no. 1), Curt Sachs, Charles Ives, and John Ford Barbour (*Stay with me, o eyes so tender*).

After a military career, Liliencron went to America (his mother having been a native of Philadelphia), where he taught painting, piano, and languages, played piano in beer halls, and trained horses. Returned to Germany, he devoted himself to writing, and became the foremost poet of his generation. He was attracted by old legends and ballads, and sought to re-create something of their atmosphere in his own poetry; but he is best remembered for his lyric gifts, his musical ear, his use of rhythm and vowel coloring. He is said to have brought a new vitality to German poetry.

IN THE CHURCHYARD

The day was rainy and blustery;
I visited many forgotten graves.
Stones and crosses crumbling, wreaths withered;
the names so overgrown they could hardly be read!

Der Tag ging sturmbewegt und regenschwer,
Auf allen Gräbern fror das Wort: Gewesen.
Wie sturmestot die Särge schlummerten,
Auf allen Gräbern taute still: Genesen.

JOHANNES BRAHMS, Op. 105, no. 4. In the second line *vergessenem*
is contracted to *vergess'nem*. The poem was also set by E. Gott
schalk.

The play upon words—the point of this poem—is quite un
translatable. Looking at the gravestones the poet sees first the word

LINGG, HERMANN, RITTER VON
1820–1905

LIED

Immer leiser wird mein Schlummer,
Nur wie Schleier liegt mein Kummer
Zitternd über mir.
Oft im Traume hör' ich dich
Rufen drauss vor meiner Tür,
Niemand wacht und öffnet dir;
Ich erwach' und weine bitterlich.

Ja, ich werde sterben müssen,
Eine andre wirst du küssen,
Wenn ich bleich und kalt;
Eh' die Maienlüfte wehen,
Eh' die Drossel singt im Wald:
Willist du mich noch einmal sehen,
Komm, o komme bald!

JOHANNES BRAHMS, Op. 105, no. 2. In the fourth line from the
end *wehen* is contracted to *weh'n*, and similarly two lines later
sehen to *seh'n*. Some forty composers include Hans Pfitzner (Op. 2
no. 6), F. Hiller (Op. 129, no. 4), H. v. Holstein (Op. 16, no. 5)

The day was blustery and rainy;
on all graves froze the word : Departed.
As though dead in the storm, the coffins slept;
on all graves silently it thawed : Recovered.

GEWESEN (past participle of the verb to be), then later in another
light GENESEN (recovered)—a parable of fundamental Christian
doctrine. There are no two such similar words in English that quite
make this point.

A military doctor who was attracted to literature by the
influence of Geibel. Though his poems show rhetorical
gifts, he was unsuccessful as a dramatist, and is remembered for his shorter verses.

SONG

Each night I sleep more lightly;
like a veil my grief
lies trembling over me.
Often in my dreams I hear you
calling outside my door.
No one wakes and lets you in;
I awaken and weep bitterly.

Yes, I shall have to die;
you will kiss another
when I am pale and cold.
Before the May breezes blow,
before the thrush sings in the wood,
If you could see me once again,
Come, o come soon!

W. Kienzl (Op. 24, no. 2), F. Wüllner (Op. 4, no. 3), L. Thuille
(Op. 4, no. 2), F. v. Liliencron (Op. 5, no. 1), and Louis Victor Saar
(Op. 14, no. 1).

MACKAY, JOHN HENRY
1864–1933

Auf, hebe die funkelnde Schale
    Empor zum Mund,
Und trinke beim Freudenmahle
    Dein Herz gesund!

Und wenn du sie hebst, so winke
    Mir heimlich zu—
Dann lächle ich, und dann trinke
    Ich still wie du . . .

Und still gleich mir betrachte
    Um uns das Heer
Der trunkenen Schwätzer—verachte
    Sie nicht zu sehr:

Nein, hebe die blinkende Schale,
    Gefüllt mit Wein,
Und lass beim lärmenden Mahle
    Sie glücklich sein.

—Doch hast du das Mahl genossen,
    Dein Durst gestillt,
Dann verlasse der lauten Genossen
    Festfreudiges Bild.

Und wandle hinaus in den Garten
    Zum Rosenstrauch—
Dort will ich dich dann erwarten
    Nach altem Brauch . . .

Und will an die Brust dir sinken,
    Eh du's erhofft,
Und deine Küsse trinken,
    Wie ehmals oft,

Scottish-German poet and novelist. Concerned himself with social problems, but is best remembered for the lyrical poems set to music by Richard Strauss.

SECRET INVITATION

Up, raise the sparkling bowl
to your lips,
and drink at the feast,
that your heart may be healed.

And as you lift it up, give me
a secret sign,
then I shall smile and drink
silently as you.

And, silent as I, consider
around us the crowd
of drunken babblers—do not despise
them too much;

no, raise the glittering bowl,
filled with wine,
and let them at their noisy meal
be happy.

But when you have had your fill
and quenched your thirst,
then leave your loud companions
to their festive scene.

And go out into the garden,
to the rosebush,
there I will be waiting for you,
as I used to do . . .

And will sink upon your breast
before you expect it,
and drink your kisses
as I often used to do,

Und flechten in deine Haare
Der Rose Pracht—
O komme, du wunderbare,
Ersehnte Nacht!

RICHARD STRAUSS, Op. 27, no. 3. The third line of the third stanza
reads: *Der trunknen Zecher.* In the stanza next before the last, line
2, *erhofft* becomes *gehofft,* and in the last stanza, line 3, *O komme*

MORGEN

Und Morgen wird die Sonne wieder scheinen,
Und auf dem Wege, den ich gehen werde,
Wird uns, die Seligen, sie wieder einen,
Inmitten dieser sonnenatmenden Erde ...

Und zu dem Strand, dem weiten, wogenblauen,
Werden wir still und langsam niedersteigen.
Stumm werden wir uns in die Augen schauen,
Und auf uns sinkt des Glückes grosses Schweigen.

RICHARD STRAUSS, Op. 27, no. 4. In the third line *Seligen* is re-

MATTHISON, FRIEDRICH VON
1761–1831

ADELAIDE

Einsam wandelt dein Freund im Frühlingsgarten,
Mild vom lieblichen Zauberlicht umflossen,
Das durch wankende Blütenzweige zittert,
Adelaide!

In der spiegelnden Flut, im Schnee der Alpen,
In des sinkenden Tages Goldgewölken,
Im Gefilde der Sterne strahlt dein Bildnis,
Adelaide!

and will twine in your hair
the splendor of the rose—
O come, wondrous,
longed-for night!

---

is shortened to *O komm'*. Another setting was made by Eugen
d'Albert (Op. 21, no. 1).

TOMORROW

And tomorrow the sun will shine again,
and on the path that I shall follow
it will reunite us, the blessed ones,
amidst this sun-breathing world . . .

And to the shore, broad and blue with the waves,
we shall go down quietly and slowly.
Mute, we shall look into each other's eyes,
and upon us will descend the great silence of happiness.

---

placed by *Glücklichen*. In the final line *grosses Schweigen* becomes
stummes Schweigen.

Matthison was an extremely popular poet in his day, and
no less a personage than Schiller found much to praise in
the melancholy sweetness of his poems and their fine
descriptions of scenery.

ADELAIDE

Lonely your friend wanders in the garden of spring blossoms,
surrounded by the magical soft light
that trembles through the moving blooming branches,
Adelaide!

In the shimmering waves, in the snow of the Alps,
in the golden clouds of sinking day,
in the field of stars shines your image,
Adelaide!

Abendlüftchen im zarten Laube flüstern,
Silberglöckchen des Mais im Grase säuseln,
Wellen rauschen und Nachtigallen flöten:
Adelaide!

Einst, o Wunder! entblüht, auf meinem Grabe,
Eine Blume der Asche meines Herzens;
Deutlich schimmert auf jedem Purpurblättchen
Adelaide!

LUDWIG VAN BEETHOVEN, Op. 46. In strong and interesting contrast to Beethoven's setting—rather a cantata than a song—is the
simpler work of Schubert (D. 95) and the near folk song of Karl

MÖRIKE, EDUARD FRIEDRICH
1804–1875

ABSCHIED

Unangeklopft ein Herr tritt abends bei mir ein:
"Ich habe die Ehr', Ihr Rezensent zu sein."
Sofort nimmt er das Licht in die Hand,
Besieht lang meinen Schatten an der Wand,
Rückt nah und fern: "Nun, lieber junger Mann,
Sehn Sie doch gefälligst mal Ihre Nas' so von der Seite
an!
Sie geben zu, dass das ein Auswuchs is."—
"Das? Alle Wetter—gewiss!"—
Ei Hasen! ich dachte nicht,
All mein Lebtage nicht,
Dass ich so eine Weltsnase führt' im Gesicht!!
Der Mann sprach noch Verschiedenes hin und her,
Ich weiss, auf meine Ehre, nicht mehr;
Meinte vielleicht, ich sollt' ihm beichten.
Zuletzt stand er auf; ich tat ihm leuchten.
Wie wir nun an die Treppe sind,
Da geb' ich ihm, ganz froh gesinnt,
Einen kleinen Tritt
Nur so von hinten aufs Gesässe mit—

The evening breezes whisper through the soft leaves,
silver May bells murmur it in the grass,
waves roar it, and nightingales warble it:
Adelaide!

Some day, o miracle, upon my grave shall spring
a flower from the ashes of my heart;
clearly it shall shine on every purple leaf:
Adelaide!

Philipp Emanuel Pilz (1794). Another was composed by V. Righini
(Op. 12, no. 3).

This worldly-wise pastor, whose works were to inspire so
many of the masterpieces of Hugo Wolf and others, was
the most gifted of the Swabian school of lyric poets,
followers of Uhland. The range of Mörike's subjects and
imagery is amazingly broad.

PARTING

Without knocking a man one evening entered my lodgings.
"I have the honor to be your critic."
Immediately he took the lamp in his hand,
inspecting at length my shadow on the wall,
he moved back and forth: "Now, my dear young man,
do me the favor to look at your nose from the side!
You will grant that it is not normal."
"That? Good gracious—really!"
My word! I never realized,
all my life long,
that I carried a world-wonder in my face!
The man spoke about this and that—
on my honor, I don't know what else;
perhaps he thought I should make a confession to him.
Finally he got up; I lighted him out.
As we stood at the head of the stairs
I gave him mischievously
A little kick,
just so, from behind on his seat—

Alle Hagel! ward das ein Gerumpel,
Ein Gepurzel, ein Gehumpel,
Dergleichen hab' ich nie gesehn,
All mein Lebtage nicht gesehn,
Einen Menschen so rasch die Trepp' hinabgehn!

HUGO WOLF (*Mörike Lieder*, no. 53). The twelfth line reads: *Der*

AN EINE AEOLSHARFE

Tu semper urges flebilibus modis
Mysten ademptum: nec tibi Vespere
  Surgente decedunt amores,
  Nec rapidum fugiente Solem.
                              —HORACE

Angelehnt an die Efeuwand
Dieser alten Terrasse,
Du, einer luftgebornen Muse
Geheimnisvolles Saitenspiel,
Fang an,
Fange wieder an
Deine melodische Klage!
Ihr kommet, Winde, fern herüber
Ach! von des Knaben,
Der mir so lieb war,
Frisch grünendem Hügel.
Und Frühlingsblüten unterwegs streifend,
Übersättigt mit Wohlgerüchen,
Wie süss bedrängt ihr dies Herz
Und säuselt her in die Saiten,
Angezogen von wohllautender Wehmut,
Wachsend im Zug meiner Sehnsucht
Und hinsterbend wieder.

Aber auf einmal,
Wie der Wind heftiger herstösst,
Ein holder Schrei der Harfe
Wiederholt, mir zu süssem Erschrecken,
Meiner Seele plötzliche Regung;
Und hier—die volle Rose streut, geschüttelt,
All ihre Blätter vor meine Füsse.

JOHANNES BRAHMS, Op. 19, no. 5. In line 12 *unterwegs* becomes
unterweges. Hugo Wolf's setting (*Mörike Lieder*, no. 11) is almost

Goodness! What a rattling!
What a tumbling! What a limping!
I never saw the like,
in all my life never saw
a man go downstairs so quickly!

Mann sprach noch Verschied'nes hin und her.

TO AN AEOLIAN HARP

But you, in tearful strains, dwell forever
on your loss of Mistes, nor do your words of
love cease when Vesper appears at evening or
flies before the swiftly moving sun.
—HORACE

Supported by the ivy-covered wall
of this old terrace,
o mysterious harp
of an aerial muse,
begin,
begin again
your sweet complaint!
Winds, you come from far away,
ah, from the fresh green grave
of the boy
who was dear to me.
And touching the spring flowers along the way
satiated with fragrance,
how sweetly you oppress my heart,
and gently sigh in the strings,
full of melodious melancholy,
swelling with my longing
and dying away again.

But all at once,
as the wind blows stronger,
a glad cry from the harp
echoes, awakening a sweet alarm
suddenly in my soul.
And lo! the full-blown rose, shaken, strews
all her petals at my feet.

equally famous. A third was composed by E. Kauffmann (Op. 13, no. 1).

AUF EIN ALTES BILD

In grüner Landschaft Sommerflor
Bei kühlem Wasser, Schilf und Rohr,
Schau, wie das Knäblein sündelos
Frei spielet auf der Jungfrau Schoss!
Und dort im Walde wonnesam,
Ach, grünet schon des Kreuzes Stamm!

HUGO WOLF (*Mörike Lieder*, no. 23).

DENK ES, O SEELE!

Ein Tännlein grünet wo,
Wer weiss, im Walde,
Ein Rosenstrauch, wer sagt,
In welchem Garten?
Sie sind erlesen schon,
Denk es, o Seele,
Auf deinem Grab zu wurzeln
Und zu wachsen.

Zwei schwarze Rösslein weiden
Auf der Wiese,
Sie kehren heim zur Stadt
In muntern Sprüngen.
Sie werden schrittweis gehn
Mit deiner Leiche;
Vielleicht, vielleicht noch eh'
An ihren Hufen
Das Eisen los wird,
Das ich blitzen sehe!

HUGO WOLF (*Mörike Lieder*, no. 39). Other settings are by Franz
(Op. 26, no. 6), C. Hauer, E. Kauffmann (Op. 6, no. 3), O. Weil
(Op. 7, no. 3), R. Kahn (Op. 12, no. 5), G. Dippe (Op. 17, no. 3), K.

ER IST'S

Frühling lässt sein blaues Band
Wieder flattern durch die Lüfte;
Süsse, wohlbekannte Düfte
Streifen ahnungsvoll das Land.

ON AN OLD PAINTING

In a green landscape, summer flowers
by the cool water, rushes and reeds—
see how the innocent boy
plays happily upon the Virgin's lap!
And yonder in the pleasant wood,
Ah! already the cross is growing.

THINK OF IT, O SOUL

A young fir is growing, where?—
who knows?—in the forest;
A rosebush, who can say
in what garden?
They are already chosen,
think of it, o soul,
upon your grave to root
and grow.

Two black colts are grazing
in the meadow;
they gambol
gaily back to town.
They will be pacing
with your body—
perhaps, perhaps before
their hoofs
lose the shoes
that I see flashing!

Kaskel (Op. 8, no. 1), W. Colsmann, S. Krehl, and Hans Pfitzner
(Op. 30, no. 4).

IT IS HE

Spring is floating his blue banner
once again on the breezes;
sweet, well-remembered scents
are portentously overrunning the land.

Veilchen träumen schon,
Wollen balde kommen.
—Horch, von fern ein leiser Harfenton!
Frühling, ja du bist's!
Dich hab' ich vernommen!

HUGO WOLF (*Mörike Lieder*, no. 6). Schumann's setting (Op. 79, no. 24) is equally well known. In it there is one textual change—line 7 is abbreviated thus: *Horch, ein Harfenton!*

Other composers include Franz (Op. 27, no. 2), Lassen (*Frühling*),

FUSSREISE

Am frischgeschnittnen Wanderstab
Wenn ich in der Frühe
So durch die Wälder ziehe,
Hügel auf und ab:
Dann, wies Vögelein im Laube
Singet und sich rührt,
Oder wie die goldne Traube
Wonnegeister spürt
In der ersten Morgensonne:
So fühlt auch mein alter, lieber
Adam Herbst- und Frühlingsfieber,
Gottbeherzte,
Nie verscherzte
Erstlings-Paradieseswonne.
Also bist du nicht so schlimm, o alter
Adam, wie die strengen Lehrer sagen;
Liebst und lobst du immer doch,
Singst und preisest immer noch,
Wie an ewig neuen Schöpfungstagen,
Deinen lieben Schöpfer und Erhalter!
Möcht es dieser geben,
Und mein ganzes Leben
Wär im leichten Wanderschweisse
Eine solche Morgenreise.

HUGO WOLF (*Mörike Lieder*, no. 10). In the third line Wolf omits the word *die*.

Violets, already dreaming,
will soon begin to bloom.
Listen! Far off the soft sound of a harp!
Spring, yes it is you!
I have heard you!

O. Scherzer (Op. 4, no. 1), G. Petzold (Op. 2, no. 1), F. v. Blon,
Th. Röhmeyer, E. d'Albert (Op. 19, no. 3), P. Seelig (Op. 5, no. 2),
Curt Sachs, and Othmar Schoeck (Op. 51, no. 4).

TRAMPING

If with my fresh-cut walking stick
in the early morning
I press through the woods,
up hill and down hill,
then as the bird in the branches
sings and moves about,
or as the golden cluster of grapes
feels the rapture
of the early morning sun,
so in me the old Adam
feels autumn and spring fever,
the god-given,
never forfeited
bliss of pristine paradise.
So you aren't such a sinner, old
Adam, as the strait-laced teachers say;
you still love and extol
and ever sing and praise,
as in the eternally new days of creation,
your dear Creator and Preserver!
O that this might be given me,
and that my whole life
could be, gently perspiring,
such a morning ramble!

GEBET

Herr! schicke was Du willt,
Ein Liebes oder Leides;
Ich bin vergnügt, dass beides
Aus deinen Händen quillt.

Wollest mit Freuden
Und wollest mit Leiden
Mich nicht überschütten!
Doch in der Mitten
Liegt holdes Bescheiden.

HUGO WOLF (*Mörike Lieder*, no. 28). Also set by C. Attenhofer
(Op. 44, no. 2), A. Stolz, K. Hösel, R. Trunk, R. Lichey, P. Prehl,

GESANG WEYLAS

Du bist Orplid, mein Land!
Das ferne leuchtet;
Vom Meere dampfet dein besonnter Strand
Den Nebel, so der Götter Wange feuchtet.

Uralte Wasser steigen
Verjüngt um deine Hüften, Kind!
Vor deiner Gottheit beugen
Sich Könige, die deine Wärter sind.

HUGO WOLF (*Mörike Lieder*, no. 46).

HEIMWEH

Anders wird die Welt mit jedem Schritt,
Den ich weiter von der Liebsten mache;
Mein Herz, das will nicht weiter mit.
Hier scheint die Sonne kalt ins Land,
Hier deucht mir alles unbekannt,
Sogar die Blumen am Bache!
Hat jede Sache
So fremd eine Miene, so falsch ein Gesicht.
Das Bächlein murmelt wohl und spricht:
Armer Knabe, komm bei mir vorüber,
Siehst auch hier Vergissmeinnicht!

PRAYER

Lord, send what Thou wilt,
good things or bad;
I am satisfied that both
come from Thy hands.

Neither with happiness
nor with affliction
do Thou overwhelm me!
For in between
lies gentle moderation.

G. Bezold, G. Böttcher, E. Nössler, and Louis Victor Saar (Op. 54,
no. 2).

WEYLA'S SONG

Thou art Orplid, my land,
that shinest afar;
from the sea thy sunny shore exhales
the mist to moisten the cheeks of the gods.

Timeless waters rise
renewed about thy slopes, child!
Before thy godhead bow
kings, who are thy guardians.

HOMESICKNESS

The world changes with every step
that takes me farther from my beloved;
my heart refuses to go on.
Here the sun shines coldly in the land;
here everything seems strange to me,
even the flowers by the brook!
Every object has
so strange a look, so false a face.
The murmuring stream seems to say:
"Poor boy, come over beside me,
here too you see forget-me-nots!"

—Ja, die sind schön an jedem Ort,
Aber nicht wie dort.
Fort, nur fort!
Die Augen gehn mir über!

Hugo Wolf (*Mörike Lieder*, no. 37). There are settings by H. von

IN DER FRÜHE

Kein Schlaf noch kühlt das Auge mir,
Dort gehet schon der Tag herfür
An meinem Kammerfenster.
Es wühlet mein verstörter Sinn
Noch zwischen Zweifeln her und hin
Und schaffet Nachtgespenster.
—Ängste, quäle
Dich nicht länger, meine Seele!
Freu dich! schon sind da und dorten
Morgenglocken wach geworden.

Hugo Wolf (*Mörike Lieder*, no. 24). Also set by H. von Herzogenberg (Op. 30, no. 5), P. Viardot-Garcia, M. Stange, O. Straus

MAUSFALLEN-SPRÜCHLEIN

(Das Kind geht dreimal um die Falle und spricht)

Kleine Gäste, kleines Haus,
Liebe Mäusin, oder Maus,
Stell dich nur kecklich ein
Heut' nacht bei Mondenschein!
Mach aber die Tür fein hinter dir zu,
Hörst du?
Dabei hüte dein Schwänzchen!
Nach Tische singen wir,
Nach Tische springen wir
Und machen ein Tänzchen:
Witt, witt!
Meine alte Katze tanzt wahrscheinlich mit.

Hugo Wolf (*Lieder nach verschiedenen Dichtern*, no. 6). In the
third line *Stell* becomes *Stelle*, and in the fourth *Heut'* becomes

Yes, they are lovely anywhere;
but not as they are *there*.
Onward, then onward!
My eyes overflow.

Herzogenberg (Op. 41, no. 3). H. Huber (Op. 38, no. 3), and E.
Kauffmann (Op. 12, no. 2).

EARLY MORNING

Still no sleep cools my eyes;
the day is already beginning to dawn
there at my bedroom window.
My troubled spirit is still tossed about
between one doubt and another,
and raises phantoms.
Be not worried, torment yourself
no longer, my soul!
Rejoice! Already here and there
morning bells have awakened.

(Op. 39, no. 2), R. Grund, S. von Hausegger, L. Brill, and Max
Reger.

MOUSETRAP INCANTATION

(The child goes three times around the trap, and says:)

Little guests, little house,
dear she-mouse or he-mouse,
appear boldly
tonight in the moonlight!
But close the door carefully after you,
do you hear?
And be careful of your tail.
After supper we will sing,
after supper we will romp
and dance a little:
Witt, witt!
My old cat might perhaps dance with us!

Heute. There are a number of repetitions in the song, appropriate
to an incantation—this is very unusual in Wolf.

NIMMERSATTE LIEBE

So ist die Lieb'! So ist die Lieb'!
Mit Küssen nicht zu stillen:
Wer ist der Tor und will ein Sieb
Mit eitel Wasser füllen?
Und schöpfst du an die tausend Jahr',
Und küssest ewig, ewig gar,
Du tust ihr nie zu Willen.

Die Lieb', die Lieb' hat alle Stund
Neu wunderlich Gelüsten;
Wir bissen uns die Lippen wund,
Da wir uns heute küssten.
Das Mädchen hielt in guter Ruh,
Wie's Lämmlein unterm Messer;
Ihr Auge bat: nur immer zu,
Je weher desto besser!

So ist die Lieb', und war auch so
Wie lang es Liebe gibt,
Und anders war Herr Salomo,
Der Weise, nicht verliebt.

HUGO WOLF (*Mörike Lieder*, no. 25). There are also settings by
E. d'Albert and M. Vogrich.

SCHLAFENDES JESUSKIND

(Gemälde von Francesco Albani)

Sohn der Jungfrau, Himmelskind! am Boden
Auf dem Holz der Schmerzen eingeschlafen,
Das der fromme Meister, sinnvoll spielend,
Deinen leichten Träumen unterlegte;
Blume du, noch in der Knospe dämmernd
Eingehüllt die Herrlichkeit des Vaters!
O wer sehen könnte, welche Bilder
Hinter dieser Stirne, diesen schwarzen
Wimpern sich in sanftem Wechsel malen!

HUGO WOLF (*Mörike Lieder*, no. 25). The first four words are
repeated at the end.

INSATIABLE LOVE

Such is love, such is love,
not to be quieted with kisses:
who is such a fool as to fill a sieve
with water?
And were you to work a thousand years,
always, always kissing,
you could never satisfy her.

Love, love has every hour
some wonderful new desire;
we bit our lips sore
today when we were kissing.
The girl takes it calmly,
like a lamb under the knife;
her eyes have led him on: so go ahead,
the more it hurts the better!

Such is love, and was indeed so
as long as love has existed,
and Lord Solomon himself, the sage,
did not love any other way.

SLEEPING CHRISTCHILD

(After a painting by Francesco Albani)

Son of the Virgin, Heavenly Child! On the ground,
asleep upon the wood of torture,
which the pious master, in a profound allegory,
laid under your peaceful dreams.
O flower, still in the bud, forebodingly
shrouded in the Father's glory!
O who could perceive what images
behind this brow, these black
eyelashes, are reflected in gentle succession!

VERBORGENHEIT

Lass, o Welt, o lass mich sein!
Locket nicht mit Liebesgaben,
Lasst dies Herz alleine haben
Seine Wonne, seine Pein!

Was ich traure, weiss ich nicht,
Es ist unbekanntes Wehe;
Immerdar durch Tränen sehe
Ich der Sonne liebes Licht.

Oft bin ich mir kaum bewusst,
Und die helle Freude zücket
Durch die Schwere, die mich drücket,
Wonniglich in meiner Brust.

Lass, o Welt, o lass mich sein!
Locket nicht mit Liebesgaben,
Lasst dies Herz alleine haben
Seine Wonne, seine Pein!

HUGO WOLF (*Mörike Lieder*, no. 12). In the third line of the third stanza *die mich drücket* is changed to *so mich drücket*.
Other composers include Franz (Op. 28, no. 5), F. Wüllner (Op. 7,

DAS VERLASSENE MÄGDLEIN

Früh, wann die Hähne krähn,
Eh' die Sternlein verschwinden,
Muss ich am Herde stehn,
Muss Feuer zünden.

Schön ist der Flammen Schein,
Es springen die Funken;
Ich schaue so drein,
In Leid versunken.

Plötzlich, da kommt es mir,
Treuloser Knabe,
Dass ich die Nacht von dir
Geträumet habe.

SECRECY

Leave me to myself, o world!
Tempt me not with love-offerings;
let this heart have alone
its joy, its suffering!

Why I grieve I do not know,
it is some unknown pain;
always through my tears I see
the beloved light of the sun.

Often I hardly know myself,
and radiant joy flashes,
through the troubles that oppress me,
blissfully within my breast.

Leave me to myself, o world!
Tempt me not with love-offerings;
let this heart have alone
its joy, its suffering!

---

no. 4), H. Abheiter, E. Lassen, C. Ressler, and A. Blomberg (Op. 8,
no. 3).

THE FORSAKEN GIRL

Early, at cockcrow,
before the stars vanish,
I must be at the hearth,
I must light the fire.

The flames make a lovely light,
the sparks fly up,
I gaze at them
sunken in grief.

Suddenly I realize,
faithless boy,
that all night long
I have dreamed of you.

Träne auf Träne dann
Stürzet hernieder;
So kommt der Tag heran—
O ging' er wieder!

HUGO WOLF (*Mörike Lieder*, no. 7). The second line reads *Eh'
die Sternlein schwinden*; the third line of the second stanza *Ich
schaue so darein*. Schumann calls his song (Op. 64, no. 2) *Das
verlass'ne Mägdelein*. His second line reads like Wolf's; the first line
of the second stanza is *Schön ist der Flamme Schein*, and the third,
Ich schaue so darein.

ZUM NEUEN JAHR

Wie heimlicherweise
Ein Engelein leise
Mit rosigen Füssen
Die Erde betritt,
So nahte der Morgen.
Jauchzt ihm, ihr Frommen,
Ein heilig Willkommen,
Ein heilig Willkommen!
Herz, jauchze du mit!

In Ihm sei's begonnen,
Der Monde und Sonnen
An blauen Gezelten
Des Himmels bewegt.
Du, Vater, Du rate!
Lenke Du und wende!
Herr, Dir in die Hände
Sei Anfang und Ende,
Sei alles gelegt!

HUGO WOLF (*Mörike Lieder*, no. 27). Others include C. Attenhofer
(Op. 44, no. 7), J. Pache, and W. Merkel.

Tears upon tears then
fall;
so the day dawns—
I wish it were over!

More than sixty other composers include I. Brüll (Op. 5), H. Götz (Op. 12, no. 5), E. Lassen, G. Pressel, C. Reinecke (Op. 19, no. 4), E. Meyer-Helmund, J. Hubay (Op. 8, no. 3), C. Bohm (Op. 326, no. 67), Robert Fuchs (Op. 26, no. 2), H. Drechsler (Op. 13, no. 2), M. Lewandowsky (Op. 6, no. 2), and Hans Pfitzner (Op. 30, no. 2).

FOR THE NEW YEAR

As stealthily
an angel, light
on rosy feet
came to earth,
so morning dawned.
Let the pious rejoice
in a holy welcome,
in a holy welcome!
My heart, rejoice with them!

Let it begin in Him
by whom the moon and the sun
in the blue tent
of heaven were caused to move.
O Father, guide us!
counsel and advise us!
Lord, in Thy hands
be the beginning and the ending—
be everything laid!

MOSEN, JULIUS

1803–1867

Es grünet ein Nussbaum vor dem Haus,
Duftig,
Luftig
Breitet er blättrig die Äste aus.

Viel liebliche Blüten stehen d'ran;
Linde
Winde
Kommen, sie herzlich zu umfahn.

Es flüstern je zwei zu zwei gepaart,
Neigend,
Beugend
Zierlich zum Kusse die Häuptchen zart.

Sie flüstern von einem Mägdlein, das
Dächte
Nächte
Tagelang, wüsste, ach! selber nicht was.

Sie flüstern,—wer mag verstehn so gar
Leise
Weise?
Flüstern von Bräut'gam und nächstem Jahr.

Das Mägdlein horchet, es rauscht im Baum;
Sehnend,
Wähnend,
Sinkt es lächelnd in Schlaf und Traum.

ROBERT SCHUMANN, Op. 25, no. 3. The third song in the *Myrten*
set. Schumann's quite senseless substitution of the word *Blätter* for
Äste in the last line of the first stanza is usually corrected in good
editions of the song—it was undoubtedly due to a slip of the pen.
For reasons of musical symmetry the two short middle lines in the
fourth stanza are expanded to *Dächte die Nächte und* . . . In the
last line of this stanza *wüsste* becomes *wusste*. Again for the benefit

For a time practiced law, then became director of the Hoftheater at Oldenburg. Influenced by Hegel, he was a prolific writer of plays and poems, some of which have passed into German folk song.

THE NUT TREE

A nut tree grows in front of the house;
fragrant,
airy,
it stretches out its leafy boughs.

Many lovely blossoms grow on it;
gentle
winds
come to fan them affectionately.

They are always whispering two by two,
bowing,
bending
prettily their soft little heads for a kiss.

They whisper about a girl who sits
meditating
night
and day, she herself does not know about what.

They whisper—who could understand
so soft
a tune?—
whisper of a bridegroom and the year to come.

The girl listens to the rustling in the tree;
longing,
imagining,
she sinks smiling into sleep and dreams.

---

of the musical scheme, and at the expense of the verse, in the fifth stanza *Weise* becomes *Weis'*. The song is especially interesting be- cause of the unusual (especially for Schumann's time) integration of the voice and piano parts—one line of the melody being given to the piano alone—but because of this treatment Mosen's striking versifi- cation is lost.

MÜLLER, WILHELM

1794–1827

DIE SCHÖNE MÜLLERIN

FRANZ PETER SCHUBERT, D. 795. Müller's little tragedy (with its direction, *Im Winter zu lesen*: to be read in winter) consists of twenty-three poems with prologue and epilogue. Schubert set twenty of the poems. The order of Müller's original is followed in Schubert's cycle.

Challier lists a cycle of ten lieder by L. Berger (Op. 11), and a setting of *Feierabend* (no. 5) by C. Streitmann (Op. 7).

DER DICHTER, ALS PROLOG

Ich lad' euch, schöne Damen, kluge Herrn,
Und die ihr hört und schaut was Gutes gern,
Zu einem funkelnadelneuen Spiel
Im allerfunkelnadelneusten Styl;
Schlicht ausgedrechselt, kunstlos zugestuzt,
Mit edler deutscher Rohheit aufgeputzt,
Keck wie ein Bursch im Stadtsoldatenstrauss,
Dazu wohl auch ein wenig fromm für's Haus:
Das mag genug mir zur Empfehlung sein,
Wem die behagt, der trete nur herein.

Erhoffe, weil es grad' ist Winterzeit,
Tut euch ein Stündlein hier im Grün nicht Leid;
Denn wisst es nur, dass heut' in meinem Lied
Der Lenz mit allen seinen Blumen blüht.
Im Freien geht die freie Handlung vor,
In reiner Luft, weit von der Städte Tor,
Durch Wald und Feld, in Gründen, auf den Höhn;
Und was nur in vier Wänden darf geschehn,
Das schaut ihr halb durch's offne Fenster an,
So ist der Kunst und euch genug getan.

This contemporary of Schubert not only influenced the composer by providing the inspiration for his two great song cycles, but also was the leader of the Berlin school of romantic poets. Heine acknowledged his debt to Müller with unaccustomed modesty. A strong humanitarian, he fought in the War of Liberation against the French and interested himself in the Greek fight for freedom. Because of its folksiness, his poetry is today considered old-fashioned, but in the cycles it provides the perfect counterpart to Schubert's music. It is interesting to recall that although poet and musician lived in Vienna at the same time, they never met.

THE BEAUTIFUL MAID OF THE MILL

THE POET, AS PROLOGUE

I invite you, beautiful ladies, clever gentlemen,
and you who appreciate good things,
to a brand new play
in a completely new style,
simply put together, fashioned without art,
decked out with noble German crudity,
cocky as a young soldier in uniform,
yet a little pious for the house.
It will be enough recommendation for me
if those it pleases only will come in.

I hope, as it is mid-winter,
that you will not mind a little time spent here in the green;
for know ye only this, that in my song today
the spring is in full bloom.
The action takes place in the open,
in the pure air, far from the town gate,
through the woods and fields, in the valleys, on the hills;
and what can only happen within four walls,
that you shall half see through the open window;
so art and you are well enough served.

Doch wenn ihr nach des Spiels Personen fragt,
So kann ich euch, den Musen sei's geklagt,
Nur eine präsentiren recht und echt,
Das ist ein junger blonder Müllersknecht.
Denn, ob der Bach zuletzt ein Wort auch spricht,
So wird ein Bach deshalb Person noch nicht.
Drum nehmt nur heut' das Monodram vorlieb:
Wer mehr giebt, als er hat, der heisst ein Dieb.

Auch ist daführ die Szene reich geziert,
Mit grünem Sammet unten tapeziert,
Der ist mit tausend Blumen bunt gestickt,
Und Weg und Steg darüber ausgedrückt.
Die Sonne strahlt von oben hell herein
Und bricht in Tau und Tränen ihren Schein,
Und auch der Mond blickt aus der Wolken Flor
Schwermütig, wie's die Mode will, hervor.
Den Hintergrund umkränzt ein hoher Wald,
Der Hund schlägt an, das muntre Jagdhorn schallt;
Hier stürzt vom schroffen Fels der junge Quell
Und fliesst im Tal als Bächlein silberhell;
Das Mühlrad braust, die Werke klappern drein,
Man hört die Vöglein kaum im nahen Hain.
Drum denkt, wenn euch zu rau manch Liedchen
    klingt,
Dass das Lokal es also mit sich bringt.
Doch, was das Schönste bei den Rädern ist,
Das wird euch sagen mein Monodramist;
Verriet' ich's euch, verdürb' ich ihm das Spiel:
Gehabt euch wohl und amüsiert euch viel!

Not set by Schubert.

I

WANDERSCHAFT

Das Wandern is des Müllers Lust
    Das Wandern!
Das muss ein schlechter Müller sein,
Dem niemals fiel das Wandern ein,
    Das Wandern.

Yet if you ask about the persons in the play
I can only (blame the muses!)
present one proper and genuine character to you:
he is the young blond miller's journeyman;
for, if the brook in the end also speaks a word,
still, this does not make the brook a person.
Therefore just be satisfied with the monodrama today:
he who gives more than he has is a thief.

Too, the stage is richly decorated for it,
carpeted with green velvet;
it is embroidered with a thousand many-colored flowers,
and roads and paths are trampled over them.
The sun shines down brightly from above,
its light shattered by dew and by tears;
and the moon too shines through the veil of clouds,
melancholy, as is the style.
A tall wood encircles the background;
the dog barks, the merry hunting horn sounds.
Here the spring gushes from the precipitous rocks,
and flows into the valley a clear and silvery stream.
The millwheel roars, the machinery clatters inside
so that one can hardly hear the birds in the nearby grove.
So you must realize, if many of the songs sound too crude
    to you,
the setting is responsible.
But what is most beautiful about millwheels
my monodramatist will tell you;
If I were to betray it to you, I would spoil his play.
Farewell and enjoy yourselves!

ROVING

Roving is the miller's delight,
roving!
It is indeed a very poor miller
who never felt the urge to rove—
roving!

Vom Wasser haben wir's gelernt,
 Vom Wasser!
Das hat nicht Rast bei Tag und Nacht,
Ist stets auf Wanderschaft bedacht,
 Das Wasser.

Das sehn wir auch den Rädern ab,
 Den Rädern!
Die gar nicht gerne stille stehn,
Die sich mein Tag nicht müde drehn,
 Die Räder.

Die Steine selbst, so schwer sie sind,
 Die Steine!
Sie tanzen mit den muntern Reihn
Und wollen gar noch schneller sein,
 Die Steine.

O Wandern, Wandern, meine Lust,
 O Wandern!
Herr Meister und Frau Meisterin,
Lasst mich in Frieden weiter ziehn
 Und wandern.

FRANZ PETER SCHUBERT, D. 795, no. 1. Titled *Das Wandern*.

2

WOHIN?

Ich hört' ein Bächlein rauschen
Wohl aus dem Felsenquell,
Hinab zum Tale rauschen
So frisch und wunderhell.

Ich weiss nicht, wie mir wurde,
Nicht, wer den Rat mir gab,
Ich musste gleich hinunter
Mit meinem Wanderstab.

Hinunter und immer weiter,
Und immer dem Bache nach,
Und immer frischer rauschte,
Und immer heller der Bach.

From the water we learned this,
from the water!
It does not rest by day or night,
but is always bent on roving,
the water!

We see it too in the mill-wheels,
the mill-wheels!
They never want to stop
and never they nor I get tired of the turning,
the mill-wheels!

Even the mill-stones, heavy as they are,
the stones!
They join in the merry dance
and want ever to go faster,
the stones!

O roving, roving, my delight,
o roving!
O master and mistress,
let me go my way in peace,
and rove!

WHITHER?

I heard a brooklet gushing
from a spring among the rocks,
gushing down into the valley,
so fresh and wonderfully clear.

I don't know how it happened,
or who gave me the idea,
but I couldn't resist following it right down
with my walking stick.

Down, always farther,
and always along the bank,
and always brisker
and clearer the brook gushed.

Ist das denn meine Strasse?
O Bächlein, sprich, wohin?
Du hast mit deinem Rauschen
Mir ganz berauscht den Sinn.

Was sag' ich denn von Rauschen?
Das kann kein Rauschen sein!
Es singen wohl die Nixen
Dort unten ihren Reihn.

Lass singen, Gesell, lass rauschen,
Und wandre fröhlich nach!
Es gehn ja Mühlenräder
In jedem klaren Bach.

FRANZ PETER SCHUBERT, D. 795, no. 2. In the third line of the second stanza *gleich* is changed to *auch*; in the first line of the fifth,

3

HALT!

Eine Mühle seh' ich blicken
Aus den Erlen heraus,
Durch Rauschen und Singen
Bricht Rädergebraus.

Ei willkommen, ei willkommen,
Süsser Mühlengesang!
Und das Haus, wie so traulich!
Und die Fenster, wie blank!

Und die Sonne, wie helle
Von Himmel sie scheint!
Ei, Bächlein, liebes Bächlein,
War es also gemeint?

FRANZ PETER SCHUBERT, D. 795, no. 3. In the first line of the song

4

DANKSAGUNG AN DEN BACH

War es also gemeint,
Mein rauschender Freund,
Dein Singen, dein Klingen,
War es also gemeint?

Is this the way I am to go,
Tell me, brooklet, whither?
You have, with your gushing,
enchanted my very soul.

What am I saying about gushing?
Gushing it cannot be!
The nixies are singing
and dancing down there.

Sing on, comrade, gush on,
and go your happy way!
There are mill-wheels turning
in every clear stream.

———————————

von becomes *vom*, and in the fourth, *Dort* is changed to *Tief*.

HALT!

I see a mill showing
through the alders;
through the gushing and singing of the water
breaks the noise of the wheel.

Welcome, welcome,
sweet song of the mill!
And the house, how comfortable it looks!
And the windows, how they glitter!

And the sun, how brightly
it shines from heaven!
O brooklet, dear brooklet,
was this what was intended?

———————————

blicken is changed to *blinken*; in the second line of the final stanza *von* becomes *vom*.

THANKS TO THE BROOK

Was this what was intended,
my gushing friend,
your singing and your sounding,
was this what was intended?

Zur Müllerin hin!
So lautet der Sinn.
Gelt, hab' ich's verstanden?
Zur Müllerin hin!

Hat sie dich geschickt?
Oder hast mich berückt?
Das möcht' ich noch wissen.
Ob sie dich geschickt.

Nun wie's auch mag sein,
Ich gebe mich drein:
Was ich such', ist gefunden,
Wie's immer mag sein.

Nach Arbeit ich frug,
Nun hab' ich genug,
Für die Hände, für's Herze
Vollauf genug!

FRANZ PETER SCHUBERT, D. 795, no. 4. In the third line of the

5

AM FEIERABEND

Hätt' ich tausend
Arme zu rühren!
Könnt' ich brausend
Die Räder führen!
Könnt' ich wehen
Durch alle Haine!
Könnt' ich drehen
Alle Steine!
Dass die schöne Müllerin
Merkte meinen treuen Sinn!

Ach, wie ist mein Arm so schwach!
Was ich hebe, was ich trage,
Was ich schneide, was ich schlage,
Jeder Knappe tut es nach.
Und da sitz' ich in der grossen Runde,
Zu der stillen kühlen Feierstunde,
Und der Meister spricht zu Allen:

To the maid of the mill!
So the meaning resounds.
Isn't that it? Have I understood it?
To the maid of the mill!

Did she send you,
or have you beguiled me?
That I want to know—
Did she send you?

Now whatever happens,
I'm yielding;
what I am seeking is found,
whatever may happen.

I applied for work;
now I have enough
for my hands and for my heart,
Enough and to spare!

---

fourth stanza *ist gefunden* is altered to read *hab' ich funden.*

AFTER WORK

If I had a thousand
arms to move!
If I could keep
the mill wheels roaring!
If I could blow
through all the groves!
If I could turn
all the mill-stones!
So that the beautiful maid of the mill
might notice my faithful nature!

Ah, how feeble is my arm!
What I can lift, what I can carry,
what I can chop, what I can strike,
any apprentice can do as well.
And there I sit in the great circle
in the quiet cool leisure hours,
and the master says to all:

Euer Werk hat mir gefallen;
Und das liebe Mädchen sagt
Allen eine gute Nacht.

FRANZ PETER SCHUBERT, D. 795, no. 5. In the second stanza, line

6

DER NEUGIERIGE

Ich frage keine Blume,
Ich frage keinen Stern,
Sie können mir nicht sagen,
Was ich erführ' so gern.

Ich bin ja auch kein Gärtner,
Die Sterne stehn zu hoch;
Mein Bächlein will ich fragen,
Ob mich mein Herz belog.

O Bächlein meiner Liebe,
Wie bist du heut' so stumm!
Will ja nur Eines wissen,
Ein Wörtchen um und um.

Ja, heisst das eine Wörtchen,
Das andre heisset Nein,
Die beiden Wörtchen schliessen
Die ganze Welt mir ein.

O Bächlein meiner Liebe,
Was bist du wunderlich!
Will's ja nicht weiter sagen,
Sag', Bächlein, liebt sie mich?

FRANZ PETER SCHUBERT, D. 795, no. 6. The third line is expanded
to *Sie können mir alle nicht sagen.*

7

DAS MÜHLENLEBEN

Seh' ich sie am Bache sitzen,
Wenn sie Fliegennetze strickt,
Oder Sonntags für die Fenster
Frische Wiesenblumen pflückt;

"Your work has pleased me."
And the dear girl says
to all a good-night.

---

four, *tut es nach* becomes *tut mir's nach*, and in line six *Zu* is
changed to *In*.

THE QUESTION

I do not ask a flower,
I do not ask a star;
they could not tell me
what I want so much to know.

Anyway, I'm no gardener;
the stars are too high.
I will ask the brooklet
if my heart was deceiving me.

O dear brooklet,
how quiet you are today!
I want to know only one thing,
one little word, over and over.

Yes is that little word—
the other one is No.
In these two words
the whole world is bound up for me.

O dear brooklet,
how strangely you behave!
I will not repeat what you say—
tell me, brooklet, does she love me?

LIFE AT THE MILL

When I see her sitting by the brook
knitting fly-screens,
or on a Sunday
gathering fresh meadow flowers for the window;

Seh' ich sie zum Garten wandeln,
Mit dem Körbchen in der Hand,
Nach den ersten Beeren spähen
An der grünen Dornenwand:

Dann wird's eng' in meiner Mühle,
Alle Mauern ziehn sich ein,
Und ich möchte flugs ein Fischer,
Jäger oder Gärtner sein.

Und der Steine lustig Pfeifen,
Und das Wasserrads Gebraus,
Und der Werke emsig Klappern,
'S jagt mich fast zum Tor hinaus.

Aber wenn in guter Stunde
Plaudernd sie zum Burschen tritt,
Und als kluges Kind des Hauses
Seitwärts nach dem Rechten sieht;

Und verständig lobt den Einen,
Dass der Andre merken mag,
Wie er's besser treiben solle,
Geht er ihrem Danke nach—

Keiner fühlt sich recht getroffen,
Und doch schiesst sie nimmer fehl,
Jeder muss von Schonung sagen,
Und doch hat sie keinen Hehl.

Keiner wünscht, sie möchte gehen,
Steht sie auch als Herrin da,
Und fast wie das Auge Gottes
Ist ihr Bild uns immer nah.—

Ei, da mag das Mühlenleben
Wohl des Liedes würdig sein,
Und die Räder, Stein und Stampfen
Stimmen als Begleitung ein.

Alles geht in schönem Tanze
Auf und ab, und ein und aus:
Gott gesegne mir das Handwerk
Und des guten Meisters Haus!

Not set by Schubert.

when I see her going to the garden
with a little basket in her hand,
looking for the first berries
along the thorny green hedge;

then the mill becomes small and narrow,
the walls all draw together,
and suddenly I wish I were a fisherman,
a hunter or a gardener.

And the happy creak of the stones,
and the roar of the water wheel,
and the busy clatter of the machinery
almost drive me out to the gate.

But when at a good time
she comes chattering up to one of the boys,
and, like the helpful daughter she is,
with a sideways glance checks on things

and judiciously praises that one
so that the other will notice
how he may do things better
to deserve her thanks—

no one feels that he is the target,
and yet she never misses her mark;
each must speak of her gentleness,
but she never dissembles.

No one wants her to go,
even though she stands there like the mistress of the house,
and almost like the eye of the Lord
her image is always with us.

Oh life at the mill
is really worthy of a song,
with the wheels, the stone, and the pounding sound
as accompaniment.

Everything goes like a beautiful dance,
up and down and in and out:
God bless the work of my hands
and the house of my good master!

8

UNGEDULD

Ich schnitt' es gern in alle Rinden ein,
Ich grüb' es gern in jeden Kieselstein,
Ich möcht' es sä'n auf jedes frische Beet
Mit Kressensamen, der es schnell verrät,
Auf jeden weissen Zettel möcht' ich's schreiben:
Dein ist mein Herz, und soll es ewig bleiben.

Ich möcht' mir ziehen einen jungen Star,
Bis dass er spräch' die Worte rein und klar,
Bis er sie spräch' mit meines Mundes Klang,
Mit meines Herzens vollem, heissem Drang;
Dann säng' er hell durch ihre Fensterscheiben:
Dein ist mein Herz, und soll es ewig bleiben.

Den Morgenwinden möcht' ich's hauchen ein,
Ich möcht' es säuseln durch den regen Hain;
O, leuchtet' es aus jedem Blumenstern!
Trüg' es der Duft zu ihr von nah und fern!
Ihr Wogen, könnt ihr nichts als Räder treiben?
Dein ist mein Herz, und soll es ewig bleiben.

Ich meint', es müsst' in meinen Augen stehn,
Auf meinen Wangen müsst' man's brennen sehn,
Zu lesen wär's auf meinem stummen Mund,
Ein jeder Atemzug gäb's laut ihr kund;
Und sie merkt nichts von all' dem bangen Treiben:
Dein ist mein Herz, und soll es ewig bleiben!

FRANZ PETER SCHUBERT, D. 795, no. 7. In the fourth line of the

9

MORGENGRUSS

Guten Morgen, schöne Müllerin!
Wo steckst du gleich das Köpfchen hin,
Als wär' dir was geschehen?
Verdriesst dich denn mein Gruss so schwer?
Verstört dich denn mein Blick so sehr?
So muss ich wieder gehen.

IMPATIENCE

I would carve it on the bark of every tree;
I would chisel it in every stone;
I would sow it in every flower bed
with watercress, which, growing quickly, would give it
  away;
on every white scrap of paper I would write it:
Thine is my heart, and shall be thine forever!

I would like to teach a young starling
until it would speak the words clearly,
until it would speak with the sound of my voice,
with the full fervent longing of my heart;
then it would sing clearly through her window:
Thine is my heart, and shall be thine forever!

To the morning wind I would breath it;
I would whisper it to the quivering trees;
O let it shine from the heart of every flower!
Let its fragrance be borne to her from near and far!
O water, can you turn nothing but millwheels?
Thine is my heart, and shall be thine forever!

I should think it must show plainly in my eyes,
on my cheeks anyone must see it burning;
it may be read upon my mute lips;
every breath I draw must proclaim it loudly
and she notices nothing of all my anxious longing:
Thine is my heart, and shall be thine forever!

---

second stanza *heissem* becomes *heissen*.

MORNING GREETING

Good morning, beautiful maid of the mill!
Why do you look away
as though something had frightened you?
Does my greeting so sorely upset you?
Do I embarrass you so by looking at you?
Then I must go away.

O lass mich nur von ferne stehn,
Nach deinem lieben Fenster sehn,
Von ferne, ganz von ferne!
Du blondes Köpfchen, komm hervor!
Hervor aus eurem runden Tor,
Ihr blauen Morgensterne!

Ihr schlummertrunknen Äugelein,
Ihr taubetrübten Blümelein,
Was scheuet ihr die Sonne?
Hat es die Nacht so gut gemeint,
Dass ihr euch schliesst und bückt und weint
Nach ihrer stillen Wonne?

Nun schüttelt ab der Träume Flor,
Und hebt euch frisch und frei empor
In Gottes hellen Morgen!
Die Lerche wirbelt in der Luft,
Und aus dem tiefen Herzen ruft
Die Liebe Leid und Sorgen.

FRANZ PETER SCHUBERT, D. 795, no. 8.

IO

DES MÜLLERS BLUMEN

Am Bach viel kleine Blumen stehn,
Aus hellen blauen Augen sehn;
Der Bach der ist des Müllers Freund,
Und hellblau Liebchens Auge scheint,
Drum sind es meine Blumen.

Dicht unter ihrem Fensterlein
Da pflanz' ich meine Blumen ein,
Da ruft ihr zu, wenn Alles schweigt,
Wenn sich ihr Haupt zum Schlummer neigt,
Ihr wisst ja, was ich meine.

Und wenn sie tät die Äuglein zu,
Und schläft in süsser, süsser Ruh',
Dann lispelt als ein Traumgesicht
Ihr zu: Vergiss, vergiss mein nicht!
Das ist es, was ich meine.

O let me only from a distance
look into your dear window,
only from a distance!
Come out, blond head,
come out from your arched gate,
blue morning stars!

O sleepy eyes,
o little flowers heavy with dew,
why do you fear the sun?
Was the night so pleasant
that you now close up and droop and weep
for quiet happiness?

Now throw off the veil of dreams
and look up fresh and free
in God's bright morning!
The lark warbles in the air,
and out of the depths of the heart
love calls grief and suffering.

THE MILLER'S FLOWERS

Along the brook many little flowers grow;
out of their bright blue eyes they look;
the brook is the miller's friend,
and light blue are my sweetheart's eyes—
therefore they are my flowers.

Close under her window,
there I plant my flowers;
call up to her when all is still,
when her head is nodding to sleep—
you know what I mean.

And when she closes her eyes
and sleeps in sweet, sweet rest,
then whisper as in a dream
to her: Forget, forget me not!
That is what I mean.

Und schliesst sie früh die Laden auf,
Dann schaut mit Liebesblick hinauf:
Der Tau in euren Äugelein,
Das sollen meine Tränen sein,
Die will ich auf euch weinen.

FRANZ PETER SCHUBERT, D. 795, no. 9. The second line of stanza
two reads: *Da will ich pflanzen die Blumen ein.*

II

TRÄNENREGEN

Wir sassen so traulich beisammen
Im kühlen Erlendach,
Wir schauten so traulich zusammen
Hinab in den rieselnden Bach.

Der Mond war auch gekommen,
Die Sternlein hinterdrein,
Und schauten so traulich zusammen
In den silbernen Spiegel hinein.

Ich sah nach keinem Monde,
Nach keinem Sternenschein,
Ich schaute nach ihrem Bilde,
Nach ihren Augen allein.

Und sahe sie nicken und blicken
Herauf aus dem seligen Bach,
Die Blümlein am Ufer, die blauen,
Sie nickten und blickten ihr nach.

Und in den Bach versunken
Der ganze Himmel schien,
Und wollte mich mit hinunter
In seine Tiefe ziehn.

Und über den Wolken und Sternen
Da rieselte munter der Bach,
Und rief mit Singen und Klingen:
Geselle, Geselle, mir nach!

And when in the morning she opens her shutters,
then look lovingly upward:
the dew in your eyes
will be the tears
that I will weep upon you.

RAIN OF TEARS

We sat so intimately together
in the cool shade of the alders;
we gazed so intimately together
down into the rippling brook.

The moon had risen
and then the stars;
and they looked so intimately together
down into the silver mirror.

I did not look at the moon,
nor at the starlight;
I only gazed at her image
only at her eyes.

And I saw her nodding and glancing
up from the blessed brook;
the flowers on the bank, the blue ones,
were nodding and glancing up after her.

And sunken in the brook,
all the light of heaven shone,
and wanted to draw me down
into its depths.

And over the clouds and the stars
the brook gurgled merrily,
and called out as it sang:
"Comrade, comrade!" after me.

Da gingen die Augen mir über,
Da ward es im Spiegel so kraus;
Sie sprach: Es kommt ein Regen,
Ade, ich geh' nach Haus.

FRANZ PETER SCHUBERT, D. 795, no. 10.

12

MEIN!

Bächlein, lass dein Rauschen sein!
Räder, stellt eur Brausen ein!
All' ihr muntern Waldvögelein,
Gross und klein,
Endet eure Melodein!
Durch den Hain
Aus und ein
Schalle heut' ein Reim allein:
Die geliebte Müllerin ist mein!
Mein!
Frühling, sind das alle deine Blümelein?
Sonne, hast du keinen hellern Schein?
Ach, so muss ich ganz allein,
Mit dem seligen Worte mein,
Unverstanden in der weiten Schöpfung sein!

FRANZ PETER SCHUBERT, D. 795, no. 11.

13

PAUSE

Meine Laute hab' ich gehängt an die Wand,
Hab' sie umschlungen mit einem grünen Band—
Ich kann nicht mehr singen, mein Herz ist zu voll,
Weiss nicht, wie ich's in Reime zwingen soll.
Meiner Sehnsucht allerheissesten Schmerz
Durft' ich aushauchen in Liederscherz,
Und wie ich klagte so süss und fein,
Meint' ich doch, mein Leiden wär' nicht klein.
Ei, wie gross ist wohl meines Glückes Last,
Dass kein Klang auf Erden es in sich fasst?

My eyes filled with tears;
the mirror of the stream was disturbed.
She said: "It is beginning to rain;
good-bye, I am going in."

MINE!

Brooklet, stop rippling!
Millwheels, stop roaring!
All you happy woodbirds,
large and small,
put an end to your songs!
Through the grove,
out and in,
let only one rhyme be heard:
The beloved maid of the mill is mine!
Mine!
Spring, have you no more flowers?
Sun, can't you shine more brightly?
Ah, so must I, all alone,
with my blessed word,
be understood by no one in all creation!

PAUSE

I have hung my lute on the wall,
and wound a green ribbon around it.
I can sing no more, my heart is too full.
I do not know how to force my feelings into rhymes.
The most intense pangs of longing
I ventured to breath out in my little songs;
and when I lamented so sweetly and so beautifully,
I really meant that my suffering was not light.
But oh, how great is the burden of my happiness,
that no sound on earth can contain it?

Nun, liebe Laute, ruh' an dem Nagel hier!
Und weht ein Lüftchen über die Saiten dir,
Und streift eine Biene mit ihren Flügeln dich,
Da wird mir bange und es durchschauert mich.
Warum liess ich das Band auch hängen so lang'?
Oft fliegt's um die Saiten mit seufzendem Klang.
Ist es der Nachklang meiner Liebespein?
Soll es das Vorspiel neuer Lieder sein?

FRANZ PETER SCHUBERT, D. 795, no. 12. Stanza one, line eight,

14

MIT DEM GRÜNEN LAUTENBANDE

"Schad' um das schöne grüne Band,
Dass es verbleicht hier an der Wand,
Ich hab' das Grün so gern!"
So sprachst du, Liebchen, heut' zu mir;
Gleich knüpf' ich's ab und send' es dir;
Nun hab' das Grüne gern!

Ist auch dein ganzer Liebster weiss,
Soll Grün doch haben seinen Preis,
Und ich auch hab' es gern.
Weil unsre Lieb ist immergrün,
Weil grün der Hoffnung Fernen blühn,
Drum haben wir es gern.

Nun schlingst du in die Locken dein
Das grüne Band gefällig ein,
Du hast ja's Grün so gern.
Dann weiss ich, wo die Hoffnung wohnt,
Dann weiss ich, wo die Liebe thront,
Dann hab' ich's Grün erst gern.

FRANZ PETER SCHUBERT, D. 795, no. 13. The first line of the last

15

DER JÄGER

Was sucht denn der Jäger am Mühlbach hier?
Bleib', trotziger Jäger, in deinem Revier!
Hier giebt es kein Wild zu jagen für dich,
Hier wohnt nur ein Rehlein, ein zahmes, für mich.
Und willst du das zärtliche Rehlein sehn,
So lass deine Büchsen im Walde stehn,

Now, my lute, rest here on your nail!
And if a breeze passes over your strings,
or if a bee touches them with his wings,
that will make me anxious and shivery.
Why have I left the ribbon hanging there so long?
It often passes over the strings with a sighing sound.
Is it the echo of my love-sorrow?
Or can it be the prelude to new songs?

---

begins *Glaubt' ich doch*, and stanza two, line four, *Da wird mir so bange*.

WITH THE GREEN LUTE-RIBBON

"It is a shame that this beautiful green ribbon
is fading here on the wall,
I am so fond of green!"
So you spoke to me today, dear.
At once I untie it and send it to you.
Now enjoy your green.

Though your miller-lover may be all white,
green also has its value;
and I like green too.
Since our love is ever green,
since hope blooms green in the distance,
therefore we are fond of it.

Now wind in your hair
nicely the green ribbon—
you are so fond of green.
Then I know where my hope lies,
then I know where love is enthroned—
then green is my favorite color.

---

stanza begins: *Nun schlinge in die Locken*.

THE HUNTER

What then does the hunter want here by the millstream?
Stay in your own country, impudent hunter!
Here is no game for you to hunt;
only one doe lives here, a tame one, for me.
And if you want to see my gentle young deer,
leave your gun in the woods,

So lass deine klaffenden Hunde zu Haus,
Und lass auf dem Horne den Saus und Braus,
Und schere vom Kinne das struppige Haar,
Sonst scheut sich im Garten das Rehlein fürwahr.

Doch besser, du bliebest im Walde dazu,
Und liessest die Mühlen und Müller in Ruh'.
Was taugen die Fischlein im grünen Gezweig?
Was will denn das Eichhorn im bläulichen Teich?
Drum bleibe, du trotziger Jäger, im Hain,
Und lass mich mit meinen drei Rädern allein;
Und willst meinem Schätzchen dich machen beliebt,
So wisse, mein Freund, was ihr Herzchen betrübt:
Die Eber, die kommen zu Nacht aus dem Hain,
Und brechen in ihren Kohlgarten ein,
Und treten und wühlen herum in dem Feld:
Die Eber die schiesse, du Jägerheld!

FRANZ PETER SCHUBERT, D. 795, no. 14.

16

EIFERSUCHT UND STOLZ

Wohin so schnell, so kraus, so wild, mein lieber Bach?
Eilst du voll Zorn dem frechen Bruder Jäger nach?
Kehr' um, kehr' um, und schilt erst deine Müllerin
Für ihren leichten, losen, kleinen Flattersinn.
Sahst du sie gestern Abend nicht am Tore stehn,
Mit langem Halse nach der grossen Strasse sehn?
Wenn von dem Fang der Jäger lustig zieht nach Haus,
Da steckt kein sittsam Kind den Kopf zum Fenster 'naus.
Geh', Bächlein, hin und sag' ihr das, doch sag' ihr nicht,
Hörst du, kein Wort, von meinem traurigen Gesicht;
Sag' ihr: Er schnitzt bei mir sich eine Pfeif' aus Rohr,
Und bläst den Kindern schöne Tänz' und Lieder vor.

FRANZ PETER SCHUBERT, D. 795, no. 15. The first line begins:

17

ERSTER SCHMERZ, LETZTER SCHERZ

Nun sitz' am Bache nieder
Mit deinem hellen Rohr,
Und blas' den lieben Kindern
Die schönen Lieder vor.

and leave your barking dogs at home,
and leave off sounding your noisy horn;
shave the unkempt beard from your chin
lest indeed you frighten the doe in her garden.

Yet it would be better for you to stay in the woods,
and leave the mill and the miller in peace.
What would a fish be doing in the green branches?
Or a squirrel in a blue pond?
So stay in the grove, impudent hunter,
and leave me alone with my three millwheels.
And if you would win the love of my sweetheart,
then know, my friend, what is troubling her heart:
It is the boars that come from the woods at night,
and break into her cabbage patch,
and tramp around and upset things in the field:
shoot the boar, hunter, if you want to be a hero!

JEALOUSY AND PRIDE

Where are you bound, so fast, so roiled and wild, my
 beloved brook?
Are you rushing angrily after that insolent brother hunter?
Come back, come back and first scold your maid of the mill
for her easy, fickle, trifling inconstancy.
Didn't you see her last night, standing by the gate,
craning her neck down the wide road?
When the hunter goes gaily home from the hunt,
no well-behaved girl would put her head out of the window.
Go tell her that, my brooklet, but don't tell her,
mind, a word about my mournful face.
Tell her: "He cuts a whistle from a reed near by,
and pipes pretty dances and songs for the children."

Wohin so schnell, so kraus und wild.

FIRST SORROW, LAST JEST

Now sit beside the brook
with your bright reed-whistle,
and pipe for the children
the loveliest songs.

Die Lust ist ja verrauschet,
Das Leid hat immer Zeit:
Nun singe neue Lieder
Von alter Seligkeit.

Noch blühn die alten Blumen,
Noch rauscht der alte Bach,
Es scheint die liebe Sonne
Noch wie am ersten Tag.

Die Fensterscheiben glänzen
Im klaren Morgenschein,
Und hinter den Fensterscheiben
Da sitzt die Liebste mein.

Ein Jäger, ein grüner Jäger,
Der liegt in ihrem Arm—
Ei, Bach, wie lustig du rauschest!
Ei, Sonne, wie scheinst du so warm!

Ich will einen Strauss dir pflücken,
Herzliebste, von buntem Klee,
Den sollst du mir stellen an's Fenster,
Damit ich den Jäger nicht seh'.

Ich will mit Rosenblättern
Den Mühlensteg bestreun:
Der Steg hat mich getragen
Zu dir, Herzliebste mein!

Und wenn der stolze Jäger
Ein Blättchen mir zertritt,
Dann stürz, o Steg, zusammen
Und nimm den Grünen mit!

Und trag' ihn auf dem Rücken
In's Meer, mit gutem Wind,
Nach einer fernen Insel,
Wo keine Mädchen sind.

Herzliebste, das Vergessen,
Es kommt dir ja nicht schwer—
Willst du den Müller wieder?
Vergisst dich nimmermehr.

Not set by Schubert

Happiness has indeed vanished,
there is always time for sorrow;
now sing new songs
of former blessedness.

The old flowers are still blooming,
the old brook still babbles on;
the sun still shines
as on the day of creation.

The windows shine
in the clear morning light;
and behind the window
there sits my love.

A hunter, a green hunter,
he lies in her arms—
O brook, how happily you ripple!
O sun, how warmly you shine!

I will pick you a bouquet,
dearest, of bright clover;
you can put it in the window
to hide the hunter from my sight.

I will strew rose-leaves
on the mill-bridge;
the bridge brought me
to you, beloved!

And if the proud hunter
steps on one of my leaves,
then collapse, bridge,
and take the Green One with you!

And take him on your back
into the sea, with a good wind,
to a distant island
where there are no girls.

Dearest, forgetting
is not so hard for you—
do you want your miller back?
He will never forget you.

18

DIE LIEBE FARBE

In Grün will ich mich kleiden,
In grüne Tränenweiden,
Mein Schatz hat's Grün so gern.
Will suchen einen Zypressenhain,
Eine Heide voll grünem Rosmarein,
Mein Schatz hat's Grün so gern.

Wohlauf zum fröhlichen Jagen!
Wohlauf durch Heid' und Hagen!
Mein Schatz hat's Jagen so gern.
Das Wild, das ich jage, das ist der Tod,
Die Heide, die heiss' ich die Liebesnot,
Mein Schatz hat's Jagen so gern.

Grabt mir ein Grab im Wasen,
Deckt mich mit grünem Rasen,
Mein Schatz hat's Grün so gern.
Kein Kreuzlein schwarz, kein Blümlein bunt,
Grün, Alles grün so rings und rund!
Mein Schatz hat's Grün so gern.

FRANZ PETER SCHUBERT, D. 795, no. 16.

19

DIE BÖSE FARBE

Ich möchte ziehn in die Welt hinaus,
Hinaus in die weite Welt,
Wenn's nur so grün, so grün nicht wär'
Da draussen in Wald und Feld!

Ich möchte die grünen Blätter all'
Pflücken von jedem Zweig,
Ich möchte die grünen Gräser all'
Weinen ganz totenbleich.

Ach Grün, du böse Farbe du,
Was siehst mich immer an,
So stolz, so keck, so schadenfroh,
Mich armen weissen Mann?

THE FAVORITE COLOR

I will dress myself in green,
the green of the weeping willow;
my sweetheart is so fond of green.
I will look for a grove of cypress,
a heath full of green rosemary;
my sweetheart is so fond of green.

Off to the jolly hunt!
Off through the meadows and hedges!
My sweetheart is so fond of hunting.
The game I am after is death,
the heath I call the sorrow of love;
my sweetheart is so fond of hunting.

Dig me a grave in the turf;
cover me over with green grass.
My sweetheart is so fond of green.
No black cross, no gaudy flowers,
green, all green around and about!
My sweetheart is so fond of green.

THE EVIL COLOR

I would like to go out into the world,
out into the wide world,
if only it weren't so green
out in the woods and the fields!

I wish I could pull down
all the green leaves from every branch;
I wish that all the green grass
could be bleached with my tears.

O green, you evil color,
why must you always look
so proudly, so pertly, so maliciously
at me, poor white man?

Ich möchte liegen vor ihrer Tür,
In Sturm und Regen und Schnee,
Und singen ganz leise bei Tag und Nacht
Das eine Wörtchen Ade!

Horch, wenn im Wald ein Jagdhorn ruft,
Da klingt ihr Fensterlein,
Und schaut sie auch nach mir nicht aus,
Darf ich doch schauen hinein.

O binde von der Stirn dir ab
Das grüne, grüne Band,
Ade, Ade! und reiche mir
Zum Abschied deine Hand!

FRANZ PETER SCHUBERT, D. 795, no. 17. In stanza four, line two,

20

BLÜMLEIN VERGISSMEIN

Was treibt mich jeden Morgen
So tief in's Holz hinein?
Was frommt mir, mich zu bergen
Im unbelauschten Hain?

Es blüht auf allen Fluren
Blümlein Vergiss mein nicht,
Es schaut vom heitern Himmel
Herab in blauem Licht.

Und soll ich's nieder treten,
Bebt mir der Fuss zurück,
Es fleht aus jedem Kelche
Ein wohlbekannter Blick.

Weisst du, in welchem Garten
Blümlein Vergiss mein steht?
Das Blümlein muss ich suchen,
Wie auch die Strasse geht.

'S ist nicht für Mädchenbusen,
So schön sieht es nicht aus:
Schwarz, schwarz ist seine Farbe,
Es passt in keinen Strauss.

I would like to lie down before her door,
in the storm, the rain and the snow,
and sing softly all day and all night
just one word—good-bye!

Listen, when a horn sounds in the woods,
I hear her at her window,
and though she doesn't see me
still I can look in at her.

O untie from your forehead
the green, green ribbon!
Good-bye, good-bye! And give me
your hand in parting!

---

n is changed to *Im*; in stanza five, line one, *ruft* is changed to
challt.

THE FORGET-ME FLOWER

What drives me out every morning
deep into the copse?
What good is it to hide myself
in the quiet grove?

It grows in every field
the flower forget-me-not;
it shines down from the clear sky
in a blue light.

And if I try to tread them down,
my foot recoils;
from the cup of every flower
a well-known face is pleading.

Do you know in what garden
the forget-me flower grows?
I must seek this flower
wherever the search may lead me.

It is not for the girls to wear,
it isn't so beautiful;
black, black is its color;
it wouldn't do for a bouquet.

Hat keine grüne Blätter,
Hat keinen Blütenduft,
Es windet sich am Boden
In nächtig dumpfer Luft.

Wächst auch an einem Ufer,
Doch unter fliesst kein Bach,
Und willst das Blümlein pflücken,
Dich zieht der Abgrund nach.

Das ist der rechte Garten,
Ein schwarzer, schwarzer Flor:
Darauf magst du dich betten—
Schleuss zu das Gartentor!

Not set by Schubert.

21

TROCKNE BLUMEN

Ihr Blümlein alle,
Die sie mir gab,
Euch soll man legen
Mit mir in's Grab.

Wie seht ihr alle
Mich an so weh,
Als ob ihr wüsstet,
Wie mir gescheh'?

Ihr Blümlein alle,
Wie welk, wie blass?
Ihr Blümlein alle,
Wovon so nass?

Ach, Tränen machen
Nicht maiengrün,
Machen tote Liebe
Nicht wieder blühn.

Und Lenz wird kommen,
Und Winter wird gehn,
Und Blümlein werden
Im Grase stehn.

It hasn't any green leaves,
it hasn't any fragrance;
it grows close to the ground
in the damp night air.

It springs up along the bank,
but there is no stream below,
and if you try to pick the flower
the abyss will draw you down.

This is the right garden,
a black, black field.
There you may make your bed—
lock the garden gate!

WITHERED FLOWERS

All you flowers
that she gave me,
you shall lie buried
with me in the grave.

How sadly you all
look at me,
as if you knew
what is happening to me?

All you flowers,
how withered? How faded?
All you flowers,
what makes you so moist?

Ah, tears do not make
the green of May,
nor cause dead love
to bloom again.

And spring will come,
and winter will go,
and flowers will spring up
in the grass.

Und Blümlein liegen
In meinem Grab,
Die Blümlein alle,
Die sie mir gab.

Und wenn sie wandelt
Am Hügel vorbei,
Und denkt im Herzen:
Der meint' es treu!

Dann Blümlein alle,
Heraus, heraus!
Der Mai ist kommen,
Der Winter ist aus.

FRANZ PETER SCHUBERT, D. 795, no. 18.

22

DER MÜLLER UND DER BACH

Der Müller

Wo ein treues Herze
In Liebe vergeht,
Da welken die Lilien
Auf jedem Beet.

Da muss in die Wolken
Der Vollmond gehn,
Damit seine Tränen
Die Menschen nicht sehn.

Da halten die Englein
Die Augen sich zu,
Und schluchzen und singen
Die Seele zu Ruh'.

Der Bach

Und wenn sich die Liebe
Dem Schmerz entringt,
Ein Sternlein, ein neues,
Am Himmel erblinkt.

And flowers will lie
on my grave,
all the flowers
she gave me.

And if she should pass
by the mound,
and think in her heart:
He was faithful to me!

Then all you flowers,
spring up, spring up!
May is here!
Winter is past!

THE MILLER AND THE BROOK

The Miller

Where a faithful heart
dies of love,
there the lilies wither
in every bed.

Then into the clouds
the full moon must ride,
so that his tears
shall not be seen by men.

Then the angels
close their eyes,
and sob and sing
the soul to rest.

The Brook

And when love
is released from sorrow,
a star, a new one
twinkles in the heavens.

Da springen drei Rosen,
Halb rot, halb weiss,
Die welken nicht wieder,
Aus Dornenreis.

Und die Engelein schneiden
Die Flügel sich ab,
Und gehn alle Morgen
Zur Erde hinab.

Der Müller

Ach Bächlein, liebes Bächlein,
Du meinst es so gut:
Ach, Bächlein, aber weisst du,
Wie Liebe tut?

Ach, unten, da unten,
Die kühle Ruh'!
Ach, Bächlein, liebes Bächlein,
So singe nur zu.

FRANZ PETER SCHUBERT, D. 795, no. 19. In line four of the third
stanza, *zu* is changed to *zur*; in the fifth stanza the second line is

23

DES BACHES WIEGENLIED

Gute Ruh', gute Ruh'!
Tu' die Augen zu!
Wandrer, du müder, du bist zu Haus.
Die Treu' ist hier,
Sollst liegen bei mir,
Bis das Meer will trinken die Bächlein aus.

Will betten dich kühl,
Auf weichem Pfühl,
In dem blauen krystallenen Kämmerlein.
Heran, heran,
Was wiegen kann,
Woget und wieget den Knaben mir ein!

There spring up three roses,
half red, half white,
never to wither,
from the prickly stems.

And the angels cut
their wings off,
and come every morning
down to the earth.

The Miller

Dear brooklet,
you mean it so well,
but brooklet, do you know
what it is to be in love?

Ah, down, down there,
the cooling rest!
Ah brooklet, dear brooklet,
just sing me to sleep.

---

changed to *Halb rot und halb weiss*, and the last word of the sixth
stanza becomes *herab*.

THE BROOK'S LULLABY

Sleep well, sleep well!
Close your eyes!
Wanderer, weary one, you have come home.
Here you will find faithfulness,
you shall lie down with me
until the sea drinks up the brooklets.

I will make you a fresh bed
on a soft pillow
in a little blue crystal room.
Come, come,
whatever can cradle,
lull and rock the boy to sleep!

Wenn ein Jagdhorn schallt
Aus dem grünen Wald,
Will ich sausen und brausen wohl um dich her.
Blickt nicht herein,
Blaue Blümelein!
Ihr macht meinem Schläfer die Träume so schwer

Hinweg, hinweg
Von dem Mühlensteg,
Böses Mägdlein, dass ihn dein Schatten nicht weckt
Wirf mir herein
Dein Tüchlein fein,
Dass ich die Augen ihm halte bedeckt!

Gute Nacht, gute Nacht!
Bis Alles wacht,
Schlaf' aus deine Freude, schlaf' aus dein Leid!
Der Vollmond steigt,
Der Nebel weicht,
Und der Himmel da oben, wie ist er so weit!

FRANZ PETER SCHUBERT, D. 795, no. 20. In the fourth stanza

DER DICHTER, ALS EPILOG

Weil gern man schliesst mit einer runden Zahl,
Tret' ich noch einmal in den vollen Saal,
Als letztes, fünf und zwanzigstes Gedicht,
Als Epilog, der gern das Klügste spricht.
Doch pfuschte mir der Bach in's Handwerk schon
Mit seiner Leichenred' im nassen Ton.
Aus solchem hohlen Wasserorgelschall
Zieht Jeder selbst sich besser die Moral;
Ich geb' es auf, und lasse diesen Zwist,
Weil Widerspruch nicht meines Amtes ist.

So hab' ich denn nichts lieber hier zu tun,
Als euch zum Schluss zu wünschen, wohl zu ruhn.
Wir blasen unsre Sonn' und Sternlein aus—
Nun findet euch im Dunkel gut nach Haus,
Und wollt ihr träumen einen leichten Traum,
So denkt an Mühlenrad und Wasserschaum,
Wenn ihr die Augen schliesst zu langer Nacht,

If a hunting horn sounds
from the green wood,
I will bluster and storm around you.
Don't look in at him,
blue flowers,
you make bad dreams for my sleeper.

Away, away
from the mill-bridge,
wicked girl, so that your shadow may not waken him!
Throw in to me
your dainty handkerchief
so that I may cover his eyes.

Good-night, good-night!
Until the day of awakening,
forget your joys in sleep, forget your sorrows!
The full moon is rising,
the mists are retreating,
and the heaven above, how wide it is!

Mägdlein becomes *Mägdelein*.

THE POET, AS EPILOGUE

Since people like things to end in round numbers,
once again I come into the full room,
for the last, twenty-fifth poem,
as Epilogue, who likes to say the cleverest things.
But the brook has already cheated me of my task
with its funeral oration in a moist mode.
From such hollow water-organ echoings
each listener can himself best draw the moral.
I leave the matter and do not enter into argument,
for it is not my function to contradict.

Therefore there is nothing better for me to do
than to wish you in conclusion a good rest.
We blow out our sun and our stars—
now find your way home safely in the dark;
and if you would dream a light dream,
think of the mill-wheel and the spray
when you close your eyes for the long night,

Bis es den Kopf zum Drehen euch gebracht.
Und wer ein Mädchen führt an seiner Hand,
Der bitte scheidend um ein Liebespfand,
Und giebt sie heute, was sie oft versagt,
So sei des treuen Müllers treu gedacht
Bei jedem Händedruck, bei jedem Kuss,
Bei jedem heissen Herzensüberfluss:
Geb' ihm die Liebe für sein kurzes Leid
In eurem Busen lange Seligkeit!

Not set by Schubert.

DIE WINTERREISE

FRANZ PETER SCHUBERT, D. 911. It is perhaps significant that
Müller's cycle of poems is entitled *Die Winterreise*; Schubert calls
his songs simply *Winterreise*. But more important are the changes
the composer has made in the order of the songs. Thus Müller's no.
6 becomes Schubert's no. 13, Müller's no. 7 Schubert's no. 6, and so
on. I doubt that there could be much question that Schubert's order
is an improvement, though the poet's sequence is followed here.

I

GUTE NACHT

Fremd bin ich eingezogen,
Fremd zieh' ich wieder aus,
Der Mai war mir gewogen
Mit manchem Blumenstrauss.
Das Mädchen sprach von Liebe,
Die Mutter gar von Eh'—
Nun ist die Welt so trübe,
Der Weg gehüllt in Schnee.

Ich kann zu meiner Reisen
Nicht wählen mit der Zeit:
Muss selbst den Weg mir weisen
In dieser Dunkelheit.
Es zieht ein Mondenschatten
Als mein Gefährte mit,
Und auf den weissen Matten
Such' ich des Wildes Tritt.

until your head begins to swim.
And he who leads a young lady by the hand,
and in parting asks a pledge of love,
if she gives today what she has often denied,
then faithfully recall the faithful miller
with every handclasp, with every kiss,
with every warm confession of affection:
may love give him, in return for his brief sufferings
lasting blessedness in your heart.

THE WINTER'S JOURNEY

GOOD NIGHT

A stranger I came,
and a stranger I depart;
May for me
was prodigal with flowers.
The girl spoke of love,
her mother even of marriage—
now the world is so gloomy,
my path covered with snow.

I cannot choose
the time for my journey;
I must find my own way
through this darkness.
A shadow in the moonlight
is my companion,
and over the snowy meadows
I follow the tracks of animals.

Was soll ich länger weilen,
Bis man mich trieb' hinaus?
Lass irre Hunde heulen
Vor ihres Herren Haus!
Die Liebe liebt das Wandern,—
Gott hat sie so gemacht—
Von Einem zu den Andern—
Fein Liebchen, Gute Nacht!

Will dich im Traum nicht stören,
Wär' Schad' um deine Ruh',
Sollst meinen Tritt nicht hören—
Sacht, sacht die Türe zu!
Ich schreibe nur im Gehen
An's Tor noch gute Nacht,
Damit du mögest sehen,
An dich hab' ich gedacht.

FRANZ PETER SCHUBERT, D. 911, no. 1. The fourth stanza, fifth and

2

DIE WETTERFAHNE

Der Wind spielt mit der Wetterfahne
Auf meines schönen Liebchens Haus.
Da dacht' ich schon in meinem Wahne,
Sie pfiff' den armen Flüchtling aus.

Er hätt' es ehr bemerken sollen,
Des Hauses aufgestecktes Schild,
So hätt' er nimmer suchen wollen
Im Haus ein treues Frauenbild.

Der Wind spielt drinnen mit den Herzen,
Wie auf dem Dach, nur nicht so laut,
Was fragen sie nach meinen Schmerzen?
Ihr Kind ist eine reiche Braut.

FRANZ PETER SCHUBERT, D. 911, no. 2. In the first line of the
second stanza *ehr* is changed to *eher*.

Why should I wait
until they drive me out?
Let prowling dogs howl
before their masters' house!
Love likes to rove—
God ordered it so—
from one to another—
dear love, good-night!

I will not disturb your dream,
It would be a shame to break your rest.
You must not hear my footsteps—
softly, softly close the door!
I only write as I leave—
"good-night"—at your gate,
so that you may see
I thought of you.

_____

xth lines, reads: *Schreib' im Vorübergehen | Ans Tor dir: gute
Nacht.*

THE WEATHERVANE

The wind plays with the weathervane
upon my fine sweetheart's house.
So, thought I in my madness,
it flouted the poor fugitive.

He should have noticed sooner
the emblem of the house;
then he never would have sought
a constant woman there.

The wind plays inside with hearts
just as on the roof, only not so loudly.
What do they care for my sorrow?
Their child is a rich bride.

3

GEFRORNE TRÄNEN

Gefrorne Tropfen fallen
Von meinen Wangen ab:
Und ist's mir denn entgangen,
Dass ich geweinet hab'?

Ei Tränen, meine Tränen,
Und seid ihr gar so lau,
Dass ihr erstarrt zu Eise,
Wie kühler Morgentau?

Und dringt doch aus der Quelle
Der Brust so glühend heiss,
Als wolltet ihr zerschmelzen
Des ganzen Winters Eis.

FRANZ PETER SCHUBERT, D. 911, no. 3. The third line of the fir
stanza is altered: *Ob es mir denn entgangen*. In the repetition of th

4

ERSTARRUNG

Ich such' im Schnee vergebens
Nach ihrer Tritte Spur,
Hier, wo wir oft gewandelt
Selbander durch die Flur.

Ich will den Boden küssen,
Durchdringen Eis und Schnee
Mit meinen heissen Tränen,
Bis ich die Erde seh'.

Wo find' ich eine Blüte,
Wo find' ich grünes Gras?
Die Blumen sind erstorben,
Der Rasen sieht so blass.

Soll denn kein Angedenken
Ich nehmen mit von hier?
Wenn meine Schmerzen schweigen,
Wer sagt mir dann von ihr?

FROZEN TEARS

Frozen drops fall
from my cheeks:
and does it only now come to me
that I have been weeping?

Ah tears, my tears,
and are you then so lukewarm
that you turn to ice
like cool morning dew?

And yet you gush from the well
of my glowing hot breast
as though you would melt
all the ice of winter.

---

last stanza, the first word is changed from *Und* to *Ihr*.

NUMBNESS

I look in vain in the snow
for a trace of her footprints,
here where we two used to stroll
across the meadow.

I want to kiss the ground,
to penetrate the ice and snow
with my hot tears
until I see the earth.

Where will I find a blossom,
where will I find green grass?
The flowers are withered,
the sod looks so faded.

Shall I then take with me
no souvenir from here?
If my sorrows are silent,
who will speak to me of her?

Mein Herz ist wie erfroren,
Kalt starrt ihr Bild darin:
Schmilzt je das Herz mir wieder,
Fliesst auch das Bild dahin.

FRANZ PETER SCHUBERT, D. 911, no. 4. The last two lines of the first stanza read : *Wo sie an meinem Arme | Durchstrich die grüne*

5

DER LINDENBAUM

Am Brunnen vor dem Tore
Da steht ein Lindenbaum:
Ich träumt' in seinem Schatten
So manchen süssen Traum.

Ich schnitt in seine Rinde
So manches liebe Wort;
Es zog in Freud' und Leide
Zu ihm mich immer fort.

Ich musst' auch heute wandern
Vorbei in tiefer Nacht,
Da·hab' ich noch im Dunkel
Die Augen zugemacht.

Und seine Zweige rauschten,
Als riefen sie mir zu:
Komm her zu mir, Geselle,
Hier findst du deine Ruh'!

Die kalten Winde bliesen
Mir grad' in's Angesicht,
Der Hut flog mir vom Kopfe,
Ich wendete mich nicht.

Nun bin ich manche Stunde
Entfernt von jenem Ort,
Und immer hör' ich's rauschen:
Du fändest Ruhe dort!

FRANZ PETER SCHUBERT, D. 911, no. 5.

My heart is as if frozen,
her cold image fixed within it:
if my heart should ever thaw,
her image also would melt.

Flur. In the last line of the song *das* is changed to *ihr.*

THE LINDEN TREE

By the well in front of the gate
there stands a linden tree:
I dreamed in its shade
many a sweet dream.

I carved in its bark
many a fond word;
in joy and in sorrow
I always felt drawn to it.

I had to pass it again just now
in the deep night,
and even in the dark
I closed my eyes.

And its branches rustled,
as if they were calling to me,
"Come here, friend,
here you will find rest!"

The cold winds blew
right into my face;
my hat flew off my head,
yet I did not turn back.

Now I am many hours
distant from that spot,
yet I always hear it rustling:
"You would find rést there!"

6

DIE POST

Von der Strasse her ein Posthorn klingt,
Was hat es, dass es so hoch aufspringt,
        Mein Herz?

Die Post bringt keinen Brief für dich:
Was drängst du denn so wunderlich,
        Mein Herz?

Nun ja, die Post kömmt aus der Stadt,
Wo ich ein liebes Liebchen hatt',
        Mein Herz!

Willst wohl einmal hinübersehn,
Und fragen, wie es dort mag gehn,
        Mein Herz?

FRANZ PETER SCHUBERT, D. 911, no. 13. In the first line of the

7

WASSERFLUT

Manche Trän' aus meinen Augen
Ist gefallen in den Schnee;
Seine kalten Flocken saugen
Durstig ein das heisse Weh.

Wann die Gräser sprossen wollen,
Weht daher ein lauer Wind,
Und das Eis zerspringt in Schollen,
Und der weiche Schnee zerrinnt.

Schnee, du weisst von meinem Sehnen:
Sag' mir, wohin geht dein Lauf?
Folge nach nur meinen Tränen,
Nimmt dich bald das Bächlein auf.

Wirst mit ihm die Stadt durchziehen,
Muntre Strassen ein und aus:
Fühlst du meine Tränen glühen,
Da ist meiner Liebsten Haus.

FRANZ PETER SCHUBERT, D. 911, no. 6. The second line of the third

THE MAIL-COACH

Along the street a post-horn sounds.
What is it that makes you so excited,
my heart?

The mail-coach brings no letter for you:
why, then, are you so strangely vexed,
my heart?

Oh, perhaps the coach comes from the town
where I had a sweetheart,
my heart!

Would you like to have a look over there,
and ask how things are going,
my heart?

third stanza *kömmt* is changed to *kommt*. By repeating *Mein Herz*
Schubert makes a kind of refrain.

THE DELUGE

Many tears from my eyes
have fallen in the snow;
its cold flakes
thirstily drink up my hot misery.

When grass is ready to grow
a gentle wind blows from thence,
and the ice breaks into chunks
and the soft snow melts.

Snow, you know of my longing:
tell me, where does your course lead?
Only follow my tears,
and the stream will carry you away.

It will carry you through the town,
in and out of the happy streets:
if you feel my tears burning,
that will be at my sweetheart's house.

stanza is changed to *Sag', wohin doch geht dein Lauf?*

8

AUF DEM FLUSSE

Der du so lustig rauschtest,
Du heller, wilder Fluss,
Wie still bist du geworden,
Giebst keinen Scheidegruss.

Mit harter, starrer Rinde
Hast du dich überdeckt,
Liegst kalt und unbeweglich
Im Sande hingestreckt.

In deine Decke grab' ich
Mit einem spitzen Stein
Den Namen meiner Liebsten
Und Stund' und Tag hinein.

Den Tag des ersten Grusses,
Den Tag, an dem ich ging,
Um Nam' und Zahlen windet
Sich ein zerbrochner Ring.

Mein Herz, in diesem Bache
Erkennst du nun dein Bild?
Ob's unter seiner Rinde
Wohl auch so reissend schwillt?

FRANZ PETER SCHUBERT, D. 911, no. 7. In the fourth line of the

9

RÜCKBLICK

Es brennt mir unter beiden Sohlen,
Tret' ich auch schon auf Eis und Schnee.
Ich möcht' nicht wieder Atem holen,
Bis ich nicht mehr die Türme seh'.

Hab' mich an jedem Stein gestossen,
So eilt' ich zu der Stadt hinaus;
Die Krähen warfen Bäll' und Schlossen
Auf meinen Hut von jedem Haus.

BY THE STREAM

You that used to ripple so happily,
clear, noisy stream,
how quiet you have become!
You give me no parting greeting.

With a hard, stiff crust
you have covered yourself.
You lie cold and motionless,
stretched out in the sand.

In your shell I carve,
with a sharp stone,
the name of my sweetheart,
with the day and hour.

The day of our first greeting,
the day of my departure—
around the name and the figure
is wound a broken ring.

My heart, in this brook
do you now recognize your own image?
Under its shell
is it too so painfully swelling?

---

second stanza *hingestreckt* is changed to *ausgestreckt*.

RETROSPECT

The soles of my feet are burning,
although I walk on ice and snow.
I don't want to draw another breath
until I can no longer see the town towers.

I stumbled over every stone,
so hurriedly did I leave the town;
the crows threw down snow and hailstones
on my head from every roof.

Wie anders hast du mich empfangen,
Du Stadt der Unbeständigkeit!
In deinen blanken Fenstern sangen
Die Lerch' und Nachtigall im Streit.

Die runden Lindenbäume blühten,
Die klaren Rinnen rauschten hell,
Und ach, zwei Mädchenaugen glühten!—
Da war's geschehn um dich, Gesell!

Kömmt mir der Tag in die Gedanken,
Möcht' ich noch einmal rückwärts sehn,
Möcht' ich zurücke wieder wanken,
Vor ihrem Hause stille stehn.

FRANZ PETER SCHUBERT, D. 911, no. 8.

10

DER GREISE KOPF

Der Reif hatt' einen weissen Schein
Mir über's Haar gestreuet.
Da meint' ich schon ein Greis zu sein,
Und hab' mich sehr gefreuet.

Doch bald ist er hinweggetaut,
Hab' wieder schwarze Haare,
Dass mir's vor meiner Jugend graut—
Wie weit noch bis zur Bahre!

Vom Abendrot zum Morgenlicht
Ward mancher Kopf zum Greise.
Wer glaubt's? Und meiner ward es nicht
Auf dieser ganzen Reise!

FRANZ PETER SCHUBERT, D. 911, no. 14. In the third line of the

11

DIE KRÄHE

Eine Krähe war mit mir
Aus der Stadt gezogen,
Ist bis heute für und für
Um mein Haupt geflogen.

How differently you welcomed me,
fickle town!
At your shining windows
the lark and the nightingale tried to outsing each other.

The rounded linden trees were blooming;
the clear brooks rippled brightly;
and ah, two girlish eyes glowed!—
then it was all over with you, my boy!

If I were to think of that day,
I would want to go back again.
I would want to go back
and stand silent before her house.

THE GRAY HEAD

The hoar-frost had given a white luster
to my hair.
I thought I was already an old man,
and it made me very happy.

But soon it thawed away—
I again have black hair.
What a horror I have of my youth—
how far it still is to the grave!

Between sunset and sunrise
many a head has turned gray.
Who would believe it? And mine has not changed
during this whole journey!

first stanza *Da meint' ich schon* is changed to *Da glaubt' ich schon*.

THE CROW

A crow followed me
out of the town;
until now, ceaselessly,
he has been flying about my head.

Krähe, wunderliches Tier,
Willst mich nicht verlassen?
Meinst wohl bald als Beute hier
Meinen Leib zu fassen?

Nun, es wird nicht weit mehr gehn
An dem Wanderstabe.
Krähe, lass mich endlich sehn
Treue bis zum Grabe!

FRANZ PETER SCHUBERT, D. 911, no. 15.

12

LETZTE HOFFNUNG

Hier und da ist an den Bäumen
Noch ein buntes Blatt zu sehn,
Und ich bleibe vor den Bäumen
Oftmals in Gedanken stehn.

Schaue nach dem einen Blatte,
Hänge meine Hoffnung dran;
Spielt der Wind mit meinem Blatte,
Zittr' ich, was ich zittern kann.

Ach, und fällt das Blatt zu Boden,
Fällt mit ihm die Hoffnung ab,
Fall' ich selber mit zu Boden,
Wein' auf meiner Hoffnung Grab.

FRANZ PETER SCHUBERT, D. 911, no. 16. The first word is changed

13

IM DORFE

Es bellen die Hunde, es rasseln die Ketten,
Die Menschen schnarchen in ihren Betten,
Träumen sich Manches, was sie nicht haben,
Tun sich im Guten und Argen erlaben:
Und morgen früh ist Alles zerflossen.—
Je nun, sie haben ihr Teil genossen,
Und hoffen, was sie noch übrig liessen,
Doch wieder zu finden auf ihren Kissen.

Crow, curious creature,
won't you leave me alone?
Do you mean, as prey, soon
to seize upon my body?

Well, I cannot go much farther
on my staff.
Crow, let me show at last
faithfulness unto the grave!

LAST HOPE

Here and there upon the trees
there is still a colored leaf to be seen.
And by the trees
I often stand musing.

I look at the one leaf
and hang my hope upon it;
if the wind plays with my leaf,
I tremble all over.

Ah, and if the leaf falls to the ground,
with it falls my hope.
I myself sink with it to the earth,
and weep upon the grave of my hope.

---

from *Hier* to *Hie,* and the second line reads *Manches bunte Blatt
zu seh'n.*

IN THE VILLAGE

The dogs bark; their chains rattle;
people are snoring in their beds.
Dreaming of many things they do not have,
they refresh themselves both with the pleasant and the
    unpleasant.
And in the morning it is all gone.
Ah well, they have enjoyed their portion,
and hope to find what is still left over
another time on their pillows.

Bellt mich nur fort, ihr wachen Hunde,
Lasst mich nicht ruhn in der Schlummerstunde!
Ich bin zu Ende mit allen Träumen—
Was will ich unter den Schläfern säumen?

FRANZ PETER SCHUBERT, D. 911, no. 17. The second line begins
Es schlafen die Menschen.

14

DER STÜRMISCHE MORGEN

Wie hat der Sturm zerrissen
Des Himmels graues Kleid!
Die Wolkenfetzen flattern
Umher in mattem Streit.

Und rote Feuerflammen
Ziehn zwischen ihnen hin.
Das nenn' ich einen Morgen
So recht nach meinem Sinn!

Mein Herz sieht an dem Himmel
Gemalt sein eignes Bild—
Es ist nichts als der Winter,
Der Winter kalt und wild!

FRANZ PETER SCHUBERT, D. 911, no. 18.

15

TÄUSCHUNG

Ein Licht tanzt freundlich vor mir her;
Ich folg' ihm nach die Kreuz und Quer;
Ich folg' ihm gern, und seh's ihm an,
Dass es verlockt den Wandersmann.
Ach, wer wie ich so elend ist,
Gibt gern sich hin der bunten List,
Die hinter Eis und Nacht und Graus
Ihm weist ein helles, warmes Haus,
Und eine liebe Seele drin—
Nur Täuschung ist für mich Gewinn!

FRANZ PETER SCHUBERT, D. 911, no. 19.

Bark me on my way, watchdogs!
Don't let me rest during the hours of sleep!
I have come to the end of all dreaming—
why should I tarry among the sleepers?

THE STORMY MORNING

How the storm has rent
the gray mantle of heaven!
Tatters of cloud drift
about in weary strife.

And red streaks of lightning
flash among them.
This I call a morning
after my own heart!

My heart sees in the heavens,
painted, its own image—
it is nothing but the winter,
the winter cold and rude!

DELUSION

A light dances cheerily before me;
I follow it this way and that.
I follow it gladly, knowing all the while
that it leads the wanderer astray.
Ah, anyone as miserable as I
gives himself willingly to the colorful deception
that points beyond the ice, the night, and its horror,
to a bright warm house,
and a loving soul within—
only delusion is left for me!

16

DER WEGWEISER

Was vermeid' ich denn die Wege,
Wo die andren Wandrer gehn,
Suche mir versteckte Stege
Durch verschneite Felsenhöhn?

Habe ja doch nichts begangen,
Dass ich Menschen sollte scheun—
Welch ein törichtes Verlangen
Treibt mich in die Wüstenein?

Weiser stehen auf den Strassen,
Weisen auf die Städte zu
Und ich wandre sonder Massen,
Ohne Ruh', und suche Ruh'.

Einen Weiser seh' ich stehen
Unverrückt vor meinem Blick;
Eine Strasse muss ich gehen,
Die noch Keiner ging zurück.

FRANZ PETER SCHUBERT, D. 911, no. 20. The first line of the third

17

DAS WIRTSHAUS

Auf einen Totenacker
Hat mich mein Weg gebracht.
Allhier will ich einkehren;
Hab' ich bei mir gedacht.

Ihr grünen Totenkränze
Könnt wohl die Zeichen sein,
Die müde Wandrer laden
In's kühle Wirtshaus ein.

Sind denn in diesem Hause
Die Kammern all' besetzt?
Bin matt zum Niedersinken
Und tödlich schwer verletzt.

THE GUIDEPOST

Why do I avoid the highways
that other wanderers travel,
and seek out hidden paths
through snowbound rocky heights?

I have done nothing
to make me avoid people—
what mad longing is it
that drives me into the wilderness?

Guideposts stand along the road
pointing to the towns;
but I trudge ceaselessly on
without rest, and seek rest.

One guidepost I see
ever fixed before my eyes:
I must travel a road
by which no one has ever returned.

anza reads: *Weiser stehen auf den Wegen*, which destroys the
yme.

THE INN

Into a graveyard
my way has led me.
Here will I stop;
I thought to myself.

The green memorial wreaths
might well be the signs
that invite weary travelers
into the cool inn.

Are then in this house
all the rooms taken?
I am so weary I can hardly stand,
and mortally wounded.

O unbarmherz'ge Schenke,
Doch weisest du mich ab?
Nun weiter denn, nur weiter,
Mein treuer Wanderstab!

FRANZ PETER SCHUBERT, D. 911, no. 21. In the last line of the thir

18

DAS IRRLICHT

In die tiefsten Felsengründe
Lockte mich ein Irrlicht hin:
Wie ich einen Ausgang finde,
Liegt nicht schwer mir in dem Sinn.

Bin gewohnt das irre Gehen,
'S führt ja jeder Weg zum Ziel:
Unsre Freuden, unsre Wehen,
Alles eines Irrlichts Spiel!

Durch des Bergstroms trockne Rinnen
Wind' ich ruhig mich hinab—
Jeder Strom wird's Meer gewinnen,
Jedes Leiden auch ein Grab.

FRANZ PETER SCHUBERT, D. 911, no. 9. In the third line of th

19

RAST

Nun merk' ich erst, wie müd' ich bin,
Da ich zur Ruh' mich lege;
Das Wandern hielt mich munter hin
Auf unwirtbarem Wege.

Die Füsse frugen nicht nach Rast,
Es war zu kalt zum Stehen,
Der Rücken fühlte keine Last,
Der Sturm half fort mich wehen.

In eines Köhlers engem Haus
Hab' Obdach ich gefunden;
Doch meine Glieder ruhn nicht aus:
So brennen ihre Wunden.

O pitiless inn,
do you refuse to take me?
Then on, ever on,
my trusty staff!

---

stanza Schubert has: *Bin tödlich schwer verletzt.*

THE WILL-O'-THE-WISP

Into the deepest rocky chasms
a will-o'-the-wisp has lured me.
How I shall find a way out
does not greatly concern me.

I am used to going astray;
every road leads to its destination:
our joys, our sorrows,
all are a will-o'-the-wisp's game.

Through the dry bed of a mountain brook
I take my way quietly down—
every stream will reach the sea,
every sorrow will find a grave.

---

second stanza *Wehen* is changed to *Leiden*, thus destroying the
rhyme. In the final line *ein* becomes *sein.*

REST

Now I notice for the first time how tired I am,
as I lie down to rest;
merely walking sustained me
along the dreary path.

My feet did not seem tired,
it was too cold to stop;
my back felt no burden,
the storm helped me along.

In a collier's little hut
I have found shelter;
but now my limbs will not rest
because they ache so.

Auch du, mein Herz, im Kampf und Sturm
So wild und so verwegen,
Fühlst in der Still' erst deinen Wurm
Mit heissem Stich sich regen!

<small>Franz Peter Schubert</small>, D. 911, no. 10.

20

DIE NEBENSONNEN

Drei Sonnen sah ich am Himmel stehn,
Hab' lang' und fest sie angesehn;
Und sie auch standen da so stier,
Als könnten sie nicht weg von mir.
Ach, meine Sonnen seid ihr nicht!
Schaut Andren doch in's Angesicht!
Ja neulich hatt' ich auch wohl drei:
Nun sind hinab die besten zwei.
Ging' nur die dritt' erst hinterdrein!
Im Dunkel wird mir wohler sein.

<small>Franz Peter Schubert</small>, D. 911, no. 23. In the fourth line *Als*

21

FRÜHLINGSTRAUM

Ich träumte von bunten Blumen,
So wie sie wohl blühen im Mai,
Ich träumte von grünen Wiesen,
Von lustigem Vogelgeschrei.

Und als die Hähne krähten,
Da ward mein Auge wach;
Da war es kalt und finster,
Es schrien die Raben vom Dach.

Doch an den Fensterscheiben
Wer malte die Blätter da?
Ihr lacht wohl über den Träumer,
Der Blumen im Winter sah?

Ich träumte von Lieb' um Liebe,
Von einer schönen Maid,
Von Herzen und von Küssen,
Von Wonn' und Seligkeit.

And you, my heart, in struggle and storm,
so fierce and so bold,
only now, in the silence, feel the worm
bestir itself with burning pangs!

THE MOCK-SUNS

I saw three suns in the sky,
and long and steadfastly I gazed at them.
They stood there so fixedly,
as if they could never leave me.
Ah, you are not my suns!
You are shining into others' faces!
Recently I too had three,
but now the best two have set.
I only wish the third would go down too!
It would be better for me in the darkness.

---

könnten sie becomes *Als wollten sie*, and in the sixth line *Andren*
becomes *Andern*.

A DREAM OF SPRING

I dreamed of colorful flowers
such as bloom in May;
I dreamed of green fields
and the happy cries of birds.

And when the cocks crew
I opened my eyes;
it was cold and gloomy,
and the ravens screamed from the roof.

But on the window panes
who painted the leaves?
Are you laughing at the dreamer
who saw flowers in winter?

I dreamed of happy love,
of a beautiful girl,
of fondling and of kissing,
of joy and bliss.

Und als die Hähne krähten,
Da ward mein Herze wach;
Nun sitz' ich hier alleine
Und denke dem Traume nach.

Die Augen schliess' ich wieder,
Noch schlägt das Herz so warm.
Wann grünt ihr Blätter am Fenster?
Wann halt' ich dich, Liebchen, im Arm?

FRANZ PETER SCHUBERT, D. 911, no. 11. In the fourth line of the

22

EINSAMKEIT

Wie eine trübe Wolke
Durch heitre Lüfte geht,
Wann in der Tanne Wipfel
Ein mattes Lüftchen weht:

So zieh' ich meine Strasse
Dahin mit trägem Fuss,
Durch helles, frohes Leben,
Einsam und ohne Gruss.

Ach, dass die Luft so ruhig!
Ach, dass die Welt so licht!
Als noch die Stürme tobten,
War ich so elend nicht.

FRANZ PETER SCHUBERT, D. 911, no. 12. In stanza 1, line 3, *Wann*
becomes *Wenn*.

23

MUT!

Fliegt der Schnee mir in's Gesicht,
Schüttl' ich ihn herunter.
Wenn mein Herz im Busen spricht,
Sing' ich hell und munter.

Höre nicht, was es mir sagt,
Habe keine Ohren.
Fühle nicht, was es mir klagt,
Klagen ist für Toren.

And when the cocks crew
my heart awoke;
Now I sit here alone
and think back over the dream.

I close my eyes again,
my heart still beats ardently.
When will the leaves turn green at the window?
When will I hold you, sweetheart, in my arms?

---

fourth stanza *Wonn'* becomes *Wonne*. The last line is changed to
Wann halt' ich mein Liebchen in Arm?

LONELINESS

Like a murky cloud
passing across the bright sky
when in the tops of the fir-trees
a light breeze is stirring:

so I go my way
onward with dragging feet,
amid the brightness and happiness of life,
lonely and friendless.

If only the air were not so calm!
If only the world were not so bright!
While the storms were still raging
I was not so miserable.

COURAGE!

If snow flies in my face,
I brush it off.
If my heart speaks within me
I sing brightly and cheerfully.

I do not hear what it is saying to me;
I have no ears.
I do not feel the cause of its complaint—
complaining is for fools.

Lustig in die Welt hinein
Gegen Wind und Wetter!
Will kein Gott auf Erden sein,
Sind wir selber Götter.

Franz Peter Schubert, D. 911, no. 22.

24

DER LEIERMANN

Drüben hinter'm Dorfe
Steht ein Leiermann,
Und mit starren Fingern
Dreht er was er kann.

Barfuss auf dem Eise
Schwankt er hin und her;
Und sein kleiner Teller
Bleibt ihm immer leer.

Keiner mag ihn hören,
Keiner sieht ihn an;
Und die Hunde brummen
Um den alten Mann.

Und er lässt es gehen
Alles, wie es will,
Dreht, und seine Leier
Steht ihm nimmer still.

Wunderlicher Alter,
Soll ich mit dir gehn?
Willst zu meinen Liedern
Deine Leier drehn?

Franz Peter Schubert, D. 911, no. 24. In the second line of the second stanza *Schwankt* is changed to *Wankt*, and in the third line of the third stanza *brummen* is changed to *knurren*. The *Leier*, as we recognize it in Schubert's music, is not what we call a barrel-organ, but a hurdy-gurdy, as described in *The Harvard Dictionary*

Gaily forth into the world,
in spite of wind and weather!
If there be no god on earth,
then we ourselves are gods.

THE HURDY-GURDY MAN

Over beyond the village
stands a hurdy-gurdy man, *very poor.*
and with his numb fingers
he grinds as best he can.

Barefoot on the ice,
he moves to and fro,
and his little tray
is always empty.

Nobody cares to hear him,
nobody looks at him;
and the dogs snarl
around the old man.

And he lets everything go
as it will;
he grinds, and his hurdy-gurdy
is never silent.

Queer old man,
shall I go with you?
Will you grind out my songs
on your hurdy-gurdy?

---

f Music: "A medieval stringed instrument in the general shape of
a lute or viol in which the strings are put in vibration, not by a bow,
ut by a rotating rosined wheel, operated by a handle at the lower
nd of the body and turned by the right hand."

PYRKER, JOHANN LADISLAUS VON
FELSÖ-EÖR
1773–1847

DIE ALLMACHT

Gross ist Jehova, der Herr: denn Himmel und Erde verkünder
Seine Macht! Du hörst sie im brausenden Sturm', in des Wald
   stroms
Lautaufrauschendem Ruf', in des grünenden Waldes Gesäusel
Sieh'st sie in wogender Saaten Gold', in lieblicher Blumen
Glühendem Schmelz', im Glanz des stern'erhelleten Himmels.
Furchtbar tönt sie im Donnergeroll, und flammt in des Blitzes
Schnellhinzuckendem Flug; doch kündet das pochende Herz dir
Fühlbarer noch, Jehova's Macht, des ewigen Gottes.
Blickst du, flehend, empor, und hoff'st von ihm Huld und
   Erbarmen!

FRANZ PETER SCHUBERT, D. 852. In Schubert's many repetitions
the original form of the poem is quite lost. In the fifth line
stern'erhelleten Himmels is changed to *sternebesäeten Himmels.* In

REINICK, ROBERT
1805–1852

LIEBESTREU

"O versenk, o versenk dein Leid, mein Kind,
in die See, in die tiefe See!"—
Ein Stein wohl bleibt auf das Meeres Grund,
mein Leid kommt stets in die Höh'.

"Und die Lieb', die du im Herzen trägst,
brich sie ab, brich sie ab, mein Kind!"
Ob die Blum' auch stirbt, wenn man sie bricht:
treue Lieb' nicht so geschwind.—

Archbishop of Venice to whom some of Schubert's songs were dedicated. The subjects of his poems are largely religious. They include long narratives based on Biblical subjects.

OMNIPOTENCE

Great is Jehovah, the Lord, for heaven and earth proclaim
His power! You hear it in the raging storm, in the torrent's
loud gushing roar, in the rustling of the verdant wood;
you see it in the gold of waving grain, in the colorful riot
of lovely flowers, in the splendor of the star-lighted heaven.
Fearful it sounds in the roll of thunder, and flames
in the quick flash of lightning. Yet your beating heart
proclaims even more clearly to you the power of Jehovah,
    the eternal God.
You look up to heaven in supplication, and hope for grace
    and mercy.

---

the last line the final words are amended to *und hoffst auf Huld und Erbarmen.*

Painter and poet; his work in both fields is homely, folksy, and healthy. Reinick wrote fables and poems for children.

FAITHFUL LOVE

"O sink, o sink your sorrow, my child,
in the sea, in the deep sea!"
A stone will stay at the bottom of the sea;
my sorrow always comes up.

"And the love you bear in your heart,
pluck it out, pluck it out, my child!"
A flower will die when we pick it,
true love not so quickly.

"Und die Treu', und die Treu'!'s war nur ein Wort,
in den Wind damit hinaus!"—
O Mutter, und splittert der Fels auch im Sturm,
meine Treu', die hält ihn aus.

JOHANNES BRAHMS, Op. 3, no. 1. In the third line of the final
stanza the word *Sturm* is changed to *Wind*. Some ten other com-

RELLSTAB, LUDWIG
1799–1860

AUFENTHALT

Rauschender Strom,
Brausender Wald,
Starrender Fels
Mein Aufenthalt.

Wie sich die Welle
An Welle reiht,
Fliessen die Tränen
Mir ewig erneut.

Hoch in den Kronen
Wogend sich's regt,
So unaufhörlich
Mein Herze schlägt.

Und wie des Felsen
Uraltes Erz,
Ewig derselbe
Bleibet mein Schmerz.

Rauschender Strom,
Brausender Wald,
Starrender Fels
Mein Aufenthalt.

FRANZ PETER SCHUBERT (*Schwanengesang*, D. 957, no. 5). There is
also a setting by Heinrich Marschner (Op. 76, no. 4).

"And your vow—and your vow—it was only a word—
into the wind with it!"
O mother, though the rock be shattered in the storm,
my vow will withstand it.

---

posers include F. Hiller (Op. 100) and J. Schmid.

A music critic noted for his biting satire as well as a
dramatist and poet. Six of Schubert's last songs were to
Rellstab texts, and of these at least two are among his best-
known works.

MY HOME

Roaring torrent,
blustering forest,
towering rock,
this is my home.

As wave
follows wave,
my tears flow
ever renewed.

As high in their crests
surging they swell,
so ceaselessly
my heart beats.

And like the rock's
ageless ore,
ever the same
remains my grief.

Roaring torrent,
blustering forest,
towering rock,
this is my home.

STÄNDCHEN

Leise flehen meine Lieder
Durch die Nacht zu dir;
In den stillen Hain hernieder,
Liebchen, komm' zu mir!

Flüsternd schlanke Wipfel rauschen
In des Mondes Licht;
Des Verräters feindlich Lauschen
Fürchte, Holde, nicht.

Hörst die Nachtigallen schlagen?
Ach! sie flehen Dich,
Mit der Töne süssen Klagen
Flehen sie für mich.

Sie verstehn des Busens Sehnen,
Kennen Liebesschmerz,
Rühren mit den Silbertönen
Jedes weiche Herz.

Lass auch Dir die Brust bewegen,
Liebchen, höre mich!
Bebend harr' ich Dir entgegen!
Komm, beglücke mich!

FRANZ PETER SCHUBERT (*Schwanengesang*, D. 957, no. 4). There
are settings by C. Arnold (Op. 14, no. 4), R. Hertzberg (Op. 3, no. 2),
F. Lachner (Op. 49, no. 6), and R. Gritzner.

RÜCKERT, FRIEDRICH
1788–1866

DU MEINE SEELE

Du meine Seele, du mein Herz,
Du meine Wonne, du mein Schmerz,
Du meine Welt, in der ich lebe,
Mein Himmel du, darein ich schwebe,
O du mein Grab, in das hinab
Ich ewig meinen Kummer gab!

SERENADE

Softly pleading, my songs go
through the night to you;
in the quiet grove down here,
dearest, come to me!

Whispering tall treetops rustle
in the moonlight;
that treacherous ears may listen,
do not fear, my dear.

Do you hear the nightingales' song?
Ah! they implore you.
With the sweet complaint of their notes
they plead for me.

They understand the longing of my heart,
know the pain of love;
they touch with their silvery voices
every tender heart.

Let your heart, too, be moved—
dearest, hear me!
Trembling I await you!
Come and make me happy!

Professor of Oriental Literature at Erlangen and Privy
Counsellor for Friedrich Wilhelm IV at Berlin from 1841
to 1848. Published a volume of poems, including sonnets
against Napoleon, in 1814. His poetic output was influenced by his interest in the Orient. Because of its fine
lyric strain his poetry is peculiarly adapted to musical
setting, a fact recognized by many leading composers.

YOU MY SOUL

You my soul, you my heart,
you my joy, you my grief;
you my world in which I live,
my heaven you, into which I soar;
O you my grave in which
I bury forever my sorrows.

Du bist die Ruh, du bist der Frieden,
Du bist der Himmel mir beschieden,
Dass du mich liebst, macht mich mir wert,
Dein Blick hat mich vor mir verklärt,
Du hebst mich liebend über mich,
Mein guter Geist, mein bessres Ich!

ROBERT SCHUMANN, Op. 25, No. 1. This first song in the collection called *Myrten* is universally known by Schumann's title, *Widmung*. The poem is the fourth in Rückert's *Liebesfrühling*, and the poet did not give it a title. In the second line of the song, for reasons of musical phrasing, there has been a slight change: *Du meine Wonn', o du mein Schmerz*, and in the eighth line the sense has been

KEHR EIN BEI MIR!

Du bist die Ruh',
Der Friede mild,
Die Sehnsucht du,
Und was sie stillt.

Ich weihe dir
Voll Lust und Schmerz
Zur Wohnung hier
Mein Aug' und Herz.

Kehr ein bei mir
Und schliesse du
Still hinter dir
Die Pforten zu!

Treib andern Schmerz
Aus dieser Brust!
Voll sei dies Herz
Von deiner Lust.

Dies Augenzelt
Von deinem Glanz
Allein erhellt,
O füll es ganz!

FRANZ PETER SCHUBERT, D. 776. Titled *Du bist die Ruh'*. There are some twenty-five other settings.

You are rest, you are consolation;
you are heaven given to me;
that you love me makes me worthy in my own eyes;
Your glance transfigures me in my own sight;
you raise me lovingly above myself—
my guardian spirit, my better self.

---

changed by the alteration—*Du bist vom Himmel mir beschieden*
(You are given to me by heaven). The musical three-part form is
completed by a repetition of the first four lines, followed by the
last line of the poem.

There are about a dozen other settings of this text, notably those
by H. Marschner (Op. 106, no. 4) and H. Litolff (Op. 58, no. 1).

COME TO ME

You are tranquility,
gentle peace,
you are longing
and that which quiets it.

I dedicate to you,
full of joy and pain,
for dwelling here
my eyes and heart.

Come to me
and close
quietly behind you
the gates!

Drive other grief
from out this breast!
Let my heart be full
of your joy.

My vision
by your radiance
alone is brightened—
oh fill it wholly!

LACHEN UND WEINENS GRUND

Lachen und Weinen zu jeglicher Stunde
   Ruht bei der Lieb' auf so mancherlei Grunde.
   Morgens lacht' ich vor Lust;
   Und warum ich nun weine
   Bei des Abendes Scheine,
   Ist mir selb micht bewusst.

Weinen und Lachen zu jeglicher Stunde
   Ruht bei der Lieb' auf so mancherlei Grunde.
   Abends weint' ich vor Schmerz;
   Und warum du erwachen
   Kannst am Morgen mit Lachen,
   Muss ich dich fragen, o Herz.

FRANZ PETER SCHUBERT, D. 777. Titled *Lachen und Weinen*.

SALIS-SEEWIS, JOHANN GAUDENE, FREIHERR VON

1763–1834

DER JÜNGLING AN DER QUELLE

Leise, rieselnder Quell!
Ihr wallenden, flispernden Pappeln!
Euer Schlummergeräusch
Wecket die Liebe nur auf.
Linderung sucht ich bei euch,
Und sie zu vergessen, die Spröde, ach,
Und Blätter und Bach
Seufzen, Luise, dir nach.

FRANZ PETER SCHUBERT, D. 300. Singers often weaken this text by the substitution of the word *Geliebte* for *Luise* in the final line.

REASONS FOR LAUGHTER AND CRYING

Laughter and crying, at different hours
have such different reasons, when one is in love.
In the morning I laugh for joy;
and why do I cry now
in the evening light?
I myself don't know.

Crying and laughter, at different hours
have such different reasons, when one is in love,
In the evening I cried for grief;
then how can you wake up
laughing in the morning?—
I must ask you, my heart.

Swiss nature poet and friend of Matthison; writer of gentle
elegiac verse.

THE YOUTH TO THE SPRING

Quiet, purling spring!
And you, rustling, whispering poplars!
Your drowsy stirring
only awakens love.
I came to you for consolation,
and to forget my coy mistress, ah,
and the leaves and the brook
sigh, Louise, for you.

SCHACK, ADOLF FRIEDRICH, GRAF VON
1815–1894

STÄNDCHEN

Mach auf, mach auf! doch leise, mein Kind,
Um keinen vom Schlummer zu wecken!
Kaum murmelt der Bach, kaum zittert im Wind
Ein Blatt an den Büschen und Hecken;
Drum leise, mein Mädchen, dass nichts sich regt,
Nur leise die Hand auf die Klinke gelegt!

Mit Tritten, wie Tritte der Elfen so sacht,
Die über die Blumen hüpfen,
Flieg leicht hinaus in die Mondscheinnacht,
Zu mir in den Garten zu schlüpfen!
Rings schlummern die Blüten am rieselnden Bach
Und duften im Schlaf, nur die Liebe ist wach.

Sitz neider! Hier dämmert's geheimnisvoll
Under den Lindenbäumen.
Die Nachtigall uns zu Häupten soll
Von unseren Küssen träumen
Und die Rose, wenn sie am Morgen erwacht,
Hoch glüh'n von den Wonneschauern der Nacht.

RICHARD STRAUSS, Op. 17, no. 2. The second line of the second
stanza is rewritten thus: *Um über die Blumen zu hüpfen.* There
are settings of the poem by F. O. Dessoff (Op. 6, no. 3), P. Hartung

Better known as a critic of art and theater than as a poet, Schack nevertheless published works in various types of verse.

SERENADE

Open! Open! But softly, my child,
that you wake no one from sleep!
The brook hardly murmurs, the wind hardly stirs
a leaf on the bushes and lattice;
then softly, my dear, that nothing may move,
lay your hand lightly on the latch.

With footsteps as gentle as the steps of elves
that skip over the flowers,
fly lightly into the moonlit night
as you slip out to me in the garden!
Around us the flowers slumber by the rippling brook,
and exhale their fragrance in their sleep; only love is awake.

Sit down! Here dusk is falling mysteriously
under the linden trees.
The nightingale above our heads shall
dream of our kisses;
and the rose, when she wakes tomorrow,
shall bloom more sublimely after the rapture of the night.

(Op. 7, no. 3), H. Berger (Op. 5, no. 2), R. Kahn (Op. 12, no. 2), J. Schäffer (Op. 18, no. 6), R. Gritzner, and others.

SCHEFFEL, JOSEPH VICTOR VON
1826–1886

BITEROLF

(Im Lager vor Akkon 1190)

Kampfmüd und sonnverbrannt
Fern an der Heiden Strand,
Waldgrünes Thüringland,
Denk' ich an dich.
Mildklarer Sternenschein,
Du sollst mir Bote sein,
Geh, grüss' die Heimat mein
Weit über Meer!

Feinden von allerwärts
Trotzt meiner Waffen Erz;
Wider der Sehnsucht Schmerz
Schirmt mich kein Schild.
Doch wie das Herz auch klagt,
Ausharr' ich unverzagt:
Wer Gottes Fahrt gewagt,
Trägt still sein Kreuz.

[Drüben am Belusbach
Ist schon die Vorhut wach;
Heut noch klingt Speerestrach
Durch Kisens Flur.
Horch, wie die Hähne krähn!
Heut bleibt das Frühmal stehn,
Heut, werter Sarazen,
Haun wir uns satt!]

HUGO WOLF (*Lieder nach verschiedenen Dichtern*, no. 15). The
third stanza is not set. Other composers include Max Bruch (Op. 33,

One of the many nineteenth-century novelists strongly influenced by Sir Walter Scott, Scheffel achieved great popularity with his sentimental *Der Trompeter von Säckingen* (made into an opera by Nessler) and *Ekkehard*, the most popular of German historical novels. Also published poems and parodies. His work has a strain of humor and on occasion a certain nobility.

BITEROLF

(In camp before Acre, 1190)

Weary of battle and burned by the sun,
far away in the heathen land,
green wooded Thuringia,
I think of you.
Mild clear starlight,
you shall be my messenger,
go, greet my homeland,
far over the sea.

On every side
my weapon's metal defies the enemy:
against the grief of longing
no shield protects me.
Yet even though my heart complains,
I endure it undismayed:
he who undertakes God's journey
silently bears his cross.

[Over there by Belus brook
the vanguard is already awake;
again today the clash of spears
resounds through Kishon's fields.
Hark! how the cocks crow!
Today breakfast shall wait!
Today, worthy Saracens,
we shall hew our fill!]

no. 1), J. Rheinberger (Op. 41, no. 1), C. Obermeyer, and W. Prantner.

SCHILLER, FRIEDRICH VON
1759–1805

GRUPPE AUS DEM TARTARUS

Horch—wie Murmeln des empörten Meeres,
  Wie durch hohler Felsen Becken weint ein Bach,
Stöhnt dort dumpfigtief ein schweres, leeres
  Qualerpresstes Ach!

Schmerz verzerret
Ihr Gesicht; Verzweiflung sperret
  Ihren Rachen fluchend auf.
Hohl sind ihre Augen, ihre Blicke
  Spähen bang nach des Cocytus Brücke,
  Folgen tränend seinem Trauerlauf,

Fragen sich einander ängstlichleise,
  Ob noch nicht Vollendung sei?—
Ewigkeit schwingt über ihnen Kreise,
  Bricht die Sense des Saturns entzwei.

FRANZ PETER SCHUBERT, D. 583.

SCHMIDT, HANS
1854–1923

GEREIMTE SAPPHISCHE ODE

Rosen brach ich nachts mir am dunklen Hage;
Süsser hauchten Duft sie als je am Tage,
Doch verstreuten reich die bewegten Äste
  Tau, der mich nässte.

Friend and chief rival of Goethe as the greatest German writer of his time, Schiller is notable for his historical dramas and philosophical works rather than for his lyric poetry, a fact attested by the comparative scarcity of songs to his texts.

GROUP IN TARTARUS

Hark—like the murmur of the swelling sea,
as through its hollowed rocky basin weeps a brook,
there sounds damp and deep a heavy, empty,
tormented cry!

Pain distorts
their faces; despair sets
their cursing jaws agape.
Empty are their eyes, their glances
peer fearfully toward the bridge of Cocytus,
weeping they follow its doleful course.

They ask each other anxiously and softly
whether there is never an end?—
Eternity swings circles over them,
breaks the scythe of Saturn in two.

Composer, pianist, teacher, and critic, Schmidt was for a time tutor in the house of Joseph Joachim. As a poet he is remembered by Brahms's setting of his *Sapphische Ode*. Brahms expressed great enthusiasm for the poems Schmidt sent him.

SAPPHIC ODE IN RHYME

Roses I gathered at night from the dark hedge
exhaled a sweeter fragrance than ever by day;
yet the stirring branches showered heavily
moist dew upon me.

Auch der Küsse Duft mich wie nie berückte,
Die ich nachts vom Strauch deiner Lippen pflückte;
Doch auch dir, bewegt im Gemüt gleich jenen,
  Tauten die Tränen!

JOHANNES BRAHMS, Op. 94, no. 4. Titled *Sapphische Ode*.

SCHOBER, FRANZ VON
1798–1883

AN DIE MUSIK

Du holde Kunst, in wieviel grauen Stunden,
Wo mich des Lebens wilder Kreis umstrickt,
Hast du mein Herz zu warmer Lieb' entzunden,
Hast mich in eine bessre Welt entrückt!

Oft hat ein Seufzer, deiner Harf' entflossen,
Ein süsser, heiliger Akkord von dir,
Den Himmel bessrer Zeiten mir erschlossen,
Du holde Kunst, ich danke dir dafür!

FRANZ PETER SCHUBERT, D. 547. This poem by Schubert's friend
and so intimately associated with the name of the composer, was
not included in Schober's collected poems when they were published

SCHUBART, CHRISTIAN DANIEL
1739–1791

DIE FORELLE

In einem Bächlein helle,
  Da schoss in froher Eil'
Die launige Forelle
  Vorüber wie ein Pfeil.
Ich stand an dem Gestade,
  Und sah in süsser Ruh'
Des muntern Fisches Bade
  Im klaren Bächlein zu.

Nor has the fragrance of kisses ever so moved me
as when I gathered them from your lips at night;
yet on you too, your soul stirred like the branches,
dropped the dew of tears.

An intimate friend of Schubert who studied law, but in his
long life tried his hand at many things—poetry, landscape
painting, lithography. For a time he was secretary to Franz
Liszt.

TO MUSIC

O sublime art, in how many gray hours,
when the wild tumult of life ensnared me,
have you kindled my heart to warm love,
have you carried me away to a better world!

Often a sigh, escaped from your harp,
a sweet, solemn chord from you,
has opened the heaven of better times for me—
o sublime art, I thank you for it!

---

in 1840 and 1855. At least three other musicians have set it: E.
Kreuz (Op. 2, no. 1), F. Siebert (Op. 10), and O. Starcke.

A musician and revolutionary, imprisoned for ten years on
account of his political opinions. His poetry is remembered in connection with Schubert's music.

THE TROUT

In a clear brooklet,
with happy haste,
a playful trout
darted about like an arrow.
I stood on the bank
and contentedly watched
the merry fish bathe
in the clear brooklet.

Ein Fischer mit der Rute
　　Wohl an dem Ufer stand,
Und sah's mit kaltem Blute,
　　Wie sich das Fischlein wand.
So lang dem Wasser helle,
　　So dacht' ich, nicht gebricht,
So fängt er die Forelle
　　Mit seiner Angel nicht.

Doch plötzlich ward dem Diebe
　　Die Zeit zu lang. Er macht
Das Bächlein tückisch trübe,
　　Und eh' ich es gedacht;—
So zuckte seine Rute,
　　Das Fischlein zappelt dran,
Und ich mit regem Blute
　　Sah die Betrogne an.

[Die ihr an goldner Quelle
　　Der sichern Jugend weilt,
Denkt doch an die Forelle;
　　Seht ihr Gefahr, so eilt!
Meist fehlt ihr nur aus Mangel
　　Der Klugheit. Mädchen seht
Verführer mit der Angel!—
　　Sonst blutet ihr zu spät.]

Franz Peter Schubert, D. 550. In the third line *launige* (playful)
is changed to *launische* (moody); in the seventh line *Fisches Bade*

A fisherman with his rod
stood on the bank
and looked on heartlessly
as the fish wriggled about.
So long as the clear water,
I thought, is not disturbed,
he will not catch the trout
with his hook.

But suddenly the thief
got tired of waiting. He
slyly muddied up the brook,
and before I realized it
he jerked his rod
and the fish struggled on the line,
and I, with my pulse beating high,
watched the betrayed one.

[You who tarry at the golden spring
of carefree youth,
remember the trout!
See your danger and hurry!
Mostly you go wrong only from lack
of caution. Girls, see
the seducers with their hooks!—
Otherwise you pay for it later!]

---

becomes *Fischleins Bade*. In the first line of the third stanza
plötzlich is changed to *endlich*. The final stanza is omitted.

SCHULZE, ERNST KONRAD FRIEDRICH
1789–1817

IM FRÜHLING

Still sitz' ich an des Hügels Hang,
  Der Himmel ist so klar,
Das Lüftchen spielt im grünen Tal,
Wo ich beim ersten Frühlingsstrahl
  Einst, ach, so glücklich war;
Wo ich an ihrer Seite ging
  So traulich und so nah,
Und tief im dunklen Felsenquell
Den schönen Himmel blau und hell,
  Und sie im Himmel sah.

Sieh', wie der bunte Frühling schon
  Aus Knosp' und Blüte blickt!
Nicht alle Blüten sind mir gleich,
Am liebsten pflückt' ich von dem Zweig,
  Von welchem sie gepflückt!
Denn alles ist wie damals noch,
  Die Blumen, das Gefild;
Die Sonne scheint nicht minder hell,
Nicht minder freundlich schwimmt im Quell
  Das blaue Himmelsbild.

Es wandeln nur sich Will' und Wahn,
  Es wechseln Lust und Streit;
Vorüber flieht der Liebe Glück,
Und nur die Liebe bleibt zurück,
  Die Lieb' und ach, das Leid!
O wär' ich doch ein Vöglein nur
  Dort an dem Wiesenhang,
Dann blieb' ich auf den Zweigen hier,
Und säng' ein süsses Lied von ihr
  Den ganzen Sommer lang.

FRANZ PETER SCHUBERT, D. 882.

Author of *Poetisches Tagebuch*, from which Schubert set
several poems.

IN SPRING

Quietly I sit on the side of the hill;
the sky is so clear;
the breeze plays in the green valley
where I in the first light of spring
once was so happy;
where I walked at her side,
so intimate and so near,
and deep in the dark rock-spring
saw the beautiful heaven, blue and bright,
and saw her in that heaven.

See how the colorful spring already
looks out of the buds and blossoms!
Not all the flowers are the same to me,
I like best to pick from the branch
from which she picked!
For all is as it used to be,
the flowers, the fields;
the sun shines no less brightly,
no less cheerfully floats in the spring
the blue image of heaven.

Only the will and the fancy change,
pleasure turns to strife;
the happiness of love flees away,
and only love remains behind—
love and alas, sorrow!
Oh, if I were only a bird
there on the hillside meadow,
then I would stay in the branches here
and sing a sweet song about her
all summer long.

SCHUMANN, FELIX

MEINE LIEBE IST GRÜN

Meine Liebe ist grün wie der Fliederbusch,
Und mein Lieb ist schön wie die Sonne;
Die glänzt wohl herab auf den Fliederbusch
Und füllt ihn mit Duft und mit Wonne.

Meine Seele hat Schwingen der Nachtigall
Und wiegt sich in blühendem Flieder,
Und jauchzet und singet vom Duft berauscht
Viel liebestrunkene Lieder.

JOHANNES BRAHMS, Op. 63, no. 5.

SEIDL, JOHANN GABRIEL
1804–1875

DER WANDERER AN DEN MOND

Auf Erden—ich, am Himmel—du,
Wir wandern beide rüstig zu,
Ich ernst und trüb, du hell und rein,
Was mag der Unterschied wohl sein?

Ich wandre fremd von Land zu Land
So heimatlos, so unbekannt,
Bergauf, bergab, waldein, waldaus,
Doch bin ich nirgend—ach!—zu Haus!

Du aber wanderst auf und ab
Aus Ostens Wieg' in Westens Grab,
Wallst länderein und länderaus,
Und bist doch, wo du bist, zu Haus!

Der Himmel, endlos ausgespannt,
Ist dein geliebtes Heimatland;—
O glücklich, wer, wohin er geht,
Doch auf der Heimat Boden steht!—

FRANZ PETER SCHUBERT, D. 870. The first line is rearranged, thus:
Ich auf der Erd', am Himmel du; in the third line *du hell und rein*

The eighteen-year-old son of Robert and Clara Schumann provided the texts for three songs of Brahms, the poet's god-father. They were never published as poems.

MY LOVE IS GREEN

My love is green like the lilac bush,
and my love is beautiful as the sun
that shines down upon the bush
and fills it with fragrance and rapture.

My soul has wings like the nightingale
and moves about among the lilac blossoms;
and drunk with the fragrance, it rejoices and sings
many love-happy songs.

Referred to as a "patriotic poet," also a numismatist and translator of Calderón.

THE WANDERER TO THE MOON

I upon earth, you in heaven,
we both go our vigorous ways;
I serious and troubled, you serene and clear—
what can be the difference?

I wander, a stranger, from land to land,
so homeless, so unknown.
Up mountains, down mountains, in and out of the forest,
Yet I am never, alas, at home!

But you go your way up and down,
from the cradle of the East to the grave of the West;
you travel from one country to another,
and wherever you are, you are at home!

The boundless heaven
is your beloved homeland;
Oh happy is he who, wherever he goes,
is always at home!

---

becomes *du mild und rein.* The second line of the third stanza is curiously changed to *Aus Westens Wieg' in Ostens Grab.*

STOLBERG, FRIEDRICH LEOPOLD, GRAF ZU
1750–1819

LIED AUF DEM WASSER ZU SINGEN

Mitten im Schimmer der spiegelnden Wellen
Gleitet, wie Schwäne, der wankende Kahn;
Ach, auf der Freude sanftschimmernden Wellen
Gleitet die Seele dahin wie der Kahn;
Denn von dem Himmel herab auf die Wellen
Tanzet das Abendrot rund um den Kahn.

Über den Wipfeln des westlichen Haines,
Winket uns freundlich der rötliche Schein;
Unter den Zweigen des östlichen Haines
Säuselt der Kalmus in rötlichen Schein;
Freude des Himmels und Ruhe des Haines
Atmet die Seel' im errötenden Schein.

Ach, es entschwindet mit tauigem Flügel
Mir auf den wiegenden Wellen die Zeit.
Morgen entschwinde mit schimmerndem Flügel
Wieder wie gestern und heute die Zeit,
Bis ich auf höherem strahlenden Flügel
Selber entschwinde der wechselnden Zeit.

FRANZ PETER SCHUBERT, D. 774. Titled *Auf dem Wasser zu singen.*
There are also settings by J. W. Kalliwoda (Op. 192), J. F. Kittl (Op.
4, no. 3), and H. Nürnberg (Op. 2, no. 2).

Brother of Christian Stolberg, also a poet, with whom he closely collaborated. Made translations of Homer, Plato, and Aeschylus, and with his brother wrote a Greek tragedy. In later life turned to the church.

A SONG TO BE SUNG ON THE WATER

Amid the shimmer of the mirroring waves,
glides, like swans, the rocking boat;
ah, on the soft shimmering waves of joy
the soul glides away like the boat;
for down from the heavens upon the waves
the evening light dances around the boat.

Over the treetops of the grove to the west
the rosy gleam beckons us on;
under the branches of the grove to the east
the iris rustles in the rosy light.
Happiness of the heavens and quiet of the groves
the soul breathes in the blushing light.

Ah, time passes with dewy wings
for me on the rocking waves.
So tomorrow may time fade with its shimmering wings
again, as yesterday and today,
until I, ascending on higher shining wings,
myself shall yield to the changing time.

UHLAND, JOHANN LUDWIG
1787–1862

DER SCHMIED

Ich hör' meinen Schatz,
Den Hammer er schwinget,
Das rauschet, das klinget,
Das dringt in die Weite
Wie Glockengeläute
Durch Gassen und Platz.

Am schwarzen Kamin
Da sitzet mein Lieber,
Doch geh' ich vorüber,
Die Bälge dann sausen,
Die Flammen aufbrausen
Und lodern um ihn.

JOHANNES BRAHMS, Op. 19, no. 4. In strong contrast to the Brahms song is that of Adolf Jensen (Op. 24, no. 6). Others include Schumann (Op. 145a, no. 11), J. Dessauer (Op. 14, no. 5), L. Héritte-

SONNTAG

So hab' ich doch die ganze Woche
Mein feines Liebchen nicht gesehn,
Ich sah es an einem Sonntag
Wohl vor der Türe stehn:
    Das tausendschöne Jungfräulein,
    Das tausendschöne Herzelein,
    Wollte Gott, ich wär' heute bei ihr.

Poet, playwright, essayist, and folklorist; trained in the law, but after a period of practice was appointed Professor of German Literature at the University of Tübingen. A leading scholar in the field of mythology and folk song, he had great influence. His original ballads and songs are well-known.

THE BLACKSMITH

I hear my lover:
he is swinging his hammer—
it roars and resounds,
sounding out
like bells
through the alleys and the square.

By the black chimney
there my lover is sitting—
but if I go past
the bellows begin to hum,
the flames leap up
and blaze around him.

Viardot (Op. 8, no. 5), C. Kreutzer (Op. 23, no. 4), R. Becker, A. Kleffel (Op. 50, no. 3), W. Platz, and T. Spiering.

SUNDAY

All week long
I haven't seen my sweetheart.
I saw her on Sunday
standing before the door:
The thousand-times beautiful girl,
the thousand-times-beautiful sweetheart,
would to God I were with her now.

So will mir doch die ganze Woche
Das Lachen nicht vergehn,
Ich sah' es an einem Sonntag
Wohl in die Kirche gehn:
   Das tausendschöne Jungfräulein,
   Das tausendschöne Herzelein,
   Wollte Gott, ich wär' heute bei ihr!

JOHANNES BRAHMS, Op. 47, no. 3. There are other settings by

WENZIG, JOSEF
1807–1876

DER GANG ZUM LIEBCHEN

Es glänzt der Mond nieder,
Ich sollte doch wieder
Zu meinem Liebchen,
Wie mag es ihr gehn?

Ach weh, sie verzaget,
Und klaget und klaget,
Dass sie mich nimmer
Im Leben wird sehn.

Es ging der Mond unter,
Ich eilte doch munter,
Und eilte, dass keiner
Mein Liebchen entführt.

Ihr Täubchen, o girret,
Ihr Lüftchen, o schwirret,
Dass keiner mein Liebchen,
Mein Liebchen entführt.

JOHANNES BRAHMS, Op. 48, no. 1. The text is a translation of a Bohemian folk song.

All week long
I cannot keep from laughing.
I saw her on Sunday
going to church:
The thousand-times-beautiful girl,
the thousand-times-beautiful sweetheart,
would to God I were with her now.

G. Hölzel (Op. 226), E. Meyer-Helmund (Op. 61, no. 1), R. Gritzner,
and Max Reger.

Czech teacher and translator of Slavic folk songs; one of
the founders of the national movement in Bohemia.

GOING TO MY SWEETHEART

The moon is shining down,
I should go again
to my sweetheart
to see how it is with her.

Alas! she is despondent,
she complains and complains
that she will never
see me in her life.

The moon went down,
I hurried more briskly,
and hurried so that no one
should steal my love away.

Coo, ye doves,
and whistle, ye breezes,
so that no one
may steal my love away.

VON EWIGER LIEBE

Dunkel, wie dunkel in Wald und in Feld!
Abend schon ist es, nun schweiget die Welt.
Nirgend noch Licht und nirgend noch Rauch,
Ja, und die Lerche sie schweiget nun auch.
Kommt aus dem Dorfe der Bursche heraus,
Giebt das Geleit der Geliebten nach Haus,
Führt sie am Weidengebüsche vorbei,
Redet so viel und so mancherlei.

"Leidest du Schmach und betrübest du dich,
Leidest du Schmach von Andern um mich,
Werde die Liebe getrennt so geschwind,
Schnell wie wir früher vereiniget sind.
Scheide mit Regen und scheide mit Wind,
Schnell wie wir früher vereiniget sind."

Spricht das Mägdelein, Mägdelein spricht:
"Unsere Liebe, sie trennet sich nicht!
Fest ist der Stahl und das Eisen gar sehr,
Unsere Liebe ist fester noch mehr.
Eisen und Stahl, man schmiedet sie um,
Unsere Liebe, wer wandelt sie um?
Eisen und Stahl, sie können zergehn,
Unsere Liebe muss ewig bestehn!"

JOHANNES BRAHMS, Op. 43, no. 1.

ZUCCALMAGLIO, ANTON WILHELM
FLORENTIN VON
1803–1869

VERGEBLICHES STÄNDCHEN

Guten Abend, mein Schatz,
Guten Abend, mein Kind!
Ich komm' aus Lieb' zu dir,
Ach, mach' mir auf die Tür!
Mach' mir auf die Tür!

OF ETERNAL LOVE

Dark, how dark in the woods and the fields!
It is evening already; now the world is quiet.
Nowhere a light and nowhere smoke,
yes, even the lark is silent now.
Out of the village comes the youth,
bringing his sweetheart home.
He leads her by the willow thickets,
talking a great deal and about so many things.

"If you are ashamed and troubled,
ashamed of me before the others,
let love be broken off as suddenly,
as quickly as we first came together.
Let us part in the rain, let us part in the wind,
as quickly as we first came together."

The girl speaks:
"Our love shall not be parted!
Iron is strong and steel very much so,
our love is even stronger.
Iron and steel are shaped in the forge,
but who shall change our love?
Iron and steel may be melted,
but our love shall endure forever!"

Folklorist who contributed articles to Robert Schumann's
Zeitschrift für Musik and published a famous collection of
folk songs. Wrote under the pseudonyms W. von Wald-
brühl and Dorfküster Wedel.

A SERENADE IN VAIN

Good evening, my dear,
good evening, my child!
I come out of love for you,
ah, open the door for me!
Open the door for me!

"Meine Tür ist verschlossen,
Ich lass dich nicht ein;
Mutter die rät' mir klug,
Wär'st du herein mit Fug,
Wär's mit mir vorbei!"

So kalt ist die Nacht,
So eisig der Wind,
Dass mir das Herz erfriert,
Mein' Lieb' erlöschen wird;
Öffne mir, mein Kind!

"Löschet dein Lieb',
Lass sie löschen nur!
Löschet sie immer zu,
Geh' heim zu Bett zur Ruh',
Gute Nacht, mein Knab'!"

JOHANNES BRAHMS, Op. 84, no. 4.

"My door is locked,
I will not let you in.
Mother warned me
that if I let you in willingly
all would be over with me!"

The night is so cold,
the wind is so icy,
that my heart is freezing.
My love will be extinguished;
open up for me, child!

"If your love is extinguished,
just let it go out!
Just keep on extinguishing it;
go home to bed, to rest!
Good night, my boy!"

FRENCH SONGS

BANVILLE, THÉODORE-FAULLAIN DE

1823–1891

NUIT D'ÉTOILES

Nuit d'étoiles,
Sous tes voiles,
Sous ta brise et tes parfums,
Triste lyre
Qui soupire,
Je rêve aux amours défunts.

La sereine Mélancholie
Vient éclore au fond de mon cœur,
Et j'entends l'âme de ma mie
Tressaillir dans le bois rêveur.

Nuit d'étoiles,
Sous tes voiles,
Sous ta brise et tes parfums,
Triste lyre
Qui soupire,
Je rêve aux amours défunts.

Dans les ombres de la feuillée,
Quand tout bas je soupire seul,
Tu reviens, pauvre âme éveillée,
Toute blanche dans ton linceul.

Nuit d'étoiles,
Sous tes voiles,
Sous ta brise et tes parfums,
Triste lyre
Qui soupire,
Je rêve aux amours défunts.

Je revois à notre fontaine
Tes regards bleus comme les cieux;
Cette rose, c'est ton haleine,
Et ces étoiles sont tes yeux.

Poet, playwright, and novelist; wrote some twenty volumes of verse and was regarded with Leconte de Lisle as a leader of the younger poets of his day. He was a classicist by inclination, and the serene quality of his work is both its strength and its weakness.

STARRY NIGHT

Starry night,
beneath your veils,
in your breeze and your fragrance,
sad lyre
that sighs,
I dream of the loves that are dead.

Serene melancholy
arises in the depths of my heart,
and I hear the soul of my beloved
starting to life in the dreamy forest.

Starry night,
beneath your veils,
in your breeze and your fragrance,
sad lyre
that sighs,
I dream of the loves that are dead.

In the shade of the foliage,
when softly I sigh to myself,
you return, poor awakened soul,
all white in your shroud.

Starry night,
beneath your veils,
in your breeze and your fragrance,
sad lyre
that sighs,
I dream of the loves that are dead.

I see again at our fountain
your eyes blue as the skies;
that rose is your breath
and those stars are your eyes.

Nuit d'étoiles,
Sous tes voiles,
Sous ta brise et tes parfums,
Triste lyre
Qui soupire,
Je rêve aux amours défunts.

CLAUDE DEBUSSY. Debussy set the refrain stanza, the first stanza, the refrain, the third stanza, and the refrain once more. Charles-Marie Widor, in his setting, used all but the last stanza and refrain. Curiously, we find this poem in Banville's *Poésies: Les stalactites*

BAUDELAIRE, PIERRE CHARLES
1821–1867

L'INVITATION AU VOYAGE

Mon enfant, ma sœur,
Songe à la douceur
D'aller là-bas vivre ensemble!
Aimer à loisir,
Aimer et mourir
Au pays qui te ressemble!
Les soleils mouillés
De ces ciels brouillés
Pour mon esprit ont les charmes
Si mystérieux
De tes traîtres yeux,
Brillant à travers leurs larmes.

Là, tout n'est qu'ordre et beauté,
Luxe, calme et volupté.

Starry night,
beneath your veils,
in your breeze and your fragrance,
sad lyre
that sighs,
I dream of the loves that are dead.

(1843–1872), Paris: Alphonse Lemerre, 1873, with the title *La dernière pensée de Weber* (*Weber's last thought*) and prefaced with a paragraph attributed to Hoffmann (see Appendix).

The first of the French *décadents,* admirer and translator of Edgar Allan Poe. His uninhibited and eccentric life and his predilection for mystic and ritualistic religion may to some extent account for the exalted and sensual qualities of his intensely personal poetry. His *Fleurs de mal,* when published in 1857, precipitated a lawsuit because of its alleged immorality.

INVITATION TO A JOURNEY

My child, my sister,
dream of the delight
of going away and living together!
Of loving at leisure,
of loving and dying
in the land that is like you!
The watery suns
of these murky skies
hold for my spirit the charms
so mysterious
of your traitrous eyes
shining through their tears.

There all is order and beauty,
splendor, calm, and delight.

[Des meubles luisants,
Polis par les ans,
Décoreraient notre chambre;
Les plus rares fleurs
Mêlant leurs odeurs
Aux vagues senteurs de l'ambre.
Les riches plafonds,
Les miroirs profonds,
La splendeur orientale,
Tout y parlerait
À l'âme en secret
Sa douce langue natale.

Là, tout n'est qu'ordre et beauté,
Luxe, calme et volupté.]

Vois sur ces canaux
Dormir ces vaisseaux
Dont l'humeur est vagabonde;
C'est pour assouvir
Ton moindre désir
Qu'ils viennent du bout du monde.
—Les soleils couchants
Revêtent les champs,
Les canaux, la ville entière,
D'hyacinthe et d'or;
Le mond s'endort;
Dans une chaude lumière.

Là, tout n'est qu'ordre et beauté,
Luxe, calme et volupté.

HENRI DUPARC. The second stanza is omitted.

LA VIE ANTÉRIEURE

J'ai longtemps habité sous de vastes portiques
Que les soleils marins teignaient de mille feux,
Et que leurs grands piliers, droits et majestueux,
Rendaient pareils, le soir, aux grottes basaltiques.

Les houles, en roulant les images des cieux,
Mêlaient d'une façon solennelle et mystique
Les tout-puissants accords de leur riche musique
Aux couleurs du couchant reflété par mes yeux.

[Shining furniture,
polished by the years,
would adorn our chamber;
the rarest flowers
would mingle their odors
with the subtle scents of amber.
The sumptuous ceilings,
the deep-reflecting mirrors,
the oriental splendor,
all would speak
to the soul in secret
in its sweet native tongue.

There all is order and beauty,
splendor, calm, and delight.]

See on the canals
the ships are asleep
whose spirit is vagrant.
It is to satisfy
your slightest desire
that they come from the ends of the earth.
The sinking suns
color the fields,
the canals, the entire town
with hyacinth and gold;
the world is asleep
in a warm light.

There all is order and beauty,
splendor, calm, and delight.

THE FORMER LIFE

I long dwelt among vast porticos,
that the sun of the sea set ablaze with a thousand fires,
and whose great pillars, straight and majestic,
made them seem in the evening like grottos of basalt.

The waves, tossing their reflection of the sky,
mingled solemnly and majestically
the powerful harmonies of their rich music
with the colors of the sunset reflected in my eyes.

C'est là que j'ai vécu dans les voluptés calmes,
Au milieu de l'azur, des vagues, des splendeurs
Et des esclaves nus, tout imprégnés d'odeurs,

Qui me rafraîchissaient le front avec des palmes,
Et dont l'unique soin était d'approfondir
Le secret douloureux qui me faisait languir.

HENRI DUPARC.

BONNIÈRES, ROBERT DE

1850–1905

LE MANOIR DE ROSEMONDE

De sa dent soudaine et vorace
Comme un chien l'amour m'a mordu . . .
En suivant mon sang répandu,
Va' tu pourras suivre ma trace . . .
Prends un cheval de bonne race,
Pars, et suis mon chemin ardu,
Fondrière ou sentier perdu,
Si la course ne te harasse!
En passant par où j'ai passé,
Tu verras que seul et blessé
J'ai parcouru ce triste monde.
Et qu'ainsi je m'en fus mourir
Bien loin, bien loin, sans découvrir
Le bleu manoir de Rosemonde.

HENRI DUPARC.

It is there that I lived amid calm delights,
surrounded by the azure sky, waves, splendors,
and naked slaves, drenched in perfumes,

who fanned my brow with palms,
and whose one care it was to fathom
the doleful secret that caused me to languish.

Educated for a diplomatic career, fought in the war of
1870 as a volunteer. Wrote political articles for *Figaro*, a
novel on Jewish society in relation to the aristocracy, an
account of travels in India, and with Jules Préval the
libretto for Vincent d'Indy's opéra-comique *Attendez-moi
sous l'orme.*

THE MANSION OF ROSAMONDE

With sudden and voracious tooth,
like a dog love has bitten me . . .
Following the blood that I have spilled,
go, you can trace my way . . .
Take a thoroughbred horse,
set out, and follow my arduous course,
by quagmire or hidden path,
if the chase does not weary you!
Passing where I have passed,
you will see that alone and wounded
I have crossed this sad world.
And that thus I have come to die,
far away, far away, without finding
the blue mansion of Rosamonde.

BOURGET, PAUL-CHARLES-JOSEPH

1852–1935

BEAU SOIR

Lorsque au soleil couchant les rivières sont roses
Et qu'un tiède frisson court sur les champs de blé,
Un conseil d'être heureux semble sortir des choses
    Et monter vers le cœur troublé.

Un conseil de goûter le charme d'être au monde
Cependant qu'on est jeune et que le soir est beau,
Car nous nous en allons, comme s'en va cette onde:
    Elle à la mer,—nous au tombeau!

CLAUDE DEBUSSY (1887).

ROMANCE

L'âme évaporée et souffrante,
L'âme douce, l'âme odorante
Des lys divins que j'ai cueillis
Dans le jardin de ta pensée,
Où donc les vents l'ont-ils chassée,
Cette âme adorable des lys?

N'est-il plus un parfum qui reste
De la suavité céleste
Des jours où tu m'enveloppais
D'une vapeur surnaturelle,
Faite d'espoir, d'amour fidèle,
De béatitude et de paix? . . .

CLAUDE DEBUSSY (1887).

Though primarily an outstanding critic and writer of social and psychological novels with a strong moralistic strain, Bourget was successful in many branches of literature. He was noted for his keen mind and unusual insight into human character.

BEAUTIFUL EVENING

When at sunset the rivers are rosy,
and a warm ripple crosses the fields of wheat,
a suggestion to be happy seems to arise from these things,
and enter into the troubled heart.

A suggestion to savor the charm of being in the world
while one is young and the evening is beautiful;
for we are moving on, even as that wave moves:
it to the sea, we to the tomb.

ROMANCE

The vanished and suffering essence,
the sweet pungent essence
of heavenly lilies that I have gathered
in the garden of your thought—
where have the winds driven it,
that adorable essence of lilies?

Is there no longer a lingering scent
of the celestial sweetness
of days when you enveloped me
in an unearthly mist,
made of hope, of faithful love,
of blessedness and of peace? ...

BUSSINE, ROMAIN
1830–1899

Dans un sommeil que charmait ton image
Je rêvais le bonheur ardent mirage,
Tes yeux étaient plus doux, ta voix pure et sonore,
Tu rayonnais comme un ciel éclairé par l'aurore;
Tu m'appelais, et je quittais la terre
Pour m'enfuir avec toi vers la lumière,
Les cieux pour nous entr'ouvraient leurs nues,
Splendeurs inconnues, lueurs divines entrevues,
Hélas! Hélas! triste réveil des songes
Je t'appelle, ô nuit, rends-moi tes mensonges,
Reviens, reviens radieuse,
Reviens, ô nuit mystérieuse!

GABRIEL FAURÉ, Op. 7, no. 1.

CAZALIS, HENRI (JEAN LAHOR)
1840–1909

CHANSON TRISTE

Dans ton cœur dort un clair de lune,
　　Un doux clair de lune d'été.
Et pour fuir la vie importune
　　Je me noierai dans ta clarté.

J'oublierai les douleurs passées,
　　Mon amour, quand tu berceras
Mon triste cœur et mes pensées
　　Dans le calme aimant de tes bras.

Trained as a singer under García and Moreau-Santi, Bussine was considered promising but did not pursue his career. His brother, Prosper-Alphonse Bussine, became a well-known vocalist; Romain taught at the Conservatoire and produced some poetry.

AFTER A DREAM

In sleep charmed by your image,
I dreamed the glowing mirage of happiness;
your eyes were more sweet, your voice pure and rich;
you shone like a sky lighted by the dawn.
You called to me, and I left the earth,
to fly with you toward the light.
The skies half-opened their clouds for us,
unknown splendours, divine lights only glimpsed.
Alas! alas! Sad awakening from dreams;
I call to you, o night, give me back your illusions!
Return, return in radiance,
return, o mysterious night!

First grouped with the *parnassiens*, he was dubbed the "*hindou du Parnasse contemporain*" because of his Orientalism. His later poetry, written under the pseudonym of Jean Lahor, has been called symbolist-pessimist.

SORROWFUL SONG

In your heart there sleeps a moonlight,
a sweet summer moonlight.
And to escape wearisome life
I shall drown myself in your limpidity.

I shall forget my past woes,
my love, when you lull
my sad heart and my thoughts
in the loving calm of your arms.

> Tu prendras ma tête malade
> Oh! quelquefois sur tes genoux,
> Et lui diras une ballade
> Qui semblera parler de nous,
>
> Et dans tes yeux pleins de tristesses
> Dans tes yeux alors je boirai
> Tant de baisers et de tendresses
> Que peut-être je guérirai . . .

HENRI DUPARC.

CORNEILLE, PIERRE
1606–1684

PSYCHÉ

[*Psyché:* Des tendresses du sang peut-on être jaloux?]

> *L'Amour:* Je le suis, ma Psyché, de toute la nature:
> Les rayons du soleil vous baisent trop souvent;
> Vos cheveux souffrent trop les caresses du vent:
> Dès qu'il les flatte, j'en murmure;
> L'air même que vous respirez
> Avec trop de plaisir passe par votre bouche;
> Votre habit de trop près vous touche;
> Et sitôt que vous soupirez,
> Je ne sais quoi qui m'effarouche
> Craint parmi vos soupirs des soupirs égarés . . .

ÉMILE PALADILHE. The text is from Corneille's drama *Psyché,* Act 3, scene 3. The song begins *Je suis jaloux, Psyché, de toute la*

You will take my aching head
oh, sometimes upon your knees,
and recite to it a ballad
which will seem to speak of us.

And in your eyes, full of sadness,
in your eyes, then, I shall drink
so many kisses and caresses
that perhaps I shall be healed ...

Educated in the law, this most famous of French dramatists
had various official posts during his lifetime. His first play
was written in 1629, but it was an elegy composed in honor
of Cardinal Richelieu that brought him to the attention of
that dignitary and, through him, to fame. *Le Cid* has been
called the "most epoch-making play in all literature."
Corneille favored noble subjects involving honor, patriot-
ism, duty, and so on.

PSYCHE

[*Psyche:* Can one be jealous of one's own kin?]

L'Amour: I am jealous, Psyche, of all nature:
   the rays of the sun kiss you too often;
   your hair allows the wind too many caresses—
   when it strokes your tresses I sulk.
   The very air you breathe
   takes too much pleasure in passing your lips;
   your garments touch you too closely.
   And whenever you sigh,
   I do not know what terror fills me,
   fear, lest from among your sighs some may go astray.

---

nature. The fourth line begins *Quand il les flatte.*

GAUTIER, THÉOPHILE
1811–1872

Reviens, reviens, ma bien-aimée;
Comme une fleur loin du soleil,
La fleur de ma vie est fermée
Loin de ton sourire vermeil.

Entre nos cœurs tant de distance!
Tant d'espace entre nos baisers!
Ô sort amer! ô dure absence!
Ô grands désirs inapaisés!

D'ici là-bas, que de compagnes,
Que de villes et de hameaux,
Que de vallons et de montagnes,
À lasser le pied des chevaux!

[Au pays qui me prend ma belle,
Hélas, si je pouvais aller;
Et si mon corps avait une aile
Comme mon âme pour voler!

Par-dessus les vertes collines,
Les montagnes au front d'azur,
Les champs rayés et les ravines,
J'irais d'un vol rapide et sûr.

Le corps ne suit pas la pensée;
Pour moi, mon âme, va tout droit,
Comme une colombe blessée,
S'abattre au rebord de son toit.

Descends dans sa gorge divine,
Blonde et fauve comme de l'or,
Douce comme un duvet d'hermine,
Sa gorge, mon royal trésor;

French poet, novelist, and notable *feuilletoniste*, leader of the younger Romantics of his day, said to have originated the slogan *L'art pour l'art*. "Pictorial and jewel-like effects" have been admired in his poetry.

ABSENCE

Return, return, my beloved!
Like a flower far from the sun,
the flower of my life is closed
far from your rosy smile.

Between our hearts how great the distance!
How far apart our kisses!
O bitter fate! Merciless absence!
O great unsatisfied desires!

From here to there how many fields,
how many cities and hamlets,
how many valleys and mountains
to weary the feet of horses!

[To the country that steals my love,
alas! if I could go there;
and if my body had wings,
like my soul, to fly!

Over the green hills,
the azure-browed mountains,
the furrowed fields and the ravines
I would go in rapid, certain flight.

The body does not follow the thought:
for me, my soul, go straight,
like a wounded dove
to throw itself upon the coping of her roof.

Alight on her divine throat,
blond and tawny as gold,
sweet as the fur of the ermine,
her throat, my royal treasure,

Et dis, mon âme, à cette belle:
"Tu sais bien qu'il compte les jours,
Ô ma colombe! à tire d'aile,
Retourne au nid de nos amours."]

HECTOR BERLIOZ, Op. 7, no. 4. From his *Nuits d'été*. In the first line of the second stanza *tant de distance* is changed to *quelle distance*. The setting actually uses the first three stanzas, the first

INFIDÉLITÉ

Bandiera d'ogni vento
conosco que sei tu.
—*Chanson italienne*

La volonté de l'ingrate est changée.
—ANTOINE DE BAÏF

Voici l'orme qui balance
Son ombre sur le sentier;
Voici le jeune églantier,
Le bois où dort le silence;
Le banc de pierre où le soir
Nous aimions à nous asseoir.

Voici la voûte embaumée
D'ébéniers et de lilas,
Où, lorsque nous étions las,
Ensemble, ô ma bien-aimée!
Sous des guirlandes de fleurs,
Nous laissons fuir les chaleurs.

[Voici le marais que ride
Le saut du poisson d'argent;
Dont la grenouille en nageant
Trouble le miroir humide;
Comme autrefois, les roseaux
Baignent leurs pieds dans ses eaux.

Comme autrefois, la pervenche,
Sur le velours vert des prés
Par le printemps diaprés,
Aux baisers du soleil penche
À moitié rempli de miel
Son calice bleu de ciel.

and say, my soul, to that charmer:
"You know well that he is counting the days;
o my dove, at the stretch of a wing,
return to the nest of our love!"]

---

reappearing twice as a kind of refrain. In a setting by Georges Bizet, stanzas 1, 2, 4, 5, 6, and 8 are used.

INFIDELITY

> Banner of every breeze,
> I know what you are.
>   *—Italian song*

The will of the ingrate is changed.
  —ANTOINE DE BAÏF

Here is the elm that casts
its wavering shadow over the path;
here is the young rose bush,
the wood where silence sleeps;
the stone bench where in the evening
we loved to sit.

Here is the fragrant arch
of ebony and lilacs
where, when we were tired,
together, o my love!
under wreathes of flowers
we would withdraw from the heat.

[Here is the marsh, rippled
by the leaping silvery fish,
of which the floating frog
disturbs the humid mirror.
As in the old days, the reeds
are bathing their feet in the waters.

As in the old days, the periwinkle
on the green velvet meadows,
brightly colored in the spring,
bends to the kisses of the sun,
half full of honey
her heaven-blue chalice.

Comme autrefois, l'hirondelle
Rase en passant les donjons,
Et le cygne dans les joncs
Se joue et lustre son aile;]
L'air est pur, le gazon doux . . .
Rien n'a donc changé que vous.

REYNALDO HAHN (1891). Only the first two stanzas and the two

LA SPECTRE DE LA ROSE

Soulève ta paupière close
Qu'effleure un songe virginal;
Je suis le spectre d'une rose
Que tu portais hier au bal.
Tu me pris encore emperlée
Des pleurs d'argent de l'arrosoir,
Et parmi la fête étoilée
Tu me promenas tout le soir.

Ô toi qui de ma mort fus cause,
Sans que tu puisses le chasser,
Toute la nuit mon spectre rose
À ton chevet viendra danser.
Mais ne crains rien, je ne réclame
Ni messe ni *De Profundis*;
Ce léger parfum est mon âme,
Et j'arrive du paradis.

Mon destin fut digne d'envie:
Pour avoir un trépas si beau,
Plus d'un aurait donné sa vie,
Car j'ai ta gorge pour tombeau,
Et sur l'albâtre où je repose
Un poète avec un baiser
Écrivit: ci-gît une rose
Que tous les rois vont jalouser.

HECTOR BERLIOZ, Op. 7, no. 2. From *Nuits d'été*. Line three of the
second stanza begins *Toutes les nuits*; line two of the third is *Et*

As in the old days, the swallow
skims the turrets in passing,
and the swan in the rushes
plays and preens its wings;]
The air is pure, the grass sweet ...
Nothing, then, has changed but you.

---

final lines of the last are set. In the fourth line of the second stanza
the exclamation *ô* is omitted.

THE PHANTOM OF THE ROSE

Open your closed eyelids
that bring to flower a maidenly dream;
I am the phantom of a rose
that you wore last night at the ball.
You took me still empearled
with silvery tears, from the watering pot,
and amid the starry assembly
you carried me all evening.

O you who were the cause of my death,
not that you could prevent it,
all night long my rosy phantom
will come to dance at your pillow.
But do not fear, I do not ask
either Mass or *De Profundis*;
this delicate perfume is my soul,
and I come from paradise.

My fate was enviable;
to have such a beautiful death,
more than one would have given his life,
for I have your throat as a tomb,
and on the alabaster where I rest
a poet, with a kiss,
has written : Here lies a rose
of which all kings will be jealous.

---

pour avoir un sort si beau; and line four, *Car sur ton sein j'ai mon
tombeau.*

GRANDMOUGIN, CHARLES-JEAN

1850–1930

POÈME D'UN JOUR

1

RENCONTRE

J'étais triste et pensif quand je t'ai rencontrée,
  Je sens moins aujourd'hui mon obstiné tourment;
Ô dis-moi, serais-tu la femme inespérée,
  Et le rêve idéal poursuivi vainement?
Ô, passante aux doux yeux, serais-tu donc l'amie
  Qui rendrait le bonheur au poète isolé,
Et vas-tu rayonner sur mon âme affermie,
  Comme le ciel natal sur un cœur d'exilé!

Ta tristesse sauvage, à la mienne pareille,
  Aime à voir le soleil décliner sur la mer!
Devant l'immensité ton extase s'éveille,
  Et le charme des soirs à ta belle âme est cher;
Une mystérieuse et douce sympathie
  Déja m'enchaîne à toi comme un vivant lien,
Et mon âme frémit, par l'amour envahie,
  Et mon cœur te chérit sans te connaître bien!

2

TOUJOURS

Vous me demandez de me taire,
  De fuir loin de vous pour jamais,
Et de m'en aller, solitaire,
  Sans me rappeler qui j'aimais!

Demandez plutôt aux étoiles
  De tomber dans l'immensité,
À la nuit de perdre ses voiles,
  Au jour de perdre sa clarté,

Demandez à la mer immense
  De dessécher ses vastes flots,
Et, quand les vents sont en démence,
  D'apaiser ses sombres sanglots!

Although trained in law, Grandmougin turned to literature under the patronage of Sully-Prudhomme. He wrote many books of poetry and dramas as well as novels. His style has been described as "at the same time very pure, very colorful, very simple and very wise"; his works range from philosophy to charming lyrics.

POEM OF A DAY

MEETING

I was sad and thoughtful when I met you;
today I feel less my persistent pain.
O tell me, could you be the unhoped-for woman
and the ideal dream, vainly pursued?
O passer-by with the sweet eyes, can you then be the friend
who will restore happiness to the lonely poet,
and will you shine upon my steadfast soul
as the native sky upon an exiled heart?

Your shy sadness, like mine,
loves to watch the sunset on the sea!
Faced with immensity, your ecstasy awakens,
and the charm of the evening is dear to your beautiful soul.
A mysterious and sweet sympathy
already binds me to you as with a living tie,
and my soul trembles, invaded by love,
and my heart cherishes you without knowing you well!

FOREVER

You ask me to be quiet,
to flee from you forever,
and to go my way alone
without remembering the one I loved!

Rather ask the stars
to fall into space,
the night to lose its mists,
the day to lose its light.

Ask of the huge sea
to dry its vast waves,
when the winds are raging,
to calm their melancholy sobs!

Mais n'espérez pas que mon âme
S'arrache à ses âpres douleurs
Et se dépouille de sa flamme
Comme le printemps de ses fleurs!

3

ADIEU

Comme tout meurt vite, la rose
Déclose,
Et les frais manteaux diaprés
Des prés;
Les longs soupirs, les bien-aimées,
Fumées!

On voit dans ce monde léger
Changer;
Plus vite que flots des grèves,
Nos rêves,
Plus vite que le givre en fleurs,
Nos cœurs!

À vous l'on se croyait fidèle,
Cruelle,
Mais hélas! les plus longs amours
Sont courts!
Et je dis en quittant vos charmes,
Sans larmes,
Presqu'au moment de mon aveu,
Adieu!

GABRIEL FAURÉ, Op. 21.

But do not hope that my soul
can tear itself from its bitter sorrows
and cast off its flame
as the spring does its flowers!

ADIEU

As everything dies quickly, the rose
in full bloom,
and the fresh dappled cloak
of the fields;
long-drawn sighs, sweethearts,
smoke!

We see in this unstable world,
change;
quicker than the waves on the shore,
our dreams;
quicker than the hoar-frost on the flowers,
our hearts!

I thought myself faithful to you,
cruel one,
but alas! the longest loves
are short!
And I say, taking leave of your charms,
without tears,
almost at the moment of my avowal,
Adieu!

HUGO, VICTOR-MARIE

1802–1885

DANS LES RUINES D'UNE ABBAYE

Seuls tous deux, ravis, chantants!
    Comme on s'aime!
Comme on cueille le printemps
    que Dieu sème!

Quels rires étincelants
    Dans ces ombres
Pleines jadis de fronts blancs,
    De cœurs sombres!

On est tout frais mariés.
    On s'envoie
Les charmants cris variés
    De la joie.

Purs ébats mêlés au vent
    Qui frissonne!
Gaîté que le noir couvent
    Assaisonne!

On effeuille des jasmins
    Sur la pierre
Où l'abbesse joint les mains
    En prière.

[Les tombeaux, de croix marqués,
    Font partie
De ces jeux, un peu piqués
    Par l'ortie.]

On se cherche, on se poursuit,
    On sent croître
Ton aube, amour, dans la nuit
    Du vieux cloître.

The most famous nineteenth-century French poet and novelist, whose influence was unbounded. His poetry represents the high-noon of Romanticism, now dealing with such subjects as nature, the Orient, or Spain, now breaking into satire, history, or comments on his own time. Always rich in imagination, his diction is exalted and intense.

IN THE ABBEY RUINS

Alone together, enraptured, singing!
How they make love!
How they gather the spring blossoms
which the Lord has sown!

What sparkling laughter
in these shadows
formerly full of white foreheads
and sombre hearts!

They are newly married.
They exchange
charming variegated cries
of joy.

Innocent sports mingled with the wind
that trembles!
Gaiety to which the old convent
gives zest!

They strip the jasmine flowers
from the stone
where the abbess clasped her hands
in prayer.

[The tombs, the crosses
take a part
in the games, a little stung
by nettles.]

They play hide and seek,
they feel growing
your dawn, love, in the night
of the old cloister.

On s'en vas se becquetant,
    On s'adore,
On s'embrasse à chaque instant,
    Puis encore,

Sous les piliers, les arceaux,
    Et les marbres.
C'est l'histoire des oiseaux
    Dans les arbres.

GABRIEL FAURÉ, Op. 2, no. 1. In stanza two, line three, the order is reversed so that it reads *Jadis pleines de fronts blancs*. In the fourth stanza *Purs ébats mêlés au vent* is changed to *Frais échos*

OH! QUAND JE DORS ...

Oh! quand je dors, viens auprès de ma couche,
Comme à Pétrarque apparaissait Laura,
Et qu'en passant ton haleine me touche ...
    Soudain ma bouche
    S'entr'ouvrira!

Sur mon front morne où peut-être s'achève
Un songe noir qui trop longtemps dura,
Que ton regard comme un astre se lève ...
    Soudain mon rêve
    Rayonnera!

Puis sur ma lèvre où voltige une flamme,
Éclair d'amour que Dieu même épura,
Pose un baiser, et d'ange deviens femme ...
    Soudain mon âme
    S'éveillera!

FRANZ LISZT. In the second stanza, the fourth line begins *Et soudain*. Also well known by the German title, *O komm' im Traum*; another translation is *O wenn ich schlaf*. There are other settings by L. Pantaleoni (*Nah' mir im Traume*), by W. Castriola-Scander-

SI MES VERS AVAIENT DES AILES

Mes vers fuiraient, doux et frêles,
Vers votre jardin si beau,
Si mes vers avaient des ailes,
Des ailes comme l'oiseau.

On they go, billing and cooing,
they adore each other,
they embrace constantly,
then again,

beneath the pillars, the archways
and the marbles.
It is the story of the birds
in the trees.

---

mêlés au vent. After the fourth stanza the first is repeated as a kind
of refrain. The sixth stanza is omitted.

OH, WHILE I SLEEP . . .

Oh, while I sleep, come to my bedside,
as Laura appeared to Petrarch,
and in passing let your breath touch me . . .
All at once
I shall smile!

On my sombre brow where perhaps there is ending
a dismal dream that has lasted too long;
let your face rise like a star . . .
All at once my dream
will become radiant!

Then on my lips, where a flame flutters,
a flash of love purified by God himself,
place a kiss, and be transformed from angel into woman . . .
All at once my soul
will awaken!

---

berg, and by Bernard van Dieren, who uses the title of the collection
of poems in which the text is found, *Les rayons et les ombres,
XXVII.*

IF MY VERSES HAD WINGS

My verses would fly, sweet and delicate,
toward your beautiful garden,
if my verses had wings,
wings, like a bird.

Ils voleraient, étincelles,
Vers votre foyer qui rit,
Si mes vers avaient des ailes,
Des ailes comme l'esprit.

Près de vous, purs et fidèles,
Ils accourraient nuit et jour,
Si mes vers avaient des ailes,
Des ailes comme l'amour.

REYNALDO HAHN (1888). The last line of each stanza is shortened by the omission of the repeated words, *Des ailes*.

LECONTE DE LISLE, CHARLES-MARIE-RENÉ
1818–1894

LYDIA

Lydia, sur tes roses joues,
Et sur ton col frais et plus blanc
Que le lait, coule étincelant
L'or fluide que tu dénoues.

Le jour qui luit est le meilleur:
Oublions l'éternelle tombe.
Laisse tes baisers de colombe
Chanter sur tes lèvres en fleur.

Un lys caché répand sans cesse
Une odeur divine en ton sein:
Les délices, comme un essaim,
Sortent de toi, jeune Déesse!

Je t'aime et meurs, ô mes amours!
Mon âme en baisers m'est ravie.
Ô Lydia, rends-moi la vie,
Que je puisse mourir toujours!

GABRIEL FAURÉ, Op. 4, no. 2. To suit his melody, Fauré has omitted part of the first stanza, and thus necessitated a slight further

They would fly, sparks,
toward your smiling hearth,
if my verses had wings,
wings, like the spirit.

Near to you, pure and faithful,
they would hasten night and day,
if my verses had wings,
wings, like love.

Leader of the *parnassien* school of French poets. Hating
the industrialism and utilitarianism of life in his time, he
broke away, too, from the lyric romanticism of its literature, seeking a union of the ideal of beauty and the learn-
ing of natural sciences. Leconte de Lisle found inspiration
in ancient Greece and in other remote civilizations. His
style was austere and beautifully balanced, and he liked to
paint grandly, often illustrating his own philosophy. His
poems, however, are not invariably remarkable for depth.

LYDIA

Lydia, on your rosy cheeks,
and on your neck, fresh and whiter
than milk, streams sparkling
liquid gold as you take down your hair.

The smiling day is the best,
let us forget the eternal tomb.
Let your kisses like doves
sing upon your flowering lips.

A hidden lily breathes forth ceaselessly
a divine fragrance within your breast.
Delights, like bees,
swarm from you, young goddess!

I love you and I die, o my love!
My soul is carried away with kisses.
O Lydia, give me back my life,
that I may ever be dying!

---

adjustment. His setting is found in the Appendix.

NELL

Ta rose de pourpre, à ton clair soleil,
  Ô Juin, étincelle enivrée;
Penche aussi vers moi ta coupe dorée:
  Mon cœur à ta rose est pareil.

Sous le mol abri de la feuille ombreuse
  Monte un soupir de volupté;
Plus d'un ramier chante au bois écarté,
  Ô mon cœur, sa plainte amoureuse.

Que ta perle est douce au ciel parfumé,
  Étoile de la nuit pensive!
Mais combien plus douce est la clarté vive
  Qui rayonne en mon cœur charmé!

La chantante mer, le long du rivage,
  Taira son murmure éternel,
Avant qu'en mon cœur, cher amour, ô Nell,
  Ne fleurisse plus ton image!

GABRIEL FAURÉ, Op. 18, no. 1. In the first line of the third stanza

LE PARFUM IMPÉRISSABLE

Quand la fleur du soleil, la rose de Lahor,
De son âme odorante a rempli goutte à goutte
La fiole d'argile ou de cristal ou d'or,
Sur le sable qui brûle on peut l'épandre toute.

Les fleuves et la mer inonderaient en vain
Ce sanctuaire étroit qui la tint enfermée:
Il garde en se brisant son arome divin,
Et sa poussière heureuse en reste parfumée.

Puisque par la blessure ouverte de mon cœur
Tu t'écoules de même, ô céleste liqueur,
Inexprimable amour, qui m'emflammis pour elle!

Qu'il lui soit pardonné, que mon mal soit béni!
Par delà l'heure humaine et le temps infini
Mon cœur est embaumé d'une odeur immortelle!

GABRIEL FAURÉ, Op. 76, no. 1.

NELL

Your purple rose in your clear sunlight,
o June, sparkles as though intoxicated;
incline to me your golden cup:
my heart is like your rose.

In the soft shelter of the shady leaves
arises a sigh of pleasure;
more than one dove sings in the lonely wood,
o my heart, its amorous lament.

How sweet is your pearl in the perfumed sky,
star of the pensive night!
But how much sweeter is the living light
that shines in my enchanted heart!

The singing sea along the shore
shall cease its eternal murmur
before in my heart, dear love, o Nell,
your image shall cease to bloom!

---

the word *parfumé* is changed to *enflammé*.

IMPERISHABLE FRAGRANCE

When the flower of the sun, the rose, of Lahore,
with its fragrant essence has filled, drop by drop,
the vial of clay, of crystal or of gold,
we could pour it all out upon the burning sand.

The tides and the sea would inundate in vain
this little sanctuary that held it imprisoned:
though shattered, it would keep its divine aroma
and its happy sands would remain perfumed.

As in the open wound of my heart
you pour yourself, o heavenly liquid,
inexpressible love with which I burn for her,

may she be pardoned, and may my pain be blest!
Beyond the human hour and infinite time
my heart is sweetened with an immortal fragrance!

PHIDYLÉ

L'herbe est molle au sommeil sous les frais peupliers,
    Aux pentes des sources moussues
Qui, dans les prés en fleurs germant par mille issues,
    Se perdent sous les noirs halliers.

Repose, ô Phidylé! Midi sur les feuillages
    Rayonne, et t'invite au sommeil.
Par le trèfle et le thym, seules, en plein soleil,
    Chantent les abeilles volages.

Un chaud parfum circule aux détours des sentiers;
    La rouge fleur des blés s'incline;
Et les oiseaux, rasant de l'aile la colline,
    Cherchent l'ombre des églantiers.

[Les taillis sont muets; le daim, par les clairières,
    Devant les meutes aux abois
Ne bondit plus; Diane, assise au fond des bois,
    Polit ses flèches meurtrières.

Dors en paix, belle enfant aux rires ingénus,
    Aux nymphes agrestes pareille!
De ta bouche au miel pur j'écarterai l'abeille,
    Je garantirai tes pieds nus.

Laisse sur ton épaule et ses formes divines,
    Comme un or fluide et léger,
Sous mon souffle amoureux courir et voltiger
    L'épaisseur de tes tresses fines!

Sans troubler ton repos, sur ton front transparent,
    Libre des souples bandelettes,
J'unirai l'hyacinthe aux pâles violettes,
    Et la rose au myrte odorant.

Belle comme Érycine aux jardins de Sicile,
    Et plus chère à mon cœur jaloux,
Repose! Et j'emplirai du souffle le plus doux
    La flûte à mes lèvres docile.

PHIDYLÉ

The soft grass tempts us to sleep under the fresh poplars
on the banks of the mossy springs,
which, in the meadows flowering with a thousand plants,
lose themselves beneath the dark copses.

Rest, o Phidylé! Noon on the leaves
is shining, and invites you to sleep.
By the clover and the thyme, alone, in the bright sun,
and fickle bees are singing.

A warm perfume pervades the winding paths,
the red flower of the wheat is bending;
and the birds, grazing the hill with their wings,
seek the shade of the eglantines.

[The copses are silent; the buck in the glades,
no longer at bay before the pack,
does not rush; Diana, sitting in the depths of the woods,
polishes her burning arrows.

Sleep in peace, beautiful child with the ingenuous smile,
so like the rustic nymphs!
From your honeyed mouth I will wave away the bee;
I will protect your bare feet.

On your shoulder and its divine forms,
like light liquid gold,
let my amorous breath play and flutter
the mat of your delicate tresses.

Without troubling your rest, on your clear brow,
free of the supple ribbons,
I will weave the hyacinth with the pale violets,
and the rose with the fragrant myrtle.

Beautiful as Erycine in the gardens of Sicily,
and dearer to my jealous heart,
sleep! And I shall fill with my sweetest breath
the flute submissive to my lips.

Je charmerai les bois, ô blanche Phidylé,
De ta louange familière;
Et les nymphes, au seuil de leurs grottes de lierre,
En pâliront, le cœur troublé.]

Mais quand l'astre, incliné sur sa courbe éclatante,
Verra ses ardeurs s'apaiser,
Que ton plus beau sourire et ton meilleur baiser
Me récompensent de l'attente!

Henri Duparc. Duparc only set the first three and the last stanzas,

LES ROSES D'ISPAHAN

Les roses d'Ispahan dans leur gaine de mousse,
Les jasmins de Mossoul, les fleurs de l'oranger
Ont un parfum moins frais, ont une odeur moins douce,
Ô blanche Leïlah! que ton souffle léger.

Ta lèvre est de corail, et ton rire léger
Sonne mieux que l'eau vive et d'une voix plus douce,
Mieux que le vent joyeux qui berce l'oranger,
Mieux que l'oiseau qui chante au bord d'un nid de
mousse.

[Mais le subtile odeur des roses dans leur mousse,
La brise qui se joue autour de l'oranger
Et l'eau vive qui flue avec sa plainte douce
Ont un charme plus sûr que ton amour léger!]

Ô Leïlah! depuis que de leur vol léger
Tous les baisers ont fui de ta lèvre si douce,
Il n'est plus de parfum dans la pâle oranger,
Ni de céleste arome aux roses dans leur mousse.

[L'oiseau, sur le duvet humide et sur la mousse,
Ne chante plus parmi la rose et l'oranger;
L'eau vive des jardins n'a plus de chanson douce.
L'aube ne dore plus le ciel pur et léger.]

I will charm the woods, o white Phidylé,
with your familiar praise;
and the nymphs, on the threshold of their ivy-covered caves,
will turn pale at the sound, troubled in heart.]

But when the sun, turning on its glittering course,
shall come to assuage the heat,
may your loveliest smile and your best kiss
recompense my waiting!

---

using as a bridge between the third and the last, three repetitions of
the words *Repose, ô Phidylé.*

THE ROSES OF ISPAHAN

The roses of Ispahan in their mossy sheaths,
the jasmines of Mossoul, the blossoms of the orange tree,
have a perfume less fresh, an odor less sweet,
O white Leïla, than your light breath.

Your lips are of coral, and your light laugh
is more musical than the water of the spring or the sweetest
    voice,
better than the joyous wind that rocks the orange tree,
better than the bird that sings beside his mossy nest.

[Yet the subtle fragrance of the roses in their moss,
the breeze that plays around the orange tree,
and the spring water flowing with its sweet complaint,
have charms more enduring than your fickle love!]

O Leïla! since in their easy flight
all kisses have flown from your sweet lips,
there is no more fragrance in the pale orange tree,
nor celestial aroma in the roses in their moss.

[The bird, on the moist down and on the moss,
no longer sings beneath the rosebush and the orange tree;
the water in the garden springs no longer has a sweet song;
the dawn no longer gilds the clear and inconstant sky.]

Oh! que ton jeune amour, ce papillon léger,
Revienne vers mon cœur d'une aile prompte et douce,
Et qu'il parfume encore la fleur de l'oranger,
Les roses d'Ispahan dans leur gaine de mousse!

GABRIEL FAURÉ, Op. 39, no. 4. The third and fifth stanzas are

LOUŸS, PIERRE

1870–1925

TROIS CHANSONS DE BILITIS

CLAUDE DEBUSSY. Debussy chose three of these "enchanting and licentious poems in prose" for his cycle, composed in 1898. Less well known are the seventeen settings of Georges Dandelot (1924–30), the texts of which are not included here.

1. LA FLÛTE

Pour le jour des Hyacinthies il m'a donné
une syrinx faite des roseaux bien taillés,
unis avec la blanche cire qui est douce à mes
lèvres comme du miel.

Il m'apprend à jouer, assise sur ses genoux;
mais je suis un peu tremblante. Il en joue après
moi; si doucement que je l'entends à peine.

Nous n'avons rien à nous dire, tant nous
sommes près l'un de l'autre; mais nos chansons
veulent se répondre, et tour à tour nos bouches
s'unissent sur la flûte.

Il est tard, voici le chant des grenouilles
vertes qui commence avec la nuit. Ma mère ne
croira jamais que je suis restée si longtemps à
chercher ma ceinture perdue.

Oh! may your young love, that fickle butterfly,
return to my heart, on swift, sweet wings,
and once again may it perfume the flowers of the orange tree,
the roses of Ispahan in their mossy sheaths!

---

mitted. There is also a setting by César Cui (Op. 54, no. 3).

After training for a military career, Louÿs achieved
notoriety by the frankness and alleged impropriety of his
novel *Aphrodite*. The *Chansons de Bilitis* were published
as a translation from the ancient Greek, and by many were
accepted as such. After their early *succès de scandale*, these
prose poems have come to be valued for their purity of
style, their imagery, their deep fervor and devotion to
beauty.

THE FLUTE

For the Hyacinthine festival he has given me
a syrinx of well formed reeds,
bound together with white wax, which is sweet to my
lips as honey.

He teaches me how to play, sitting on his knees;
but I am a little nervous. He plays after
me, so softly I can scarcely hear.

We have nothing to say to each other, so
close are we to one another; but in songs
we converse, and sometimes our lips
come together on the flute.

It is late; that is the song of the green frogs
that begins with the night. My mother
will never believe I have been so long
looking for my lost girdle.

2. LA CHEVELURE

Il m'a dit: "Cette nuit, j'ai rêvé.
J'avais ta chevelure autour de mon cou.
J'avais tes cheveux comme un collier noir
autour de ma nuque et sur ma poitrine.

"Je les caressais, et c'étaient les miens;
et nous étions liés pour toujours ainsi, par
la même chevelure la bouche sur la bouche,
ainsi que deux lauriers n'ont souvent qu'une racine.

"Et peu à peu, il m'a semblé, tant nos
membres étaient confondus, que je devenais
toi-même ou que tu entrais en moi comme mon
songe."

Quand il eut achevé, il mit doucement ses
mains sur mes épaules, et il me regarda d'un
regard si tendre, que je baissai les yeux
avec un frisson.

3. LE TOMBEAU DES NAÏADES

Le long du bois couvert de givre, je marchais;
mes cheveux devant ma bouche se fleurissaient de
petits glaçons, et mes sandales etaient lourdes
de neige fangeuse et tassée.

Il me dit: "Que cherches-tu?—Je suis la trace
du satyre. Ses petits pas fourchus alternent
comme des trous dans un manteau blanc." Il me dit:
"Les satyres sont morts."

"Les satyres et les nymphes aussi. Depuis
trente ans il n'a pas fait un hiver aussi terrible.
La trace que tu vois est celle d'un bouc. Mais
restons ici, où est leur tombeau."

Et avec le fer de sa houe il cassa la glace de
la source où jadis riaient les naïades. Il prenait
de grands morceaux froids, et les soulevant vers le
ciel pâle, il regardait au travers.

THE HAIR

He said: "Last night I dreamed.
I had your hair around my throat.
I had your tresses like a black collar
around my neck and upon my breast.

"I caressed them, and they were mine;
and we were bound together forever thus, by
that same hair, mouth to mouth,
as two laurel bushes often have a single root.

"And little by little, it seemed to me, our
limbs so lost their identity that I became
you, or you entered into me like my dream."

When he had finished, he softly put his
hands upon my shoulders, and looked at me with
so tender a gaze that I lowered my eyes,
with a shudder.

THE TOMB OF THE NAIADS

Through the wood covered with hoar frost I walked;
my hair before my mouth blossomed with
little icicles, and my sandals were heavy
with muddy lumps of snow.

He said to me: "What are you looking for?"—"I
am following the tracks of a satyr. The prints of his
little cloven hoofs are spaced like holes in
a white cloak." He said: "The satyrs are dead."

"The satyrs and the nymphs too. For thirty
years there has not been so terrible a winter.
The tracks that you see are those of a he-goat. But
let us stop here, for here is their tomb."

And with the head of his hoe he broke the ice on
the spring where the naiads used to laugh. He took
up the big frozen pieces, and holding them toward the
pale sky, he looked through them.

MALLARMÉ, STÉPHANE
1842–1898

SAINTE

À la fenêtre recélant
Le santal vieux qui se dédore
De sa viole étincelant
Jadis avec flûte ou mandore,

Est la Sainte pâle, étalant
Le livre vieux qui se déplie
Du Magnificat ruisselant
Jadis selon vêpre et complie:

À ce vitrage d'ostensoir
Que frôle une harpe par l'Ange
Formée avec son vol du soir
Pour la délicate phalange

Du doigt que, sans le vieux santal
Ni le vieux livre, elle balance
Sur le plumage instrumental,
Musicienne du silence.

MAURICE RAVEL (1896). Stanza one, line four has *selon flûte*, and

Leader of the French *symbolistes*, Mallarmé developed under such varied influences at Lamartine, Baudelaire, Poe, Gautier, Verlaine, and Hegel. Each of his poems is built around an idea, or symbol, with secondary images to help develop the idea. Though respecting the accepted rules of prosody, he brought to his poems a new plasticity.

THE SAINT

In the window concealing
the old sandalwood, with the tarnished gilt,
of her glittering viol—
once with flute or mandora—

is the pale saint, holding
the old book open
to the glittering Magnificat—
once for vespers and compline—

In this stained-glass window like a monstrance,
which a harp touches—formed by the angel
poised for her evening flight—
for the delicate row

of fingers, which, without the sandalwood
and the antique book, she balances
on her feather-formed instrument,
musician of silence.

---

stanza two, line four, *vêpre ou complie.*

MAROT, CLÉMENT
ca.1497–1544

D'ANNE JOUANT DE L'ESPINETTE

Lorsque je voi en ordre la brunette,
Jeune, en bon point, de la ligne des dieux,
Et que sa voix, ses doigts et l'espinette
Meinent un bruit doux et mélodieux,
J'ai du plaisir, et d'aureilles et d'yeux
Plus que les saints en leur gloire immortelle:
Et autant qu'eux je deviens glorieux,
Dès que je pense être un peu aimé d'elle.

MAURICE RAVEL, *Epigrammes de Clément Marot*, no. 2 (1898).

RICHEPIN, JEAN
1849–1926

AU CIMETIÈRE

Heureux qui meurt ici
    Ainsi
Que les oiseaux des champs!
Son corps près des amis
    Est mis
Dans l'herbe et dans les chants.

French poet of the court of Francis I, remembered no less for his metrical translations of the Psalms than for his graceful lyrics. He is said to have introduced the sonnet into the French language. A Protestant at a Catholic court, he ended his life as an exile in Geneva.

ANNE PLAYING THE SPINET

When I look upon the well-groomed, dark,
　young and plump descendant of the gods,
　and her voice, her fingers, and the spinet
make a sweet and melodious sound,
I feel pleasure of both ears and eyes
more than the saints in their immortal glory:
and I become as blest as they,
　believing myself a little loved by her.

A handsome and successful journalist, whose first book of poems, *Chansons des Gueux*, created a celebrated scandal and led to the author's imprisonment for a month. Richepin's aim was to become a sort of modern Villon, to live unconventionally, and to write a kind of vagabond verse, in expression akin to folk song. After a period as a sailor he returned to literature, even producing a drama with himself and Sarah Bernhardt in the leading roles. His work has won admiration for variety, power, and pathos, but has also been criticized for its lack of substance.

AT THE CEMETERY

Happy he who dies here
like
the birds in the fields!
His body near his friends
is laid
in the sod with songs.

Il dort d'un bon sommeil
Vermeil
Sous le ciel radieux.
Tous ceux qu'il a connus,
Venus,
Lui font de longs adieux.

À sa croix les parents
Pleurants
Restent agenouillés;
Et ses os, sous les fleurs,
De pleurs
Sont doucement mouillés.

Chacun sur le bois noir
Peut voir
S'il était jeune ou non,
Et peut avec de frais
Regrets
L'appeler par son nom.

Combien plus malchanceux
Sont ceux
Qui meurent à la mé,
Et sous le flot profond
S'en vont
Loin du pays aimé!

Ah! pauvres, qui pour seuls
Linceuls
Ont les goëmons verts
Où l'on roule inconnu,
Tout nu,
Et les yeux grands ouverts.

Heureux qui meurt ici
Ainsi
Que les oiseaux des champs!
Son corps près des amis
Est mis
Dans l'herbe et dans les chants.

GABRIEL FAURÉ, Op. 51, no. 2. Richepin's last stanza is a simple
repetition of his first. To round out his musical repetition, Fauré

He sleeps a good
roseate sleep
under the radiant sky.
All those he knew
are come
to make their long farewells.

By his cross his kinsmen,
weeping,
remain kneeling;
and his bones under the flowers
with tears
are gently watered.

Anyone, on the black wood,
can see
whether he was young or not,
and can with renewed
sorrow
call him by his name.

How much more unfortunate
are those
who die at sea,
and under the deep wave
go down
far from the land they love!

Ah! poor ones, who for
shrouds
have only the green seaweed,
where they roll unknown,
all naked,
and with eyes wide open.

Happy he who dies here,
like
the birds in the fields!
His body near his friends
is laid
in the sod with songs.

---

also repeats the second.

RONSARD, PIERRE DE
1524–1585

À SON ÂME

Amelette Ronsardelette,
Mignonnelette, doucelette,
Très-chère hôtesse de mon corps,
Tu descends là-bas foiblelette
Pâle, maigrelette, seulette,
Dans le froid royaume des morts,
Toutesfois simple, sans remords
De meurtre, poison, et rancune,
Méprisant faveurs et trésors
Tant enviés par la commune.
    Passant, j'ai dit; sui ta fortune,
Ne trouble mon repos: je dors!

MAURICE RAVEL. The song is called *Ronsard à son âme.*

SILVESTRE, PAUL ARMAND
1837–1901

AURORE

Des jardins de la nuit s'envolent les étoiles,
Abeilles d'or qu'attire un invisible miel;
Et l'aube, au loin, tendant la candeur de ses toiles
Trame de fils d'argent le manteau bleu du ciel.

Du jardin de mon coeur qu'un rêve lent enivre,
S'envolent mes désirs sur les pas du matin,
Comme un essaim léger qu'à l'horizon de cuivre,
Appelle un chant plaintif, éternel et lointain.

Leading member of the group of poets who called themselves the *pléiade*. As a boy he was page at the court of Francis I, and later became official court poet under Henry II and Charles IX. Influenced by Petrarch, Pindar, Theocritus, and Propertius, he in turn influenced the Elizabethans. He excelled in the writing of sonnets and odes and was much admired for the lightness and grace of his amorous verse.

TO HIS SOUL

Little soul of little Ronsard,
little darling, little sweetheart,
dearest hostess of my body,
you go down yonder weakly,
pale, thin, alone,
into the cold kingdom of the dead,
nonetheless unspoiled, without remorse
for murder, poison or malice,
scorning favors and treasures
so much desired by the common people.
In passing I say: Follow your fortune,
do not trouble my rest—I sleep.

Intended for a military career, Armand Silvestre worked in the Ministry of Finance before publishing his first poems. His works contain drama and art criticism as well as Rabelaisian tales. His poetry and prose have been much admired for the fecundity of his talent, the finish of his style, and passages of ethereal beauty.

DAWN

From the gardens of night the stars take wing,
golden bees drawn to an invisible honey;
and the dawn, in the distance, drawing its white curtains,
streaks with threads of silver the blue cloak of the sky.

From the garden of my heart, drugged by a dull dream,
my desires flee on the steps of the morning,
like a swift swarm of bees which at the copper horizon
calls with a plaintive song, eternal and distant.

Ils volent à tes pieds, astres chassés des nues,
Exilés du ciel d'or où fleurit ta beauté,
Et, cherchant jusqu'à toi des routes inconnues,
Mêlent au jour naissant leur mourante clarté.

GABRIEL FAURÉ, Op. 39, no. 1.

AUTOMNE

Automne au ciel brumeux, aux horizons navrants,
Aux rapides couchants, aux aurores pâlies,
Je regarde couler, comme l'eau du torrent,
Tes jours faits de mélancolie.

Sur l'aile des regrets mes esprits emportés,
Comme s'il se pouvait que notre âge renaisse!
Parcourent en rêvant les coteaux enchantés,
Où, jadis, sourit ma jeunesse!

Je sens, au clair soleil du souvenir vainqueur,
Refleurir en bouquet les roses déliées,
Et monter à mes yeux des larmes qu'en mon cœur,
Mes vingt ans avaient oubliées.

GABRIEL FAURÉ, Op. 18, no. 3.

LE SECRET

Je veux que le matin l'ignore
Le nom que j'ai dit à la nuit,
Et qu'au vent de l'aube, sans bruit,
Comme une larme il s'évapore.

Je veux que le jour le proclame
L'amour qu'au matin j'ai caché,
Et sur mon cœur ouvert penché
Comme un grain d'encens il l'enflamme.

Je veux que le couchant l'oublie
Le secret que j'ai dit au jour,
Et l'emporte avec mon amour,
Aux plis de sa robe pâlie!

GABRIEL FAURÉ, Op. 23, no. 3.

They fly to your feet, stars driven from the sky,
exiled from the golden heaven where your beauty
   flourishes,
and seeking unknown paths to you,
mingle their dying light with the dawning day.

AUTUMN

Autumn with your hazy sky, your heart-breaking horizons,
with your quick sunsets, with your pale dawns,
I watch flow away, like the water of a torrent,
your days made up of melancholy.

My spirits are born on the wings of regret,
as though our age could be young again!
Dreaming they cross the enchanted hills
where once my youth smiled!

It seems to me in the clear sun of conquering memory
the fallen roses bloom again in a bouquet,
and to my eyes rise the tears which in my heart
my twenty years had forgotten.

THE SECRET

I want the morning not to know
the name I have spoken to the night,
and that in the breeze of the dawn, silently,
like a tear it shall evaporate.

I want the day to proclaim it,
the love I hid in the morning,
and leaning upon my open heart
ignite it like a grain of incense.

I want the sunset to forget
the secret I have spoken to the day,
and to carry it with my love
in the folds of her pale robe!

SULLY-PRUDHOMME, RENÉ FRANÇOIS ARMAND PRUDHOMME

1839–1907

LE LONG DU QUAI

Le long du quai les grands vaisseaux,
Que la houle incline en silence,
Ne prennent pas garde aux berceaux
Que la main des femmes balance.

Mais viendra le jour des adieux,
Car il faut que les femmes pleurent,
Et que les hommes curieux
Tentent les horizons qui leurrent.

Et ce jour-là les grands vaisseaux,
Fuyant le port qui diminue,
Sentent leur masse retenue
Par l'âme des lointains berceaux.

GABRIEL FAURÉ, Op. 23, no. 1, titled *Les Berceaux.*

SOUPIR

Ne jamais la voir ni l'entendre,
Ne jamais tout haut la nommer,
Mais, fidèle, toujours l'attendre,
 Toujours l'aimer.

Ouvrir les bras et, las d'attendre,
Sur le néant les refermer,
Mais encor, toujours les lui tendre,
 Toujours l'aimer.

Ah! ne pouvoir que les lui tendre,
Et dans les pleurs se consumer,
Mais ces pleurs toujours les répandre,
 Toujours l'aimer!

Turned to poetry after education in science and law; later went over to philosophy and criticism. In 1901 he was awarded the first Nobel Prize for literature. Representative of the *parnassiens*, Sully-Prudhomme showed in his work some leaning towards the older Romanticists, though his point of view is free of pessimism and his comprehension of science and metaphysics is unique in his time.

ALONG THE QUAY

Along the quay the great ships,
bending silently with the surge,
take no thought of the cradles,
rocked by the hands of the women.

But the day of parting will come,
for it is ordained that women shall weep,
and that inquisitive men
shall try the shining horizons.

And on that day the great ships,
leaving the receding harbor,
feel their hulks restrained
by the soul of the distant cradles.

SIGH

Never to see her or hear her,
never to breathe her name aloud,
but, faithful, always to wait for her,
always to love her.

To open my arms, and, weary of waiting,
to close them again on nothing,
but again, always to hold them out,
always to love her!

Ah! to be able only to hold them open,
and to consume myself with tears,
but always to shed these tears,
always to love her!

Ne jamais la voir ni l'entendre,
Ne jamais tout haut la nommer,
Mais d'un amour toujours plus tendre
Toujours l'aimer.

HENRI DUPARC. This once popular verse is now best remembered in Duparc's music, though there are also settings by Respighi,

VERLAINE, PAUL
1844–1896

LA BONNE CHANSON

GABRIEL FAURÉ's cycle of nine songs is set to texts chosen from Verlaine's twenty-one poems published under this same title. Fauré's order in Verlaine's numbers is 8, 4, 6, 20, 15, 5, 19, 17, 21.

I

Une sainte en son auréole,
Une Châtelaine en sa tour,
Tout ce que contient la parole
Humaine de grâce et d'amour;

La note d'or que fait entendre
Un cor dans le lointain des bois,
Mariée à la fierté tendre
Des nobles Dames d'autrefois!

Avec cela le charme insigne
D'un frais sourire triomphant
Éclos dans des candeurs de cygne
Et des rougeurs de femme-enfant;

Des aspects nacrés, blancs et roses,
Un doux accord patricien.
Je vois, j'entends toutes ces choses
Dans son mon Carlovingien.

GABRIEL FAURÉ, Op. 61, no. 1. In stanza two, line two, *Un cor* is

Never to see her or hear her,
never to breathe her name aloud,
but with a love ever more tender,
always to love her!

Bemberg, Widor, and others, and the text also turns up (in French)
in the Russian opera *Dubrovsky* by Napravnik.

Certainly the greatest musician's poet in French literature.
First classed among the *parnassiens,* Verlaine was the
immediate forerunner of the *symbolistes.* Personally erratic
and undisciplined, he wrote verses of the utmost delicacy,
grace, and musicality, among the purest gems of lyric
poetry in any language. Inspired by the spirit of the
eighteenth century, and of Watteau in particular, much of
his work is vague and nebulous, owing not a little of its
charm to its moonlight effects.

A saint with her halo,
a chatelaine in her tower,
all that human words contain
of grace and of love,

the golden note sounded by
a horn far off in the woods,
blended with the tender pride
of noble ladies of other days!

With that the sheer charm
of a fresh smile of triumph,
born of the ingenuousness of a swan
and the blushes of a youthful woman;

alternating white and rose like a pearl,
a sweet patrician consent:
I see, I hear all these things
in her Carlovingian name.

---

changed to *Le cor.*

2

Puisque l'aube grandit, puisque voici l'aurore,
Puisque, après m'avoir fui longtemps, l'espoir veut bien
Revoler devers moi qui l'appelle et l'implore,
Puisque tout ce bonheur veut bien être le mien.

[C'en est fait à présent des funestes pensées,
C'en est fait des mauvais rêves, ah! c'en est fait
Surtout de l'ironie et des lèvres pincées
Et des mots où l'esprit sans l'âme triomphait.

Arrière aussi les poings crispés et la colère
À propos des méchants et des sots rencontrés;
Arrière la rancune abominable! arrière
L'oubli qu'on cherche en des breuvages exécrés!

Car je veux, maintenant qu'un Être de lumière
A dans ma nuit profonde émis cette clarté
D'une amour à la fois immortelle et première
De par la grâce, le sourire et la bonté,]

Je veux, guidé par vous, beaux yeux aux flammes douces,
Par toi conduit, ô main où tremblera ma main,
Marcher droit, que ce soit par des sentiers de mousses
Ou que rocs et cailloux encombrent le chemin;

[Oui, je veux marcher droit et calme dans la vie,
Vers le but où le sort dirigera mes pas,
Sans violence, sans remords et sans envie.
Ce sera le devoir heureux aux gais combats.]

Et comme, pour bercer les lenteurs de la route,
Je chanterai des airs ingénus, je me dis
Qu'elle m'écoutera sans déplaisir sans doute;
Et vraiment je ne veux pas d'autre Paradis.

GABRIEL FAURÉ, Op. 61, no. 2. The second, third, fourth, and sixth
stanzas are omitted.

Now that day is breaking, now that the dawn is here,
now that, having forsaken me for a long time, hope will
come back to me who am calling and imploring,
now that all this happiness is to be mine,

[I am through now with mournful thoughts,
I am through with bad dreams, ah! I am through
above all with the irony of prim lips
and words in which the mind triumphed without the soul.

Behind me too are the clenched fists and anger
over the malicious and stupid people we have met;
forgotten the abominable rancor! Forgotten
the oblivion sought in detested drinks!

For I want, now that a radiant being
has shed in my dark night this brightness
of a love at once eternal and pristine,
by grace, smile and favors,]

I want, guided by you, beautiful eyes with the gentle
   flames,
led by you, o hand trembling in my hand,
to walk straight, be it through mossy paths
or a way obstructed by rocks and stones;

[yes, I wish to walk straight and calm in life,
toward the end to which fate shall lead my steps,
without violence, without remorse and without desire.
That shall be my happy duty in the high-spirited struggle.]

And as, to while away the long journey,
I shall sing simple songs, I tell myself
that she will hear me without displeasure, without doubt,
and truly I wish no other paradise.

3

La lune blanche
Luit dans les bois;
De chaque branche
Part une voix
Sous la ramée . . .

Ô bien-aimée.

L'étang reflète,
Profond miroir,
La silhouette
Du saule noir
Où le vent pleure . . .

Rêvons, c'est l'heure.

Un vaste et tendre
Apaisement
Semble descendre
Du firmament
Que l'astre irise . . .

C'est l'heure exquise.

GABRIEL FAURÉ, Op. 61, no. 3. One of the most popular Verlaine texts, this poem is perhaps best known in Reynaldo Hahn's *L'heure exquise* (*Chansons grises*, no. 5). Others who have set it include N. Sokolow (Op. 31, no. 5 and Op. 32, no. 1), M. Capllonch (Op. 10,

4

J'allais par des chemins perfides,
Douloureusement incertain.
Vos chères mains furent mes guides.

Si pâle à l'horizon lointain
Luisait un faible espoir d'aurore;
Votre regard fut le matin.

Nul bruit, sinon son pas sonore,
N'encourageait le voyageur.
Votre voix me dit: "Marche encore!"

The white moon
shines in the woods;
from every branch
goes forth a voice
under the leaves ...

O my beloved.

The pond reflects,
deep mirror,
the silhouette
of the black willow
in which the wind weeps ...

Let us dream, it is the hour.

A great and tender
peace
seems to descend
from the heavens
irised by the star ...

It is the enchanted hour.

----

no. 5), R. Pick-Mangiagalli, Allen van Höveln (Op. 46), S. B. Schlesinger, A. Flégier (*Apaisement*), Werner Josten, Igor Stravinsky (Op. 9, no. 2), and Ethelbert Nevin (Op. 28, no. 6, *The silver moon*).

I walked the treacherous ways,
miserably uncertain.
Your dear hands were my guide.

So pale on the distant horizon
shone a feeble hope of dawn;
your eyes were the morning.

No sound save that of his own steps
encouraged the traveler.
Your voice said: "Go on!"

Mon cœur craintif, mon sombre cœur
Pleurait, seul, sur la triste voie;
L'amour, délicieux vainqueur,

Nous a réunis dans la joie.

GABRIEL FAURÉ, Op. 61, no. 4.

5

J'ai presque peur, en vérité,
Tant je sens ma vie enlacée
À la radieuse pensée
Qui m'a pris l'âme l'autre été.

Tant votre image, à jamais chère,
Habite en ce cœur tout à vous,
Mon cœur uniquement jaloux
De vous aimer et de vous plaire;

Et je tremble, pardonnez-moi,
D'aussi franchement vous le dire,
À penser qu'un mot, un sourire
De vous est désormais ma loi,

Et qu'il vous suffirait d'un geste,
D'une parole ou d'un clin d'œil,
Pour mettre tout mon être en deuil
De son illusion céleste.

Mais plutôt je ne veux vous voir,
L'avenir dût-il m'être sombre
Et fécond en peines sans nombre
Qu'à travers un immense espoir,

Plongé dans ce bonheur suprême
De me dire encore et toujours,
En dépit des mornes retours,
Que je vous aime, que je t'aime!

GABRIEL FAURÉ, Op. 61, no. 5. In the third line of the second stanza *Mon cœur* is changed to *Ce cœur*; and in the third line of the third stanza *un sourire* becomes *qu'un sourire*.

My fearful heart, my melancholy heart
wept, lonely, along the unhappy way;
love, delightful victor,

has reunited us in joy.

I am almost afraid, to tell the truth,
so much do I feel my life bound up
in the radiant emotion
that took possession of my soul last summer.

So much does your very dear image
inhabit this heart, dedicated to you,
my heart anxious only
to love you and to please you;

and I tremble, forgive me
for telling you so frankly,
to realize that one word, one smile
from you henceforth is my law;

and that one gesture would suffice,
one word or one wink,
to put my whole being in mourning
for its divine illusion.

But I would rather not see you—
if my future should be melancholy
and full of numberless sorrows—
except through an immense hope

that, deep in this supreme happiness,
I can say again and always,
in spite of dismal vicissitudes,
that I love you! I love you!

6

Avant que tu ne t'en ailles,
Pâle étoile du matin,
 —Mille cailles
Chantent, chantent dans le thym.—

Tourne devers le poète,
Dont les yeux sont pleins d'amour,
 —L'alouette
Monte au ciel avec le jour.—

Tourne ton regard que noie
L'aurore dans son azur;
 —Quelle joie
Parmi les champs de blé mûr!—

Puis fais luire ma pensée
 Là-bas,—bien loin! oh! bien loin,
 —La rosée
Gaîment brille sur le foin.—

Dans le doux rêve où s'agite
Ma mie endormie encor . . .
 —Vite, vite,
Car voici le soleil d'or!—

GABRIEL FAURÉ, Op. 61, no. 6. The first words of the fourth stanza are changed from *Puis fais luire* to *Et fais luire*. The poem has also

7

Donc, ce sera par un clair jour d'été:
Le grand soleil, complice de ma joie,
Fera, parmi le satin et la soie,
Plus belle encor votre chère beauté;

Le ciel tout bleu, comme une haute tente,
Frissonnera somptueux à longs plis
Sur nos deux fronts heureux qu'auront pâlis
L'émotion du bonheur et l'attente;

Before you fade,
pale morning star,
    —a thousand quails
are singing, singing in the thyme.—

Turn to the poet,
whose eyes are full of love,
    —the lark
mounts up to heaven with the day.—

Turn your glance, which
the dawn drowns in its blue;
    —what joy
among the fields of ripened grain!—

Then make my thoughts shine
yonder—far away, o far away!
    —the dew
sparkles brightly on the hay.—

In the sweet dream that occupies
my still-sleeping love . . .
    —haste, haste,
for the golden sun is here.—

---

been set by N. Sokolow (Op. 31, no. 7) and R. Koczalski (Op. 69, no. 9).

Then, it shall be one bright summer day:
the great sun, accomplice of my happiness,
will make your dear beauty, in satin and silk,
even lovelier;

the sky, all blue, like a high tent,
shall vibrate sumptuously in its long folds
over our two happy brows, grown pale
with the emotion of pleasure and expectancy;

Et quand le soir viendra, l'air sera doux
Qui se jouera, caressant, dans vos voiles,
Et les regards paisibles des étoiles
Bienveillamment souriront aux époux.

GABRIEL FAURÉ, Op. 61, no. 7. In the third line of the second
stanza the word *heureux* is omitted. There is a setting by Reynaldo

8

[N'est -ce pas? en dépit des sots et des méchants
Qui ne manqueront pas d'envier notre joie,
Nous serons fiers parfois et toujours indulgents.]

N'est -ce pas? nous irons, gais et lents, dans la voie
Modeste que nous montre en souriant l'Espoir,
Peu soucieux qu'on nous ignore ou qu'on nous voie.

Isolés dans l'amour ainsi qu'en un bois noir,
Nos deux cœurs, exhalant leur tendresse paisible,
Seront deux rossignols qui chantent dans le soir.

[Quant au Monde, qu'il soit envers nous irascible
Ou doux, que nous feront ses gestes? Il peut bien
S'il veut, nous caresser ou nous prendre pour cible.

Unis par le plus fort et le plus cher lien,
Et d'ailleurs, possédant l'armure adamantine,
Nous sourirons à tous et n'aurons peur de rien.]

Sans nous préoccuper de ce que nous destine
Le Sort, nous marcherons pourtant du même pas,
Et la main dans la main, avec l'âme enfantine

De ceux qui s'aiment sans mélange, n'est-ce pas?

GABRIEL FAURÉ, Op. 61, no. 8. The first, fourth and fifth stanzas
are omitted. Another setting has been published by R. Koczalski
(Op. 69, no. 10).

and when the evening comes the air will be sweet
that plays caressingly in your garments,
and the peaceful stars looking down
will smile benevolently upon our union.

Hahn called *Tous deux* (*Chansons grises*, no. 2), and one by N.
Sokolow (Op. 32, no. 4).

[Isn't it so? In spite of fools and schemers
who will not fail to envy our happiness,
we shall be proud now and then and indulgent always.]

Isn't it so? We shall go, merrily and slowly, down
the modest path which smiling hope points out to us,
little caring whether we are ignored or seen.

Alone in our love as in a deep forest,
our two hearts, breathing their quiet tenderness,
shall be two nightingales singing in the evening.

[As for the world, whether it be irritable toward us
or kind, what will its attitude mean to us? It may well,
if it wishes, either caress us or make a target of us.

United by the strongest and the dearest bonds,
moreover, possessed of impenetrable armor,
we shall smile at all and shall fear nothing.]

Without concerning ourselves with
what fate sends, we shall still walk with the same step,
and hand in hand, with the simple spirit

of those who love with singleness of heart, shall we not?

9

L'hiver a cessé: la lumière est tiède
Et danse, du sol au firmament clair.
Il faut que le cœur le plus triste cède
À l'immense joie éparse dans l'air.

[Même ce Paris maussade et malade
Semble faire accueil aux jeunes soleils
Et comme pour une immense accolade
Tend les mille bras de ses toits vermeils.]

J'ai depuis un an le printemps dans l'âme
Et le vert retour du doux floréal,
Ainsi qu'une flamme entoure une flamme,
Met de l'idéal sur mon idéal.

Le ciel bleu prolonge, exhausse et couronne
L'immuable azur où rit mon amour.
La saison est belle et ma part est bonne
Et tous mes espoirs ont enfin leur tour.

Que vienne l'été! que viennent encore
L'automne et l'hiver! Et chaque saison
Me sera charmante, ô Toi que décore
Cette fantaisie et cette raison!

GABRIEL FAURÉ, Op. 61, no. 9. The second stanza is omitted.

C'EST L'EXTASE LANGOUREUSE

Le vent dans la plaine
suspend son haleine.
—FAVART

C'est l'extase langoureuse,
C'est la fatigue amoureuse,
C'est tous les frissons des bois
Parmi l'étreinte des brises,
C'est, vers les ramures grises,
Le chœur des petites voix.

Winter is past: the light is mild
and it dances from the sun in the bright sky.
The saddest heart must yield
to the great joy that fills the air.

[Even this Paris, disagreeable and sick,
seems to welcome the young suns,
and as if for an immense accolade,
holds out the thousand arms of its ruddy roofs.]

For a year I have had spring in my soul,
and the green return of sweet Floreal,
as a flame encompasses a flame,
adds an ideal to my ideal.

The blue sky expands, exalting and crowning
the steadfast azure where my love smiles.
The weather is lovely and my lot is happy,
and all my hopes have at last been realized.

Let summer come, let
autumn and winter come again! And every season
will be charming to me, o you adorned by
this fantasy and this reason.

IT IS THE ECSTASY OF LANGUOR

> The wind on the plain
> holds its breath.
> —FAVART

It is languorous ecstasy,
it is amorous fatigue,
it is all the thrills of the forest
embraced by the breezes;
it is, about the gray branches,
the chorus of little voices.

Ô le frêle et frais murmure!
Cela gazouille et susurre
Cela ressemble au cri doux
Que l'herbe agitée expire . . .
Tu dirais, sous l'eau qui vire,
Le roulis sourd des cailloux.

Cette âme qui se lamente
En cette plainte dormante
C'est la nôtre, n'est-ce pas?
La mienne, dis, et la tienne,
Dont s'exhale l'humble antienne
Par ce tiède soir, tout bas?

CLAUDE DEBUSSY (*Ariettes oubliées*, no. 1). Fauré made a setting titled simply *C'est l'extase* . . . (Op. 58, no. 5). In the third line of the second stanza *cri doux* is changed to *bruit doux*, and in the

CLAIR DE LUNE

Votre âme est un paysage choisi
Que vont charmant masques et bergamasques
Jouant du luth et dansant et quasi
Tristes sous leurs déguisements fantasques.

Tout en chantant sur le mode mineur
L'amour vainqueur et la vie opportune,
Il n'ont pas l'air de croire à leur bonheur
Et leur chanson se mêle au clair de lune,

Au calme clair de lune triste et beau,
Qui fait rêver les oiseaux dans les arbres
Et sangloter d'extase les jets d'eau,
Les grands jets d'eau sveltes parmi les marbres.

GABRIEL FAURÉ, Op. 46, no. 2. Fauré's song is a piano minuet with commentary by the voice, so apparently inevitable and at the same time so impersonal that his music seems the perfect complement of the poem. Very different, but also very fine, is the quietly ecstatic setting of Debussy (*Fêtes galantes*, ser. 1, no. 3), with its wonderful

COLLOQUE SENTIMENTAL

Dans le vieux parc solitaire et glacé,
Deux formes ont tout à l'heure passé.

O the delicate fresh murmur!
It chirps and whispers,
it is like the sweet cry
breathed out by the waving grass ...
You would say, under the changing tide,
the heavy rolling of stones.

The spirit lamenting
in this dull complaint,
it is ours, is it not?
Mine, tell me, and yours,
breathing its lowly anthem
on this mild evening, so quietly?

---

second line of the third stanza *En* is changed to *Et*. There is another
setting by N. Sokolow (Op. 32, no. 2).

MOONLIGHT

Your soul is a rare landscape
with charming maskers and mummers
playing the lute and dancing, almost
sad beneath their fantastic disguises.

While singing in minor mode
of victorious love and life in its season,
they do not seem to believe in their happiness,
and their song mingles with the moonlight.

With the calm moonlight, sad and lovely,
that sets the birds in the trees to dreaming,
and the fountains to sobbing in ecstasy,
the great fountains, svelte among the marbles.

---

soaring final line. Also well known is the song of Jósef Szulc, in
which the picture seems to be centered around the fountain
described at the end. Other settings include a very early one by
Debussy, quite different from that mentioned above, one by A.
Diepenbrock, and one by A. Teichmüller.

SENTIMENTAL COLLOQUY

In the old park, deserted and frozen,
two forms just now passed by.

Leurs yeux sont morts et leurs lèvres sont molles,
Et l'on entend à peine leurs paroles.

Dans le vieux parc solitaire et glacé,
Deux spectres ont évoqué le passé.

— Te souvient-il de notre extase ancienne?
— Pourquoi voulez-vous donc qu'il m'en souvienne?

— Ton cœur bat-il toujours à mon seul nom?
Toujours vois-tu mon âme en rêve? — Non.

— Ah! les beaux jours de bonheur indicible
Où nous joignions nos bouches! — C'est possible.

— Qu'il était bleu, le ciel, et grand l'espoir!
— L'espoir a fui, vaincu, vers le ciel noir.

Tels ils marchaient dans les avoines folles
Et la nuit seule entendit leurs paroles.

CLAUDE DEBUSSY (*Fêtes galantes*, ser. 2, no. 3). Also set by

EN SOURDINE

Calmes dans le demi-jour
Que les branches hautes font,
Pénétrons bien notre amour
De ce silence profond.

Fondons nos âmes, nos cœurs
Et nos sens extasiés,
Parmi les vagues langueurs
Des pins et des arbousiers.

Ferme tes yeux à demi,
Croise tes bras sur ton sein,
Et de ton cœur endormi
Chasse à jamais tout dessein.

Laissons -nous persuader
Au souffle berceur et doux
Qui vient à tes pieds rider
Les ondes de gazon roux.

Their eyes are dead and their lips are flabby,
and one can hardly hear their words.

In the old park, deserted and frozen,
two ghosts were recalling their past.

"Do you remember our old ecstasy?"
"But why do you want me to remember it?"

"Does your heart still beat at the very mention of my name?
Do you always see my spirit in your dreams?" "No."

"Ah! the beautiful days of unutterable happiness
when our lips met!" "It is possible."

"How blue the sky was, and how great our hope!"
"Hope has flown, vanquished, to the black sky."

So they walked on through the wild oats,
and only the night heard their words.

Charles Bordes and by Henry K. Hadley (Op. 82, no. 2).

MUTED

Calm in the twilight
which the high branches make,
let us steep our love
in this deep silence.

Let us fuse our souls, our hearts,
and our enraptured senses
among the vague languors
of the pines and the arbutus trees.

Half-close your eyes,
cross your arms upon your breast,
and from your sleeping heart
banish all purpose.

Let us persuade ourselves
in the quieting soft breeze
that comes around your feet to ruffle
the waves of ruddy grass.

Et quand, solennel, le soir
Des chênes noirs tombera,
Voix de notre désespoir
Le rossignol chantera.

GABRIEL FAURÉ, Op. 58, no. 2. The first line of the second stanza reads: *Mêlons nos âmes, nos cœurs.* Debussy made two settings, the more familiar being no. 1 of his first set of *Fêtes galantes*; the second, published in 1944, is called *Calme dans le demi-jour.*

FANTOCHES

Scaramouche et Pulcinella
Qu'un mauvais dessein rassembla,
Gesticulent, noirs sur la lune.

Cependant l'excellent docteur
Bolonais cueille avec lenteur
Des simples parmi l'herbe brune.

Lors sa fille, piquant minois,
Sous la charmille en tapinois
Se glisse demi-nue, en quête

De son beau pirate espagnol
Dont un langoureux rossignol
Calme la détresse à tue-tête.

CLAUDE DEBUSSY (*Fêtes galantes*, ser. 1, no. 2). In the next to last line *langoureux* becomes *amoureux.*

GREEN

Voici des fruits, des fleurs, des feuilles et des branches,
Et puis voici mon cœur, qui ne bat que pour vous.
Ne le déchirez pas avec vos deux mains blanches
Et qu'à vos yeux si beaux l'humble présent soit doux.

J'arrive tout couvert encore de rosée
Que le vent du matin vient glacer à mon front.
Souffrez que ma fatigue, à vos pieds reposée,
Rêve des chers instants qui la délasseront.

And when, solemnly, evening
shall fall from the dark oaks,
voice of our hopelessness,
the nightingale will sing.

Reynaldo Hahn also set the poem as no. 4 of his *Chansons grises*.
German versions have been set by C. F. Karthaus and F. E. Simon
(*Breiten, schattenden Zweige*).

PUPPETS

Scaramouche and Pulcinella,
maliciously met,
gesticulate, black against the moon.

Meanwhile the excellent Bolognese Doctor
is slowly gathering
simples among the brown grass.

Then his daughter, lively little creature,
under the arbor stealthily
glides half-naked in search

of her handsome Spanish buccaneer,
whose distress a languorous nightingale
calms at the top of its voice.

GREEN

Here are fruits, flowers, leaves, and branches,
and here too is my heart, which beats only for you.
Do not tear it with your two white hands,
and to your lovely eyes may the humble present be sweet.

I arrive, still all covered with dew,
which the morning wind has frozen on my brow.
Let my weariness, resting at your feet,
dream of the dear moments when I shall be refreshed.

Sur votre jeune sein laissez rouler ma tête
Toute sonore encor de vos derniers baisers;
Laissez-la s'apaiser de la bonne tempête,
Et que je dorme un peu puisque vous reposez.

CLAUDE DEBUSSY (*Ariettes oubliées*, no. 5). *Ariettes* five and six are subtitled *Aquarelles*, title and subtitle are Verlaine's. In the second line of the final stanza *encor* is expanded to *encore*.

IL PLEURE DANS MON CŒUR

Il pleut doucement sur la ville.
—ARTHUR RIMBAUD

Il pleure dans mon cœur
Comme il pleut sur la ville,
Quelle est cette langueur
Qui pénètre mon cœur?

Ô bruit doux de la pluie
Par terre et sur les toits!
Pour un cœur qui s'ennuie
Ô le chant de la pluie!

Il pleure sans raison
Dans ce cœur qui s'écœure.
Quoi! nulle trahison?
Ce deuil est sans raison.

C'est bien la pire peine
De ne savoir pourquoi,
Sans amour et sans haine,
Mon cœur a tant de peine!

CLAUDE DEBUSSY (*Ariettes oubliées*, no. 2). In the last line of the second stanza *le chant* is changed to *le bruit*. Fauré (Op. 51, no. 3) calls his song *Spleen*. In the third stanza, second line, he has *Dans*

MANDOLINE

Les donneurs de sérénades
Et les belles écouteuses
Échangent des propos fades
Sous les ramures chanteuses.

Upon your young breast let me roll my head,
still ringing with your last kisses;
let it calm itself after the delightful tempest,
and let me sleep a bit while you are at rest.

GABRIEL FAURÉ, Op. 58, no. 3.
REYNALDO HAHN (1891). Hahn calls his setting *Offrande*.

THERE IS WEEPING IN MY HEART

It is raining gently on the town.
—ARTHUR RIMBAUD

There is weeping in my heart
like the rain on the town.
What is this languor
that penetrates my heart?

O sweet sound of the rain,
on the ground and on the roofs!
To a weary heart,
o the song of the rain!

Tears fall without reason
in my sick heart.
What! no treachery?
This mourning is without reason.

Indeed it is the worst pain
not to know why,
without love and without hate,
my heart has so much pain!

---

mon cœur . . . and in the fourth line, *Mon deuil est sans raison.*
There is also a setting by Sokolow (Op. 32, no. 3).

MANDOLIN SERENADE

The men serenading
and the lovely ladies listening
exchange affected pleasantries
under the singing branches.

C'est Tircis et c'est Aminte,
Et c'est l'éternel Clitandre,
Et c'est Damis qui pour mainte
Cruelle fait maint vers tendre.

Leurs courtes vestes de soie,
Leurs longues robes à queues,
Leur élégance, leur joie
Et leurs molles ombres bleues

Tourbillonnent dans l'extase
D'une lune rose et grise,
Et la mandoline jase
Parmi les frissons de brise.

CLAUDE DEBUSSY (1880). Most important of the other settings are those of Fauré (Op. 58, no. 1), Hahn (1892), and Gabriel Dupont. Fauré repeats the first stanza at the end, and in the fourth line of the

L'OMBRE DES ARBRES

Le rossignol qui du haut d'une branche se regard dedans, croit être tombé dans la rivière. Il est au sommet d'un chène et toutefois il a peur de se noyer.—CYRANO DE BERGERAC

L'ombre des arbres dans la rivière embrumée
  Meurt comme de la fumée,
Tandis qu'en l'air, parmi les ramures réelles
  Se plaignent les tourterelles.

Combien, ô voyageur, ce paysage blème
  Te mira blème toi -même,
Et que tristes pleuraient dans les hautes feuillées
  Tes espérances noyées!

CLAUDE DEBUSSY (*Ariettes oubliées*, no. 3); REYNALDO HAHN (*Chansons grises*, no. 6).

LE CIEL EST, PAR-DESSUS LE TOIT

Le ciel est, par-dessus le toit,
  Si bleu, si calme!
Un arbre, par-dessus le toit,
  Berce sa palme.

Tircis is there and Aminte,
and the inevitable Clitandre;
and there is Damis, who for many
a cruel maid makes many tender verses.

Their short silk jackets,
their long gowns with trains,
their elegance, their joy
and their soft blue shadows

whirl in the ecstasy
of a rose and gray moon,
and the mandolin babbles on
in the quiverings of the breeze.

---

second stanza changes *fait* to *fit*. Hahn, whose song is called *Fêtes galantes*, makes this same change. Other composers include Gabriel Grovlez, Bernard de Lisle, and R. Pick-Mangiagalli.

THE SHADOW OF THE TREES

The nightingale, who from the high branches sees his reflect-tion below, believes that he has fallen into the river. He is at the top of an oak, yet he is afraid of drowning.—CYRANO DE BERGERAC

The shadow of the trees in the misty river
is dissipated like smoke,
while in the real branches above
the turtle-doves lament.

How this pale landscape, o traveler,
reflected your pale self,
and how sad was the lamenting in the lofty foliage
of your drowned hopes!

THE SKY, ABOVE THE ROOFS

The sky, above the roofs,
is so blue, so calm!
A tree over the roofs
waves its branches.

La cloche dans le ciel qu'on voit
　　Doucement tinte.
Un oiseau sur l'arbre qu'on voit
　　Chante sa plainte.

Mon Dieu, mon Dieu, la vie est là,
　　Simple et tranquille.
Cette paisible rumeur-là
　　Vient de la ville.

— Qu'as-tu fait, ô toi que voilà
　　Pleurant sans cesse,
Dis, qu'as-tu fait, toi que voilà,
　　De ta jeunesse?

REYNALDO HAHN (1892). Titled *D'une prison*. Fauré calls his setting (Op. 83, no. 1) *Prison*. That of Ettore Panizza is known by

VILLON, FRANÇOIS
1431–ca.1463

TROIS BALLADES DE FRANÇOIS VILLON

BALLADE DE VILLON À S'AMYE

Faulse beauté, qui tant me couste cher,
Rude en effect, hypocrite doulceur,
Amour dure, plus que fer, à mascher;
Nommer te puis de ma deffaçon soeur,
Charme felon, la mort d'ung povre cueur,
Orgueil mussé, qui gens met au mourir;
Yeulx sans pitié! ne veult droict de rigueur,
Sans empirer, ung povre secourir?

The bell in the sky I can see
is softly ringing.
A bird on the tree I can see
sings his sad song.

My God! My God! life is there,
simple and tranquil.
That peaceful sound
comes from the town.

"What have you done, you there,
ceaselessly weeping,
say, what have you done, you there,
with your youth?"

---

its first line, *Le ciel est pardessus le toit*. There are other settings by
S. Pantschenko (Op. 11, no. 1) and R. Pick-Mangiagalli.

The proverbial vagabond poet, whose real name was
François de Montcorbier, or perhaps François des Loges.
As a student at the Sorbonne he led a wild and erratic life
and was not infrequently arrested for participation in street
brawls involving murder and robbery. Much of his career
as we know it is undoubtedly legendary, but it has inspired
stories, novels, poems, dramas, and operettas. His poems
are masterpieces of form and expression.

BALLADE OF VILLON TO HIS LOVE

False beauty, who costs me so dear,
rude, indeed, false sweetness,
love harder to chew than iron;
I might call you, sister of my undoing,
criminal charm, the death of my poor heart,
hidden pride that puts men to death;
eyes without pity! would not justice,
without making him worse, come to the aid of a poor man?

Mieulx m'eust valu avoir esté crier
Ailleurs secours, c'eust esté mon bonheur;
Rien ne m'eust sceu de ce fait arracher;
Trotter m'en fault en fuyte à deshonneur.
Haro, haro, le grand et le mineur!
Et qu'est cecy? mourray sans coup ferir,
Ou pitié peult, selon ceste teneur,
Sans empirer, ung povre secourir?

Ung temps viendra, qui fera desseicher,
Jaulnir, flestrir, vostre espanie fleur:
J'en risse lors, se tant peusse marcher,
Mais las! nenny: Ce seroit donc foleur,
Vieil je seray; vous, laide et sans couleur.
Or, beuvez fort, tant que ru peult courir,
Ne donnez pas à tous ceste douleur
Sans empirer, ung povre secourir.

Envoi

Prince amoureux, des amans le greigneur,
Vostre mal gré ne vouldroye encourir;
Mais tout franc cueur doit, par Nostre Seigneur,
Sans empirer, ung povre secourir.

BALLADE QUE VILLON FEIT À LA REQUESTE DE SA MÈRE POUR PRIER NOSTRE-DAME

Dame du ciel, régente terrienne,
Emperière des infernaulz palux,
Recevez-moy, vostre humble chrestienne,
Que comprinse soye entre vos esleuz,
Ce non obstant qu'oncques rien ne valuz.
Les biens de vous, ma dame et ma maistresse
Sont trop plus grans que ne suys pecheresse,
Sans lesquelz bien ame ne peult merir
N'avoir les cieulx, je n'en suis menteresse.
En ceste foy je vueil vivre et mourir.

Better to have cried
elsewhere for help that would have been my happiness;
nothing could keep me from acting thus;
now I must flee in dishonor.
For shame! For shame! The great and the small!
And what is this? I shall die without striking a blow.
Or will pity, in this plight,
without making him worse, come to the aid of a poor man?

A time will come that will dry up,
discolor and wither your full-blown flower;
I will laugh, if I still can,
but no! that would be folly.
Old I shall be, you ugly and colorless.
Then drink deep, as long as the stream runs;
do not give to everyone this misery.
Without making him worse, come to the aid of a poor man.

Envoy

Prince of love, lord of lovers,
I would not want to incur your displeasure;
but every noble heart should, by Our Lord,
without making him worse, come to the aid of a poor man.

BALLADE WHICH VILLON WROTE AT THE REQUEST
OF HIS MOTHER TO PRAY TO OUR LADY

Lady of heaven, Regent of the earth,
Ruler of the infernal swamps,
receive me, your humble Christian,
that I may be numbered among your chosen ones,
although in me there is no value.
Your mercies, my Lady and my Mistress,
are so much greater than my sinfulness,
without which mercies my soul would not be worthy
to enter heaven—in this I am not lying—
in this faith I wish to live and die.

A vostre Filz dictes que je suys sienne;
De luy soyent mes pechez aboluz:
Pardonnez-moy comme à l'Egyptienne,
Ou comme il feit au clerc Theophilus,
Lequel par vous fut quitte et absoluz,
Combien qu'il eust au diable faict promesse.
Preservez -moy que je n'accomplisse ce!
Vierge portant sans rompure encourir
Le sacrement qu'on celebre à la messe.
En ceste foy je veuil vivre et mourir.

Femme je suis povrette et ancienne,
Qui riens ne sçay, oncques lettre ne leuz;
Au moustier voy dont suis paroissienne,
Paradis painct où sont harpes et luz,
Et ung enfer où damnez sont bouluz:
L'ung me faict paour, l'aultre joye et liesse.
La joye avoir fais-moy, haulte Deesse,
A qui pecheurs doibvent tous recourir,
Comblez de foy, sans faincte ne paresse.
En ceste foy je vueil vivre et mourir.

Envoi

[Vous portastes, digne Vierge, princesse,
Iesus regnant, qui n'a ne fin ne cesse.
Le Tout-Puissant, prenant nostre foiblesse,
Laissa les cieulx et nous vint secourir,
Offrit à la mort sa tres chiere jeunesse.
Nostre Seigneur tel est, tel le confesse,
En ceste foy je vueil vivre et mourir.]

BALLADE DES FEMMES DE PARIS

Quoy qu'on tient belles langagières
Florentines, Veniciennes,
Assez pour estre messaigières,
Et mesmement les anciennes;
Mais, soient Lombardes, Romaines,
Genevoises, à mes perils,
Piemontoises, Savoysiennes,
Il n'est bon bec que de Paris.

Say to your Son that I am His;
by Him may my sin be absolved:
pardon me as He did the Egyptian,
or the clerk Theophilus,
who by you was pardoned and absolved,
although he had pledged himself to the devil.
Preserve me that I may never do such a thing!
Virgin Mother, who carried undefiled
the Sacrament we celebrate at Mass.
In this faith I wish to live and die.

A woman I am, poor and old,
ignorant and unable to read.
In the convent where I am a parishioner
is a painted paradise, where there are harps and lutes,
and a hell where the damned are boiled.
The one frightens me, the other gives me joy and mirth.
Let that joy be mine, High Goddess
to whom sinners should all return
full of faith, without pretense or weariness.
In this faith I wish to live and die.

Envoy

[You bore, Worthy Virgin, Princess,
Jesus the King, who has no end or ceasing.
The All-Powerful, taking on our weaknesses,
left the heavens and came to our aid,
offered unto death His most precious youth.
Such is Our Lord, and such I do confess Him.
In this faith I wish to live and die.]

BALLADE OF THE WOMEN OF PARIS

Though they are accounted good talkers,
the women of Florence and of Venice,
enough to make their meanings clear—
even the old ones—
still, be they Lombards, Romans,
Genovese, I say to my peril,
Piedmontese or Savoyards,
there is no good mouth except in Paris.

De beau parler tiennent chayeres,
Ce dit-on Napolitaines,
Et que sont bonnes cacquetières
Allemandes et Bruciennes;
Soient Grecques, Egyptiennes,
De Hongrie ou d'aultre païs,
Espaignolles ou Castellannes,
Il n'est bon bec que de Paris.

Brettes, Suysses, n'y sçavent guères,
Ne Gasconnes et Tholouzaines;
Du Petit-Pont deux harangères
Les concluront, et les Lorraines,
Anglesches ou Callaisiennes,
(Ay-je beaucoup de lieux compris?)
Picardes, de Valenciennes . . .
Il n'est bon bec que de Paris.

Envoi

Prince, aux dames parisiennes
De bien parler donnez le prix;
Quoy qu'on die d'Italiennes,
Il n'est bon bec que de Paris.

CLAUDE DEBUSSY. There are so many variant editions of the Villon ballades—each with its own obscurities—that it has seemed best for our purpose to copy the texts from the published scores of

Good at holding lectures,
they say, are the women of Naples,
and very good prattlers
are the Germans and the Prussians;
be they Greeks, Egyptians,
from Hungary or other countries,
Spaniards or Castilians,
there is no good mouth except in Paris.

Bretons, Swiss know hardly anything of this,
or Gascons or Toulousians;
two spouters from the Petit-Pont
would shut them up; and the Lorrains,
women from England or Calais
(have I mentioned a lot of places?)
Picards, Valencians:
there is no good mouth except in Paris.

Envoy

Prince, to the Parisian women
give the prize for talk;
whatever they say of the Italians,
there is no good mouth except in Paris.

---

the Debussy settings. However, the *Envoy* to the second ballade, which Debussy did not set, has been restored.

ITALIAN SONGS

AGANOOR POMPILJ, VITTORIA
1855–1910

PIOGGIA

Piovea; per le finestre spalancate
A quella tregua di ostinati ardori
saliano dal giardin fresche forlate
d'erbe risorte e di risorti fiori.

S'acchetava il tumulto dei colori
sotto il vel delle gocciole implorate;
E intorno ai pioppi ai frassini agli allori
Beveano ingorde le zolle assertate.

Esser pianta, esser foglia, esser stello
E nell' angoscia dell' ardor (pensavo)
Cosi largo ristoro aver dal cielo
Sul davanzal protesa io gli arboscelli,
i fiori, l'erbe guardavo . . .
mi battea la pioggia sui capelli.

OTTORINO RESPIGHI.

CARPANI, GIUSEPPE
1752–1825

IN QUESTA TOMBA OSCURA

In questa tomba oscura
Lasciami riposar;
Quando vivevo, ingrata,
Dovevi a me pensar.

Lascia che l'ombre ignude
Godansi pace almen,
E non bagnar mie ceneri
D'inutile velen.

LUDWIG VAN BEETHOVEN. This arietta was Beethoven's contribution to a collection of sixty-three settings of the same poem published by T. Mollo, Vienna, in 1808. Luigi Cherubini, Antonio Salieri, Bonifazio Asioli, Vincenzo Righini, Nicola Antonio Zingarelli, Joseph Weigl, Ferdinando Paër, and Carl Czerny were

Italian poetess whose works are marked by restlessness and
a seeking after spiritual calm.

RAIN

It rained; through the windows thrown open,
in truce to persistent ardors,
mount from the garden fresh bursts of fragrance
of revived grass and of revived flowers.

The tumult of colors is subdued
under the veil of prayed-for dewdrops;
and around the poplars, the ash trees, the laurels,
the thirsty roots drink greedily.

To be a plant, to be a leaf, to be a star,
and in the anguish of ardor (I thought)
such liberal restoration to have from heaven.
On the sheltered window sill I looked at the trees,
the flowers, the grass . . .
The rain beat upon my head.

The esteem enjoyed by Carpani in his own time is evi-
denced by the story of the song below. He is remembered
today also as the author of the biography of Haydn translated into French by Stendhal and published as his own.

IN THIS MURKY TOMB

In this murky tomb
let me rest;
when I was living, ungrateful woman,
you should have thought of me.

Let the naked shadows
enjoy peace there,
and do not bathe my ashes
with useless venom.

---

among the most distinguished contributors; some were mere ama-
teurs, and some gave the verses a number of settings. Beethoven's
song is among his best known; none of the others is remembered
today.

D'ANNUNZIO, GABRIELE
1863–1938

L'ALBA SEPÀRA DALLA LUCE L'OMBRA

L'alba sepàra dalla luce l'ombra,
e la mia voluttà dal mio desire.
O dolci stelle, è l'ora di morire.
Un più divino amor dal ciel vi sgombra.

Pupille ardente, o voi senza ritorno
stelle tristi, spegnetevi incorrotte!
Morir debbo. Veder non voglio il giorno,
per amor del mio sogno e della notte.

Chiudimi, o Notte, nel tuo sen materno,
mentre la terra pallida s'irrota.
Ma che dal sangue mio nasca l'aurora
e dal sogno mio breve il sole eterno!

FRANCESCO PAOLO TOSTI.

I PASTORI

Settembre, andiamo. È tempo di migrare.
Ora in terra d'Abruzzi i miei pastori
lascian gli stazzi e vanno verso il mare:
scendono all'Adriatico selvaggio
che verde è come i pascoli dei monti.

Han bevuto profondamente ai fonti
alpestri, che sapor d'aqua natia
rimanga ne' cuori esuli a conforto,
che lungo illuda la lor sete in via.
Rinnovato hanno verga d'avellano.

E vanno pel tratturo antico al piano,
quasi per un erbal fiume silente,
su le vestigia degli antichi padri.
O voce di colui che primamente
conosce il tremolar della marina!

The most famous of modern Italian writers, D'Annunzio was successful as poet, novelist, and dramatist. Throughout his eventful life—the incident of his leading the Italian occupation of Fiume and his ardent championship of Mussolini will be remembered—his art was always concerned with the senses.

THE DAWN SEPARATES THE LIGHT FROM THE SHADOW

The dawn separates the light from the shadow,
and my pleasure from my desire.
O sweet stars, it is the hour to die.
A love more divine drives you from the sky.

Ardent eyes, oh you unreturning
sad stars, quench yourselves still uncorrupted!
I should die. I do not wish to see the day,
for love of my dream and of the night.

Close me, o night, in your maternal bosom,
while upon the pale earth the dew descends.
But let the dawn from my blood be born,
and from my brief dream the eternal sun!

THE SHEPHERDS

September; let us go. It is the time to migrate.
Now in the country of the Abruzzi my shepherds
leave their places and go toward the sea;
they go down to the wild Adriatic
which is green like the pastures on the mountains.

They have drunk deeply at the mountain springs
so that the taste of the native water
remains to comfort their exiled hearts,
long deceiving their thirst along the way.
They have made new staffs from the tree.

And they go by the old drove-path to the plain,
as if by a grassy silent river
in the steps of their ancient fathers.
O voice of the one who first
knows the swelling of the shore!

Ora lungh'esso il litoral cammina
la greggia. Senza mutamento è l'aria.
Il sole imbionda sì la viva lana
che quasi dalla sabbia non divaria.
Isciacquìo, calpestìo, dolci romori.

Ah perchè non son io co' miei pastori?

ILDEBRANDO PIZZETTI.

NEGRI, ADA

1870–1945

NEBBIE

Soffro.—lontan lontano
Le nebbie sonnolente
Salgono dal tacente
          Piano.

Alto gracchiando, i corvi,
Fidati all'ali nere,
Traversan le brughiere
          Torvi.

Dell'aere ai morsi crudi
Gli addolorati tronchi
Offron, pregando, i bronchi
          Nudi.

Come ho freddo! Son sola;
Pel grigio ciel sospinto
Un gemito d'estinto
          Vola;

E mi ripete: Vieni,
È buia la vallata.
O triste, o disamata,
          Vieni!

OTTORINO RESPIGHI.

Now along the coast
goes the herd. The air is unchanging.
The sun turns the living wool to gold
that is hardly different from sand.
Sweet sounds of the sea and of the tramping.

Ah, why am I not with my shepherds?

Considered the greatest of Italian women poets and one of
the finest literary artists of modern Italy. Her life was
tempestuous, and her poems are filled with restlessness and
despair. As a young woman she worked for social betterment, but finally resigned herself to hopelessness. Her last
works took on a religious tone.

MISTS

I suffer. Far in the distance
the sleeping mists
rise from the silent
plain.

Croaking above, the crows,
relying on their black wings,
fly over the moorland,
desolate.

Into the air like crude jaws
the suffering tree trunks
lift, praying, their branches
so bare.

How cold I am! I am alone.
Impelled by the gray sky
a moan of the dead
flies;

and says again to me: Come,
it is dark in the valley,
O sad, o friendless one,
come!

NOTTE

Sul giardino fantastico
profumato di rosa
la carezza de l'ombra
posa.

Pure ha un pensiero e un palpito
la quiete suprema;
l'aria, come per brivido,
trema.

La luttuosa tenebra
una storia di morte
racconta a la cardenie
smorte?

Forse—perché una pioggia
di soavi rugiade
entro socchiusi petali
cade.—

... Su l'ascose miserie,
su l'ebbrezze perdute,
sui muti sogni e l'ansie
mute,

Su le fugaci gioie
che il disinganno infrange,
la notte le sue lagrime
piange.

OTTORINO RESPIGHI. The third line in the fourth stanza reads:
entro i socchiusi petali.

NIGHT

Upon the fantastic garden,
fragrant with roses,
the caress of the shadow
lies.

Even so a thought and a sigh disrupt
the deadening silence;
the air, quivering,
shudders.

The mournful shadow
a story of death
tells to the pale
gardenias.

Perhaps—because a rain
of soft dews
into the half-closed petals,
falls—

... Over the hidden miseries,
after the lost joys,
after the silent dreams and the anxiety,
silent.

Over the fleeting joys
that disenchantment destroys,
the night weeps
its tears.

RUSSIAN SONGS

CONSTANTINE, GRAND DUKE OF RUSSIA
1858–1915

RASTVORIL YA OKNO

Rastvoril ya okno—stalo grustno ne v moch',
Opustilsya pred nim na koleni,
I v litzo mne pakhnula vesennyaya noch'
Blagovonnym dykhan'iem sireni.

A vdali gde to chudno tak pel solovei,
Ya vnimal yemu s grust'yu glubokoï
I s toskoyu o rodine vspomnil svoyeï;
Ob otchisne ya vspomnil daliokoï,

Gde rodnoï solovei pesn' rodnuyu poiot
I ne znaya zemnykh ogorcheniï,
Zalivaietsya tzeluyu noch' na proliot
Nad dushistoyu vetkoï sireni.

PIOTR IL'ICH TCHAIKOVSKI, Op. 63, no. 2. The first line reads: *Rastvoril ya okno—stalo dushno ne v moch'*; and the fifth: *A*

GALINA, G.
1873–

ZDES' KHOROSHO

Zdes' khorosho . . . Vzǵlyani,
Vdali oǵniom ǵorit reka,
Tzvetnym kovrom luga leǵli,
Beleyut oblaka.

Zdes' net lyudeï . . . Zdes' tishina . . .
Zdes' tol'ko Boǵ da ya,
Tzvety da staraya sosna,
Da ty, mechta moya!

SERGEI RACHMANINOFF, Op. 21, no. 7. This song is known in various translations as *How fair this spot, How sweet the place,*

Poet, playwright, and literary critic.

I OPENED THE WINDOW

I opened the window—sadness overwhelmed me.
I knelt before it;
and the spring night blew in my face
the aroma of lilacs in bloom.

And somewhere in the distance the nightingale began to
    sing;
I listened to the song sadly
and with longing remembered my homeland,
my far-away native land,

where our native nightingale sings our native song,
and, not knowing any earthly worries,
sings all night long
above the fragrant lilac branch.

---

vdali gde to chudno zapel solovei.

Pseudonym of Glafira Adol'fovna Einerling, poetess,
novelist, and translator. One of her poems, *Les rubyat*
(The woods are being chopped down), having for its
theme the unrest of the students in 1901, was long cir-
culated in manuscript and then printed abroad.

IT'S LOVELY HERE

It's lovely here . . . look,
the river is shimmering in the distance,
the meadows are a carpet of flowers,
and the clouds are white.

There are no people here . . . It is quiet . .
Here are only God and I,
flowers and the old pine tree,
and you, my dream!

Here beauty dwells, etc.

GOLENISHCHEV-KUTUZOV, COUNT ARSENIĬ ARKAD'YEVICH
1848–1913

PESNI I PLYASKI SMERTI—1
(Songs and Dances of Death)

TREPAK

Les, da polyany, bezlyud'ye krugom;
V'yuga u plachet i stonet;
Chuyetsya, budto vo mrake nochnom,
Zlaya kovo to khoronit.
Glyad'! Tak i yest'!
V temnote muzhika
Smert' obnimayet, laskayet;
S p'yanen'kim plyashet vdvoiom trepaka,
Na ukho pesn' napevayet:
Okh muzhichok, starichok ubogoĭ,
P'yan napilsya, poplelsya domoĭ;
A myatel' to, ved'ma, podnyalas', vzygrala,
S polya v les dremuchiĭ nevznachaĭ zagnala.
Gorem, toskoĭ, da nuzhdoĭ tomimyĭ!
Lyag, prikorni, da usni rodimyĭ!
Ya tebya, golubchik moĭ, snezhkom sogreyu,
Vkrug tebya velikuyu igru zateyu.
Vzbeĭ ka postel', ty myatel' lebedka,
Geĭ, nachinaĭ, zapevaĭ, pogodka;
Skazku, da takuyu, chtob vsyu noch' tyanulas',
Chtob p'yanchuge krepko pod neio zasnulos'.
Oi, vy lesa, nebesa, da tuchi,
Tem', veterok, da snezhok letuchiĭ,
Sveites' pelenoyu, snezhnoĭ pukhovoyu
Yeyu, kak mladentza, starichka prikroyu.
Spi, moĭ druzhok, muzhichok schastlivyĭ,
Leto prishlo, rastzvelo! Nad nivoĭ
Solnyshko smeyetsya, da serpy gulyayut;
Pesenka nesetsya, golubki letayut . . .

MODEST PETROVICH MUSORGSKI.

Lyric poet, very popular at the end of the nineteenth century. He began to publish in 1869, under the influence of Pushkin and Lermontov. The themes of pessimism, weariness and desire to flee into the past are characteristic of his poems.

TREPAK

The forest and fields are deserted;
only the storm is moaning and weeping.
It seems as though in the darkness
the evil one were burying someone.
And behold, so it is!
There in the darkness is death
embracing a poor old drunken man,
dancing a trepak with him,
and whispering in his ear:
"You have had too much to drink,
you poor old peasant,
and the blizzard has driven you
deep into the forest.
You are tired and weary;
lie down here and go to sleep.
I'll warm you up under a cover of snow
and will start a great game around you.
Storm, make him a soft bed;
winds, sing him a song
that will last all night,
so as to make him sleep more soundly.
And you, forests, heavens and clouds,
darkness and falling snow,
weave a blanket for him,
so that I can tuck him in like a baby.
Sleep, my friend, and enjoy yourself."
Summer has come again. Everything is in bloom.
The sun is smiling over the harvest fields.
A song sounds through the air, and the birds are flying
    around.

2

KOLYBEL′NAYA

Stonet rebionok. Svecha nagaraya,
Tusklo mertzayet krugom.
Tzeluyu noch′, kolybel′ku kachaya,
Mat′ ne zabylasya snom.

Ranym raniokhon′ko v dver′, ostorozhno,
Smert′ serdobol′naya stuk!
Vzdrognula mat′, oglyanulas′ trevozhno . . .
"Polno pugat′sya, moï drug!

Blednoye utro uzh smotrit v okoshko.
Placha, toskuya, lyubya
Ty utomilas′. Vzdremni ka nemnozhko,
Ya posizhu za tebya.

Ugomonit′ ty ditya ne sumela,
Slashche tebya ya spoyu."
Tishe! Rebionok moï mechetsya, b′iotsya,
Dushu terzayet moyu!

"Nu, da so mnoyu on skoro uïmiotsya,
Bayushki, bayu, bayù."
Shchechki bledneyut, slabeyet dykhan′ye . . .
Da zamolchi-zhe, molyu!

"Dobroye znamen′ye: stikhnet stradan′ye
Bayushki, bayu, bayù."
Proch′ ty proklyataya!
Laskoï svoyeyu sgubish′ ty radost′ moyu.

"Net, mirnyï son ya mladentzu naveyu;
Bayushki, bayu, bayù."
Szhal′sya, pozhdi dopevat′ khot′ mgnoven′ye,
Strashnuyu pesnyu tvoyu!

"Vidish′, usnul on pod tikhoye pen′ye.
Bayushki, bayu, bayù!"

MODEST PETROVICH MUSORGSKI.

3

SERENADA

Nega volshebnaya, noch′ golubaya,
Trepetnyï sumrak vesny . . .
Vnemlet, poniknuv golovkoï bol′naya
Shopot nochnoï tishiny.
Son ne smykayet blestyashchiye ochi,
Vsio pritailos′ krugom;

CRADLE SONG

The child is moaning. The candle burning low
casts a dim light.
The mother has sat up all night,
rocking the cradle.
With the first light of dawn
death knocks on the door.
Trembling, the mother looks around,
and hears: "Don't fear, my dear.
It is morning,
and with crying, worrying and loving
you are tired. Rest and sleep for a while.
I'll watch in your place.
You have failed to soothe the child.
I'll sing him a better song."
"Be quiet, the baby is restless again.
It breaks my heart."
"He'll soon be asleep in my arms.
Hush, baby, hush!"
The child gets paler; his breathing becomes weaker ...
Oh do keep silent, I beg thee.
"These are good signs—soon his suffering will be over.
Hush, baby, hush."
"Go away, accursed death,
you will kill my child with your caresses."
"No, I'll only put him to sleep peacefully.
Hush, baby, hush!"
"Have pity on me! Stop your terrible singing,
if only for a moment."
"You see I have put your child to sleep with my song.
Hush, baby, hush!"

THE SERENADE

Enchanting languor, blue night,
trembling twilight of spring ...
With bowed head the sick girl listens
to the murmurs in the stillness.
Sleep has not closed her eyes.
Everything remains quiet around.

V strastnom molchan'i vesenneĭ polnochi
Pesnya zvuchit pod oknom.
"V mrake nevoli surovoĭ i tesnoĭ,
Molodost' vyanet tvoya.
Rytzar' nevedomyĭ, siloĭ chudesnoĭ
Osvobozhu ya tebya.
Vstan', posmotri na sebya: krasotoyu
Lik tvoĭ prozrachnyĭ blestit,
Shchioki rumyany, volnistoĭ kosoyu
Stan tvoĭ, kak tucheĭ obvit;
Pristal'nykh glaz goluboye siyan'ye,
Yarche nebes i ognya;
Znoyem poludennym veyet dykhan'ye,
Ty obol'stila menya.
Slukh tvoĭ plenilsya moyeĭ serenadoĭ,
Rytzarya shopot tvoĭ zval.
Rytzar' prishol za beztzennoĭ nagradoĭ
Chas upoyen'ya nastal.
Nezhen tvoĭ stan, upoitelen trepet.
O zadushu ya tebya
V krepkikh ob'yat'yakh; lyubovnyĭ moĭ lepet
Slushaĭ . . . molchi . . . Ty moya!"

MODEST PETROVICH MUSORGSKI. Several changes in this poem

4

POLKOVODETZ

Grokhochet bitva, bleshchut broni,
Orud'ya mednyye revut,
Begut polki, nesutsya koni
I reki krasnyye tekut.
Pylayet polden', lyudi b'yutsya!
Sklonilos' solntze, boĭ sil'neĭ!
Zakat bledneyet, no derutsya
Vragi vsio yarostneĭ i zleĭ!
I pala noch' na pole brani.
Druzhiny v mrake razoshlis' . . .
Vsio stikhlo i v nochnom tumane
Stenan'ya k nebu podnyalis'.
Togda ozarena lunoyu,
Na boyevom svoiom kone,
Kosteĭ sverkaya beliznoyu,
Yavilas' smert' i v tishine,

And in the passionate silence of the spring midnight
a song is heard under her window:
"In the darkness of cruel captivity
your youth is fading away.
I, an errant knight, unknown to you, by magic power
will free you.
Come, look at yourself!
You are beautiful,
with rosy cheeks and dark tresses
that envelop your body as a cloud.
The light of your blue eyes
is brighter than the skies and the fires.
Your breath is hot as midday air.
You charm me.
I have cast a spell over you with my song.
Your whisper was calling me,
and now your knight is here to claim his supreme reward.
The hour of bliss has come.
Your body is soft and your charm enchanting.
Oh, I will strangle you
in my strong embrace; to my passionate whisper
listen . . . be silent . . . you're mine!"

---

can be found in the Appendix.

THE COMMANDER

The battle is raging. Armor gleams
and cannon roar.
The soldiers rush onward, the horses stampede
and rivers flow red with blood.
In the glaring midday they fight.
The sun is going down. They still fight;
the twilight fades,
but the warriors still fight fiercely.
Only when night falls
do the armies separate and retreat.
All is quiet, and in the night fog
the moans of the dying are heard.
And now death
rides forward,
his white bones glittering
in the moonlight.

Vnimaya vopli i molitvy
Dovol'stva gordovo polna,
Kak polkovodetz, mesto bitvy
Krugom ob'yekhala ona.
Na kholm podnyavshis' oglyanulas',
Ostanovilas', ulybnylas',
I nad ravninoĭ boyevoĭ
Razdalsya golos rokovoĭ:
"Konchena bitva! Ya vsekh pobedila!
Vse predo mnoĭ vy smirilis' boĭtzy!
Zhizn' vas possorila, ya pomirila,
Druzhno vstavaĭte na smotr, mertvetzy!
Marshem torzhestvennym mimo proĭdite,
Voĭsko moye ya khochu soschitat'.
V zemlyu potom, svoi kosti slozhite,
Sladko ot zhizni v zemle otdykhat'!
Gody nezrimo proĭdut za godami,
V lyudyakh ischeznet i pamyat' o vas.
Ya ne zabudu! I gromko nad vami
Pir budu pravit' v polunochnyĭ chas!
Plyaskoĭ, tyazholoyu, zemlyu syruyu
Ya pritopchu, chtoby sen' grobovuyu
Kosti pokinut' vo vek ne mogli,
Chtob nikogda vam ne vstat' iz zemli!"

MODEST PETROVICH MUSORGSKI. Line twenty-four: *pronessya golos rokovoĭ.*

ZABYTYĬ (BALLADA)

On smert' nashol v krayu chuzhom,
V krayu chuzhom, v boyu s vragom;
No vrag druz'yami pobezhdion,
Druz'ya likuyut, tol'ko on
Na pole bitvy pozabyt,
Odin lezhit.
I mezhdu tem kak zhadnyĭ vran
P'iot krov' yevo iz svezhikh ran,
I tochit nezakrytyĭ glaz,
Grozivshiĭ smert'yu v smertnyĭ chas,
I, nasladivshis', p'yan i syt,
Doloĭ letit . . .
Dalioko tam, v krayu rodnom,
Mat' kormit syna pod oknom:
"A-gu . . . a-gu! Ne plach', synok,

He listens to the wailing and praying,
and as a proud commander
rides on top of a hill;
looking over the battle ground,
he smiles with contempt
and proclaims in a loud voice:
"The battle is over.
I defeated you all,
you are all subdued.
You were enemies in life, and I have united you.
Rise now, and march past me
in a triumphal review.
I want to count my armies.
Then lie down;
bury your bones in the ground.
It will be sweet for you to rest.
Years will pass;
people will forget about you.
But I will remember
and celebrate in the midnight hours.
Dancing with heavy steps
I will stamp on the damp ground
over your graves
so that you will never rise again."

THE FORGOTTEN ONE (A BALLAD)

He met his death in a foreign land,
fighting the foe in a foreign land.
But his friends defeated the enemy
and are celebrating their victory.
Only he lies forgotten on the battle field,
lies alone.
The greedy raven
drinks the blood from his wounds
and pecks at his still-open eyes,
the eyes that had challenged death,
till, drunk and satisfied,
he flies off.
Meanwhile far away in his native land
the mother feeds his son sitting by the window,
and she comforts the child: "Do not cry, little one,

Verniotsya tyatya, pirozhok,
Togda na radostyakh, druzhku
Ya ispeku" . . .
A tot zabyt, odin lezhit.

MODEST PETROVICH MUSORGSKI. Known in various translations

KUKOL'NIK, NESTOR VASIL'YEVICH
1809–1868

SOMNENIYE

Uïmites' volneniya strasti
Zasni beznadiozhnoye serdtze
Ya plachu, ya strazhdu
Dusha utomilas' v razluke
Ya strazhdu, ya plachu
Ne vyplakat' gorya v slezakh.

Naprasno nadezhda mne schast'ye gadayet
Ne veryu, ne veryu obetam kovarnym
Razluka unosit lyubov'.
Kak son neotstupnyï i groznyï
Mne snitsya sopernik schastlivyï
I taïno i zlobno oruzhiya ishchet ruka.
Naprasno ismenu mne revnost' gadayet,
Ne veryu, ne veryu kovarnym navetam,
Ya schastliv, ty snova moya.
Minuyet pechal'noye vremya
My snova obnimem drug druga
I strastno i zharko
Zab'yot'sya voskressheye serdtze,
I strastno i zharko
S ustami sol'yutsya usta.

MIKHAIL IVANOVICH GLINKA.

daddy will come back soon,
and I'll bake a cake
to welcome him home."
But the other one lies alone and forgotten.

---

as *After the battle, Forgotten, Left alone,* etc. The poem was never
published.

Russian playwright and novelist.

THE DOUBT

Stop, you turmoils of passion,
go to sleep, restless heart.
I cry, I suffer,
my soul is made tired by our parting.
I suffer, I cry,
I cannot exhaust my sorrow in tears.

Hope, in vain, promises me happiness;
I do not trust, I do not trust these insidious promises.
Parting takes away love.
As a persistent and terrible dream,
I dream of a happy rival
and secretly and furiously my hand seeks a weapon.
The vain jealousy foretells perfidy to me.
I do not believe, I do not believe these wily calumnies.
I am happy, you are mine again.
The sad times will pass,
again we will embrace each other
and passionately and ardently
the resurrected heart will beat;
and passionately and ardently
our lips will meet.

LERMONTOV, MIKHAIL YUR'YEVICH
1814–1841

OTCHEVO

Mne grustno potomu, chto ya tebya lyublyu
I znayu molodost' tzvetushchuyu tvoyu
Ne poshchadit molvy kovarnoye gonen'ye.
Za kazhdyĭ svetlyĭ den', il' sladkoye mgnoven'ye
Slezami i toskoĭ zaplatish' ty sud'be.
Mne grustno . . . potomu, chto veselo tebe!

ALEKSANDR SERGEYEVICH DARGOMYZHSKI. Also known as *I grieve*.

MEREZHKOVSKI, DMITRI SERGEYEVICH
1865–1941

KHRISTOS VOSKRES

"Khristos voskres" poyut vo khrame;
No grustno mne . . . dusha molchit.
Mir polon krov'yu i slezami,
I étot gimn pred altaryami
tak oskorbitel'no zvuchit.

Kogda-b on byl mezh nas i videl,
chevo dostig nash slavnyĭ vek,
kak brata brat voznenavidel,
kak opozoren chelovek.

I yesli-b zdes' v blestyashchem khrame
"Khristos voskres" on uslykhal,
kakimi-b gor'kimi slezami
pered tolpoĭ on zarydal!

SERGEI RACHMANINOFF, Op. 26, no. 6.

Called "the poet of the Caucasus" because he was twice sent to that land as an exile. On the wave of Byronism then sweeping the literary world, Lermontov wrote romantic and revolutionary poems. He is known as the most tragic of the Russian poets.

WHY

I grieve because I love you,
and because I know that malicious talk
will not spare your youth.
And every happy moment of your life
you must repay with tears and sorrow.
I grieve . . . because you are gay.

A follower of Nadson and the leader of the Russian Symbolists. In his search for "eternal truths" he found himself in opposition successively to the tsarist and the Soviet regimes in Russia. A strong figure in his day, he lost most of his influence during his lifetime.

CHRIST IS RISEN

"Christ is risen," they sing in the temple;
but I feel sad . . . my soul is silent.
The world is full of blood and tears,
and that hymn before the altars
sounds like an insult.

If He were here among us and should see
what our brilliant age has accomplished,
how brother hates brother,
how defamed is man,

and if here, in this bright temple,
He should hear "Christ is risen,"
oh what bitter tears He would shed
before that mob.

PLESHCHEYEV, ALEKSEĬ NIKOLAYEVICH

1825–1893

STEP′YU IDU YA UNYLOYU

Step′yu idu ya unyloyu:
Net ni zvetochka na neĭ,
Netu zelionovo dereva,
Gde by mog spet′ soloveĭ.
Mrachno tak vecher nasupilsya,
Zvezd—ni sleda v vyshine . . .
Sam ya ne znayu, chto vspomnilas′
Vdrug, v ètu poru, ty mne . . .
Vspomnilas′ ty, moya milaya,
S krotkim i yasnym litzom . . .
Vizhu tebya . . . i, mne kazhetsya,
Mgla uzh redeyet krugom,
I budto pesn′ solov′inaya
V chashche zelenoĭ zvuchit,
Volny tzvetov kolykhayutsya.
V zviozdakh vsio nebo gorit.

ALEXANDER GRECHANINOFF, Op. 5, no. 1. The poem is after the Hungarian of Petöfi. In Grechaninoff's setting line three reads:

POLYUBILA YA NA PECHAL′ SVOYU

Polyubila ya
No pechal′ svoyu
Sirotinushku
Bestalannovo.
Uzh takaya mne
Dolya vypala.

Razluchili nas
Lyudi sil′nyye;
Uvezli yevo
Sdali v rekruty . . .

Russian poet and translator of Western poets into Russian.

OVER THE STEPPE

Over the steppe I trudge;
no flower blooms here,
and no green grass grows
in which a nightingale might sing.
The dark night falls,
and not a star lights the sky . . .
I do not know why at this moment
I thought of you, dear one,
I remember you, my dear,
with your frank and gentle face.
I see you . . . and it seems to me
as though the gloom had dispersed,
as though the nightingale were singing
in the green groves;
as though the flowers were moving like waves
and the skies were aglow with stars.

Derevtza nety zelionovo; and line ten: *S krotkim i yasnym chelom.*

THE SOLDIER'S BRIDE

I fell in love
to my sorrow
with an orphan,
a luckless one—
such is
my fate.

We were parted
by influential people;
he was driven away,
recruited into the army.

I soldatkoï ya,
Odinokoï ya,
Znat′ v chuzhoï izbe
I sostareyus′
Uzh takaya mne
Dolya vypala.

SERGEI RACHMANINOFF, Op. 8, no. 4. The fifth and sixth lines, and

PUSHKIN, ALEKSANDR SERGEYEVICH
1799–1837

TZARSKOSEI′SKAYA STATUYA

Urnu s vodoï uroniv, ob utios yeio deva razbila.
Deva pechal′no sidit, prazdnyï derzha cherepok.
Chudo! ne syaknet voda, izlivayas′ iz urny razbitoï;
Deva, nad vechnoï struioï, vechno pechal′na sidit.

CESAR ANTONOVICH CUI, Op. 57, no. 17. Also called *The statue of Tzarskoye Selo.*

UZNIK

Sizhu za reshotkoï v temnitze syroï.
Vskormlionnyï v nevole oriol molodoï,
Moï grustnyï tovarishch, makhaya krylom,
Krovavuyu pishchu klyuyot za oknom.
Klyuyot i brosayet, i smotrit v okno,
Kak budto so mnoyu zadumal odno;
Zoviot menya vzglyadom i krikom svoim,
I vymolvit′ khochet: "davaï uletim!
My vol′nyya ptitzy; pora, brat, pora!
Tuda, gde za tucheï beleyet gora,
Tuda, gde sineyut morskie kraya,
Tuda, gde gulyaem—lish′ veter da ya!"

ALEXANDER GRECHANINOFF, Op. 20, no. 4. There are also settings

And as a soldier's wife,
a lonely one,
in strangers' house,
I'll grow old.
Such is
my fate.

---

the final two, are changed to *Uzh takaya dolya mne vypala.*

The first great writer of modern Russia, poet, dramatist, novelist, and short story writer. He was at first influenced by Byron and the Romantics, but developed a strongly original style capable of depicting life in all its phases. Perhaps it is his directness and charm which have established his fame so securely among the Russians.

THE FOUNTAIN AT TZARSKOYE SELO

The maiden has dropped her urn and broken it on the rock.
Now she sits sadly holding the useless pieces.
But o miracle! The water does not stop flowing from the broken urn.
And over the unfailing stream the sad maiden sits forever.

THE CAPTIVE

I sit behind the bars of my dungeon.
An eagle, raised in captivity,
my poor comrade, beating his wings,
tears his food down below my window,
tears and throws it and glances at me
as though sharing my thoughts.
With his looks and his cries he is calling to me
as though to say: "Let us flee,
we were free born. It is time, brother, it is time.
Let us flee to the mountains beyond the clouds,
from where you can see the expanses of blue sea,
where only I and the wind roam."

---

by Anton Rubinstein (Op. 78, no. 6), and Nicolai Medtner (Op. 52, no. 7).

NENASTNYĬ DEN´ POTUKH

Nenastnyĭ den´ potukh; nenastnoĭ nochi mgla
Po nebu steletsya odezhdoyu svintzovoĭ;
Kak prividyeniye za roshcheyu sosnovoĭ
Luna tumannaya vzoshla . . .
Vsio mrachnuyu tosku na dushu mne navodit.
Dalioko, tam, luna v siyanii voskhodit;
Tam vozdukh napoion vecherneĭ svezheĭ mgloĭ;
Tam more dvizhetsya roskoshnoĭ pelenoĭ
Pod golubymi nebesami
Vot vremya: po gore teper´ idiot ona
K bregam, potoplennym shumyashchimi volnami,
Tam, pod zavetnymi skalami,
Teper´ ona sidit pechal´na i odna.
Odna . . . Nikto pred neĭ ne plachet, ne toskuyet,
Nikto yeio kolen v zabven´i ne tzeluet,
[Odna, nich´ im ustam ona ne predaiot
Ni plech, ni vlazhnykh ust, ni perseĭ belosnezhykh]
Nikto yeio lyubvi nebesnoĭ ne dostoin,
Ne pravda l´: ty odna . . . ty plachesh´ . . . ya spokoyen;
No yesli . . .

NIKOLAI RIMSKI-KORSAKOV. In the fifteenth line the word *kolen*
(knees) is changed to *usta* (lips); two lines immediately following

NE POĬ, KRASAVITZA

Ne poĭ, krasavitza, pri mne
Ty pesen Gruzii pechal´noĭ:
Napominayut mne one
Druguyu zhizn´ i bereg dal´noĭ,
Uvy, napominayut mne
Tvoi zhestokiye napevy
I step´, i noch´, i pri lune—
Cherty dalekoĭ bednoĭ devy.
Ya prizrak milyĭ rokovoĭ
Tebya uvidev, zabyvayu;
No ty poyosh´—i predo mnoĭ
Yevo ya vnov´ voobrazhayu.

THE GLOOMY DAY IS ENDED

The gloomy day is ended; the darkness of the gloomy night
envelops the skies in a cloth of lead;
as a ghost, from behind the pine grove,
the nebulous moon is rising . . .
Everything bestows dark sadness on my soul.
There, in a far-away land, the moon shines brightly,
the air is filled with fresh twilight;
the sea spreads a rich mantle
under the blue skies.
This is the time: now she comes over the mountain
to the shores drowned in the noisy waves.
There, under these sacred rocks,
she sits now sad and alone.
Alone . . . Nobody cries or suffers before her,
nobody kisses her knees in oblivion.
[Alone, she does not permit other lips to touch
her shoulders, mouth, or breast.]
Nobody deserves her heavenly love . . .
Is that not right: you are alone . . . you are crying . . . I am
    at peace;
But if . . .

---

this are omitted in the setting.

O DO NOT SING

O do not sing, beautiful maiden,
the sad songs of Georgia.
They remind me
of another life and of a distant shore.
Alas, your cruel melodies
bring to my memory
the steppe, and night and by moonlight
the features of the poor girl,
that dear, fatal ghost.
I forget, seeing you,
but then you sing—and before me
my imagination brings her back again.

Ne poï, krasavitza, pri mne
Ty pesen Gruzii pechal′noï:
Napominayut mne one
Druguyu zhizn′ i bereg dal′noï.

SERGEI RACHMANINOFF, Op. 4, no. 4. Also known as *O cease thy singing, maiden fair*, and as *Georgian song*. There are other settings

SURIKOV, IVAN ZAKHAROVICH
1840–1880

YA LI V POLE DA NE TRAVUSHKA BYLA

Ya li v pole da ne travushka byla?
Ya li v pole ne zelenaya rosla?
Vsyali menya travushku skosili
Na solnyshke v pole issushili
Okh ty gore, moio goryushko,
Znat′ takaya moya dolyushka.

[Ya li v pole ne pshenichushka byla?
Ya li v pole ne vysokaya rosla?
Vzyali menya srezali serpami
Sklali menya na pole snopami
Okh ty gore, moio goryushko
Znat′ takaya moya dolyushka.]

Ya li v pole ne kalinushka byla?
Ya li v pole da ne krasnaya rosla?
Vzyali kalinushku, polomali,
I v zhgutiki menya posvyazali!
Okh ty gore, moio goryushko,
Znat′ takaya moya dolyushka.

Ya l′ u batyushki ne dochen′ka byla,
U rodimoï ne tzvetochek ya rosla;
Nevoleï menya, bednuyu vzyali
Si nemilym sedym povenchali!
Okh ty gore, moio goryushko,
Znat′ takaya moya dolyushka.

PIOTR IL′ICH TCHAIKOVSKI, Op. 47, no. 7. Also known as *The bride's complaint*. The second stanza is not in the musical setting.

O do not sing, beautiful maiden,
the sad songs of Georgia.
They remind me
of another life and of a distant shore.

by Rimski-Korsakov (Op. 51, no. 2), Glinka, Balakirev (*Georgian song*), and Lazare Saminski (*A Georgian song*, Op. 2, no. 1).

Born of peasant stock, Surikov spent his early years working in his father's store. Encouraged by meeting A. N. Pleshcheyev, he produced his first play in 1863 and became known as a dramatist and poet.

WAS I NOT A BLADE OF GRASS

Was I not a blade of grass in the field?
Did I not grow green in the field?
They cut me down,
dried me in the sun.
Oh you sorrow, my sorrow,
such is my fate.

[Was I not wheat in the field?
Did I not grow tall in the field?
They cut me down with sickles
and gathered me on the field into sheaves.
O you sorrow, my sorrow,
such is my fate.]

Was I not a guelder-rose in the field?
Did I not grow red in the field?
They broke the guelder-rose bush
and tied me into plaits.
Oh you sorrow, my sorrow,
such is my fate.

Was I not my father's little daughter,
growing like my mother's flower?
They broke me, poor girl, by force,
and married to an old unwanted one!
Oh you sorrow, my sorrow,
such is my fate.

TOLSTOĬ, COUNT ALEKSEĬ
KONSTANTINOVICH
1817–1875

SRED' SHUMNAVO BALA

Sred' shumnavo bala, sluchaĭno,
V trevoge mirskoĭ suyety,
Tebya ya uvidel, no taĭna
Tvoi pokryvala cherty;
Lish ochi pechal'no glyadeli,
A golos tak divno zvuchal,
Kak zvon otdalionnoĭ svireli,
Kak morya igrayushchiĭ val.
Mne stan tvoĭ ponravilsya tonkiĭ
I ves' tvoĭ zadumchivyĭ vid,
A smekh tvoĭ, i grustnyĭ i zvonkiĭ,
S tekh por v moiom serdtze zvuchit.
V chasy odinokiye nochi
Lyublyu ya ustalyĭ, prilech';
Ya vizhu pechal'nyye ochi,
Ya slyshu vesioluyu rech',
I grustno ya tak zasypayu,
I v griozakh nevedomykh splyu . . .
Lyublyu li tebya ya ne znayu—
No kazhetsya mne, chto lyublyu!

PIOTR IL'ICH TCHAIKOVSKI, Op. 38, no. 3. Line seventeen reads:
I grustno ya, grustno tak zasypayu.

UZH TY, NIVA MOYA

Uzh ty, niva moya, nivushka,
Ne skosit' tebya s makhu yedinovo,
Ne svyazat' tebya vsyu vo yedinyĭ snop,
Uzh vy dumy moi, dumushki,
Ne stryakhnut' vas razom s plech doloĭ,
Odnoĭ rech'yu to vas ne vyskazat'!

Poet, playwright, novelist. Though he moved in court circles, his poems often touch on the theme of rebellion.

AT THE BALL

I met you by chance
amid the music and splendor of the ball,
but your features
were shrouded in mystery.
Your eyes looked so sad,
and your voice sounded so wonderful,
like the music of reed-pipes
or of waves at play.
I loved your graceful bearing,
your pensive expression;
and your laughter so glad and clear
is still ringing in my heart.
And when I go to rest
in the lonely hours of night
I see your sad eyes
and I hear your gay voice.
And as I fall asleep,
in my dreams I ask myself
whether I love you or not,
and yet it seems to me that I do.

THE HARVEST OF SORROW

Oh you, my wheat field,
you cannot be reaped with one stroke,
you cannot be tied into one sheaf.
Oh you, my thoughts,
you cannot be forgotten at once,
you cannot be expressed in one word.

Po tebe—l', niva, veter razgulival,
Gnuł kolos'ya tvoi do zemli,
Zrely ziorna vse razmiotyval;
Shiroko vy, dumy, porassypalis',
Kuda padala kakaya dumushka,
Tam vskhodila lyuta pechal' trava,
Vyrostalo gore goryucheye.

SERGEI RACHMANINOFF, Op. 4, no. 5. A well-known translation is
O thou billowy harvest field.

TYUTCHEV, FIODOR IVANOVICH
1803–1843

VESENNIYE VODY

Yeshcho v polyakh beleyet sneg,
A vody uzh vesnoï shumyat—
Begut i budyat sonnyï breg,
Begut i bleshchut i glasyat—
One glasyat vo vse kontzy:
"Vesna idiot, vesna idiot!
My molodoï vesny gonzy,
Ona nas vyslala vpered!
Vesna idiot, vesna idiot!"
I tikhikh, teplykh, maïskikh dneï
Rumyanyï, svetlyï khorovod,
Tolpitsya veselo za neï.

SERGEI RACHMANINOFF, Op. 14, no. 11. Best known as *Floods of
spring.*

The wind was blowing over you, my field,
bending your spikes to the ground,
dispersing the ripe grains.
Wide apart you fell, my thoughts,
and where each thought fell
grew wild grass,
grew up deep sorrow.

One of the best known Russian poets of his day, Tyutchev
was the first to translate the poems of Heine. He served as
a clerk in the Russian embassies, and spent twenty-two
years abroad. As a poet he was not prolific; he left only
some 300 poems.

SPRING WATERS

The fields are still covered with snow,
but already the brooks are filled with the murmur
   of spring.
They flow, and the sleepy shores awake;
they run and ripple and cry out;
they cry out everywhere:
"Spring is coming! Spring is coming!
We are harbingers
sent forth by the young spring!
Spring is coming! Spring is coming!"
And for a gay escort,
in a rosy, light ring of dancing,
come the calm and balmy days of May.

SCANDINAVIAN SONGS

ANDERSEN, HANS CHRISTIAN
1805–1875

MIN TANKES TANKE

Min Tankes Tanke ene du er vorden,
Du er mit Hjertes første Kjærlighed,
Jeg elsker dig som Ingen her paa Jorden
Jeg elsker dig i Tid og Evighed.

EDVARD GRIEG, Op. 5, no. 3. Grieg's song is called *Jeg elsker dig*. First published in Germany, it became internationally famous as *Ich liebe dich*, or *I love thee*. It is worth noting that the second stanza of the German and English versions does not exist in the

BENZON, OTTO
1856–1927

EROS

Hør mig, I kølige Hjærter i Nord,
I, som vil Fryd i Forsagelsen finde,
I gaar i Blinde, I gaar i Blinde,
vil plukke Roser hvor Roser ej gror.
Aarene rinde,
Kræfterne svinde,
hvor er vel Sneen som faldt ifjor?
Ej I det Tabte tilbage vinde,
læg Jer paa Sinde
da mine Ord:

Favne hende, som helt gav sig hen,
hende, hvem helt du dig gav igjen,
favne hende med al den Ild
som i dit bankende Hjærte bor,
det er den største—
nej mere end det!
det er den eneste virkelig store Lykke paa Jord.

EDVARD GRIEG, Op. 70, no. 1.

The beloved writer of fairy tales is well remembered in his native Denmark as a poet, novelist, and dramatist. Andersen's first love was the theater, and it was as a playwright that he first became known.

THOUGHT OF MY THOUGHTS

You alone have become the thought of my thoughts,
You are my heart's first love;
I love you as no one on this earth,
I love you for all time and eternity.

original, but was added for fear the song might seem too brief. The repeat signs in the published music do not apply when the original text is sung.

Noted chiefly as a writer of stage comedies, this Norwegian was also a poet of some ability.

EROS

Hear me, ye cold hearts in the North,
you who would find joy in renunciation,
you are blind, you are blind,
you would pluck roses where no roses grow.
The years roll by,
your strength fails,
where is the snow that fell last year?
You cannot win back what is lost,
mark well
then my words.

To embrace her, who gave herself completely,
her, to whom you gave yourself completely,
to embrace her with all the fire
that lives in your beating heart,
that is the greatest—
no, more than that:
that is the only truly great happiness on earth.

BJØRNSON, BJØRNSTJERNE

1832–1910

DET FØRSTE MØDE

Det første mødes sødme
det er som sang i skogen,
det er som sang på vågen
i solens siste rødme—
det er som horn i uren,
de tonende sekunder,
hvori vi med naturen
forenes i et under.

EDVARD GRIEG, Op. 21, no. 1.

FRA MONTE PINCIO

Aftenen kommer, solen står rød,
farvende stråler i rummet henskylle
lyslængsel'ns glans i uendelig fylle;—
fjældet forklares, som åsyn i død.
Kuplerne gløder, men længere borte
tågen langs markernes blålige sorte
vugger opover som glæmselen før:
over hin dal dækker tusen års slør.

Aft'nen, hvor rød og varm!
blusser av folkelarm,
glødende hornmusik
blomster og brune blik.—
[Fortidens store står rundtom, knapt kjænte,
bundne i marmor og vænte!

Known in his time as Norway's leading journalist and an orator of great eloquence, Bjørnson devoted his life and his writings to humanitarianism and social betterment. He was active in the movement to break with the Danish language, and he advocated a strong bond between literature and real life. As a director of the theater at Bergen he founded a new school of drama, striving to make the people aware of their heritage in the ancient sagas. He became known as the national poet of Norway and wrote his country's national anthem.

THE FIRST MEETING

The first meeting's sweetness
is like song in the forest,
it is like song on the waves
in the sun's last blazing—
it is like a horn on the rocky mountainside
in the resounding seconds
when we with nature
are wondrously united.

FROM MONTE PINCIO

Evening is coming, the red sun pours
its gleaming rays through space,
the brilliance of light longing, infinitely rich;
the mountain is transfigured as a countenance in death,
the cupolas are aglow, while in the distance
the fog over the deep blue of the fields
waves upwards like oblivion:
over the valley is spread the veil of a thousand years.

How red and warm the evening
glows with the swarm of people,
flaring horn music,
flowers and brown eyes.
[The great men of old stand around, scarcely remembered,
bound in marble, waiting.

Vesper det ringer, i rødmende luft
tonernes offer-damp tåger og spredes,
kirkernes hellige halvmørke bredes,
aftenbøn bæver i ord og i duft.

Ildbæltet over Sabinerne spændes
blus på Kampagnen av hyrderne tændes,
Roma med lamperne frembryder mat,
ligesom sagn av historiens nat.
Gænnem den unge kvæld
hopper en saltarell';—
sværmere knaller til
latter og morra-spil;—]
tankerne stræber i farver og toner
trofast mot det, som forsoner.

[Lyset har tabt i sin lydløse kamp,
himmelen hvælver de dunkelblå buer,
dybt fra dens evighed stjærnerne luer,
jordmassen synker i tåge og damp.
Øjnene flygter fra mørket mod staden,
møder et ligtog med fakler i gaden;
natten det søger, men lysenes flag
vifter dog håb fra den evige dag.

Muntert en mandolin
lyder til dans og vin,
munkesang, gadeleg,
døves av tappenstreg;—
gænnem det drømmende livsårens banken
glimter med daglys i tanken.]

Stille det bliver, æn dunklere blå
himmelen våger og vænter—opunder
fortid som drømmer, og fræmtid som stunder,
usikre blus i det rugende grå.
Men—de vil samle sig! Roma fræmstige
lystændt en nat for Italiens rige:
klokkerne kime, kanonerne slå,
minnerne flamme på fræmtidens blå!—

Through the roseate air the vespers are ringing,
Offerings of music float and vanish like the mists,
the holy twilight spreads out from the churches,
with evening prayer trembling in words and in incense.

Over the Sabines lies a belt of flame,
on the Campagna the shepherds light their fires;
dimly the lamps of Rome break forth
as shadowy legends from the night of history.
In the young night
they are dancing a saltarelle
amid fireworks,
laughter and mora-games.*]
In the colors and the music thoughts strive
steadfastly toward the power of mercy.

[Silently the light has died away;
the dark blue vaults of heaven arch above;
from the deep infinity of heaven the stars flame forth;
the masses of earth sink in the fog and the vapor.
From the darkness our eyes turn toward the city,
to meet a funeral cortege with its torches in the street,
seeking the night while like flags the lights
wave with the hope of eternal day.

Gaily a mandolin
sounds to dancing and wine,
the singing of the monks, the noise of the street
are drowned by drum beats;
the pulse of life beats in all the drums,
always looking to the day.]

Silence falls, ever deeper blue
heaven watches and waits—
the past with its dreams, and the approaching future,
gleam uncertain, above in the brooding gray!
But they will unite and Rome will stand forth
radiantly one night from a united Italy;
the bells shall ring and the cannons sound,
memories flame against the blue of the future!

* An ancient counting game.

Yndig om håb og tro
op mot nygifte to,
jubler en sanger til
cither og fløjtespil.
Stærkere længsler får barnesød hvile
mindre tør vågne og smile.

EDVARD GRIEG, Op. 39, no. 1.

PRINSESSEN

Prinsessen sad højt i sit jomfrubur,
smågutten gik nede og blåste på lur.
"Hvi blåser du altid, ti stille, du små,
det hæfter min tanke, som vide vil gå,
nu, når sol går ned."

Prinsessen sad højt i sit jomfrubur,
smågutten lod være at blåse på lur.
"Hvi tier du stille, blås mere, du små,
det løfter min tanke, som vide vil gå,
nu, når sol går ned."

Prinsessen sad højt i sit jomfrubur,
smågutten tog atter og blåste på lur.
Da græd hun i aftnen og sukkede ud:
"o, sig mig, hvad er det, mig feiler, min Gud!—
nu gik solen ned."

EDVARD GRIEG. Also set by Frederick Delius.

FRÖDING, GUSTAF

1860–1911

SÄV, SÄV, SUSA

Säv, säv, susa,
våg, våg, slå,
I sägen mig var Ingalill
den unge månde gå?

Singing of hope and faith
to a young married couple above,
jubilantly a singer shouts
to the cither and the flute.
Like children our strongest longings are laid to rest;
the lesser ones dare awaken and smile.

THE PRINCESS

The princess sat high up in her bower,
the little boy walked below and blew his horn.
"Why must you keep on blowing? Be quiet, little one,
you hinder my thoughts which would wander far away,
now that the sun is setting."

The princess sat high up in her bower,
the little boy stopped blowing his horn.
"Why are you so quiet? Blow more, little one,
it lifts my thoughts which would wander far away,
now that the sun is setting."

The princess sat high up in her bower,
the little boy again began to blow his horn.
Then she wept in the evening and sighed:
"O tell me what ails me, God,
now that the sun has set."

Fröding was said to owe his lively imagination and gifts of
fantasy to the fact that he was a native of picturesque and
colorful Värmland. Under the literary influence of Burns,
Heine, and Byron, he became a poet of nature, Sweden's
leading lyric artist and by some considered one of the
greatest poets of Europe. His verse is vivid, tense, and ex-
citing, with touches of humor.

SIGH, SIGH, RUSHES

Sigh, sigh, rushes,
beat, waves, beat,
you tell me where Ingalill
the young has gone?

Hon skrek som en vingskjuten and, när hon sjönk i
sjön,
det var när sista vår stod grön.

De voro henne gramse vid Östanålid,
det tog hon sig så illa vid.

De voro henne gramse för gods och gull,
och för hennes unga kärleks skuld.

De stucko en ögonsten med tagg,
de kastade smuts i en liljas dagg.

Så sjungen, sjungen sorgsång,
I sorgsna vågor små,
säv, säv, susa,
våg, våg, slå!

JEAN SIBELIUS, Op. 36, no. 4.

GARBORG, ARNE

1851–1924

HAUGTUSSA

1

EDVARD GRIEG, Op. 67. Grieg's cycle is a selection from Garborg's poetic romance. *Haugtussa*—"hill-lady," pixy—is a supernatural being who lives in the hills. *Veslemøy*, our heroine, was visionary, and the things she "saw" frightened her so that she became queer, and spent most of her life in the mountains and hills, away from other people. Wherefore she was called *Haugtussa*. Catharinus Elling also published two sets of six *Haugtussa* songs (Op. 52 and Op. 60), which have been very popular in Norway.

DET SYNG

Aa veit du den draum, og veit du den song,
so vil du tonane gøyme;
og gilja det for deg so mang ein gong,
rett aldri so kan du det gløyme.
Aa hildrande du!
Med meg skal du bu;
i Blaahaugen skal du din sylvrokk snu.

She cried like a winged duck as she sank into the sea,
that was when last spring was green.

They hated her at Ostanalid,
that filled her with grief.

They begrudged her goods and gold,
and her young love.

They stabbed an eyeball with thorns,
they threw mud on the dew of a lily.

So sing, sing your mournful song,
you sad little waves,
sigh, sigh, rushes,
beat, waves, beat!

Son of a strict religious peasant father, Garborg first won attention by writing in reaction, advocating free love and atheism. His poetic cycle *Haugtussa* is considered the chief classic of Norwegian Landsmaal, and has been admired for its true picture of peasant life, its elevated tone, and its fine verbal painting.

IT SINGS

If you know the dream, if you know the song,
then you will conceal the tune;
so often has it beguiled you
that you can never forget it.
Oh fascinating one!
With me shall you live;
in the blue hill you shall turn your silver spinning wheel.

[Du skal ikkje fæle den svale nott,
daa røtane gror ned i jordi;
du saag i draumen det maane-slott
og høyrde dei leikar-ordi.
Det frævest i blund,
det grønkar i lund,
og dagen ei kjenner den sæle-stund.]

Du skal ikkje fæle den mjuke nott,
daa draumen slær ut sine vengir
i linnare ljos enn dagen hev aatt
og tonar fraa stillare strengir.
Det voggar um lid,
det svævest av strid,
og dagen ei kjenner den sæle-tid.

[Du skal ikkje fæle den djupe nott,
som søv under svivande eimar
og ser gjenom gru og ser gjenom graatt
langt inn i dei draumhulde heimar
og voggar deg linn
og lullar deg inn
fraa dagen den trøytte, av soli blind.]

Du skal ikkje ræddast den elskhug vill,
som syndar og græt og gløymer;
hans famn er heit og hans hug er mild,
og bjønnen arge han tøymer.
Aa hildrande du!
Med meg skal du bu;
i Blaahaugen skal du din sylvrokk snu.

2

VESLEMØY

Ho er mager og myrk og mjaa
med brune og reine drag
og augo djupe og graa
og stilslegt, drøymande lag.

Det er som det halvt um halvt
laag ein svevn yver heile ho;
i rørsle, tale og alt
ho hev denne døyvde ro.

[You shall not fear the mild night
when the roots grow into the earth;
in your dream you saw the moon-castle
and heard playful words.
The grove is sprouting
and becoming green
and the day does not know such happiness.]

You shall not fear the soft night
when dreams spread their wings,
in softer air than ever by day
and music from softer strings.
It ripples around the hillside,
it lulls you to sleep,
and the day never knows such happiness.

[You shall not fear the deep night,
which sleeps under billowing mists
and looks through horror and looks through grayness
far into dream-happy worlds;
and rocks you gently,
and lulls you to sleep
from the weary day, blinded by the sun.]

You shall not fear the wild love
that sins and weeps and forgets;
his embrace is hot and his mind is mild,
and he tames the wild bear.
Oh fascinating one!
With me you shall live;
in the blue hill you shall turn your silver spinning wheel.

VESLEMØY

She is thin and dark and slender,
with features brown and pure,
eyes deepened and gray,
and quiet, dreamy manners.

It is as if she were
half asleep;
in gestures, speech, and everything
she has this gentle quietness about her.

Under panna fager men laag
lyser augo som att-um eim;
det er som dei stirrande saag
langt inn i ein annan heim.

[Ho gjeng aat sin omnskraabenk
og set seg, men veit det knapt,
og tek denne mjølkeskjenk
og sit der roleg fortapt.]

Berre barmen gjeng sprengd og tung
og det bivrar um munnen bleik.
Ho er skjælvande sped og veik
midt i det ho er ven og ung.

3

BLAABÆRLID

Nei, sjaa kor det blaanar her!
No maa me roe oss, kyra!
aa nei, slike fine bær;
og dei som det berre kryr a'!
Nei maken eg hev ikkje set!
sumt godt her er daa til fjells.
No vil eg eta meg mett;
her vil me vera til kvelds.

[As nam-nam, so søtt og godt!
Ja naar det slik seg lagar!—
Og allestad blaatt i blaatt!
Her hev eg for mange dagar.
Slik smak so frisk og so fin!
Eg er som paa kongens slott.
D'er plent som den beste vin;
aa nam-nam, so søtt og godt!]

Men kom nu den bjørnen stor!
—her fekk bli rom aat oss baae.
Eg torde ikkje segja eit ord
til slik ein rysjeleg vaae.
Eg sa berre: ver so god;
no maa du kje vera bljug!
Eg læt deg so vel i ro;
tak for deg etter din hug.

Under her forehead, beautiful but low,
her eyes shine as through a mist;
it is as if they gazed
far into another world.

[She goes to her bench in the chimney corner
and sits down, hardly aware;
she takes a cup of milk
and sits there lost in thought.]

Only her bosom heaves heavily,
and her pale mouth trembles.
She is tremulous and slight and weak
because she is beautiful and young.

BLUEBERRY HILL

Oh look how blue it is here!
Now we must rest, cows!
Oh, such fine berries!
And what a lot of them there are!
I never saw the like of it!
There is something good in the mountains after all!
Now I will eat my fill;
here we shall stay till night.

[Oh my, how sweet and good!
Yes, when it turns out like this!
And everywhere it is blue!
Here I have enough for many a day.
They taste so fresh and fine!
I feel as though I were in the king's castle.
It is just like the best wine;
oh me, how sweet and good!]

But if the big bear should come!
There would have to be room for us both.
I would not dare say a word
to such a dreadful dare-devil.
I should only say: "Please,
now you must not be bashful!
I will leave you in peace;
help yourself as much as you like."

Men var det den reven raud,
so skuld' han faa smaka staven;
eg skulde banke han daud,
um so han var bror til paven.
Slikt skarve, harmelegt sleng!
Han stel baade kje og lamb.
Men endaa so fin han gjeng
hev korkje agg hell skam.

Men var det den stygge skrubb,
so arg og so hol som futen,—
eg tok meg ein bjørkekubb
og gav han ein god paa snuten.
Han reiv sund sauir og lomb
for mor mi so traadt og tidt;
ja sant! um han berre kom,
so skuld' han so visst faa sitt.

Men var det den snilde gut
der burte fraa Skarebrote,—
han fekk vel ein paa sin trut,—
men helst paa ein annan maate.
Aa tøv, kva tenkjer eg paa!
Det lid nok paa dagen alt . . .
Eg maa til buskapen sjaa;—
ho Dokka drøymer um salt.

4

MØTE

Ho sit ein sundag lengtande i lid;
det strøymer paa med desse søte tankar;
og hjarta fullt og tungt i barmen bankar,
og draumen vaknar, bivrande og blid.
Daa gjeng det som ei hildring yvi nuten;
ho raudnar heit;—der kjem den vene guten.

Burt vil ho gøyme seg i ørska braa,
men stoggar tryllt og augo mot han vender;
dei tek einannan i dei varme hender
og stend so der og veit seg inkje raad.
Daa bryt ho ut i dette undringsord:
"men snille deg daa . . . at du er so stor!"

But if it were the red fox,
he should get a thrashing;
I should knock him dead,
even if he were brother to the Pope.
Such a good-for-nothing provoking scamp!
He steals both kid and lamb,
but even so he is quite unconcerned,
feels neither uneasiness nor shame.

But if it were the bad wolf,
as ugly and greedy as the sheriff,
I would take a birch log
and knock him on the snout.
He tore to death sheep and lamb
so many a time for my mother;
yes, truly! if only he would come
he would get his.

But if it were the nice boy
from Skarebrote yonder,
he would also get one on the mouth,
but in a rather different way.
Oh, nonsense, what am I thinking of!
The day is wearing on.
I must look after the herd;
Dokka, my cow, is dreaming of salt.

MEETING

She sits of a Sunday on the hill, filled with longing;
sweet thoughts pour over her;
and her heart beats full and heavy in her bosom,
and dreams awaken, quivering and sweet.
Then suddenly the whole world becomes transfigured;
she blushes hotly, for there comes the handsome boy.

In sudden confusion she wants to hide,
but stops fascinated, and turns her eyes toward him;
they take each other by the hot hand,
and stand there, and don't know what to do.
Then she breaks out in a cry of wonder:
"But dear me . . . how big you are!"

[Han smiler raud og strekkjer led og legg;
"det er vel so, naar guten kar maa vera,
han lærer au som vaksin kar seg bera."
—"Og tenk, eg trur at du hev fengi skjegg!"
"Det var der fyrr," han svarar stø og sann;
"men kanskje det hev vaksi litegrand."

Han mjuk seg ned attunder steinen slengjer,
og upp or lumma nistemat han dreg;
og gild han vera skal som andre drengir:
"sjaa her er egg! Deim tok eg med til deg."
Ho lær og set seg, so ho nett kann sjaa han.
I barm det gjeng; ho fær kje augo fraa han.

So sit dei der i denne varme dag;
han lentug er, og ho maa læ i eino;
ho er saa glad som fuglen millom greino,
men kan kje koma rett i svalle-lag.
No, daa dei rett skal hava gildt og gaman,
ho sit der hjelpelaus og er som framand.

Han bed um sogur, men kan inkje faa;
alt det ho stundom saag og langysnt drøymde,
det kan ho liksom ikkje koma paa;
det er som alle slike ting ho gløymde.
"Nei, lat no trolli," bed ho, "gaa for seg.
I dag eg heller høyre vil paa deg."

Han gjerne daa fortel um Skarebrote.
der upp han vaks, og som han eingong fær;
dei fire kyr skal maklegt føde der,
naar han fær stelt det paa den rette maate.
Kvart orde hans ho trygt kan stole paa;
og alt ho spyrr um; alt ho vita maa.

So dreg dei rundt um lid og logne strendar
med snilde smale og den kloke ku;
og naar eit bil dei kann seg tryggje tru,
so tek dei fisk i bekk med berre hendar.
Den steikjer dei paa glod som best dei rekk,
og tømer so den gode nistesekk.

[He smiles blushingly, and stretches his legs;
"I suppose when the boy grows up,
he learns to behave like a man."
"And fancy, I believe you have grown a beard!"
"It was there before," he answers steadily,
"but perhaps it has grown a little."

Lithely he flings himself behind the rock,
and out of his pocket he pulls a parcel of food;
and he wants to be grand like other boys:
"See, here are eggs! I brought them for you."
She laughs and sits down where she can just see him.
Her bosom heaves; she cannot take her eyes from him.

Thus they sit in the warm day;
he is gay, and she is constantly laughing.
She is happy as the bird in the tree,
but cannot get into the mood for talking.
Now that they should be happy and gay,
she sits there helpless, and is like a stranger.

He asks for stories, but in vain;
all that she sometimes has seen and dreamed,
now somehow escapes her;
it is as though she has forgotten all such things.
"No," she begs, "let the trolls go their own way.
Today I would rather listen to you."

Gladly then he tells her about Skarebrote,
where he grew up and which some day will be his;
they could easily feed four cows there,
when he gets things arranged as they should be.
She can safely trust every word he speaks,
and she asks about everything; everything she must know.

Then they walk about the hills and the strands,
with the nice sheep and the wise cow;
and when they feel safe
they capture fish in the brooks with their bare hands.
They roast them in the embers as best they can,
and empty the good lunch box.

D'er gildt;—naar berre ikkje dette var,
at ingen av deim lenger fri og kyrr
den andre kan i augo sjaa som fyrr;—
han og er brydd, som skulde vera kar.
Naar berre ikkje dette eine skilde,
aa nei, so godt som daa det vera vilde!

Men upp det dreg; og døyvde toremaal
i bergi brumlar; snart vil regne drive;
ved Gjetleberge snøgt dei maa seg live;
der under heller er eit livadahòl.
Det er kje stort! nett so det vel er vitjande.
Der inn dei kryper, og der vert dei sitjande.]

Og som det lid til svale kveldings stund,
alt meir og meir i lengt dei saman søkjer;
og braadt um hals den unge arm seg krøkjer,
og øre sjelv dei saman munn mot munn.
Alt svimrar burt. Og der i kvelden varm
i heite sæle søv ho i hans arm.

5

ELSK

Den galne guten min hug hev daara
eg fanga sit som ein fugl i snora;
den galne guten, han gjeng so baus;
han veit at fuglen vil aldri laus.

Aa gjev du batt meg med bast og bende;
aa gjev du batt meg so bandi brende!
As gjev du drog meg saa fast til deg,
at heile verdi kom burt for meg!

Ja kunde rett eg mi runelekse
eg vilde inn i den guten vekse;
eg vilde vekse meg i deg inn,
og vera berra hjaa guten min.

As du som bur meg i hjarta inne,
du makti fekk yver alt mitt minne;
kvart vesle hugsviv som framum dreg
det berre kviskrar um deg, um deg.

It is wonderful—if only it were not for one thing—
that neither can look freely any more
into the other's eyes as before;
he who should be a man is also embarrassed.
If only this one thing did not part them,
Oh, how good it would be then!

But a storm is brewing; and thunder
rumbles in the mountains; soon it will be pouring;
suddenly they must hide; at Gjetle Mountain
there is a shelter there.
It is not large—just big enough to hold them.
They creep in and there they remain.]

And as it wears toward the cool of the evening,
more and more they seek each other;
and suddenly the young arm bends around his neck,
and dizzily they tremble together, mouth to mouth.
Everything fades away, and there in the warm evening
in hot happiness she sleeps in his arms.

LOVE

The mad boy has captivated my mind,
like a bird I am caught in the snare;
the mad boy, he struts so proudly;
he knows that the bird never wants to get loose.

I wish you would put me in fetters;
I wish you would bind me so that the fetters would burn me!
I wish you would draw me so tightly to you
that the whole world would be lost to me!

Yes, if I could conjure with runes
I would grow into that boy;
I would grow into you
and be one with you.

Oh you who live in my heart,
you have power over my mind;
every little thought that comes to me
whispers only of you, of you.

Um soli lyser paa himlen blanke,
no ser ho deg, det er all min tanke;
um dagen dovnar og skuming fell,
skal tru han tenkjer paa meg i kveld?

[Um vinden strid yvi heidi susar,
det gule haaret ditt visst han krusar;
um regne dryp med sin døyvde graat,
so stakkars guten, no vert du vaat.

Aa berre timane vilde skride,
og berre dagane vilde lide!
Men eg vil kveda og vera glad;
for um sundag kjem han, trala, trala!]

6

(*This poem is a study in onomatopœia and therefore untranslatable. Many of the words were made up by the poet. Christian Rynning, in his analysis of* Haugtussa, *calls it "an impressionistic suggestive concentration of light and sound and movement". Our translation aims to give some of its flavor.*)

KILLINGDANS

Aa hipp og hoppe,
og tipp og toppe
paa denne dag;
aa nipp og nappe,
og tripp og trappe
i slikt eit lag.
Og det er kjæl-i-sol,
og det er spel-i-sol,
og det er titr-i-lid,
og det er glitr-i-lid,
og det er kjæte
og lurvelæte
ein solskinsdag.

Aa nupp i nakken
og stup i bakken,
og tipp paa taa;
aa rekk i ringen,
og svipp i svingen,
og hopp-i-haa.

If the sun shines in the bright heaven,
"Now he sees you," is my only thought;
if the day dies and dusk falls,
"Does he think of me tonight?"

[When the stiff wind whistles over the heath,
"It is surely blowing in your yellow hair";
if the rain falls like silent tears,
"My poor boy, now you'll get wet."

Oh, if only the hours would pass,
and the days would wear on!
But I'll sing and be merry,
for on Sunday he comes, trala, trala!]

DANCING GOATS

They skip and jump,
and frolic and run
on this day;
They lock horns,
they trip and trample
every which way.
And there is playing-in-the-sun,
and there is glittering-on-the-hill;
there is gaiety
and abandoned joy
on a sunshiny day.

There is playful fighting
and somersaults,
and balancing-on-tip-toe
and dancing-in-a-ring
and swinging around
and jumping up and down.

Og det er sleik-i-sol,
og det er leik-i-sol,
og det er glim-i-lid,
og det er stim-i-lid,
og det er kvitter
og bekkje-glitter
og lognt i kraa.

Aa trapp og tralle,
og puff i skalle,
den skal du ha.
Og snipp og snute,
og kyss paa trute,
den kann du ta.
Og det er rull-i-ring,
og det er sull-i-sving,
og det er lett-paa-taa,
og det er sprett-paa-taa,
og det er hei-san,
og det er hopp-san,
og tra-la-la.

7

VOND DAG

Ho reknar dag og stund og seine kveld
til sundag kjem; han hev so trufast lova,
at um det regnde smaastein yvi fjell,
so skal dei finnast der i "Gjætarstova."
Men sundag kjem og gjeng med regn og rusk;
ho eismal sit og græt attunder busk.

[So vel ho veit han aldri svike kan,
um det kjem gode dagar eller vonde;
han veit at daa ho aldri liva kunde,
men sokk og dreiv som kalde lik i land.
Men tungt er hjarta i den unge bringe,
og rædde graaten kan ho ikkje tvinge.

Daa kjem ho heim ein sundags kveld mot haust,
av hugverk mødd og sjuk av ank og otte
og trøytt og tung. All dagen hev det aust
med regn, so reint i flaum ho vassa maatte.
Ho berre skundar seg og vil i seng.
Det er det einaste ho veit og treng.

And there is basking-in-the-sun,
and there is playing-in-the-sun,
and there is glittering-on-the-hill,
and it is crowded on the hill,
and there is chirping of birds
and shimmering of the brook
in this sheltered corner.

Stamping
and butting,
that you shall have.
And a kiss
on the snout,
that you can take.
And there is dancing-in-a-ring
and somersaults.
They are light on their toes;
they leap and frisk,
and it is hey and ho,
and it is hopp-sasa,
and tra-la-la.

BAD DAY

She counts the days and hours and late nights
until Sunday comes; so faithfully he has promised
that even if it should rain pebbles over the mountains
they shall meet there in the shepherd's shelter.
But Sunday comes and goes with rain and bad weather;
alone she sits and weeps under the bush.

[Surely she knows he never could fail her,
come good days or bad;
he knows that then she could not go on living,
but would sink and drift ashore as a cold corpse.
But heavy is the heart in her young bosom,
and she cannot stop her frightened weeping.

Then home she comes on a Sunday night towards autumn,
troubled, her head aching, sick with fright,
and tired and heavy. All day long it has poured down
with rain so that she has had to wade through the floods.
She hurries, wanting to go to bed.
It is the only thing she knows and wants.

Men nett er gamlen komin heim fraa kyrkja;
og no med pipa nøgd han nytt fortel:
"jau daa var Jon i Skarebrote sæl,
um hans ho vart, den kaute velstands-fyrkja!"
Ho kjenner styng i bryst og skjelv i kne;
i vanmagt trøytt ho sig paa stolen ned.

Daa fær ho høyre meir enn sjølv ho vilde;
ho høyre maa, att denne guten staut,
som so ho truddle, lett sin lovnad braut
og floksa fritt med alle gjentur gilde.
Men no han vankar klok paa bele-raas
til sjølve rike Megga ifraa Aas.

Og denne etter Jon er reint som gali;
ho lokkar han so alle kann det sjaa;
og han so vel som andre vita maa,
at ho er best av alle gifte-vali.
Og so med denne drosi eine dansar han,
og andre gode gjentur aldri ansar han.]

Som fuglen saara under varme veng
so blode tippar lik den heite taare,
ho dreg seg sjuk og sjelvande i seng
og vrid seg natti lang i graaten saare.
Det slit i hjarta og det brenn paa kinn.
No maa ho døy; ho miste guten sin.

8

VED GJÆTLE-BEKKEN

Du surlande bekk,
du kurlande bekk,
her ligg du og kosar deg varm og klaar.
Og speglar deg rein
og glid yvi stein,
og sullar so godt
og mullar so smaatt,
og glitrar i soli med mjuke baar'.
—Aa her vil eg kvile, kvile.

Du tiklande bekk,
du siklande bekk,
her gjeng du so glad i den ljose lid.
Med klunk og med klukk,

But the old man has just come home from church,
and now, sitting contentedly with his pipe he tells the news:
"Jon of Skarebrote surely would be glad
if she becomes his, the wealthy catch!"
She feels a stab in her bosom, her knee trembles;
powerless and tired she sinks down into a chair.

Then she must hear more than she wants;
she must hear how this fine boy
in whom she believed so surely, has lightly broken his promise.
and flirted with all the girls.
But now prudently he is courting
the rich Magga from Aas.

And *she* is madly in love with Jon;
she leads him on for all to see;
and he knows, as everyone else does,
that she is the best catch among the eligible girls.
And so he dances only with this woman,
and never looks at the other nice girls.]

Like a bird wounded under its warm wing
until the blood streams like hot tears,
so she drags herself to bed, sick and trembling,
and writhes the night long in sore weeping.
It tears at her heart, and it burns on her cheek,
now she must die—she has lost her boy.

AT THE GJETLE BROOK

O humming brook,
o cooing brook,
you lie there so comfortable and warm and clear.
You mirror so clearly
as you glide over the stones,
crooning pleasantly
and mumbling faintly
while the sun glitters on your soft waves.
O here I will rest, rest . . .

O rippling brook,
o purling brook,
here you run so merrily on the sunny hillside,
gurgling and chuckling,

med song og med sukk,
med sus og med dus,
gjenom lauvbygt hus,
med underlegt svall og med svæving blid.
—Aa, her vil eg drøyme, drøyme.

Du hullande bekk,
du sullande bekk,
her fekk du seng under mosen mjuk.
Her drøymer du kurt
og gløymer deg burt
og kviskrar og kved
i den store fred
med svaling for hugsott og lengting sjuk.
—Aa her vil eg minnast, minnast.

Du vildrande bekk,
du sildrande bekk,
kva tenkte du alt paa din lange veg?
Gjenom aude rom?
millom busk og blom?
Naar i jord du smatt,
naar du fann deg att?
Tru nokon du saag so eismal som eg.
—Aa, her vil eg gløyme, gløyme.

Du tislande bekk,
du rislande bekk,
du leikar i lund, du sullar i ro.
Og smiler mot sol
og lær i ditt skjol,
og vandrar so langt
og lærer so mangt . . .
aa syng kje um det som eg tenkjer no.
—Aa, lat meg faa blunde, blunde.

singing and sighing,
rushing and frolicking
through your leafy house,
with strange chatter lulling me softly to sleep.
O here I will dream, dream.

O murmuring brook,
o crooning brook,
here you have found a bed under the soft moss.
Here you dream so quietly
and forget yourself
and whisper and sing
in the great peace
with comfort for sorrow and sick longing.
O here I will remember, remember.

O wandering brook,
o rippling brook,
what have you been thinking on your long road?
In the desolate spaces,
among the shrubs and the blossoms,
when you slipped into the earth,
and when you came out again?
I wonder if you have found anyone so lonely as I?
Oh, here I will forget, forget.

O rippling brook,
o purling brook,
you play in the grove, you murmur quietly.
And smile toward the sun,
and laugh in your hiding place,
and wander so far away,
and learn so much . . .
O do not sing about what I am thinking of now.
O let me sleep, sleep.

IBSEN, HENRIK

1828–1906

MED EN VANDLILJE

Se, min bedste, hvad jeg bringer,
blomsten med de hvide vinger.
På de stille strømme båren
svam den drømmetung i våren.

Vil du den til hjemmet fæste,
fæst den ved dit bryst, min bedste,
bag dens blade da sig dølge
vil en dyb og stille bølge.

Vogt dig, barn, for tjernets strømme,
farligt, farligt der at drømme!
Nøkken lader som han sover—
liljer leger ovenover.

Barn, din barm er tjernets strømme.
Farligt, farligt der at drømme—
liljer leger ovenover;
nøkken lader som han sover.

EDVARG GRIEG, Op. 25, no. 4. The first line reads: *Se, Marie,*

EN SVANE

Min hvide svane,
du stumme, du stille;
hverken slag eller trille
lod sangrøst ane.

Angst beskyttende
alfen, som sover,—
altid lyttende
gled du henover.

Norway's most famous writer and the leading dramatist of his time. Ibsen was a sensitive child and rebellious by nature. He got his start in the theater as stage manager first in Bergen and then in Christiania. His first dramas created a scandal because of their outspokenness, and many of his works had great influence on social reform. As a poet he is best known for the dramas *Brand* and *Peer Gynt*, which established his reputation in his native land.

WITH A WATERLILY

See, my dear, what I bring,
the flower with the white wings.
On the quiet streams floating
it was swimming, laden with dreams, in the springtime.

So that it may be at home,
pin it on your breast, my dear;
beneath its leaves then will be hidden
a deep and peaceful wave.

Careful, child, of the currents of the lake,
dangerous, dangerous there to dream!
The water sprite pretends to be asleep,
lilies play above him.

Child, your bosom is the current of the lake.
Dangerous, dangerous there to dream!
Lilies play on the surface;
the water sprite pretends to be asleep.

---

hvad jeg bringer; and the first and second lines of the second stanza:
Vil du den til hjemmet vie, fæst den ved dit bryst, Marie.

A SWAN

My white swan,
still and silent one,
neither song nor trill
hinted that you could sing.

Anxiously guarding
the sleeping water sprite,
ever listening
you glided above.

Men sidste mødet,
da eder og øjne
var lønlige løgne,—
ja da, da lød det!

I toners føden
du slutted din bane.
Du sang i døden;—
du *var* dog en svane!

EDVARD GRIEG, Op. 25, no. 2. According to the Ibsen authority
Francis Bull (cf. his *Nordisk kunstnerliv i Rom*, Oslo, 1961), Ibsen
met Thea Brunn in Rome in 1864. Her brother Christopher Brunn
was one of the relatively few Norwegians who went to war when
Denmark was attacked by Prussia in 1864 (the rest of the intel-
lectuals, Ibsen among them, had qualms for the rest of their lives
about their own lack of courage). Ibsen was alone in Rome at the
time, and when his wife Suzannah was not with him he was sus-
ceptible to feminine charms. Says Bull, Suzannah was "a self-sacri-
ficing companion, of strong character, a grand valkyrie type; but she
had little feminine charm, and when Ibsen—in his wife's absence—
met Thea Brunn, his mind was attuned to a new mode. Her tender

JOSEPHSON, ERNST ABRAHAM

1851–1906

SVARTA ROSOR

Säg, varför är du så ledsen i dag,
du, som alltid är så lustig och glad?
Och inte är jag mera ledsen i dag
än när jag tyckes dig lustig och glad,
ty sorgen har nattsvarta rosor.

I mitt hjärta där växer et rosendeträd,
som aldrig nånsin vill lämna mig fred,
och på stjälkarna sitter det tagg vid tagg,
och det våller mig ständigt sveda och agg,
ty sorgen har nattsvarta rosor.

Men av rosor blir det en hel klenod,
än vita som döden, än röda som blod.

But at the last meeting,
when vows and eyes
were secret lies,—
yes, then, then it sounded!

In the birth of song
you ended your life,
you sang in death—
you *were* indeed a swan.

---

grace, her soulful look, her capacity for listening, became the main characteristics of the new female character he created" (i.e., Agnes in *Brand*).

Memories of Thea Brunn are found in the poem *Borte* (also set by Grieg—Op. 25, no. 5); ". . . but there is another poem by him which has some of the same rhythm and emotional intensity: *The swan*—and even if one does not, as in the case of *Borte*, have any information from his Roman friends about the background and meaning of this strange poem, I feel inclined to guess that it also is connected with Thea Brunn, who left Rome with her mother in the summer of 1865, and died of tuberculosis at home in Norway before the end of the year."

A Swedish painter who published two notable collections of poetry.

BLACK ROSES

Say, why are you so sad today,
you who are always so gay and happy?
Oh, I am no more sad today
than when I seem to you to be gay and happy;
for sorrow has roses black as the night.

In my heart grows a rose tree
which never will leave me in peace,
and the stems are covered with thorns,
and it always causes me anxiety and pain,
for sorrow has roses black as the night.

But of roses there are a whole treasure,
some white as death, some red as blood.

Det växer och växer, jag tror jag förgår,
i hjärtträdets rötter det rycker och slår,
ty sorgen har nattsvarta rosor.

JEAN SIBELIUS, Op. 36, no. 1.

JYNGE, ANDREAS GRIMELUND

1870–1955

MOT KVELD

Alle de duggvåte blomster har sendt
solen det sidste godnat,
sanktehansormen sin lykte har tendt,
sitter og lyser i krat.
Sommerfugl tatt sine duggsokker på,
lagt sig til hvile i klokken den blå,
drømmer så deilig om solen,
drømmer om duft av fiolen.

AGATHE URSULA BACKER-GRØNDAHL, Op. 42, no. 7.

KRAG, VILHELM ANDREAS WEXELS

1871–1933

DER SKREG EN FUGL

Der skreg en fugl over øde hav,
langt fra lande.
Den skreg saa saart i den høstgraa dag,
flakset paa brute, avmægtige slag,
seiled paa sorte vinger
bortover hav—

CHRISTIAN SINDING, Op. 18, no. 5. Less well known than the
Sinding setting is that by Edvard Grieg, Op. 60, no. 4.

It grows and grows, I think I shall perish,
the roots of the heart-tree pull and beat,
for sorrow has roses black as the night.

A Norwegian public official and writer, Jynge was noted
for his deep and sincere love of nature. His writings include
Viser of vers (1896), a collection of unpretentious children's songs, *Egne veie* (1903), a book of poems, and
Hester i fjellet (1947), a collection of short stories.

TOWARDS EVENING

All the flowers, wet with dew, have sent
the sun a last goodnight;
the glowworm has lighted his lantern,
and sits and glows in the bushes.
The butterfly has put on her dewy socks,
has laid herself to rest in the blue harebell,
dreaming delightfully of sunshine,
dreaming of the fragrance of violets.

Krag's plays, novels, and poems have been admired for
their fine landscape painting, their truth in depicting the
life of simple fisher folk, their humor, and their human
sympathy.

A BIRD CRIED

A bird cried over the desolate sea,
far from land.
It cried so piteously in the gray autumn day;
flapped brokenly, feebly;
sailed on black wings
out over the sea—

MENS JEG VENTER

Vildgjæs, vildgjæs i hvide flokker,
solskinsveir,
ællingen spanker i gule sokker,
fine klær.
Ro, ro til fiskeskjær,
lunt det er omkring holmen her.
Sjøen ligger saa stille.
Bro, bro brille.

Løs dit guldhaar og snør din kyse,
du min skat.
Saa skal vi danse den lune, lyse juninat.
Vent, vent til Sanktehans
staar vort bryllup i lystig dans.
Alle giger skal spille.
Bro, bro brille.

Vug mig, vug mig du blanke vove
langt og let.
Snart gaar min terne paa dans i skove
søndagsklædt.
Vug, vug i drøm mig ind,
hver tar sin, saa tar jeg min.
Bro, bro brille.
[Hør hvor gigerne spille.]

EDVARD GRIEG, Op. 60, no. 3. The last two lines are reversed. The song is well known in its German and English versions, as *Im Kahne* or *In the boat*.

OG JEG VIL HA MIG EN HJERTENSKJÆR

Og jeg vil ha mig en silkevest,
ja, ja en silkevest.
Og jeg vil ha mig en snehvid hest,
prustende, snehvid hest.

Og jeg vil ha mig en stigebøil,
ja, ja en stigebøil.
Og jeg vil ha mig en bluse av fløil,
sølvknappet bluse av fløil.

WHILE I WAIT

Wild geese, wild geese in white flocks
in the sunshine,
the duckling struts in yellow socks
and fine clothes.
Row, row to the fishing bank,
it is sheltered around this islet,
the sea is quiet.
Bro, bro brille!

Let down your golden hair and tie your hood,
you, my treasure!
Then we shall dance in the light mild June night.
Wait, wait until Saint John's Day;
then we shall celebrate our wedding with joyous dance;
all the fiddles will play!
Bro, bro brille.

Toss me, toss me, you shimmering wave,
long and gently.
Soon my sweetheart goes to dance in the forest
in her Sunday clothes.
Toss me, toss me into a dream,
each one takes his and I take mine,
Bro, bro brille.
[Hear how the fiddles play!]

I SHALL HAVE A SWEETHEART

And I shall have a silken waistcoat,
yes, yes, a silken waistcoat.
And I shall have a snow-white horse,
a snorting, snow-white horse.

And I shall have a stirrup,
yes, yes, a stirrup.
And I shall have a velvet blouse,
a velvet blouse with silver buttons.

En heirefjær vil jeg ha i min hat,
ja, ja i min røde hat.
Og det skal være en jonsoknat—
Gud—for en jonsoknat!

Og jeg vil ha mig en hjertenskjær,
ja, ja en hjertenskjær.
Saa svinger jeg hatten med heirefjær,
i sadlen jeg løfter den jomfru skjær,
og fremover duggvaade marker det bær
den deilige jonsoknat!

EDVARD GRIEG, Op. 60, no. 5. Also known under the title *Saint John's Eve.*

LANGE, THOR
1851–1915

I WÜRZBURG RINGE DE KLOKKER TIL FEST

I Würzburg ringe de Klokker til Fest;
I Würzburg hue mig Pigerne bedst.

Forneden i Dalen gaa Bækkene smaa,
der gaar og hun, min Hu ligger paa.

De Bække de vorde den stride Flod—
det hjælper mig intet, jeg er Dig saa god.

Og Floden rinder i salten Hav—
dér rinder med hvert Ord, Du mig gav.

Hundrede Ord og Løfter ti,
lidt Falskhed er der altid deri.

Dog var Du min Kærest en ringe Tid,
derfor gøre Gud din Lykke blid!

PETER ERASMUS LANGE-MÜLLER, Op. 34, no. 6. The poem is based on the German folk song best known as *Da unten im Tale.*

A heron's feather shall I have in my hat,
yes, yes, in my red hat.
And it shall be Midsummernight—
God! what a Midsummernight!

And I shall have a sweetheart,
yes, yes, a sweetheart.
Then I flourish my hat with the heron's feather.
Into the saddle I lift the pure maiden,
and over the dewy fields we ride
in the beautiful Midsummernight!

A Danish poet and essayist who was interested in antiquity,
he made numerous translations from the Greek.

THE BELLS OF WÜRZBURG

In Würzburg the bells are ringing for the feast;
the girls of Würzburg are the ones I like best.

Down in the valley the brooklets flow;
there too goes the one of whom I am thinking.

The brooks become the rushing river—
there is no help for it, I love you so much.

And the river runs into the salt sea,
there too runs every word you have given me.

A hundred words and ten promises,
there is always a little falsehood in it.

But you were my sweetheart for a little while,
so may God send you luck!

PAULSEN, JOHN OLAF
1851–1924

MED EN PRIMULA VERIS

Du vårens milde, skjønne barn,
tag vårens første blomme,
og kast den ej, fordi du ved,
at somrens roser komme.

Ak, vist er somren lys og smuk,
og rig er livets høst,
men våren er den dejligste
med elskovs leg og lyst.

Og du og jeg, min ranke mø,
står jo i vårens rødme,
så tag da min blomst,
men giv igjen dit unge hjertes sødme.

EDVARD GRIEG, Op. 26, no. 4. Some translations call it *With a primrose.*

RODE, HELGE
1870–1937

SNE

Der er ingenting i Verden saa stille som Sne,
naar den sagte gennem Luften daler,
dæmper dine Skridt,
tysser, tysser blidt
paa de Stemmer, som for høilydt taler.

Der er ingenting i Verden af en Renhed som Sne,
Svanedun fra Himlens hvide Vinger.
Paa din Haand et Fnug
er som Taaredug.
Hvide Tanker tyst i Dans sig svinger.

A friend of Grieg and a writer of fiction, essays, and poetry.

WITH A VIOLET

Oh modest, lovely child of spring,
take the first spring flower,
and do not throw it away because you know
that summer's roses are coming.

Of course the summer is bright and beautiful,
and rich is life in autumn;
yet spring is the most delightful,
with love's sport and joy.

And you and I, my fine young maid,
stand in the blaze of spring,
so take my flower,
but give in return the sweetness of your young heart.

Danish poet, dramatist and critic. Rode was prominent in
the Symbolist movement in Denmark in the 90's, a seeker
after truth in nature.

SNOW

There is nothing in the world so still as snow
when it falls softly through the air,
deadening your steps,
muting, gently muting
the voices that speak too stridently.

There is nothing in the world as pure as snow,
swan's down from the wings of heaven.
On your hand a flake
is like the dew of tears.
White thoughts dancing silently.

Der er ingenting i Verden, der kan mildne som Sne.
Tys, du lytter, til det Tavse klinger.
O, saa fin en Klang,
Sølverklokkeklang,
Inderst inde i dit Hjerte ringer.

SIGURD LIE.

RUNEBERG, JOHAN LUDVIG

1804–1877

FLICKAN KOM FRÅN SIN ÄLSKLINGS MÖTE

Flickan kom från sin älsklings möte,
kom med röda händer.—Modern sade:
"Hvaraf rodna dina händer, flicka?"
Flickan sade: "Jag har plockat rosor,
och på törnen stungit mina händer."
Åter kom hon från sin älsklings möte,
kom med röda läppar.—Modern sade:
"Hvaraf rodna dina läppar, flicka?"
Flickan sade: "Jag har ätit hallon,
och med saften målat mina läppar."
Åter kom hon från sin älsklings möte,
kom med bleka kinder.—Modern sade:
"Hvaraf blekna dina kinder, flicka?"
Flickan sade: "Red en graf, o moder!
Göm mig der och ställ et kors deröfver,
och på korset rista som jag säger:
En gång kom hon hem med röda händer,
ty de rodnat mellan älskarens händer.
En gång kom hon hem med röda läppar,
ty de rodnat under älskarens läppar.
Senast kom hon hem med bleka kinder,
ty de bleknat genom älskarens otro."

JEAN SIBELIUS, Op. 37, no. 5. The theme of this poem appears in various languages and guises, notably in A. Walter Kramer's song,

There is nothing in the world which can comfort like snow.
Quietly you listen until the silence sounds.
Oh, such a delicate sound,
the peal of silver bells
ringing in your innermost heart.

A Swedish-Finnish poet, outdoor man, hunter, born ob-
server and realist, Runeberg is acknowledged Finland's
national poet. His works are said to have done much to
awaken and strengthen Finnish nationalism and inde-
pendence. Besides many smaller poems, Runeberg wrote
dramas and a series of larger works.

THE MAIDEN CAME FROM THE TRYST

The maiden came from the tryst;
she came with red hands. The mother said:
"Why are your hands red, girl?"
The maiden replied: "I have been picking roses,
and my hands were pricked by the thorns."
Again she came from the tryst;
came with red lips. The mother said:
"Why are your lips red, girl?"
The maiden said: "I have been eating raspberries,
and the juice has painted my lips."
Again she came from the tryst;
came with pale cheeks. The mother said:
"Why are your cheeks pale, girl?"
The maiden said: "Make a grave, mother,
hide me there under a cross,
and on the cross engrave what I say:
Once she came home with red hands,
made red by her lover's hands.
Once she came home with red lips,
made red by her lover's lips.
At last she came home with pale cheeks,
made pale by her lover's faithlessness."

The faltering dusk, Op. 45, no. 1, set to a text my Louis Untermeyer.

STUCKENBERG, VIGGO HENRIK FOG
1863–1905

LYKKEN MELLEM TO MENNESKER

Lykken mellem to mennesker
er hverken hu! eller hei!
Snarest er den et ensomt græs
der grønnes paa stenet vei!

Lykken mellem to mennesker
er hverken kys eller klap;
snarest er den et skumringssus,
der aander, hvor dagen slap.

Lykken mellem to mennesker
er som den dunkle nat,
stille, men med de tusinde,
tause stjerner besat.

EYVIND ALNAES.

VINJE, AASMUND OLAVSEN
1818–1870

VAAREN

Enno ei gong fekk eg vetren at sjaa for vaaren at røma;
heggen med tre, som det blomar var paa, eg atter saag bløma.
Enno ei gong fekk eg isen at sjaa fraa landet at fljota,
snjoen at braana og fossen i aa at fyssa og brjota.
Graset det grøne eg enno ei gong fekk skoda med blomar,
enno eg høyrde at vaarfuglen song mot sol og mot sumar.

Danish novelist and poet born in Zealand. Stuckenberg's lyric gifts were dedicated to a rationalistic realism, a courageous will to face the bitterness and trials of life. His poetic diction is greatly admired.

HAPPINESS BETWEEN TWO PEOPLE

Happiness between two people
is not a spoken greeting, neither hu! nor hei!
Rather it is a bit of grass blade
growing on a rocky road!

Happiness between two people
is neither kiss nor caress;
rather it is a murmur in the evening twilight,
breathing as the day dies.

Happiness between two people
is like the dark night,
quiet, but set with a thousand
silent stars.

A childhood friend of Ibsen who devoted his life to the development of Norwegian national culture. The foundation of his work was always cultural or social significance. He wrote in the Norwegian Landsmaal and worked toward the establishment of that language.

SPRING

Once again I saw winter flee before the spring;
again I saw the wild cherry in bloom.
Once again I saw the ice float out from the shore,
the snow melt, and the falls in the river roar and break.
The green grass I saw once again dotted with flowers;
once again I heard the birds of spring herald the sun and
    the summer.

[Enno ei gong den velsignad eg fekk at gauken eg høyrde,
enno ei gong ut paa aakren eg gjekk, der plogen dei køyrde.
Enno ei gong fekk eg skoda meg varm paa lufti og engi,
jordi at sjaa som med lengtande barm at sukka i sængi.
Vaarsky at leika dertil og ifraa, og skybankar krulla,
so ut av banken tok tora til slaa og kralla og rulla.]

Saagidren endaa meg unntest at sjaa paa vaarbakken dansa,
fivreld at floksa og fjuka ifraa, der blomar seg kransa.
Alt dette vaarliv eg atter fekk sjaa, som sidan eg miste.
Men eg er tungsam og spyrja meg maa: tru det er det siste?
Lat det so vera! Eg mykit av vænt i livet fekk njota,
meire eg fekk enn eg hadde fortent, og alting maa trjota.

[Ei gong eg sjølv i den vaarlege eim, som mættar mit auga,
ei gong eg der vil meg finna ein heim og symjande lauga,
Alt det, som vaaren i møte meg bar, og blomar eg plukkad,
federnes aandir eg trudde det var, som dansad' og sukkad'.
Derfor eg fann millom bjørkar og bar i vaaren ei gaata;
derfor det ljod i den fløyta eg skar, meg tyktest at graata.]

EDVARD GRIEG, Op. 33, no. 2. The second and fourth stanzas are
omitted.

[Once again I was blessed to hear the cuckoo sing;
once again I wandered in the field where they were ploughing.
Once again I saw the air and the field with pleasure,
the earth I saw in its bed, sighing with longing.
Spring clouds drifted to and fro, and the cloudbanks rolled
    up;
then out of the bank the thunder began to resound.]

Once again I saw the spring mist dancing on the vernal
    hillside,
the butterfly flitting among the garland of flowers.
All this spring life I saw once again before I lost it,
but I am heavy in my mind, and I ask myself: could this be
    the last time?
So be it! I have enjoyed much of beauty in my life,
I have gotten more than I deserved, and everything must end.

[Sometime in the spring mist that fills my eyes,
I shall find a home and I shall bathe and swim.
All that spring offered me, and the flowers I picked,
seemed to me the spirits of my ancestors, dancing and
    sighing.
Therefore in the spring, among pines and birches, I found
    an enigma;
therefore the sound of the whistle I cut seemed to weep.]

VED RUNDANE

No ser eg atter slike Fjøll og Dalar,
som deim eg i min fyrste Ungdom saag,
og same Vind den heite Panna svalar,
og Gullet ligg paa Snjo, som fyrr det laag.
Det er eit Barnemaal som til meg talar,
og gjer meg tankefull, men endaa fjaag.
Med Ungdomsminni er den Tala blandad.
Det strøymer paa meg so eg knapt kan anda.

Ja, Livet strøymer paa meg som det strøymde,
naar under Snjo eg saag det grøne Straa.
Eg drøymer no, som fyrr eg altid drøymde,
naar slike Fjøll eg saag i Lufti blaa.
Eg gløymer Dagsens Strid, som fyrr eg gløymde,
naar eg mot Kveld af Sol eit Glimt fekk sjaa.
Eg finner vel eit Hus som vil meg hysa,
naar Soli heim til Natti vil meg lysa.

[Alt er som fyrr, men det er meir forklaarat,
so Dagsens ljos meg synest meire bjart,
og det, som beit og skar meg, so det saarat,
det gjerer sjølve Skuggen mindre svart;
sjølv det, som til at synda tidt meg daarat,
sjølv det gjer harde Fjøllet mindre hardt.
Forsonad' koma atter gamle Tankar,
det same Hjarta er som eldre bankar.

Og kvar ein Stein eg som ein Kjenning finner,
for slik var den, eg flaug ikring som Gut.
Som det var Kjæmpur spyr eg, kven som vinner
af den og denne andre haage Nut.
Alt minner meg, det minner og det minner,
til Soli burt i Snjoen sloknar ut.
Og inn i siste Svevn meg eingong huggar
dei gamle Minni og dei gamle Skuggar.]

EDVARD GRIEG, Op. 33, no. 9. Though the setting is strophic, only
the first two stanzas appear in the printed music.

AT RUNDANE

Now I again see such fountains and valleys
as I saw in the early days of my youth;
and the same wind cools my heated brow,
and the snow is covered with gold as before.
It is the language of childhood that speaks to me,
and makes me thoughtful and yet gay.
Memories of my youth are mixed into that language.
It overwhelms me so that I scarcely can breathe.

Yet life overwhelms me as it did
when under the snow I saw the green grass.
I dream now, as before I always dreamed,
when I saw such hills against the blue sky.
I forget the toil of the day, as before I forgot,
when towards evening I got a glimpse of the sun.
No doubt I shall find a house that will take me in,
when before the night the sun will lead me home.

[Everything is as it was, but it is transfigured,
so the light of the day seems clearer to me,
and that which wounded me
the very shadow makes less black;
even that which often led me into sin,
even that the mountain softens.
Reconciled, the old thoughts come back;
it is the same heart that beats, though older.

And every stone seems to me an old acquaintance,
for it was such a one I ran around as a boy.
As if they were fighters I ask them who is winning
this or that other high top?
Everything brings back memories,
until the sun flickers out in the snow.
And into my last sleep I shall be lulled one day
by these old memories and these old shadows.]

SPANISH SONGS

GÓNGORA Y ARGOTE, LUIS DE
1561–1627

O excelso muro, o torres coronadas
De honor, de majestad y gallardía!
O gran Río, gran Rey de Andalucía,
De arenas nobles, ya que no doradas!

O fertil llano, o sierras levantadas,
Que privilegia el cielo y dora el día!
O siempre glorïosa patria mia,
Tanto por plumas cuanto por espadas!

Si entre aquellas ruinas y despojos
Que enriquece Genil y Dauro baña,
Tu memoria no fué alimento mío,
Nunca merezcan mis ausentes ojos
Ver tu muro, tus torres y tu Río,
Tu llano y sierra, o patria, o flor de España!

MANUEL DE FALLA.

PERIQUET Y ZUAZNABAR, FERNANDO
1873–1940

AMOR Y ODIO

Pensé que yo sabría ocultar la pena mía
Que por estar en lo profundo no alcanzará
á ver el mundo este amor callado
que un majo malvado en mi alma encendió.

Y no fué así porque el vislumbró
el pesar oculto en mí
Pero fué en vano que vislumbrara
pues el villano mostróse ajeno de que le amara.

Originally destined for the law, Góngora early turned to
poetry, and was hailed by Cervantes as a "rare and match-
less genius." His work was marked by unusually fine
craftsmanship and skillful satire and a precious and
metaphorical style which became proverbial. *Gongorismo*
in Spanish literature is parallel to the English Euphuism
or the French *précieux*.

SONNET TO CORDOVA

Oh sublime wall, oh towers crowned
with honor, majesty and gallantry!
Oh, great river, great king of Andalusia,
of noble sands, yet golden no longer.

Oh fertile plain, oh lofty mountains
that grace the sky and gild the day;
oh my eternal fatherland, glorious
as much for your plumage as for your sword!

If among yonder ruins and spoils
that enrich Genil and bathe Dauro,
your memory did not nourish me,
my absent eyes would not deserve
to see your wall, your towers and your river,
your plain and mountain, oh flower of Spain.

Was a part of the movement in Spain concerned with the
revival of interest in the art and customs of earlier days.
Wrote librettos for Albéniz and Granados, most notably
for the latter's *Goyescas*. His researches in Spanish song
account for the writing of his *tonadillas*, which Granados
set to music.

LOVE AND HATE

I thought I would know how to hide my pain—
that because it was so deep in me
the world would never see the mute love
a wicked majo has kindled in my soul.

And yet it was not thus because he glimpsed it,
the hidden sorrow in me.
But it was in vain that he glimpsed it,
for the villain showed himself a stranger to love.

Y esta es la pena que sufro ahora
sentir mi alma llena de amor por quien me olvida
sin que una luz alentadora surja en las sombras de mi
vida.

ENRIQUE GRANADOS. The word *tonadilla* usually refers to a brief comic opera introduced between the acts of more ambitious works in eighteenth-century Spain. The name was derived, however, from the type of song of which these intermezzi were mainly composed.

CALLEJEO

Dos horas ha que callejeo
pero no veo nerviosa ya
sin calma el que le
dí confiada el alma.

No ví hombre jamás
que mentiera mas
que el majo que hoy me engaña
más no le ha de valer
pues siempre fuí mujer
de maña y si es menester
correré sin parar tras él entera España.

LA MAJA DOLOROSA (I)

O! muerte cruel
porqué tu á traición
mi majo arrebataste a mi pasión?
No quiero vivir
sin él porque es morir
porque es morir así vivir!

No es posible ya
Sentir más dolor:
en lagrimas deshecha mi alma está
Oh Dios! torna mi amor
porque es morir
porque es morir así vivir!

And this is the pain that I suffer now,
to feel my soul filled with love for one who forgets me,
to be without a comforting light to shine through the
    shadows of my life.

It is to this original meaning that Granados and his friend Periquet
returned in their well-known collection. Seven of the ten numbers
in their set are included here.

A WALK

Two hours have I walked the streets—
nervous, now, and without calm—
But I do not see him
to whom I entrusted my soul.

Never have I seen a man
who would lie more
than the majo who today betrays me.
He does not value
that I was always a woman
of courage—and if necessary
I will pursue him relentlessly through all Spain.

THE PITEOUS MAJA (I)

Oh cruel death
why did you so treacherously
carry off the majo of my passion?
I do not desire to live
without him because it is death,
because it is death to live thus.

No longer is it possible
to feel more pain!
My soul is dissolved in tears
Oh God, restore my love
because it is death,
because it is death to live thus.

LA MAJA DOLOROSA (II)

Ay! majo de mi vida
no, no, tu no has muerto;
Acaso yo existiese
si fuera eso cierto?
Quiero loca besar tu boca!
Quiero segura gozar mas de tu ventura,
Ay! de tu ventura.

Más Ay! deliro, sueño,
mi majo no existe,
En torno mio el mundo
Lloroso está y triste.
A mi duelo no hallo consuelo!
Más muerto y frío
siempre el majo será mio
Ay! siempre mio!

LA MAJA DOLOROSA (III)

De aquel majo amante que fué mi gloria
guardo anhelante dichosa memoria
El me adoraba vehemente y fiel
Yo mi vida entera dí á el
Y otras mil diera
sí el quisiera
Que en hondos amores
martirios son flores
Y al recordar mi majo amando
van resurgiendo ensueños
de un tiempo pasado.

Nien el Mentidero
nien la Florida
majo más majo paseó en la vida
Bajo el chambergo sus ojos vi
con toda el alma puestos en mí
Que á quien miraban
enamoraban.
Pues no halle en el mundo
mirar más profundo.
Y al recordar mi majo amando
van resurgiendo ensueños
de un tiempo pasado.

THE PITEOUS MAJA (II)

Oh majo of my life,
no, no, you are not dead.
Would I exist
if that were true?
I am wild to kiss your mouth,
I want to enjoy more of your danger,
oh more of your danger.

Again no, delirium, dream,
my majo does not live.
Around me the world
is tearful and sad.
For my grief I find no consolation.
Only death and cold.
Forever my majo will be mine,
oh, always mine.

THE PITEOUS MAJA (III)

Of that loving majo who was my glory,
I keep longingly a happy memory.
He loved me intensely and faithfully,
I gave him my whole life,
and a thousand others I would have given
if he so desired.
For in profound love
martyrs are flowers,
and remembering my majo of love,
dreams rise up again
of a time gone by.

No more Mentidero,
no more Florida;
majo of majos he lived his life,
beneath his soft hat I saw his eyes
fixed on me with all his soul.
Whomever they looked at
became enamored,
for there is not in this world
a look more profound.
And remembering my majo of love
dreams rise up again
of a time gone by.

EL MAJO DISCRETO

Dicen que mi majo es feo,
Es posible que sí que lo sea,
que amor es deseo que ciega y marea
ha tiempo que sé que quien á mano vé.

Más sí no es mi majo un hombre,
que por lindo descuelle y asombre
En cambio es discreto y guarda un secreto
que yo posé en el sabiendo que es fiel.

Cual es el secreto que el majo guardó?
Seria indiscreto contarlo yo,
No poco trabajo costara saber
secretos de un majo con una mujer.
Nació en Lavapies.
Eh! Eh! Es un majo un majo es.

EL MAJO OLVIDADO

Cuando recuerdes los dias pasados
piensa en mí, en mí
Cuando de flores se llene tu reja
piensa en mí, piensa en mí.
Ah!
Pobre del Majo olvidado que duro sufrir!
sufrir! sufrir!
pues que la ingrata le deja no quiere
no quiere vivir no quiere vivir
Ah!
Cuando las noches serenas cante el ruiseñor
piensa en el Majo olvidado que muere de amor.

THE DISCREET MAJO

They say my majo is ugly;
yes, that may be so.
Love is desire that blinds and bewilders;
sometimes I know whom I see before me.

But if my majo is not the kind of man
who being handsome, impresses and astonishes.
On the other hand, he is discreet and guards the secret
which I entrusted to him knowing he is faithful.

What is the secret the majo guarded?
It would be indiscreet to tell you—
How difficult it is to understand
the secrets of a majo with a woman.
He was born in Lavapies.
Oh! He is a majo, a majo is he.

THE FORGOTTEN MAJO

When you remember those days of the past,
think of me, think of me.
When the flowers fill your lattice,
think of me, think of me.
Oh!
Poor forgotten majo who so deeply suffers,
suffers, suffers!
When an ungrateful wench leaves him he doesn't,
he doesn't want to live, he doesn't want to live.
Oh!
When in serene nights the nightingale sings,
think of the forgotten majo who dies of love.

EL MAJO TIMIDO

Llego á mi reja y me mira por la noche un majo
que en cuanto me ve y suspira se va calle abajo
Ay! que tió más tardío
Sí así se pasa la vida estoy divertida.

EL MIRAR DE LA MAJA

Porqué es en mis ojos
tan`hondo el mirar?
Que á fin de cortar desdenes
y enejos
los suelo entornar.
Que fuego dentro llevarán
Que sí acaso con calor
los clavo en mi amor
sonrojo me dan.

Por eso el chespero
á quien mi alma dí
al verse ante mí
me tira el sombrero
y diceme así
Mi maja! no me mires más
que tus ojos rayos son
y ardiendo en pasión
la muerte me dan.

THE TIMID MAJO

At night a majo comes to my lattice and gazes at me;
when he sees me he sighs and goes down the street.
Oh, what a slow fellow!
If I spend my life like this, how amusing!

THE MAJA'S GLANCE

Why do my eyes
Have so deep a look?
Because to hide disdain
and anger I usually
half-close them.
What inner fire they would reveal
if by chance with fury
I should fix them on my love.
It would make me blush.

For this, that devil,
to whom I gave my soul,
on seeing me before him
tips his hat at me
and says to me:
My maja, don't look at me any more.
For your eyes are like rays
that burning with passion
give me death.

SEVEN SPANISH FOLK SONGS

MANUEL DE FALLA

EL PAÑO MORUNO (I)

Al paño fino en la tienda
Una mancha le cayó;
Por menos precio se vende,
Porque perdió su valor, Ay!

SEGUIDILLA MURCIANA (II)

Cualquiera que el tejado tenga de vídrio,
No debe tirar piedras al del vecino.
Arrieros somos,
Puede que en el camino
Nos encontremos.
Por tu mucha inconstancia
Yo te comparo
Yo te comparo por tu mucha inconstancia
Yo te comparo
Con peseta que corre de mano en mano;

Que al fin se borra
Y creyéndola falsa
Nadie la toma.

It has been frequently pointed out that Falla, modern Spain's most distinguished composer, was inspired by the folk music of his country. Nevertheless, it would seem that only in this set of songs did he actually make use of folk material. The seven songs are a prime example of the transformation of folklore into art; unquestionably they lead all Spanish art songs in popularity.

THE MOORISH CLOTH (I)

On the delicate fabric in the shop
there fell a stain;
for a lower price it sells
because it lost its value. Ay!

SEGUIDILLA OF MURCIA (II)

Whoever has a glass roof
should not throw stones at his neighbor's.
Mule drivers are we,
perhaps on the road
we shall meet.
Because of your inconstancy
I compare you,
I compare you because of your inconstancy,
I compare you
to a peseta that passes from hand to hand;

that finally becomes so rubbed down,
that believing it false,
no one will take it.

ASTURIANA (III)

Por ver si me consolaba,
Arriméme a un pino verde;
Por verme llorar, lloraba.
Y el pino, como era verde,
Por verme llorar, lloraba.

JOTA (IV)

Dicen que no nos queremos
Porque no nos ven hablar;
A tu corazón y al mío
Se lo pueden preguntar.
Ya me despido de tí,
De tu casa y tu ventana
Y aunque no quiera tu madre,
Adiós, niña, hasta mañana.

NANA (V)

Duérmete, niño, duerme,
Duerme, mi alma,
Duérmete, lucerito
De la mañana
Nanita, nana.
Nanita nana
Duérmete, lucerito
De la mañana.

ASTURIANA (III)

To see if I could be consoled
I sought comfort of a green pine tree;
seeing me weep, it wept too.
And the pine tree, since it was green,
seeing me weep, wept too.

JOTA (IV)

They say we don't love each other
because they never see us talking;
but of your heart and mine
they have only to ask.
Now I bid you farewell,
your house and your window too,
even though your mother may not like it,
farewell, little girl, until tomorrow.

LULLABY (V)

Sleep, little baby, sleep,
sleep, my soul,
sleep, little star
of the morning.
Nanita, nana,
nanita nana.
Sleep, little star
of the morning.

CANCIÓN (VI)

Por traidores, tus ojos,
Voy a enterrarlos;
No sabes lo que cuesta,
"Del aire," niña, el mirarlos
"Madre, a la orilla,"
Niña, el mirarlos.
"Madre."
Dicen que no me quieres,
Ya me has querido . . .
Váyase lo ganado
"Del aire" por lo perdido,
"Madre, a la orilla," por lo perdido.
"Madre."

POLO (VII)

Guardo una "ay"
Guardo una pena en mi pecho
Ay!
Que a nadie se la diré!
Malhaya el amor, malhaya!
Ay!
Y quien me lo dió a entender!
Ay!

SONG (VI)

Because they are traitors, your eyes,
I will bury them;
you don't know how painful it is,
"From heaven," little one, to look at them.
"Mother, from their edge"—
little one, to look at them.
"Mother."
They say you don't love me,
yet once you did love me!
Gone is my love!
"From heaven," it is lost.
"Mother, from their edge!" It is lost.
"Mother!"

POLO (VII)

I am hiding an "ay"—
I am hiding a pain in my breast,
Ay!
That to no one will I reveal!
Cursed love, cursed!
Ay!
And the one who taught it to me!
Ay!

APPENDIX

ALTERNATE VERSIONS OF
SEVERAL POEMS

French poem from which Chamisso translated *Die Karten-legerin*:

BÉRANGER, PIERRE JEAN DE
1780–1857

LES CARTES, OU L'HOROSCOPE
Air de la petite gouvernante

Tandis qu'en faisant sa prière,
Au coin du feu maman s'endort,
Peu faite pour être ouvrière,
Dans les cartes cherchons mon sort.
Maman dirait: Craignez les bagatelles!
Le diable est fin; tremblez, Suzon!
Mais j'ai seize ans: les cartes seront belles.
Les cartes ont toujours raison,
Toujours raison, toujours raison.

Amour, enfant ou mariage,
Sachons ce qui m'attend ici.
J'ai certain amant qui voyage:
Valet de cœur? Bon! le voici.
Pour une veuve, aux pleurs il me condamne.
L'ingrat l'épouse, ô trahison!
J'entre au couvent; mon confesseur se damne.
Les cartes ont toujours raison,
Toujours raison, toujours raison.

Au parloir, témoin de mes larmes,
Le roi de carreau vient souvent.
C'est un prince épris de mes charmes;
Il m'enlève de mon couvent.
Par des cadeaux son altesse m'entraine
Jusqu'à sa petite maison.
La nuit survient, et je suis presque reine.
Les cartes ont toujours raison,
Toujours raison, toujours raison.

Je suis le prince à la campagne;
On vient lui parler contre moi.
En secret un brun m'accompagne;
Tout se découvre: adieu mon roi!
Un de perdu, j'en vois arriver douze;
J'enflamme un campagnard grison:
Je suis cruelle, et celui-là m'épouse,
Les cartes ont toujours raison,
Toujours raison, toujours raison.

En ménage d'une semaine,
Dans un char je brille à Paris.
C'est le roi de trèfle qui mène;
Mon mari gronde, et je m'en ris.
Dieu! l'amour fuit à l'aspect d'une vieille!
En ai-je passé la saison?
Eh! non vraiment, c'est maman qui s'éveille.
Les cartes ont toujours raison,
Toujours raison, toujours raison.

Hans Christian Andersen poem from which Chamisso translated *Der Soldat*:

ANDERSEN, HANS CHRISTIAN
1805–1875

SOLDATEN

Med dæmpede Hvirvler Trommerne gaae,
—ak, skal vi da aldrig til Stedet naae,
at han kan faa Ro is sin Kiste?
—Jeg troer mit Hjerte vil briste!

For sidste Gang skuer han nu Guds Sol,
—Der sidder han alt paa Dødens Stol;
de binder ham fast til Pælen.
—Forbarme dig, Gud over Sjælen!

Jeg havde i Verden en eeneste Ven.
Ham er detm man bringer til Døden hen
med klingende Spil giennem Gaden.
Og *jeg* er med i Paraden!

Paa eengang sigte de alle Ni,
de Otte skyde jo reent forbi;
de rysted' paa Haanden af Smerte,
—kun *jeg* traf midt i hans Hjerte!

Russian translation of Goethe's *Mignon-Lieder-3*:

MEĬ, LEV ALEKSANDROVICH
1822–1862

Net tol'ko tot, kto znal
   Svidan'ya zhazhdu,
Poĭmiot, kak ya stradal
   I kak ya strazhdu.

Glyazhu ya v dal' . . . net sil—
   Tuskneyet oko . . .
Akh, kto menya lyubil
   I znal—dalioko!

Vsya grud' gorit . . . kto znal
   Svidan'ya zhazhdu,
Poĭmiot, kak ya stradal
   I kak ya strazhdu.

Gérard de Nerval's translation of *Dichterliebe-13*:

GÉRARD DE NERVAL
1808–1855

J'AI PLEURÉ EN RÊVE

J'ai pleuré en rêve; je rêvais que tu étais morte;
je m'éveillai, et les larmes coulèrent de mes joues.

J'ai pleuré en rêve; je rêvais que tu me quittais;
je m'éveillai, et je pleurai amèrement longtemps après.

J'ai pleuré en rêve; je rêvais que tu m'aimais encore;
je m'éveillai, et le torrent de mes larmes coule toujours.

Remaining two stanzas of Heine's later version of *Dichterliebe-15*:

Wo alle Bäume sprechen
Und singen, wie ein Chor,
Und laute Quellen brechen
Wie Tanzmusik hervor;—

Und Liebesweisen tönen,
Wie du sie nie gehört,
Bis wundersüsses Sehnen
Dich wundersüss betört!

Ach, könnt' ich dorthin kommen, etc.

Heine's own French version of *Die Grenadiere*:

LES DEUX GRENADIERS

Longtemps captifs chez le Russe lointain
Deux grenadiers retournaient vers la France.
Déjà leur pied touche le sol germain,
Mais on leur dit: Pour vous plus d'espérance,
L'Europe a triomphé, vos braves ont vécu!
C'en est fait de la France et de la grande armée!
Et, rendant son épée
L'Empereur est captif et vaincu!

Ils ont frémi; chacun d'eux sent tomber
Des pleurs brûlants sur sa mâle figure.
"Je suis bien mal," dit l'un, "je vois couler
Des flots de sang de ma vieille blessure!"
—"Tout est fini," dit l'autre, "oh! je voudrais
         mourir!
Mais, au pays, mes fils m'attendent, et leur mère,
       Qui mourrait de misère;
J'entends leur voix plaintive; il faut vivre et
souffrir!"

   —"Femmes, enfants, que m'importe! Mon cœur
Par un seul voeu tient encore à la terre;
Ils mendieront, s'ils ont faim! L'Empereur,
  Il est captif, mon Empereur! . . . O frère,
Écoute-moi; je meurs! . . . Aux rives que j'aimais,
Rends du moins mon cadavre, et du fer de ta lance,
      Au soldat de la France
Creuse un funèbre lit sous le soleil français! . . .

  Fixe à mon sein glacé par le trépas
La croix d'honneur que mon sang a gagnée;
Dans le cercueil couche-moi l'arme au bras,
  Mets sous ma main la garde d'une épée;
De là, je prêterai l'oreille au moindre bruit,
Jusqu'au jour, où, tonnant sur la terre ébranlée,
      L'écho de la mêlée
M'appellera du fond de l'éternelle nuit!

  Peut-être bien qu'en ce choc meurtrier,
Sous la mitraille et les feux de la bombe,
Mon Empereur poussera son coursier
  Vers le gazon qui couvrira ma tombe.
Alors, je sortirai du cercueil, tout armé,
Et, sous les plis sacrés du drapeau tricolore,
     J'irai défendre encore
La France et l'Empereur, l'Empereur bien-aimé!

Original version of Hölty's *Minnelied*:

MINNELIED

Süsser klingt der Vogelsang,
Wann die gute, reine,
Die mein Jünglingsherz bezwang,
Wandelt durch die Haine.

Röter blühen Tal und Au,
Grüner wird der Wasen,
Wo die Finger meiner Frau
Maienblumen lasen.

Freude fliesst aus ihrem Blick
Auf die bunte Weide,
Aber fliehet sie zurück,
Ach, so flieht die Freude.

Alles ist dann für mich tot,
Welk sind alle Kräuter
Und kein Sommerabendrot
Dünkt mir schön und heiter.

Liebe, minnigliche Frau,
Wollest nimmer fliehen,
Dass mein Herz, gleich dieser Au,
Immer möge blühen.

Paragraph which prefaces Banville's *Nuit d'Étoiles* (entitled *La dernière pensée de Weber* in *Poésies: Les stalactites*). This passage is attributed to Hoffmann:

Je me promenais dans un jardin délicieux: sous l'épais gazon on voyait des violettes et des roses dont le doux parfum embaumait l'air. Un son doux et harmonieux se faisait entendre, et une tendre clarté éclairait le paysage. Les fleurs semblaient tressaillir de bonheur et exhaler de doux soupirs. Tout à coup je crus m'apercevoir que j'étais moi-même le chant que j'entendrais, et que je mourais.

I was walking in a delightful garden: under the thick turf I could see violets and roses whose perfume sweetened the air. A sweet and harmonious sound was heard, and a delicate light illumined the countryside. The flowers seemed to tremble with happiness, and to exhale soft sighs. All at once it came to me that I myself was the song I heard, and that I was dying.

Gabriel Fauré's setting of first stanza of Leconte de Lisle's *Lydia*:

> *Lydia, sur tes roses joues,*
> *Et sur ton col frais et si blanc,*
> *Roule étincelant*
> *L'or fluide que tu dénoues . . .*

Musorgski's changes in Golenishchev-Kutuzov's *Serenada*:

Lines five to eight read:

Son ne smykayet blestyashchiye ochi
Zhizn' k naslazhden'yu zoviot;
A pod okoshkom v molchan'i polnochi
Smert' serenadu poiot.

And line twenty-three:

Rytzar' prishol za posledneĭ nagrodoĭ.

COMPOSERS

COMPOSERS

TITLES AND
FIRST LINES

TITLES AND FIRST LINES